BATTERED BLESSINGS

Surviving My Abusive, Toxic Relationship

SHANNON EZZO

BATTERED BLESSINGS: SURVIVING MY ABUSIVE, TOXIC RELATIONSHIP

1405 SW 6th Avenue • Ocala, Florida 34471 • Phone 352-622-1825 • Fax 352-622-1875
Website: www.atlantic-pub.com • Email: sales@atlantic-pub.com
SAN Number: 268-1250

Library of Congress Control Number: 2020908185

Printed in the United States

PROJECT MANAGER: Crystal Edwards
INTERIOR LAYOUT AND JACKET DESIGN: Nicole Sturk

Trigger Warning

The following story is not intended for all audiences. Some scenes in this story describe graphic physical, sexual, and emotional abuse that may cause negative or emotional reactions. If you or a loved one currently are or ever have experienced abuse or have been in a domestic violence situation, please proceed with caution. This story is not recommended for children or anyone who suffers from PTSD due to domestic violence or sexual abuse. To preserve the authenticity of the story, please be advised that there is strong language used that may be offensive to some readers.

Although the names have all been changed to protect the innocent, this is the author's true story. The purpose of sharing this story is to not only bring awareness to different forms of abuse, but to possibly help someone who may be in a similar situation. If you are in need of help, please refer to the help page in the back of this book for references. Thank you.

Book Dedication

I would like to dedicate this book to some especially important influences in my life. First and foremost, I would like to thank God for leading me to the life he wanted for me. Had it not been for his guidance and abundant blessings, I do not know where I would be.

Secondly, I dedicate this to my amazing daughter. You are far too young to understand this, but one day I hope you know how much you saved me. Had it not been for your surprising arrival in this world, I would never have been strong enough to make the changes needed to save myself. I love you more than any words can describe! *Everything* I do, I do for you, my sweet.

Third, I dedicate this to my loving family and closest friends, who stood by me through this horrific time of my life, those of you who helped encourage and support me and still cheer me on now. I love you all; I know a lot of you will never read this book because it is too hard. But you can never understand how much your being there for me helped make me who I am today. I love you all very much!

Last but most certainly *not* least, I dedicate this book to my amazing husband. Had it not been for your initial interest in helping me get a safe place to live and care for me in the lowest part of my whole life, I cannot imagine where I would be. You are the most amazing father in the world, and you did not have to be. I never expected to fall so in love with you but thank God I did. I love you more than you could possibly know, and everything I do in life is for you and our daughter. You have helped inspire the woman I am today, and I will keep making you proud and making our family as happy as you all have made me. I love you babe! Thank you for always supporting me!

Table of Contents

Chapter One: How It All Started 3

Chapter Two: Red Flags 15

Chapter Three: Control 21

Chapter Four: The Boys 29

Chapter Five: Changes to be Made 37

Chapter Six: So It Begins 43

Chapter Seven: Outside Influences 53

Chapter Eight: Good Times 75

Chapter Nine: Cards on the Table 85

Chapter Ten: Well, That Got Weird 93

Chapter Eleven: Goodbye Baby Bear 103

Chapter Twelve: Beginning of the End 113

Chapter Thirteen: A Losing Battle 125

Chapter Fourteen: Was That Necessary? 135

Chapter Fifteen: When Will I Learn? 149

Chapter Sixteen: New Orleans 157

Chapter Seventeen: Here We Go..............................173

Chapter Eighteen: Make a Plan...............................195

Chapter Nineteen: Blast from the Past 213

Chapter Twenty: Really? Now? 229

Chapter Twenty-One: False Hope.............................. 251

Chapter Twenty-Two: Okay, Now What? 273

Chapter Twenty-Three: Here for the Sex 285

Chapter Twenty-Four: Final Days 303

Chapter Twenty-Five: New Life.................................327

Chapter Twenty-Six: Nobody Told Me!?....................351

Chapter Twenty-Seven: Head games. 373

Chapter Twenty-Eight: I didn't know 403

Chapter Twenty-Nine: Cut Off. 429

Chapter Thirty: New Me. 459

Chapter Thirty-One: One man's loss is another man's gain. 483

Epilogue...513

Helpful resources...517

About the Author..519

"If you're going to kill yourself just do it already. I'm sick of you threatening me with suicide to control me," I said to him, not expecting what he was going to do next.

As he stormed off to the back bedroom, I took a deep breath of relief, thinking that I had won. I had finally shut his tantrum down and gotten away with standing up for myself without even a backhand or being shoved in a wall or through a door! It was a small victory, but a victory nonetheless...or so I believed.

Less than 30 seconds later, he came back out with my 45-caliber handgun. I always kept it in my purse, and my purse was in the bedroom where he had gone.

I didn't know for sure what was about to happen, but I was fully aware of the fact that my gun was loaded...and I had just told this man to kill himself. I knew two things. 1) I didn't want to die, and 2) I didn't want to watch anyone kill themselves—especially with *my* gun after what I had just said.

He came over to me, grabbed my hair by the roots at the nape of my neck, and pulled me onto the floor. He said, "You want me dead, bitch? You're coming with me." Then he put his head against mine and placed the gun to his head.

CHAPTER ONE

How It All Started

It was 2015 when I joined an all-women's gym near my apartment. I loved the positive atmosphere and not having to worry about being gawked at by any men while I was working out. I attended a bunch of classes almost daily and naturally started to meet some new ladies and even make some new friends. I work in what you might call a 'man's field,' so it wasn't easy to make female friends.

I started working in a cabinet shop two days before my 18th birthday as my dad's helper. That developed into learning how to paint and stain. So, I made a career of being a cabinet-finisher. It came naturally to me, and I enjoyed it. So, I have always been one of the guys.

I didn't have many close girlfriends at the time. I noticed a lady in there a few times who caught everyone's attention—for good and bad. She was very loud all the time, no matter what she was talking about. She had a strong Jersey accent and didn't care about what people thought of her. She was a heavy-set Italian lady. I could tell she was older than me, but she looked great for her age. My first impression of her was that she was annoying and distracting in class, but the more I saw her, the more she grew on me.

Her name was Gia. Yes, she was extremely loud and borderline rude with most of the things that she said, but I have been described similarly in the past. So, naturally, we gravitated toward each other. We mostly worked out together to start, then we would go out for a few drinks or dinner. There was a little Italian restaurant next to the gym that we would walk to on occasion and have a glass of wine after we worked out. We got along well, so we decided to actually go out one night.

In the beginning of 2015, she posted a selfie of us out at a local bar. One of the men commenting on it showed a rather great interest in me.

Gia explained that the guy was a married biker who was involved with a motorcycle club. That's all I really needed to know. I was not in the slightest bit interested in sneaking around with a married man. So, when he would try to send me friend requests, I just declined them and kept on with my everyday life.

Then, on May 5, 2015, Gia and I went to a Mexican restaurant to enjoy some tacos and margaritas for Cinco De Mayo. After dinner, we decided to go to the bar next door and get another drink with another friend of ours from the gym. Gia had posted on social media where we were throughout the evening.

Next thing we knew, the married biker who was champing at the bit to know me walked through the door. He came straight over to our table and sat next to Gia. Surprised that he was there, she said a quick hello and introduced him to the table.

His name was Hector. He sat directly across from me. The first thing I noticed about him was his smile. He didn't have perfect white teeth or any-thing, but there was something charming about it—almost like an insecure teenager talking to his secret crush. He wasn't dressed to impress by any means. He was wearing blue jeans and a white t-shirt, some riding boots, and a ball cap. He wasn't fit but also wasn't overweight—just an average guy with sort of a dangerous charm about him.

He was very polite and dove right into the table's conversation. He ad-mitted that he had seen where we were and wanted to meet me, so he just decided to show up. I had enough drinks to disregard that red flag, so I interpreted it as being kind of cute that he wanted to meet me so bad.

At one point, Gia asked him how the wife and kids were.

He laughed uncomfortably and squirmed a bit in his seat. I remember him breaking eye contact with me and answering uncomfortably. I made sure to look directly at him while they chatted, so he knew I was aware that he was married. But he then started talking about how he and his wife were 'swingers' and had an open relationship.

He talked about the bike club he was a member of. I remember how proud of himself he seemed to be to tell me he was president of his chapter—as if that were supposed to make my panties drop right then.

I just nodded and listened, and eventually, the evening came to an end. He walked Gia and me to the car and gave her a big hug. He then gave me a hug and said it was nice to finally meet me. I politely said the same and told him to have a safe night, not thinking much of it.

The next day he sent me another friend request. I told Gia, and she wasn't surprised at all. She said that he was an extremely persistent kind of guy.

I thought, *What the hell…where's the harm?*

Within minutes of accepting his friend request, he started messaging me. It started out very dry and innocent—the usual: *How are you? Did you have a good day? What do you do for a living?*

Then, he started to ask more personal questions and made it clear that he was interested in me. I told him several times that I was not available to a married man. I explained that we could be friends on social media if he wanted to, but that was all.

We talked every day for about a week or so. Then, he started telling me about his problems at home. He told me about how unhappy he was and how he felt depressed all the time. He said that the two boys he was raising weren't his kids but that he felt obligated to be there since he was the one who raised them from a very young age. He explained how toxic his marriage was and how violent his wife was towards him. I started to notice very quickly that he was always going through a lot. He constantly need attention—not just from me, but anyone who was willing to give it to him. He was always in need of a shoulder to cry on, so to speak.

He started to tell me a bit about his past and about how he had basically grown up in foster care. He told me crazy horrible stories about what he remembered as a very young child. His biological father had punched him so hard in the face when he was 4 years old that it caused his left eye to almost go blind. I was surprised to hear that because I knew his father was also a member of the biker club he was in. I saw pictures of them, and I thought they seemed close. He explained that his father was in prison for 13 years, and he was in foster care during that time. But his dad found him when he got out of prison and wanted to reconnect.

It was the stories of his past that brought me closer to him. For some reason, the more I learned about him, the more I was hoping that someday he would experience real unconditional love since not even his parents had given that to him. I began to think of him as a poor guy who gotten a bad start in life or a wounded child who just need a mother's love.

I continued to talk with him daily. Then, one Saturday, I was at work when my phone chime went off. When I saw who it was, I immediately knew he had been trying to be sneaky. It was Hector's wife, and she was livid to say the least. She had seen some of our messages and was adamant that he was married, and she wasn't having this. She asked me a few questions, and I answered them honestly. I told her that he had tracked me down and had made it clear that they had an open relationship. I told her that nothing had happened between us and that I had clearly been misled. I explained that she needed to be mad at her husband, because I wasn't the one trying to involve myself in his life.

I screenshot the conversation with her and sent it to Gia. She wasn't very surprised since she had a run in or two with his wife before, as well. She was known for being insane and having an explosively violent temper. When Gia met Hector, she had no idea he was married. She slept with him a few times, but then one night, he invited her out to his clubhouse and when she got there, he introduced her to his wife. So, obviously, he was a slime ball.

I messaged Hector and told him not to contact me again. I told him what happened and sent him the conversation. He tried to apologize and talk his way out of it, but I wasn't interested in hearing any more. He had lied to both me and his wife, so why would I want to communicate with him and cause myself unwanted drama over a man I didn't even know? I deleted him from social media immediately.

About two weeks later, I got a message from Gia. Hector had contacted her and wanted to know if it was okay to message me. He said that he had left his wife and they weren't even married. Apparently, they had gotten divorced a few years prior to that during one of their other many breakups and nobody knew. After Gia got onto him for being a sneaky, lying dog, she listened to his story and told him that she would see if I was comfortable with him contacting me. He had a talent for making people believe he was a helpless victim and pulling at people's heartstrings. Gia called me and explained what was going on. She said it was up to me, but she did feel kind of bad for him because he was in a bad spot. She had been friends with him for years. So, I agreed to let him apologize to me.

Not even two minutes later, he was messaging me. He wanted to see me face-to-face to apologize. I declined that offer and told him that messaging would be fine for now. I just wasn't comfortable being around him with all his drama at the time. Plus, I didn't even know if I liked him yet. So far, I just felt so bad for him.

He apologized up and down but not exactly for lying. It was more of a "sorry my wife busted me and went crazy on you" apology. He told me that they had divorced two years prior, but she wouldn't stop stalking him and used the kids to get him back after he had moved to California for a year. He told me that it was public record, and I could look it up if I thought he couldn't be trusted.

So, I did. He was correct, they had been divorced and she did have quite a reputation for being "crazy."

I forgave him, and we went on talking for a couple of weeks. He was always trying to invite himself over or go grab a drink, but I just kept blowing him off. I still didn't know if I really wanted this kind of mess in my life. But he was incredibly persistent.

Eventually, I agreed to let him be my date to one of my girlfriends' birthday dinners. It was going to be in public with friends, one of whom was Gia, so I thought what the heck? He met me and Gia at my apartment, and we rode to the restaurant together. He told us that he was staying on his friend's couch until he found his own place. To be honest, it was more Gia and him having a conversation with me just listening in.

The restaurant was one of those cool places where you sit on the floor on a bunch of pillows. We ordered some drinks and a hookah and watched the belly dancer. He chatted with all my friends and kind of snuggled up to me more and more as the night went on.

After dinner, everyone wanted to go back to my place for another drink, so we did. We chatted, and I got to know him a little more on my couch. Eventually most people were tired and ready to go. So, I walked them out and said my goodbyes. When I came back in, Gia and Hector were sitting on the couch talking. I went to the bathroom, and when I came out, I was shocked to find Gia on her knees in front of him, trying to pull his dick out! Feeling unsure and uncomfortable, I asked if they needed some alone time. They both said no, and she proceeded to suck his dick. He was looking at me the whole time with an uncomfortable smile. He told me to come sit down, so I did—away from them.

He asked me to come closer so he could touch me, but I said no. I think that turned him on more. I told him to enjoy himself but explained that he wouldn't be touching me. She stopped what she was doing and told him that she wanted him inside her. That made things awkward really quick. He said he didn't want to because he really liked me and that would ruin his chance with me. Then he said he didn't even have a condom. It almost turned into an argument at that point because she was offended that he wanted to use one when they never had before.

I awkwardly offered them a condom, and she said, "No, we don't need one. I have an IUD, and we've fucked raw every other time."

It felt very much like Gia was marking her territory. She had slept with him a couple of times in the past, but it never developed into anything. Her behavior made it seem like she was jealous, but I was interested in seeing what he was going to do, so I let it play out. After a brief back and forth between the two, he finally agreed to give her what she wanted—she wasn't taking no for an answer.

So, she bent over and got what she wanted. It was basically like having live porn. Although it was a little awkward because it was clear why Gia wanted to do this in front of me, it was still kind of hot to watch people have sex. While they did what they were doing, I pleasured myself while he watched me. He was staring into my eyes the whole time with a desperately hungry look. It didn't last very long, and when he finished, he asked where my bathroom was and if he could take a shower. I told him yes and pointed him in the right direction.

"You are so fucking hot," he whispered in my ear when I went to give him a towel. "I didn't want to do that," he said even quieter. Ignoring him, I went back out to the couch where Gia was. We had another drink but soon heard Hector yelling over the phone to someone.

She knocked on the door to see if everything was okay. He was yelling at a club member. It was a Friday night, and the club hadn't made any money, and he wasn't happy. On Friday and Saturday nights, the clubhouse was open so friends and support clubs could come hang out and buy some drinks to support the club. But nobody showed, so he was displeased. Then he sat on the couch in my towel and started venting about how difficult it was to get people to come to the clubhouse. He said he was getting in trouble with the higher-up members because he needed to pull in more numbers and cash if he wanted to maintain his chapter. Gia, having been there several times before, started to make some suggestions. We got into a long conversation about some things she could help with if he wanted. Then eventually she had to call it a night since she had a date the next day and needed some sleep.

He didn't get up. I walked her to the door and told her goodnight. I came back into the living room, and he asked if he could stay the night.

I laughed uncomfortably and said, "I hardly know you, and I literally just watched you fuck my best friend on my couch the second time I ever saw you in person, and you're asking to stay the night?"

"You know I didn't want to do that. She attacked me and wouldn't take no for an answer!"

I told him I didn't really care. I was tired and just wanted to go to sleep, so I said that he could sleep on the couch. He got up and went to my bed. Too tired to fight at this point, I told him he was *not* to touch me and was to stay on his side of the bed. I built a pillow fortress between us and put my dog between us, as well.

The next morning, I took a shower and made breakfast as usual. We sat on the couch all morning and talked. It was strange how we both acted like nothing had happened the night before, and neither of us brought it up. We talked about how his ex-wife wouldn't let him see or talk to the kids. We talked about the club, the clubhouse, pretty much everything. He had to go to the clubhouse and asked me to go with him. I didn't really want to and sent him on his way. I went to the gym and the grocery store, walked the dog, and just did the usual stuff. Then he messaged me that he wanted to come back over.

It was still early in the evening, so I agreed to let him come by for a drink or two. Next thing you know he's staying the night again. He still respected my boundaries and stayed on his side of the bed. He never tried to touch me or even suggest anything like that. Then, we spent the entire day together on Sunday, talking, laughing, and watching movies.

Later, he told me that he had to go to 'church' at the clubhouse. It was basically a weekly club meeting to discuss club politics and plan for upcoming events. He asked me to drive him so I could meet his club. I wasn't allowed to stay, of course, because no girls are allowed when they're having church, but I came in long enough to have a beer and meet his bros in that chapter. He said he'd get a ride back to my place if I didn't want to pick him up.

Weeks later, he and I went to Gia's house to have a pool day. On the way to her car from the pool, a bike pulled up. It was Gia's ex-boyfriend who was also Hector's V.P. I had heard a lot about him from Gia, of course, but had never met him in person. People called him Big. That was his biker name. He rolled up on his motorcycle in full gear, and you could tell he had an amazing body even though it was fully covered. He stopped and pulled off his helmet, and he and Hector started talking.

Then he turned to me and said, "Who's this?"

So, my stupid ass said, "Hi, I'm Gia, Savannah's friend."

Gia busted out laughing. "She meant that she is Savannah, Gia's friend," she said, correcting me.

Hector jokingly said, "Wow! He got you so flustered you forgot your own name?"

Obviously, I felt like a heel, but we all made light of it and laughed it off.

When we got back up to Gia's apartment, Hector wouldn't stop talking about it. At first it seemed playful, but then we started to see that he was very jealous, and it became quite annoying. Gia told him, "All right, that's enough. It was stupid, and you're acting like a crazy person! She's not even your girlfriend, Hector. Drop it."

So, he did. From there on out he would act ridiculous every time Big was around. I would have to go out of my way not to talk to him or interact with him at all so Hector wouldn't get upset. But he would invite Big over to my apartment to hang out and then start little fights about it after the man left.

I was in the kitchen one time, and Big went to leave, so I followed him to the door to lock it behind him. It was a matter of maybe 15 seconds, but as soon as he was out the door, Hector was in my face asking me what had happened in the kitchen. What could have possibly happened in 15 seconds of being out of his sight?

I told him he was being ridiculous, but to that, all he said was, "Yeah you all say that and then cheat on me or leave me for another dude."

That was the beginning of having to walk on eggshells in order to not upset him.

Finally, one night, when we went to bed, I lay down on my side and he went to his. I said good night and suddenly felt his hand on my ass. "What are you doing?" I asked.

"We've been dating for weeks now," he said, crawling over the pillow fortress I had. "I really want to be with you," he said, planting a kiss on me. It wasn't the best kiss I ever had, but it was nice.

"I don't know if I'm ready for this yet," I whispered.

Ignoring me, he kept kissing me. He rolled me over onto my back and climbed in between my legs. He kissed all over my neck and down my chest.

"Hector…" I said, becoming aroused but still nervous to go there with him.

"Shh, I just want to taste you," he whispered, pulling my tank top down to expose my breasts.

He nipped at my nipples hungrily, but not too rough. My back arched in response letting him know I wanted more. He moved his way down further kissing my lower stomach and inner thighs.

"You have no idea how bad I've wanted this," he growled, moving my panties to the side. When he put his mouth on me, he seemed a little lost.

I don't think he did this a lot, but he was trying, so I helped him along. "Move down a little and lick harder," I directed him.

He did as I asked and found his mark. It took me a while to climax, but eventually he got me there. He climbed back on top of me pulling his boxers down.

"Wait," I said nervously.

"I'll go slowly," he said.

I sighed, feeling his dick poking at me. "It's been a while since I've done this."

"Good!" Slowly, he started sinking into me. His size wasn't mind-blowing, but it had a decent girth to it. But after how much he described how well-endowed he was, I now knew he was being quite generous with his self-description.

"Wait, I have a condom," I said, stopping him. Annoyed by the disruption, he continued. "Stop, you need to put a condom on," I said.

"I'm about to come," he whispered, pulling out of me. I felt the hot semen on my lower stomach while he let out a relieved sigh.

That's it? I thought to myself. That didn't last two whole minutes. *Maybe he was just excited.*

"Holy shit, that was fast," he laughed nervously.

"Can you get me a wet rag, please?" I asked, annoyed by the mess I didn't want.

"Yeah," he said and kissed me quickly before running to the bathroom. "Sorry that was so fast—you made me wait so long," he said nervously.

"It's fine," I said.

"Don't tell Gia I did that."

"Did what?" I asked.

"Went down on you. I would never do that to her," he said dramatically.

"Why would she care?"

"Because she's a jealous bitch," he responded.

"I thought you liked her," I said, confused.

"No, I can't fucking stand her."

"Then why were you sleeping with her?" I asked, even more confused.

"Because she's easy. Everyone fucks her. She'll hang out all night, buying you drinks, and then take you home and let you do whatever the hell you want to her—you don't have to wear a condom or anything," he said, laughing uncomfortably. "She's just the guaranteed lay if you don't find anyone else by the end of the night," he said.

"Wow, that's fucked up. I thought you were friends."

"Not at all, she's fucking annoying," he replied.

CHAPTER TWO

Red Flags

Since it was clear that he wasn't going anywhere, I decided to start introducing Hector to people.

Although my father and brother didn't seem to really care for him, they tolerated him. It wasn't unusual for them to not like a guy I was seeing; they're both very protective of me—my brother especially. One night, we were drinking and hanging out at my dad and brother's apartment. I don't remember why it came up, but Hector said one of his most common phrases, which was completely idiotic to everyone around him.

"My hands are bisexual; I don't care if you're a man or a woman, I'll beat your ass if you come at me."

My brother, being who he is, was not a fan of this statement and immediately reacted. He got closer to Hector and told him, "Yeah? Well, let me tell you something, boy. If you ever touch my sister, and I find out about it, I'll pop your eyes out and skull-fuck you to death."

Hector, clearly uncomfortable, just nervously laughed and played it like he was joking. Meanwhile, my brother had the death stare on him and kept looking over at me with a 'what the fuck are you doing with this douchebag' look. It was clear that it was time to leave.

We all lived in the same apartment complex at the time. It wasn't the best neighborhood, but it wasn't the worst either and was very affordable. I took comfort in my dad and brother being so close to me. But very much enjoyed having my own place.

The moment we walked out the door and headed to my apartment, Hector very calmly and very quietly said, "Real talk, if your brother ever talks to me like that again I'll have him killed."

I laughed—obviously I didn't take him seriously. I could tell his little ego took a hit, so I just thought it was ridiculous. "You don't know my brother. Don't threaten my family or you can get your shit and get out of my apartment." I will never forget the look he gave me when I said that. I could tell he wanted to say or do something to me right then, but he had an end game in sight, so he wasn't about to risk losing his free place to live. I honestly believe that's the only reason he controlled himself that night.

Shortly after that, one of my older girlfriends, Lulu, came to town to get her son Trey, who is just a few years younger than me, out of jail. Unfortunately, the state of Georgia wouldn't allow him to go with her to Florida since he was still on probation. He had to wait to get approval and a transfer to be legally allowed to go live with her.

I invited them over to my place for dinner while she was in town. I wanted her to meet Hector. So, they came over, and we ate and had some wine. Lulu explained that Trey wasn't allowed to go with her, and he needed a place to stay. It needed to be somewhere safe and clean that his P.O. could have the address for to show residence. She asked me if she could leave him to stay with me.

My first response was no—I had a one-bedroom apartment, and Trey had always had a bit of a crush on me. I'd known them forever and had nothing but love for them, but I knew how much drama this could cause with Hector being so jealous and insecure with his own male friends around me. I could only imagine how bad it would be with a man he didn't know living on my couch for who knows how long. But Hector pulled me aside and said it was the right thing to do. He said he would stay with me the entire time Trey was here to make sure nothing happened. But he was certain the probation transfer would only take a few weeks at the most.

Well it didn't; it was more like a few months. At first, it wasn't that bad. Trey didn't work so he helped keep the apartment clean and cooked dinners for us. Then, one night we had some of my friends over, and Hector sat down on the couch and pulled up a show on Netflix that we'd been watching together.

Trey jokingly yelled, "Savannah, he's trying to watch our show without us! Tell him he can't!"

My friends and I thought it was funny until Hector looked at Trey and said, "Bitch, don't tell me what I can and can't do in my own house." That made everyone go silent and look at me.

I spoke up and said, "Actually this is *my* apartment and since nobody in this bitch is paying a damn bill, y'all can both chill."

Hector got up and grabbed his keys. "Okay, if it's like that, fuck this!" He walked out the front door and slammed it as hard as he could, causing the picture that was hung on the wall next to it to fall and smash on the floor. Now everyone was concerned.

I just made excuses for his ridiculous tantrum and told everyone that he was just having a hard time. I thought I calmed everyone down enough, but a few days after that, the same group of friends tried a sort of intervention with me. They told me that his actions that night had scared them and that there was something off about him. They were concerned for my safety, which at the time I thought was ridiculous. I just saw his outbursts as childlike tantrums—just a kid making noise. Nothing dangerous. I assured them that he wasn't abusing me, and everything was fine. But the relationships had already changed. I didn't realize what was beginning then. But that's when the separations started. People began being pushed out of my everyday life if they didn't like him or feel comfortable around him.

That one instance changed Hector's entire attitude towards Trey. After that, he started going out of his way to make Trey uncomfortable. He told him he needed to start making money and pitching in.

Trey said, "Then shouldn't you be doing the same? How long have you lived here for free?"

It was a constant back and forth. Hector wanted Trey gone. But we were stuck with him until his probation got cleared. Things just kept building and building between them. On the few occasions Hector was out, Trey would try to talk some sense into me. He was growing more and more concerned about Hector's temper. He even said, at one point, that he was scared to leave because he didn't know what Hector was going to do to me. I, again, thought it was ridiculous. I don't know why I didn't see what everyone else was seeing. It was right in front of my face the whole time.

Finally, in about mid-July 2015, the probation came through, and Lulu came to pick up Trey. I was indescribably relieved to see him go, because it had gotten to the point that Hector was constantly telling me that he was going to beat Trey's ass.

When we were at the clubhouse, he'd tell all his bros how he wanted to just go over there and leave him bloody outside the doorstep and let him die in the streets. He told them he was a low-life piece of shit who was taking advantage of me and that one way or another he was going to be gone. At that point in our relationship, I had already learned that I was not allowed to speak up or disrespect him when we were at the clubhouse. When I did, those were the times that he scared me. He was relentless about not being embarrassed in front of his bros.

Shortly after Trey left, we had a fight on the way home from the clubhouse. He was upset that I had been sarcastic or something, and he felt disrespected. It was so stupid to me, but the fact that I didn't take it seriously enraged him all the more. He swerved the car and told me that he would crash it and kill us both—he didn't care.

When we got home, he was still yelling at me, so I went to the bathroom to get away from him. He burst through the door threatening me. He said that he was going to punch me in the face while I was walking past him. I stopped and turned around, looked him dead in the eye, and said, "Do it! I fucking dare you. I promise I'll be the last women you ever lay your hands on."

He punched the wall and screamed in my face. I told him to leave. I didn't threaten him or try to get him even more upset I just asked for his set of apartment keys and told him to leave. He stormed out the door, so I followed him and told him that he was not taking my car (he didn't have one of his own) and that I wanted my house key. I told him I would call the cops and my dad and brother if he took one more step without giving me my keys. He told me I was a stupid whore and handed me my keys.

When I went inside, I called Gia and told her that we'd had a big fight. About a minute into our conversation, he knocked on the door. Not banging, just a casual knock. I told Gia that I would call her back. She said that if I needed her, she would be right over. I hung up and answered the door.

His whole demeanor had changed. He looked like a sad little boy whose mommy had just told him that she didn't love him anymore. There were tears in his eyes as he calmly asked if he could get his clothes. I let him in. He went to the drawers where his clothes were and started moving things around. When I asked him if he need a container or a bag to put his stuff in, he broke down and started crying. He sat on my bed holding his head and apologizing. He said that he was trying to be a better man for me. He said he knew he had a temper, and he didn't want to be that way with me. He told me that he had never met a woman like me, and he would do anything not to lose me. He asked if I could forgive him and just hold him. He was being so open and vulnerable with me that I saw him as a broken boy.

I sat next to him on the bed and put my arm on his back. "Thank you for apologizing. I'm sorry I got you so upset. I don't want to fight with you," I told him.

He reached over and wrapped his arms around me, still crying. "I'm no good for you. I know that, but I'm trying so hard. I want to be with you, but I understand if you don't want me anymore," he said.

I told him he needed to stop being so jealous and controlling, or it was going to ruin our relationship. But I understood that he was going through a lot, and I was trying to be there for him. I held him until he fell asleep, and then I eventually drifted off myself.

CHAPTER THREE

Control

After that fight we seemed to get along better. He was so sweet to me—so loving and affectionate. I really saw some good changes in him, and it gave me some hope. I was starting to believe that I was having a positive impact on him. I would go to the clubhouse with him more and get my friends to come up there and buy drinks and hang out. Things seemed to be going almost fairytale-like for about a week and a half.

Then, one day, we were out trying to get Hector a car of his own. I was sitting in my car in the parking lot waiting for him to finish up his chat with someone he knew at the car dealership, when my phone rang. It was Gia. I knew something was off with her the moment I answered the phone. She tried to make it casual and asked me what I was up to and how my day was. I told her that we were car hunting and that everything was fine. I asked her what was up, and she said she needed to see me. I told her I wasn't going to be able to come by today and asked if she wanted to meet us at my place later when we got home.

"No, Savannah, I need to see you alone. I need to talk to you face to face." That's when I knew it was serious. I begged her to tell me what was wrong. After telling her that she was starting to scare me, she finally spoke up.

"I went to the doctor last week for my regular checkup and pap…" she said. "While I was there, I got a full STD test, because I always get tested."

There was what felt like a very long pause before I said, "Okay?" urging her to get to the point.

"I tested positive for herpes," she started crying. I tried to comfort her and tell her it was going to be okay, but she stopped me and said, "Savannah, you need to get tested. I slept with Hector that night at your apartment without a condom, remember? You are at risk, and I am *so* sorry! I will pay for your test, but you need to go as soon as possible. I have to let everyone know who is at risk."

I had honestly forgotten all about that night. It never even crossed my mind that I could be affected by her news, but she was right. I needed to get tested. And so did Hector.

"I'm not paying for Hector to get tested," she said bitterly. "He's a ho, so who knows? I could have gotten it from him. I'm not worried about his ass—I'm worried about *you!*"

When he got in the car, he could tell that something had happened. I quietly started driving and simply said, "We're going home."

He asked me what was wrong, but I couldn't formulate the words. He already spoke poorly of Gia and didn't want me to be friends with her. I knew this news was going to make him lose his shit. It was eating away at me so I couldn't wait until we got home to tell him. Atlanta traffic is always crap, so it was an easy 30 minutes at least that we would be in the car.

I pulled up to a red light and took a deep breath. "I just got a call from Gia," I said calmly.

"Oh? And what's that bitch want?" he responded.

"She just got an STD test and tested positive for herpes." I spat it out like it was poison in my mouth.

His first reaction was, "Not surprised. I told you she's a slut. Serves her ho ass right."

I tried to remain calm and said, "You fucked her without a condom two or three weeks before she went to the doctor, Hector. We are both at risk. We both need to get tested."

I thought he was going to break out my windows. He started banging his fists on everything and moved the seat so he could kick my windshield. I told him to calm down or get out of the car. Eventually, he stopped kicking and said, "That fucking cum dumpster is going to pay for our tests!"

I told him that she had already told me that she was going to pay for *my* test…but that she wasn't paying for his.

That sent him into a whole new level of rage. He got out his phone and started looking for something. I asked what he was doing, and he said, "I'm calling all the guys I know she fucked and telling them that she's an STD-riddled whore!"

I grabbed his phone and told him that that was unnecessary. She was already calling everyone herself and doing the responsible thing by letting people know.

He said, "I know Big just fucked her recently because he told me! He's my best friend, and he has a girl that doesn't deserve herpes from your nasty-ass friend! I'm calling Big!"

I told him it wasn't his place to trash her name. "Right now, we need to just be focused on making sure we're clean."

I was hoping that he'd have cooled down by the time we got to the apartment, but he hadn't. He started throwing my stuff and smashing glasses on my floating shelves and kicking furniture. It scared me and my dog, Rafiki. He told me that he was going to make her pay and that he would ruin her life.

I asked him to calm down and took Rafiki for a walk to get away from him. I took my sweet time walking around my building. I was really scared and really upset and wanted to go run to my daddy and my brother and tell them what happened. I wanted them to go get this crazy kid out of my apartment. I wanted to feel safe, but I was embarrassed. I didn't want them to know that Gia and Hector had slept together on my couch while I watched. I didn't want them to see how bad his temper was. I didn't want anyone getting hurt. So, I walked back home.

When I came back inside, he seemed to be much calmer. He was on the phone with someone, and it didn't seem like he was pissed at them, so I knew that it wasn't Gia. Rafiki and I went to the kitchen and I gave him his usual treat for being a good boy and pooping outside. He happily accepted it and went to the living room to enjoy it. I followed and sat on the couch waiting for Hector to finish his phone call.

"It's gonna be all right, Big. That stank-ass bitch is gonna get what she deserves. I'll see you at the clubhouse later." Big had called Hector as soon as he'd gotten off the phone with Gia. Big had a reputation of his own for sleeping with anything that had a wet hole, so Hector said he could have been the one who was giving out this STD. Still, he looked at me and said, "I hope you enjoyed your little friendship, because you ain't talking to that dirty bitch again after she pays for our tests."

I told him that I was in charge of who I was friends with and to not put me in the position of choosing, because I would choose my friend. He didn't like hearing that.

"You would choose a nasty whore over your man?"

I said, "If she's such a nasty whore, why did *you* fuck her?"

We argued back and forth for at least an hour or two. I was exhausted. Finally, I asked him, "What's the real issue here, Hector? She told us the day she found out. It's not like she knew she had it and deliberately tried to pass it to anyone. People make mistakes. Shit happens. We don't even know if we have it yet, so why are you acting so crazy?"

"Because if that bitch gave me something, I can't be a swinger anymore! It would ruin my life!"

Shocked by his answer, I said, "Are you fucking kidding me? First, I'm not a swinger, so if you're going to be with me, that shouldn't matter. Secondly, you're more upset that you can't go around fucking everyone than you are at the fact that *you* could have given this to *me*—your girlfriend? I'm not a ho. I don't go around sleeping with everyone, and I know I'm STD-free! You should be more upset that you may have given this to me!"

I couldn't believe his thinking. He didn't seem the least bit bothered that he could have passed this to me.

I got my appointment, and Gia gave me the money to get tested. My test came back clean, but I was advised to retest in six months. I told Hector the news, and he was relieved. I asked him when he planned to get tested and he said he didn't need to. If I was clean, he was clean. I explained to him that that wasn't exactly true. I told him that the doctor said that he could still have it and he needed to go get tested, but Hector just said that the doctor was wrong, and we were fine.

After he strutted around telling everyone that we were unaffected by this outbreak, I thought he would be over everything enough to not be an ass if I went to see my friend, but that's when he started making rules. At the time, he called it compromising. He didn't want to see Gia at all, so I had to go to her house or the gym to see her. He tried to tell me she wasn't allowed at my apartment. I told him she was always allowed there, and if he didn't want to see her, he could leave. So, she would come over when he would go to the clubhouse. Then we weren't allowed to go out anywhere unless I had someone else that he knew and trusted with us.

One night, his aunt, (we called her Titi), whom I had just recently met, wanted to go do a girl's dinner. Hector had recently gotten her a job working with him, so I was getting to know her a little bit since she would come to the house and pick him up and drop him off every day for work. I invited Gia so they could meet each other. Hector put up a fight at first but then I told him, "Who better to be out with than your aunt?"

He agreed to let us all go to dinner, but that was it. This was going to be the first time Gia met his aunt. It started out fine, but Gia'd had one too many drinks, and after Titi asked what the story was with her and Hector and why I needed a chaperone, she started crying.

"He treats me like I am nothing. Like I have no place in his life. I've known Hector for years and have been a good friend to him. This is how he treats me? Like I don't even matter? He tried to ruin my friendship with Savannah and my reputation."

Titi said, "I'm sorry, but the only woman who has a place in Hector's life right now is Savannah. You aren't his girl—she is."

Gia was really emotional and said she understood all that, but she didn't feel like she deserved the way he was treating her. I had to agree on that. He was awful. We all went out and had a cigarette, and Gia calmed down and apologized for getting so emotional. Titi handled the awkward situation well. But I could tell by the looks she gave me that there was plenty she wanted to say.

I really liked Titi. She was a strong Puerto Rican woman and had a mouth on her that was relentless when she needed it to be. There was no bullshitting this woman. I found her realness very refreshing; she didn't sugar coat anything, and I loved that about her. The first thing she said when we were driving home was, "You gotta watch out for that one honey. She's in love with your man."

"You know, Titi, I never got that vibe from her before. But after what just happened, I honestly don't know what I'm feeling."

She told me that Hector had already told her about the STD thing and that I had been tested. I didn't know she knew that, so it was a little embarrassing, but also almost refreshing to have someone to talk to about that situation. Out of respect for Gia, I had kept it to myself. I couldn't talk to Hector about it because it always started a fight.

After I got over the embarrassment of it, she asked me if I was okay with everything.

"How else can I be? So far, I'm clean, and right now, I'm just trying to keep my friendship and my man."

"It shouldn't be this hard to have a man and a best friend. That should tell you that something isn't right here. It's toxic. I know Hector, and you seem like a nice girl, so listen to me, Savannah. Watch your back. I love my nephew, but I know what he's capable of." For now, that was all she said.

One day, I mentioned to Hector that my dad had invited us over, but he said that he wasn't going over there. He wouldn't step foot over there or be around my family again until my brother apologized for disrespecting him. I told my dad what happened and why Hector was uncomfortable around my brother. In the next day or two, my brother did what he thought he had to do and had a face to face discussion with him. I knew he didn't want to, nor should he have had to. But I didn't want my time with my family limited. So, I was glad they hashed it out. It seemed like I didn't have many friends anymore, so I needed my family to still want us around at least.

CHAPTER FOUR

The Boys

One day in October 2015, we had just put some pigs in a blanket in the oven and sat on the couch to talk about going to one of those haunted houses they do every year. Hector was telling me that he loved getting scared and that we should try to get a group together and go. I was a fan of haunted houses as well, so we were talking about who to go with when his phone rang.

It was Tasha. I didn't really know her that well, but she was Big's girlfriend. She was calling to tell him that she had been driving behind Big up a hill on a side road when his motorcycle slid from under him and he ended up wrecking. She told him that he'd been thrown from the bike, and had rolled and hit a fire hydrant. She'd gotten out of the car and ran to him. He was still talking, so she was trying to remain calm, but asked Hector to meet them at the hospital. She was following the ambulance. We turned off the oven and rushed to the E.R.

Tasha seemed as calm as she could be when we got there, but they still didn't know anything. Hector started calling all the members of his club to get them there to show support.

Coincidentally, a gay couple I was close to was at the same hospital in the ICU. I knew they were still there, and since I really didn't know Hector's circle that well, I figured I'd go visit Juan and see how Sergio was doing. I called Juan and told him that I was there and asked if I could come sit with him. Excitedly, he said yes and told me where to meet him. I told

Hector what I was doing and where to find me when he was ready or if he needed me.

I got to the ICU and was so happy to see Juan. Unfortunately, I couldn't go in the room and visit Sergio because I wasn't family and he was very ill and battling pneumonia. He hadn't been very conscious for days, and Juan was worried. He tried to put on a strong positive front, but I could see it in his eyes. At one point, a nurse announced, "Code blue in ICU," over the loudspeaker, and Juan jumped out of his seat and ran to his partner's room. I didn't know what was going on, but when he came back a few minutes later, he explained to me that "code blue" meant that someone was dying.

I was telling Juan why I was there when Hector called me. "Hey, do you have the number of that kid who lives with Big and Tasha?" He was a friend of Gia's whom I'd met a few times, but I didn't know him like that, so I told him I would ask Gia. When I called her, she was upset to hear about Big. She wanted to come to the hospital but felt like it may not be the right time. Instead, she agreed to get ahold of her friend and get him there.

When I called Hector back, I told him what she had said, and he said, "Yeah, that ho ain't welcome here. Oh, by the way, Genna's here. So, you need to stay in the ICU because she doesn't want to see you."

I was shocked that he would tell *me* to stay away to make his ex-wife comfortable, so I told him I really didn't give a shit how she felt. Furthermore, I didn't appreciate him putting *her* request over *my* feelings. We started arguing and I told him that he was a pussy and I would just head home when I felt like it since he was going to stay until they got more news about Big.

I told Juan about what he just said, and Juan agreed that his actions were inappropriate but probably not worth fighting over now. Hector called me back and asked me to leave the hospital. He said that Genna had left but he didn't want any drama, and since she was close to Big and a good friend of Tasha's that she'd be back. He wanted me to leave so she didn't start anything with me. It infuriated me, but I left.

Hector finally came home at 3 AM. They had found some internal damage on Big, and he had been moved to the ICU just a couple doors down from where my friend was. He told me that he and Genna agreed that it was best for me and her new boyfriend to avoid coming to the hospital since the wounds were still fresh.

I laughed and told him two of my best friends are there, so until Sergio gets out, I will visit him whenever I damn well please. I was up there with Juan a day or two later.

Juan thought the whole thing was messy. He said he thought there was something fishy about it so he would keep an eye on things in my absence. He was friendly to everyone, and Hector even confided in him a time or two. Juan advised him as best as he could on how to be respectful of our relationship.

Hector decided to plan a fundraising event at his clubhouse for Big. The night of, Genna showed up. She kept her distance from me all night until a big fight broke out among the guys. The women and guests were ushered outside and told to wait there. So, she asked if she could speak to me one-on-one. I asked someone to hold my purse and went to chat with the ex.

She was very short and scrawny compared to me—pretty in the face, but no curve to her body at all. She had dark hair, tattoos, and boots that made her legs look like toothpicks. She looked like she was on drugs. After all I had heard about her, I was expecting her to attack me the second she got me away from the crowd. But she didn't come at me like that at all. For someone who had such a reputation of being so crazy and scary, I didn't see it.

She told me that she just wanted to introduce herself and clear the air between us; I was fine with that. She proceeded to tell me that she had heard a lot about me and about how I was a good woman. She said that I seemed to have a positive impact on Hector and was happy he was happy. She told me that she had a man, and they were very happy, as well. She felt the need to make it clear, though, that she and Hector hadn't been swingers; they'd just had some threesomes together. Mostly, he just cheated on her all the time, which is why she didn't ever want him back. She went on to say that she wasn't keeping him from her children. They didn't want to talk to him or see him because he was so abusive to them and their mother. They didn't want to deal with anymore back and forth drama, so she felt like it was a good thing to finally have it be over. She said that I had actually done her a favor by giving him something else to focus on so she could finally move on. I just listened and nodded. When she was done, we shook hands and went back inside.

When we did, Hector told me to go home. Confused as to why he would ask ME to leave knowing his ex-wife was there, I told him no. I said that we had come together so we would leave together. And, of course, that started the tantrum. The louder and more aggressive he got, the more people were looking at me with that "this poor girl" look on their faces. He was adamant that I leave.

I told him I would but that was going to be the end of our relationship. I proceeded to tell him to come get his clothes the next day and give me my key back. He said he didn't have it on him. I wished him a good night and went home. He was messaging me right after I left telling me that he was sorry, but he couldn't handle being around me like this; he didn't want me to see him this way. I told him that I was done, and he needed to come get his things the next day.

Then next morning, my friend Kia called me. She had heard what had happened through the grape vine and couldn't believe what an idiot Hector was being. I vented out the entire evening to her. When I hung up the phone, I got up to take Rafiki out and was shocked to find Hector passed out on my couch. Clearly, he had my key and didn't want to give it up. As I walked Rafiki, I wondered how I was going to get him out of my apartment.

When I came in, he was still passed out, so I took a shower. I finally woke him up and told him he needed to leave and give me my key. He rolled over and ignored me. I told him again that he wasn't welcome there and he needed to go. He finally sat up and said that he wasn't leaving. He started telling me how he was an emotional wreck the night before. He didn't want his best friend to die. He didn't know how to deal with Genna and I being in the same room. He said he handled it all wrong and that he was sorry. He told me that he never wanted to hurt me and he just needed me to not give up on him. It seemed genuine at the time, so I forgave him.

A day or two after that, the announcement was made that Big wasn't going to pull through and everyone needed to come say their goodbyes before they unplugged him. Hector was devastated; he went straight to the hospital from work. When he got there, he was surprised to find that his ex-wife had brought her new man along to say goodbye to Big. Hector was inappropriately livid; he believed that Genna must have been cheating on him with the man while they were married since they got together almost immediately after she kicked Hector out.

After Genna left, I went up to the hospital to see Juan and Sergio. Juan told me that his mother was kicking them out of her house, so when and if Sergio pulled through, they would have no place to live. I was shocked. I had met his mother a few times and been to her house. She knew they were gay and in love before, so why kick them out now? I told him that they could stay with me until they find their own place. He was so happy and grateful that I was willing to take them in. I had to run it by Hector, but he was surprisingly cool with the idea, so once again, my little apartment was about to be full!

Big died the next day. It hit everyone hard. Hector took it especially hard. We went to the funeral together and I remember him being both mad and disgusted that Gia "had the nerve" to come pay her respects. He still hated her and didn't want her around at all. For whatever reason, Genna decided to sit right behind us. She was there alone.

Outside, everyone was talking about going in one direction or the other. I wanted to go with Gia; I had no desire to go to the clubhouse. So, I asked if that would be okay. Surprisingly, Hector said that it was fine, and he would see me later. So, off I went.

Shortly after that, Sergio got healthy enough to be released, so the boys came to live with us. I had a sunroom in my apartment. It was small, but they were able to set up a little bedroom with a blow-up mattress in there. Sergio was skinny and fragile but still had a sweet positive smile, and the two of them were always fun to be around. Juan was the more blunt of the two, who told it like it was; Sergio was more careful with his delivery, usually, but I suspect that it was because he sometimes struggled with English.

I was curious to know why Juan's mom had kicked them out, so I asked while Hector wasn't home. Sergio came straight out with it. "I have AIDS."

I was shocked. "What?"

Juan came out of the bathroom and saw the look on my face. He looked and Sergio, then back to me and said, "He told you, didn't he?"

I nodded my head, speechless.

Juan went on to explain that Sergio had been diagnosed with AIDS and that he himself had gotten tested and was HIV positive. They didn't know who had given it to whom, but they both loved each other so much that they both tried to take the blame. For Juan's family, though, it was too much to accept. With his mother's beliefs, she could no longer support them.

I started crying. I had never known anyone with this disease, and the only thing I knew was it was a death sentence. Juan calmed me down and explained that it didn't mean they were going to die, but they did have to be more careful. They assured me that they would be very clean and that I would not be at risk of contracting it by just living with them. We all cried, hugged each other, and told each other how much we loved one another the rest of the night.

A few days later, Hector made me go to work with him. While we were in the van, he asked me what was wrong. He could tell that something had changed in me, and he wanted me to be honest with him. So, I started sobbing and told him.

He immediately laughed and said, "Is that all? I figured that's what was going on with them. Hey, it's no big deal. The medicine they have for that nowadays can almost reverse it. They even qualify for all kinds of government benefits and programs! They're going to be fine! I'll talk to them when we get home and tell them where to go to get started."

Confused, I asked, "Why do you seem to have so much knowledge and personal experience with AIDS?"

He told me that his uncle had AIDS and had been living with it for almost 10 years. He said that his uncle had hid it for a long time, but Hector found the bottle of medicine in his uncle's bedroom. He told his uncle, and they had a discussion.

At the time, I didn't have any reason to suspect he was lying. When we got home, he and the boys discussed what options he knew of that they could take advantage of. They were a little sad that I had told him, but after the conversation, everyone felt better.

CHAPTER FIVE

Changes to be Made

Out of nowhere one day, Hector decided it was time for us to get a house together. I explained to him that I was in a lease, and in order to move, I would have to buy myself out. He didn't care; he was adamant that we have a house—a place that belonged to both of us—so he didn't feel like he was just a guest all the time.

So, we started searching. His original idea was to bring the boys with us and find something with a basement or separate living area. We would split everything four ways, so it was affordable for everyone. At first, the boys were on board, but as the weeks went on and they saw more of how he was, they started to bring things to my attention. It was little things at first, like an inappropriate comment he made to them or how he was making them feel uncomfortable. They even suspected him of being bisexual but not wanting me to know. Hector had said to Juan that he must have a huge dick because he could always see the outline in his pants and would ask them personal questions about sex or their relationship.

Of course, I told them it was nothing and said to ignore him. I apologized for them being uncomfortable. But I knew I had to say something to Hector. He was furious. That started a very rapid downfall. They began having verbal disagreements, and Hector even threatened them physically. That was all they needed; they packed up and got out of there.

The day they came to get the last of their things was emotional. Hector was still at work, but one of his bros named Thor from the bike club had come in from out of town; he was a club member from out of state. It wasn't uncommon to house out-of-state members, but he was our first. He was going to stay on my couch for a day or two and came straight to my apartment. It was a little strange meeting some new man this way. Thor was very tall and towered over me. He was black and built like a football player, but had a sweet smile and a baby face, which put me at ease as he introduced himself.

I let him in and led him to the living room. He told me that Hector had explained that there was an uncomfortable situation going on and didn't want me to be alone when the boys came by to get their stuff. I told him that the boys were close friends of mine and that they had issues with Hector, not me. I would never be in any danger around them, no matter the situation.

They showed up soon after. Juan barely spoke at first; he just started grabbing stuff. Sergio was crying. I asked if there was anything I could do, and Juan said, "No, unlike you, I don't negotiate with terrorist."

I told him that I understood how he felt but and asked that he be respectful of me and my man while he in my house.

"Fine, but what the hell are you doing with this jackass, Savannah? You're smarter than this; you're better than this. He is taking advantage of you and turning you against all of your friends."

That's when Thor stood up. I put my hand up and just said, "Please." He stayed standing but didn't say anything.

Juan said, "I can see it's time to go. We love you, and we hope that you will be okay. Do not let this asshole destroy you!" He gave me a big hug, and I walked them to the door. Sergio and I were both in tears. I gave them both one more hug. Sergio told me that he loved me, and I told him the same, not knowing if I would never see them again. When I closed the door, my new giant friend was there to give me a big hug. I never cry in front of anyone if I can avoid it, but for some reason I didn't feel ashamed in front of Thor. He made me feel safe and comforted. I very much enjoyed having him around. Hector never behaved badly toward me in front of him. So, I was sad to see him go when he had to leave a few days later. He had discussed possibly moving to Georgia soon, so I was hopeful that he would be a good influence on Hector. But for the time being, he had to go back home.

I eventually found us a house another town over. I paid out my lease, and we had a move-in date of January 1, 2016. Hector flew his cousin Barb down to stay with us during that time. He said that it was so she could help us with the move, but it turned out that she was just young and a bit of a troublemaker looking to escape. Barb was stunning—she had a beautiful body and gorgeous dark hair. She was very friendly and easy to get along with, but she was in her early twenties and wanted to party all the time.

She did end up being very helpful with packing and helping us move, so I was glad she had come. I didn't know when she was going home, but she had already been there about a week before we moved. She was thrilled to get to our new house.

It was huge compared to my apartment. Only two floors, but they were very well laid out. We had three bedrooms and two bathrooms on the top level. There was also a big living room, another bedroom, an office, a two-car garage, and an area I turned into my shop on the bottom level. I absolutely loved that house. We put a pool table and bar in downstairs. We were set up for home life and party life. I thought we were going to be happy there.

The first day in our new home, he had the cable guy out to hook up the internet and cable, and I don't know why, but Hector was being really mean to me all day. I didn't do anything to him, so I didn't understand why he was behaving like he hated me. He told me to come out to the living room and talk to the cable guy. Jokingly, I said, "Don't tell me what to do." His cousin and I giggled when I said it.

He turned around grabbed both of my arms and shoved me into an empty bedroom and slammed the door. He slammed me against the wall and put his forearm in my neck so that I couldn't talk or breath, got up against me, and said very low, "From now on you're going to learn how the fuck to talk to me. Don't you ever disrespect me like that again, or I'll beat your fucking ass in front of everyone and throw you outside. This is *my* house and you belong to *me*. Now, shut your big fucking mouth and go deal with the cable guy."

He shoved off my neck so hard that I was coughing for about 15 seconds and had to catch my breath. I heard him very politely tell the cable man that I was coming and told Barb that they were going to take a motorcycle ride. I went to the living room to talk to the cable man and he could tell something was wrong. I tried to pull myself together and answer his questions. Before he left, the cable guy turned to me and said, "Are you okay, ma'am? Are you in trouble?"

I was honestly shocked that he asked me that. I thought I was holding it together well. I politely said I was fine and that I wasn't feeling well and sent him on his way.

I went to the bathroom and could see that my neck was still red. My eyes were holding back tears and my hands were shaking. Hector had never put his hands on me before. It was literally the first day in our new house, and that's how we were starting out? I had already given up my apartment and freedom. I was farther away from my family and friends and was financially stuck in this house. I told myself that maybe it was just a fluke and he was having a bad day or something. Besides what's a shove into a wall, really? He didn't actually hurt me, so it's not like he was abusing me, right?

Then, one night, we all decided to go to a bar where some of his bros were shooting pool. It started off okay. Barb started drinking heavily and was chatting with some of the bros. I don't remember why, but she started getting verbally aggressive. The bros though it was funny, and we could all see she was drunk, but Hector told her she needed to settle down.

To that she said, "Don't be gay."

He got in her face and said, "What the fuck did you just say to me? Watch your fucking mouth!" He grabbed her face and pushed her backwards. Instantly, two of his bros stepped in and separated them.

She started screaming drunken pissed off slurs at him. They're escorting him away while he's yelling, "Do you know who I am, bitch? I'll beat your fucking ass!"

She yelled back at him that he better not ever touch her again and called him a pussy. I tried to calm her down, but she was understandably upset. Then, about two minutes later, after I had calmly explained to her that her mouth was only making things worse and maybe it was time to call it a night, here came Hector. He pushed me out of the way and grabbed her by her arm and the back of her hair. Pulling her out to the front so he could take her outside. I'm yelling at him to stop and screaming that she's a girl and he can't put his hands on her like that. He just ignored me and walked off. I tried to follow, but the bros stopped me. They wouldn't let me follow them and told me that I would just make things worse but they would look after her.

Finally, Hector came back in. Alone. I asked him where Barb was, and he said, "She's fucking gone. That stupid bitch can get her shit out of my house and go the fuck back home."

I asked again where was she and if he had just left her outside? He told me he had to slap some sense into her and sent her to Titi's house. I asked him if he was joking, and he looked at me and said, "No. I told you, my hands are bisexual. You should learn from this." He picked up a beer and walked off like nothing had happened.

Obviously concerned, I messaged Barb to see if she was okay. She was very upset. She said that he had picked her up and slammed her against the brick wall outside. The back of her head and her arms hurt. I told her that I was so sorry. I knew Titi was not going to be happy about this.

Titi cussed Hector out as soon as he got to work the next day. She was about the only family member he had that called him out and told him when he was wrong. Unfortunately, though, when everyone else around him turned a blind eye and enabled him, she had no effect. The day before Barb was leaving, their cousin Jimmy, who lived with Titi, came to let her get her things from my house. I was happy to see her and glad that she was going home. She didn't need to be around Hector. She showed me the bruises and clear marks of handprints down the backs of her arms. It made my heart ache. I felt horrible—both that it had happened and that I couldn't do anything to stop it.

Jimmy invited me to go eat some Mexican food with them. Since Hector wasn't home and I didn't know when to expect him, I said sure. We went and enjoyed a nice dinner. We talked a little about Hector's behavior, but it seemed like they were both just used to it. It was what it was, and that's who Hector was. I still can't understand why everyone allowed this his whole life.

While we were at dinner, Hector started messaging me. He was home and wanted to know where the hell I was, who I was with, and why his dinner wasn't ready. I explained that I had gone to dinner to say goodbye to Barb and asked if he wanted something from there. He was pissed. Apparently, I wasn't allowed to do anything without checking with him first. We all thought it was ridiculous, but, again, they weren't surprised.

After they dropped me off and said their goodbyes, I felt a bit relieved. We had moved into our house weeks ago but hadn't spent any time in it alone yet. I would learn very soon that being alone with Hector wasn't very fun. I knew he was pissed at me for going to dinner, so I just asked him how his day was and made small talk. I already learned that it was better to just move on and act like things were fine, especially when they weren't. He still felt the need to reiterate that I was no longer allowed to do anything without first getting his permission. He told me there would be consequences next time and not to test him. I just walked away and ran myself a nice hot bubble bath.

CHAPTER SIX

So It Begins...

In mid-April 2016, my brother and dad invited us to join them at a little carnival that had popped up near our houses. My brother and his girlfriend at the time had moved into a house not too far from Hector and me. My dad was staying with them, and my brother had his son that weekend. I asked Hector if we could go, and he said sure.

It was a beautiful, sunny Saturday. We all had a great time. We rode all the rides, and Hector and my brother played some of the games with my nephew. Everyone was so happy. Then Hector got a call. It was his cousin Jimmy's birthday a few days prior, so his president wanted us all to go out and celebrate.

The day was already great, so we were more than up to celebrating. Hector arranged for us all to meet at this little Latin hookah lounge. He knew the owner, so he liked to go and act like a big shot. We rode up there on his Harley and met everyone. I chatted with some of the other girlfriends and wives I didn't get to see often. I got along really well with the wife of the president of the club Jimmy was in. Her name was Angel, and she was tall, with dark hair and a curvy build. She had a beautiful face and, to me, a beautiful personality. We hit it off well, which Hector hated.

He told me several times that I was not allowed to be friends with her and to stay far away from her. He said all she did was start drama and bullshit and that I shouldn't trust anything she said. But it's hard not to talk to the women you seem to have to be around all the time. We didn't see her often because they had two kids; she was busy being a mom, which I respected.

Everything was going well that night until we went out on the patio to smoke a cigarette and see what the guys were up to. At this point in our relationship, Hector showed ridiculous signs of jealousy towards my ex-boyfriend Bruce. He would go out of his way to try to cause an issue with him. The whole thing started because when I first started dating Hector, I had a picture hanging on my wall of a group of my closest friends and Bruce. He got so mad that I still had a picture of him that he took a picture of Bruce and sent it out to everyone he knew to see if anyone knew him. He wanted to pick a fight with him because of his reputation for being a badass. Bruce and I had spent a passionate seven years together, but more than that, he had been my best friend for a very long time. I had met him when I was 18 years old. We were just friends for years, until we developed into something much more. I hadn't been physical with Bruce in a couple of years. But he and I still maintained a phone friendship. We never saw each other but would occasionally call one another to make sure the other was doing okay. Bruce didn't trust many people, so it wasn't uncommon for him to reach out to me if he just needed to talk or get a different perspective on something he was dealing with. I didn't see why this was a problem for Hector since not only was he still talking to his ex-wife every chance he got but also every other chick in the world that would show him attention. I told him that I would stop answering my phone when Bruce called me when he stopped talking to all his exes. It only seemed fair. Bruce and I didn't discuss anything inappropriate. He knew I respected my relationship and didn't cross any lines.

That night at the hookah lounge, Hector was drunk enough to ask all the guys if they wanted to go to another bar down the street. When he told them what bar it was, he looked back at me with his evil stare and mischievous smile. He knew that was Bruce's bar and that he would most likely run into him. But since he was a shit-starting coward, he only wanted to make a scene as long as his bros were there to protect him.

I said, "We aren't going there." His bro asked him why he wanted to go, and I answered, "Because that's the bar my ex works at, and he has a bug up his ass about him. So, he wants to go act like a badass and start some shit."

Now, at that time, I was new "Property," which meant I was his personal property with a club-issued vest. This was my first time out in public wearing my property vest, and, while wearing it, you are expected to follow certain guidelines.

"Take that fucking vest off, you disrespectful cunt. Don't you ever talk to me like that."

Immediately, the president of the Jimmy's club stepped between us and told him to chill.

We spat a few more hateful words at each other, but for the most part, the subject was dropped. We continued drinking and hanging out. At one point, Hector told me that one of his bros, Little Bit, needed a quick place to crash with his girlfriend, so he told them to go to our house. Apparently, he had left the door unlocked. I wasn't a fan of this young man. He acted like a spoiled little brat whose daddy always cleaned up after him. He would throw ridiculous fits over literally anything. He even tried to intimidate me one time by pulling out a gun and putting it on the table pointed at me while he was lecturing me on some nonsense. I laughed and asked if I was supposed to be intimidated. He put the gun back in his pocket and walked away.

When we finally went to leave, we quickly realized that the guys were too drunk to get us home. They were dropping their bikes before they could even get on them. Still fighting that they were fine, I called an Uber to come get me. I wasn't going to die on a motorcycle tonight. Angel had her own vehicle and was screaming at them about how stupid they were being and that they should just get in the car.

Finally, the owner came out to offer Hector safe storage of the bikes for the night. He agreed to put the bikes in his building after they closed so we could all get home safe. This ridiculous drunken scene went on long enough that we had already gotten the attention of the police officers that were in the area. My Uber arrived, and I told Hector it was time to go. I was leaving with or without him.

I got in the car and asked the lady if she could wait a minute. I explained that he was very drunk, and I needed to get him home. She agreed to wait and took a look at our vests. She asked me how long we had been in the bike life. I told her that he was the member and it was his lifestyle; I had only been around about a year.

She turned around and looked at me and said, "You know, I used to be in that life, hun, so let me give you some advice. Get out. Get as far away from this as you can as fast as you can. They treat their woman like trash. I'm going to be praying for you."

The door opened, and Hector climbed in. The lady faced forward and asked if we were ready to go. What she had said got my attention, but I was too tired to think, so I just shrugged it off.

I was relieved to get home. What had started out as such a beautiful day had turned into something long, dramatic, and unnecessary. As I brushed my teeth and took my contacts out, I looked down at my sweet Rafiki and loved on him when he stretched up for me.

That's when Hector stormed into the bathroom. Right away, I noticed that he was suddenly more sober than the drunken guy I had just helped into the house minutes before. His pupils were dilated, making his eyes seem really dark. It made me think of a character in a movie who was possessed by a demon or something.

"You fucking whore," he spat at me. "Why don't you go fuck Bruce and get the hell out of my life?"

I rolled my eyes looking at him behind me in the mirror and told him that he was drunk and being ridiculous. I said that it was late, so I was going to bed.

I turned around to leave, but he pushed me backwards into the counter, making me step on Rafiki. So, I pushed his ass right back. My push was a bit more aggressive; I landed both hands in the middle of his chest and put all my weight into it, knocking him on his ass. He looked up at me, stunned.

"Don't *ever* touch me again. I'm not a bitch you wanna put your hands on." I pointed my shaky finger at him. I backed up to let him up and turn off the light. He jumped up from the floor and lunged at me, grabbing my throat with both hands and strangling me. He slammed the back of my head against the wall behind me, turned me around, and slammed me to the floor, hitting my head against the wall and my left elbow into my garden tub. He smashed my head against the door twice while still strangling me and screaming in my face. "How dare you take his side in front of my friends! I told you not to challenge me, and now look what you made me do!" He threw himself off of me and stormed out of the bathroom.

I was in complete shock. Pandora's box was open. He really just put his fucking hands on me, so I switched into fight mode. I stepped into our bedroom but saw no sign of him. I walked down the hall past the room Little Bit and his girl were in and stepped into the living room.

He was sitting on the couch, turning on the TV. I walked right up to him and punched him twice in the face, knocking off his glasses. He tackled me and got on top of me. I wrapped my right leg over his left shoulder and around his neck, pulling him down backwards.

Everything from then on was a blur. We fought right there on the floor for what seemed like 30 minutes. I was screaming at him, and he was screaming at me. His friend never made a sound. Never once did he come to see if I was okay or try to stop it. The coward was in *my* guest bedroom, pretending he couldn't hear us.

Finally, I broke away from Hector and stood up. I started crying, not because I was hurt physically, but because I was so mad.

"Why did you do this to me? Why did you make me get rid of my apartment and lose friendships and change my whole life for you to treat me like this? I was fine before you came into my life, and I wish I never met you!"

I went to my room and locked the door, looking around for my purse. I had to make sure that he hadn't gotten my gun. While I was checking to see if it was there, I heard the door handle jiggle—he was trying to get in. He told me to unlock the door. I told him no and said to leave me alone.

Hector burst through the door, shattering the frame. He literally tore the door down. It hung barely attached by to the frame, which was busted and had torn-off pieces of sheet rock stuck to it. He looked at me and simply said, "Don't ever lock a door in this house." He walked to his side of the bed, grabbed his phone charger, and walked back out to the living room.

I didn't hear any noise, and he didn't turn on any lights. I knew he was still in the house because none of the doors opened. I went into the bathroom with Rafiki and sat in my empty tub, pulling my sweet pup in with me. I was shaking and crying. I was so shocked at what had taken place. I had to be dreaming, right? This couldn't be real…

I sat crying into my dog's fur for what seemed like hours. Before long, I started to feel the physical effects from our altercation. My adrenaline was pumping so hard while everything was happening that it didn't faze me while he was hitting and kicking me, but now that the adrenaline was ebbing, I could feel it all. The first thing I noticed was my throbbing head. I reached up and started feeling around in my hairline. I could feel four tender spots that were starting to swell a bit. My throat was raw from being choked and screaming at the top of my lungs. My left thigh was red and beginning to swell from being kicked repeatedly. My stomach hurt, and I had scrapes and carpet burn on my knees and elbows. Still, overall, I felt like I came out of it like a champion. He was careful to avoid my face. He punched me in the head and pulled my hair a lot to control me, like a little bitch, but he never touched my face.

Finally, I got out of the tub to face myself in the mirror. I looked like I had just been drug down the street. My hair was all over the place, and there wasn't much of my body that wasn't slightly swollen and red; some of it was already bruising. I tried to clean myself up a little and calm down enough to maybe go to bed. Still curious about where he was lurking, I mustered up the courage to tiptoe out to the living room and see if he was there. He was lying on the couch facing away from me. It looked like he was asleep, so I went back to the bedroom.

I tried to close the door as best as I could, but it was in shambles. I lay down in bed and called Rafiki up. I curled up to him under the covers and started crying again. I started going over everything I had said and how I was reacting to him and began thinking that maybe it had been my fault. He *had* warned me several times about my mouth and my smart-ass comments. He told me that he used to fight his ex-wife all the time for the same reasons. I knew how insecure he was, and I started to feel like I was to blame; I shouldn't have said this or that; I need to work on being more understanding; I need to work on not provoking him; I need to make him feel secure and loved with me. Otherwise he would never change. He would never feel comfortable trusting me if I was constantly combative. I fucked this up. Now I need to be the one to fix it. I didn't want him to compare me to his ex because he spoke so poorly of her. He made her out to be a monster. So, I felt like trying a different approach would work.

Since I knew I couldn't sleep anyways and I wanted to fix this, I went back out to the living room.

"Babe?" I said just above a whisper in a shaky voice. I got down on my knees and started crying. He didn't move. "I'm so sorry," I sobbed. "I know I upset you. I know this was my fault, and I'm so sorry."

He turned over and said, "I'm sorry too. I just love you so much, and I'm so afraid that you're going to realize that I'm no good and leave me like everyone else in my life has."

I asked him to come to bed. He acted like his entire body was bruised and battered, so I helped him up and to the bedroom. I turned off the lights and settled in next to him, both of us crying slightly.

He said, "My whole body hurts, babe. You're fucking tough," and let out a sort of uncomfortable laugh. I told him my whole body hurt as well, and I never want to feel like this again.

He turned to me, put his hand on my face, and said, "Then don't ever try to leave me."

He grabbed the back of my sore head and pushed his hand through my hair as he climbed on top of me. I could feel how aroused he was and thought to myself, *What a strange time to be turned on.* But I had to make things right with him. I had to show him how much he could rely on me; that I wanted to do better. His kisses were a kind of kiss I hadn't really had from him before. There was a hunger about him. He kissed me as if my kiss were the only thing that could make him better. It was aggressive and forceful but not in a bad way. He tore at my panties, unable to wait any longer to have me. So, I let him. I gave myself to him completely. We had fought several times before, but makeup sex had *never* been this hot. I felt like my whole body was on fire. I couldn't get enough. I wanted it to last forever. I had never felt so close to him. Finally, we wrapped our arms around one another and drifted off to sleep. I knew it was late because the sun was already starting to come up. But I felt safe and happy in that moment, ironically.

When we finally woke up, it was like nothing bad had happened. We even joked about the door being smashed and compared bruises and scratches on our bodies. I told him that I would ask my brother to come fix the door and see what he would charge us. We agreed to tell him we came home drunk and Hector had fallen through the door before I could open it. I knew we had to be believable for my brother. He was the last person I needed to find out.

Our guests had apparently left before we woke up. I was thankful for that. I wasn't ready to face them after everything they must have heard. I made us food and we watched movies snuggled on the couch. It was like we had finally connected. We were finally on the same page and things were going to be better. There had been so much tension between us since we moved into the house, that this was the first time I felt like we were both completely comfortable around each other. I decided not to tell anyone about what happened. I knew that if I did, they would overreact and blow things out of proportion. I told myself that it wouldn't happen again, and we were fine.

CHAPTER SEVEN

Outside Influences

Back in January, I heard of an old friend of mine named Bessie who had recently had her heart broken.

She was a little shorter than me— probably about 5'6". When I met her, she was overweight, wore glasses, and had hair so long it looked like she had never cut it. She hadn't known how to apply makeup or dress like a girl. So, I took her under my wing and we became very close over the years. I did everything for this chick. I drove her everywhere, paid for her to go out and have fun. Wherever I went, she went with me. We'd had a bit of a falling out about a year and a half prior to this time and had stopped speaking.

When I heard she wasn't doing well, I reluctantly reached out to her. I sent her a message and told her that I heard she was having a tough time and that I was sorry for the way things had gone between us. I really just wanted to let her know that I wished her nothing but happiness.

She messaged me back very quickly and thanked me, apologizing as well. We chatted back and forth here and there and eventually started talking all the time again. At the time, she lived inside the perimeter in Atlanta, so her apartment was about 40 minutes from my new house. She hadn't met Hector yet and since we were getting along well, I decided that we should try to hang out. It felt good to rekindle our friendship. She was someone I had always been really honest with, and she spent years being my ride-or-die best friend.

We fell back into place naturally. She had a busy schedule and worked on the weekends, so we didn't see her that much at first. But then she would pack a bag and come camp out at our house with her dog on the weekends. She liked going to the clubhouse at first because she didn't mind the male attention, but that got old to her pretty quickly. There were too many rules to follow, and she just wanted to be free. I understood that.

When Bessie started coming around, though, Gia was not happy. She didn't like her at all. I think it upset her that Hector didn't mind having Bessie around. I was still on a tight leash with Gia. Even though she was able to come around more now that she and I were made properties, Hector still didn't like us being too close.

One day, Hector came home in a bad mood. I asked him what was wrong, but, of course, it was none of my business. I moved along and told him Bessie was coming over. He said that he was tired and didn't want any noise, so she didn't need to come over this weekend. Since Bessie was already on her way, I told him it was too late to change plans, but we could go downstairs or just go out and get a drink or see a movie. He grabbed the remote and threw it directly into my relatively new 55" flat screen TV as hard as he could. The screen shattered instantly and there was a big hole where it had hit.

Shocked, I said, "What the hell was that for?"

He said, "I fucking told you I was tired and going to bed. If I'm staying in, you're staying in."

Ignoring his command, I said, "Well, I hope you're happy, because now you get to go buy me a new TV since you had to throw a tantrum."

He said, "That's what happens when you want to be a fucking smart ass," as if it were *my* fault he reacted that way. He walked back to our bedroom and slammed the door so hard the house shook.

When Bessie got to the house, he was already passed out in bed. I told her what happened when she saw the TV, and she put her stuff down in the bedroom and came back out. "Well, fuck him, let's go out."

I was reluctant to disobey him at first, but he just shattered my TV, so yeah…fuck him.

We went to the movies. Then we decided we were hungry and went to Denny's. I hadn't heard from him, so I knew he was still passed out cold, but Bessie noticed that I kept checking my phone.

"This isn't you, Savannah," she said to me as I was looking for the 20th time to see if I was in trouble.

Putting my phone down, I said, "What do you mean?"

"Bitch, I've known you for years and have never seen you cower to a man like this. What's going on?"

Not knowing how to answer, I just said, "Nothing. Everything is okay."

"That man just smashed your fucking TV over you saying I was coming over, and that's okay? That's not something a grown-ass man would do. That's a little boy throwing a fit because Mommy wouldn't let him have ice cream before bed."

She was absolutely right.

We wrapped up dinner and went back to the house. We stayed down in the bar and had some drinks; we had a lot of catching up to do. It was nice to have my friend back. Nice to have someone who knew me so well before all this craziness started. But she saw straight through it. I knew eventually that it was going to be a problem.

We finally said our goodnights and went to bed. I crawled into bed as carefully as I could, trying desperately not to wake him up. As soon as I got in, he rolled over and wrapped his body around mine lovingly. I breathed a sigh of relief, feeling like I had gotten away with something. Then, his right hand was around my throat, and his left hand grabbed my hair. He wrapped his legs around me and put all his weight on me so that I couldn't move.

He quietly said in my ear, "I told you that you weren't going out. Where the fuck were you?"

"We just went to the movies and to Denny's," I squeaked with his hand just loose enough to let me breath.

"You better not be fucking lying to me; I will snap your fucking neck and stab your fat-ass friend if she has a problem with it."

Remaining calm, I squeaked, "I have movie tickets and the receipt from dinner, babe. I'm not lying, I swear. I love you! You were sleeping, and we didn't want to wake you up. Since the TV is broken, we decided to go watch a movie."

Seeming satisfied, he loosened his grip on me and told me to take off my clothes. I ripped my clothes off as fast I could, hoping he wouldn't make a scene. I didn't want Bessie to suspect any more than she already did.

"Ride my dick, and don't even think about coming. This is for me, not for you to enjoy."

Like the puppet I was, I did as commanded. Luckily, it never took more than a couple of minutes, so I just thought of it as one of my chores. Even if I wanted to enjoy it, it was rare that he would last long enough for me to finish anyway. If trying to make me feel degraded and like I didn't matter turned him on, then so be it. I was tired and wanted to go to sleep.

As soon as he was done, he swiped me off of him and rolled over. Thankful it was over, I went to the bathroom. I put my hair up and hopped into a hot shower. Sex with him was either hot or made me feel dirty, shameful, and unsatisfied. So, I couldn't wait to wash him off me when he was finished. That night, like so many other nights, it felt like he had gone to the bathroom on me, so I made the water extra hot.

While I was in the shower, I started crying. *Maybe I should tell someone what I'm going through. Maybe I can tell Bessie and she won't overreact. Maybe she'll just listen and advise me and be there for me,* I thought. No. Even after all the time we spent not talking, I knew how protective my friends were of me. I knew that if they knew the truth, they would create a war. So, I told myself that the less they knew, the better.

I was in this situation because I had allowed myself to be. I ignored the warnings and the signs. I wasn't some victim; I was a grown-ass woman who made my own decisions. I just needed to do better—be less mouthy, less sarcastic. Pleasing him and fixing him were the only things that mattered. I got frustrated with myself in these weak moments when I would start crying and feeling sorry for myself. I knew I was bringing on some of this behavior myself. I didn't have to be rebellious all the time; I didn't have to be so mouthy and critical of him, knowing how insecure he was. It seemed easier to tell myself that in order to help *him,* I needed to change *my* behavior. How could I expect him to change if I wasn't willing to do the same? I couldn't, it didn't make sense to me.

Soon after that, Hector sat me down and told me that Thor had a really great job offer here in Atlanta. Thor used to be a football player. He was semi-pro and was even going to be in the NFL until a knee injury took him out of the game. Instead, he got an assistant-coaching job that he really wanted. It was such short notice, though, that he didn't have a place to stay. Since he was able to leave his daughter with her mother and keep her in the school and environment she was used to, he just needed to rent a room for a few months, so Hector told him that he could stay with us. I was actually happy to hear this. I didn't know Thor well yet, but I did know that he was kind, and Hector wouldn't be so awful to me if he were here. I agreed to let him stay for as long as he needed.

When Thor showed up, Rafiki and I went out to greet him and help him carry in his things since Hector wasn't home yet. I had recently quit my fulltime job since I had a shop set up at home. I still worked for companies when they needed me to; I just charged a daily rate instead of hourly since I was so fast at getting jobs done that it was more lucrative for me this way. When Thor opened the door and stepped out, he was smiling and friendly just as I remembered. He gave me a big hug and told me that he was very grateful to be able to stay with us. I asked him if he needed help bringing anything in. He said, "No mama, I got it. I would never ask you to carry my stuff. You're doing enough as it is." He opened his trunk and I started grabbing stuff. He laughed. "Well, all right."

He hadn't seen the house yet, so he was excited to get the tour. Rafiki and I showed him all around and helped him get his things into his room. I asked him if he needed anything else, and he politely said no, so I left him to get settled in while I started dinner.

I really liked having him stay with us. He didn't leave messes anywhere, he ate whatever I cooked if he was there, and he was always considerate of my home.

He even called and asked for permission when he was having a lady friend come by. He told me on the phone, "Hector said it was fine, but I know how the lady of the house can turn into a lioness over unknown females in her territory!" That made me laugh because it was so true. But he was smart enough to ask, and the ladies I met were all very respectful of our home.

He really wasn't home often because of his job, so he was the perfect room-mate. I remember we all went out one night and Bessie came. She instantly liked Thor. They flirted all night while she looked up at him with dreamy eyes. She stayed with him that night. I don't think they had sex, just snuggled. But she was really crushing on him after that.

Since he was a club member, we saw him at the clubhouse often. Gia took a liking to him as well. She took him home one night, and that disgusted Bessie. Bessie hated Gia just as much as Gia hated her. It was usually a little uncomfortable to hang out with them both. But once they'd had a few drinks they were typically more tolerant of each other.

One night we had a small gathering, and Bessie had a little too much whiskey. I had told her several times she needed to leave that shit alone. It made her argumentative and messy. But when the boys are shoving drinks in your face, it's hard to say no. She was all over Thor, and we could see that he wasn't really feeling it. So he came downstairs to play pool. Knowing Bessie had gone up there after him and seeing him come down alone, I asked where she was.

"Up there pouting," he said. Everyone laughed and she came downstairs.

We had a projector screen downstairs that Hector hooked up to his PlayStation so we could watch YouTube. Adele's "Hello" came on and Bessie went to change it halfway through. They guys yelled at her not to touch it and continued belting out the song like a bunch of silly boys. Drunken Bessie was immediately offended; she got up and walked upstairs.

A few minutes later, Hector and Thor decided to make a beer run. As soon as I heard the garage door open, Hector called my phone.

"Come get your drunk-ass friend out of her car. She isn't driving like that. Put her ass to bed somewhere; she's embarrassing me."

I didn't even know she had been trying to leave, so I ran out to stop her. As the boys drove off, me and the one other girl that was there tried to get her out of the car back inside. She was crying angrily and having a total drunken breakdown. Finally, I got her inside and up to a guest room. She just kept crying the whole way. I guess all the stuff she was going through and hadn't dealt with yet had finally come crashing down.

Hector burst into the room to see what was going on. He said, "Enough catering to this bitch. Get up—we have company, and she's not going to ruin our good time."

I told him I would be out in a minute; I just wanted to let her vent and make sure she didn't leave.

"I'm not going to tell you again. Get your ass up! Fuck that sloppy bitch. I'm your man. So unless you want me to come over there and drag your ass out of this room, you better move *now*!"

I shot up off the floor where I'd been sitting and said, "Okay."

Bessie was shouting, "Fuck you, asshole!" at Hector as I apologetically closed the door.

I turned to follow him, and he grabbed me by the arms and forced me into our bedroom. He shoved me onto the bed and climbed on top of me, getting right in my face and holding my head so I had to look right at him. It was dark but the door was still open so there was just enough light to see his face. He had that same look in his eye from the night we beat the shit out of each other. I froze.

"Why do you bitches never learn? Why do you make me do this? You will *not* embarrass me in front of my friends! That bitch is no longer allowed here. She leaves first thing in the morning, and she won't be staying weekends in this house again, do you understand?"

"Yes. I'm sorry, babe," I said shakily.

We heard Thor coming down the hall looking for us. He immediately let my face go and started kissing me and running his hands all over my body.

I heard Thor say, "Oh my bad!" and laugh.

Hector sat up and laughed too. "Nah, you good. I just needed a little taste real quick. We're coming." He jumped off of me, laughing, and said, "Come on, babe." He reached his hand out lovingly to help me off the bed.

Thor said, "I'm not mad at you, bro—she's a beautiful woman. You're a lucky man."

"Shit she's lucky too!" Hector laughed while wrapping his arms around me from behind and kissing my cheek. "Right babe?"

I laughed uncomfortably and said, "Of course."

He slapped me on the ass and said, "Let's go downstairs. We'll have plenty of time for fucking later!"

I laughed and asked if I could use the bathroom first.

"Did you just ask permission to use the bathroom in your own home?" Thor asked jokingly. But I could see that he had noticed the panic in my face. It was only an instant, but I could tell by the way he looked at me that he had seen a red flag. I just laughed and went to my bathroom, telling them I'd be right down.

After that night Thor started asking questions. But questions weren't something I wanted. I was good at acting like nothing was wrong. But I am the *worst* liar. You can see it in my face and body language as soon as I even try.

It started out with him noticing frequent bruises or marks on my body. He would ask what happened, and I would always say it was work-related. "Oh, I'm just a klutz," I would say. "Not much space in my shop, so I probably hit myself on something."

He wouldn't push me much because Hector was usually around, but I could tell by the look on his face that he wasn't buying it.

He stayed with us for a few months, but eventually the season came to an end, and he had to head back home to be with his daughter. A few days before he left, I remember him coming home before Hector. He sat on the couch across from me, and we started talking. First it was just about family stuff and general small talk. Then he hit me with it.

"Is he putting his hands on you?"

Stunned by the directness of the question, I asked what makes him think that.

"Well you sure seem to have a lot of strange marks on your body, and you jump up like a soldier when he tells you to do something. I know he has a history of violence with his ex-wife, so all signs point to concern."

I got nervous and started tearing up. All I could say is: "I'm fine." I got up and went to the kitchen, hoping he hadn't noticed my tears. He respectfully gave me a minute and then followed behind.

"Come here, mama," he said in a disappointed tone while wrapping his arms around me. "You are a beautiful, amazing woman. Any man would be blessed to have you. Hell, we all wish we had a woman like you. Don't let this man destroy you."

I was now full on crying in his giant embrace.

"I'm going to talk to him before I leave," he said.

Immediately, panic set in, and I ripped away from him. "Please don't do that!" I yelled much louder than needed. "I'm begging you, please! I'm fine! This is nothing I can't handle. I'm helping him! You'll only make things worse, and then I'll be here with him alone!" My whole body was shaking. I would have gotten on my knees and begged if that's what it took for him to stay silent.

"Okay, mama, okay. Calm down. I won't say anything to him if you don't want me to, but you can't keep doing this. I can see how strong you are. You have a great career; you're hardworking and gorgeous. Why are you putting up with him?" he asked.

"He needs me," I whimpered, wiping my nose.

"Okay, but what about you?" he asked.

"Does anyone know about this? Your dad and brother strike me as the kind of men that would have charges already brought against them if they knew," he laughed.

I said no.

He asked if Gia knew.

I told him that she knew he had a temper and threw his hissy fits. But I wasn't really trying to let anyone know. I told him that Bessie was starting to ask questions, and that was about it.

"Maybe you should at least tell Gia or Bessie the truth. You need someone to talk to, at least."

"They'll tell my dad and brother. I can't let them hurt Hector." I could see how disappointed in me he was. That was the exact look I didn't want from anyone. I didn't feel like a victim of anything. I felt like I was the only one strong enough to stand by a broken boy who needed to heal. But people were starting to notice more and more, so I had to do a better job.

Shortly after Thor moved away, Hector took me to a little hookah bar we hadn't been to yet. One of his friends who worked there as a bartender and waitress had invited us over to check the place out. It was small but cozy. I liked his friend right away; she reminded me of myself in many ways. She was beautiful and funny, laid back, and had a responsible vibe to her that I found refreshing. Most of the female 'friends' of his I had met were unimpressive to say the least. This woman was a single mother and was working her butt off to support her child. She didn't seem to be interested in drama, drugs, or sleeping with every guy who paid her attention—I respected that.

Hector and I were having a nice time and the drinks were flowing. At one point, we were outside and I noticed him looking through his Instagram feed.

"Why haven't you accepted my follow request on Instagram yet?" I asked.

He laughed nervously, locking his phone. "Because I don't want you on there," he said.

We had been together for over a year. He and I lived together the entire time, and the fact that he didn't want me to see it made me more curious.

"Why? What would you possibly post on social media that I can't see?" I asked.

"None of your business. Don't start a fight right now." he said.

"I'm not starting a fight. I'm just wondering why I have so many rules that I have to follow, and you think you can do whatever you want," I said, getting irritated.

"You don't need to see my Instagram. I'm not hiding shit; I just don't feel the need for you to have access to everything I do," he said obviously getting annoyed with me.

"Well, it feels a little bit shady, and I don't like it," I said.

"Fine! You want to see it? Fuck it!" he said, pulling out his phone.

A moment later, I got a notification that he had finally accepted my follow request.

I unlocked my phone and started scrolling through his page. Now I see why he didn't want me on there. He was acting completely single on there! If the posts weren't about naked women being tied up and beaten or some stupid photo of him trying to be sexy, they were pictures of him and his ex-wife. I was nowhere to be found. Anyone following him on his Facebook knew he was with me, but I didn't exist on his Instagram. There was a naked selfie of him in my bathtub with candles. He wasn't showing his penis, but he had bedroom eyes and the caption said, "Need someone to share this with." That made me furious. He *never* took a bath without me, so clearly I was there; I just hadn't gotten into the tub yet. There he was in *our* tub, in *our* house, where *we* lived as a couple.

"What the hell, Hector? You are looking *really* single on this page!" I said showing him the post.

He rolled his eyes. "Whatever. It's *my* page" he said arrogantly.

Then I stumbled across one of the pictures I had taken of him. In the picture, he was completely naked, holding his dick and staring sexily at the camera. He had cropped out his penis, of course, but why the hell would he post this if it weren't to get some female attention?

"*Really?!*" I asked showing him the post.

"See, this is why I didn't want you on there! You blow everything out of proportion," he said.

"You would literally beat my ass if I was pulling this shit!" I yelled at him.

"Lower your fucking voice," he said in a warning tone.

"Fuck you," I said, walking towards my car.

"You're drunk. You aren't driving," he said.

"Well, I'm leaving," I said stubbornly.

"I knew you would be a drama queen and ruin our night. This is why I don't want to take your ass anywhere," he said getting into the driver seat of my car.

"How are *you* mad at *me* right now? You're literally trying to be a ho on Instagram, and *I'm* the asshole?" I asked as he drove off angrily.

"I knew I shouldn't have let you see my shit," he said to himself shaking his head.

"No, you shouldn't have been posting a bunch of thirsty-ass posts, trying to get the attention of these groupies of yours," I said, equally disgusted. "You're so pathetic," I said, shaking my head.

He slammed on the brakes and pulled off to the side of the road. "I'm pathetic?" he asked, looking at me with the dark eyes that told me I was in trouble.

"Why do you feel the need to do shit like this? I give you all the attention you want; I fuck you when you want me to; I've done everything you have asked me to do! Why am I not good enough for you?" I asked.

"You called me pathetic, right?" he said, unbuckling his seatbelt. "Okay, you can get the fuck out of my life, you fat bitch!" He shoved my head backwards into the door and window of my car. He slammed my head three times, spat in my face, called me a whore, and got out of the car.

It was the middle of the night, and we were on a very popular street in Gwinnett County, Georgia, which is known to have plenty of police activity. I didn't want him to get in trouble; he was drunk—we both were—so I got out of the car and chased after him.

"Babe, get back in the car. We're going to get arrested out here. Stop!" I yelled, grabbing his arm.

He turned around and shoved me to the ground. "Get the fuck out of here!" he said, turning away from me.

I got up and tried again. "Babe, I'm sorry. We can talk about this later. I didn't mean to upset you. Let's just get home! This is stupid!" I said, trying to get him in the car.

He turned around and shoved to the ground again, this time kicking me in the back of the leg twice. He towered over me and said, "We don't have anything to discuss! I will do whatever the fuck I want! You want to go home? Okay, fine," he said, grabbing my hair. He tried to drag me but wasn't very successful because of the broken asphalt and dirt I was lying on. I could feel the hair being pulled out of my head.

I screamed, "*Stop! I'm fucking sorry!*" and started crying.

"Not yet, but you're gonna be," he said. "Get your ass up, and get in the car—you're driving." He pulled me to my feet by my hair.

"I can't drive, I'm drunk," I said.

"I don't fucking care," he said, leading me back to the car by my hair and opening the driver-side door. "Get in," he said, throwing me into the car. He got into the back seat and moved to the middle so that he could see my face in the mirror. "Drive," he barked, smacking the back of my head so hard that my hair went into my face.

Not wanting to escalate the situation, I said a quick prayer to God while putting the car in drive. *Please God just get us home safely,* I prayed silently. We were only about 12 minutes from our house, so as long as I didn't get pulled over, I figured that I would make it; I just had to focus.

"How dare you speak to me the way you do!" he said, shaking his head angrily. "Do you know how many bitches would *love* to be you? How many want to be with me? Shit, your fat whore best friends would *love* to take your place," he said. "Why do you think Gia made me fuck her when we were at your apartment that night? Why do you think she was so upset and cried when she talked about me at dinner with Titi? She was pissed because I wouldn't be with that bitch if you fucking paid me to be. Nobody wants that fat whore, but I wanted *you*; she's fucking jealous of you, of *us*. She's mad I didn't want her ass," he continued.

I didn't respond. I was just trying to focus on getting home safely. I hated driving at night anyways, and I was in no way sober at the moment. I was focusing on the lines in the road and my speed, so I wasn't able to pay attention to what he was saying.

BAM! He punched me hard in the right side of my head just behind my right ear. The car swerved in response, and I slowed down almost to a stop. Thank God the road was clear.

"Babe, I'm fucking driving!" I said, looking back at him.

He slapped me in the face. "If you stop this car again I will drag you out of it and leave you on the side of the road," he growled at me. "*Drive bitch!*" he screamed.

I was shaking and crying; my head was already throbbing and hitting me in the head was only making it more impossible for me to drive. "I'm sorry babe," I said, grabbing the steering wheel.

"Don't you know how lucky you are? You have a good-looking man who loves you, and all you do is bitch. I'm never enough for you, am I?"

I didn't know what to say. If I responded with anything other than what he wanted to hear, I was in trouble; if I didn't respond at all, I was in trouble. There was no winning for me. I had felt like such a different person a few minutes ago as I called him pathetic. "Babe, I love you. I didn't mean to say that."

"Didn't mean to say what?" he demanded, moving closer to me aggressively.

I pulled up to a red light only maybe five minutes from my house. "I didn't mean to call you that," I said, looking down at my hands.

BAM! He punched me again in the same throbbing spot on the back of my head, this time hitting my ear, making the pain sharper. I put my hand up to block him from hitting me there again and cowered toward my window.

"Please stop," I begged, crying. "I said I was sorry!"

"Quit fucking crying!" he spat at me, sitting back in his seat. "It's fucking green, stupid. Drive!" he said angrily.

I did as I was told and made it to the next red light—the last red light before we were home.

"I have had a hundred bitches finer than you. You aren't even my type, you know. I settled for you," he said.

Tears were pouring out of my eyes. *Don't say anything, Savannah. You'll only upset him more,* I thought to myself.

BAM! He punched me behind my left ear. I was almost relieved he hadn't chosen to keep attacking the same spot. "Drive!" he yelled as the light turned green.

"I'm sorry!" I said in a loud whisper. Finally, I saw our house. "Thank you, Jesus," I whispered silently.

"I should make you sleep in the fucking car," he said, laughing.

I pulled in and closed the garage door, stepping out of the car cautiously. "Can I please come inside? I won't say anything." I sounded like a cowering dog.

He laughed and lit a cigarette. "Now who's pathetic?" he asked arrogantly as he walked into our home with his nose in the air.

I knew I was pathetic. I had never been so weak in my entire life. Why was I doing this? Who was I? I didn't even recognize myself. I hated myself; I hated who I was becoming; I hated that no matter what I did, I could not please him. I just wanted to be happy; I just wanted him to be happy with me. Why did I keep fucking this up? Why was I acting so insecure?

So what if he wanted to put on some fake face on social media? I knew he was insecure and craved constant attention—who was that really hurting?

Way to go, Savannah. You really fucked this night up, I told myself.

I walked cautiously into the house, creeping up the stairs. Hector was out on the back porch, smoking a cigarette and looking through his phone. I walked quietly back to our room. I took a handful of Advil for my throbbing head and undressed carefully. I turned on the shower and stepped in. The stream was freezing, but I thought that might help the swelling in the back of my head and my right hip where he had tried to drag me along the broken asphalt. My skin was shredded and dirty; I'd only been wearing a skimpy skirt. I knew he wouldn't let me put ice on myself. It upset him for me to 'lick my wounds' in front of him—I had already learned that lesson—so cold showers were becoming my new friend.

When I came out of the bathroom, Hector was lying in bed, still scrolling through his phone. I went to my drawers to get a tank top to wear to bed, but without looking up from his phone, he barked, "Don't bother. I want you naked."

I knew where this was headed, so I took a deep, shaky breath and turned off the bathroom light.

"Drop the towel," he said sternly.

I did as commanded.

"Come over here, and get on your knees," he said, pointing to the floor next to him. Not wanting any more drama, I obliged. He put his phone down on the nightstand next to him. "Apologize," he said, folding his arms behind his head looking at the ceiling and crossing his legs.

"I'm sorry," I said quietly. I didn't want to do this, but I knew there was no escaping it.

"I don't believe you," he said, rolling over putting his back to me while I remained kneeling on the floor.

I sighed with disappointment, looking down at my entangled fingers. *I'm tired, my head hurts, and I just want to go to bed.* "I love you so much, babe. I'm so sorry I upset you. How can I make this better?" I asked pathetically.

He didn't respond right away. "Come get on the bed," he demanded with his back still towards me.

I got up and went to my side of the bed. I lay on my back on top of the covers. My hair was wet from my icy shower, so I was starting to shiver.

"Why do you make me punish you?" he asked me, putting his warm hand on my nervous stomach.

"Because I'm stupid and stubborn," I said.

He laughed, moving towards me. I was happy to feel the warmth of his body—I was freezing. "Why are you so cold?" he asked.

"I just took a shower," I said. He stroked my wet hair.

"What am I going to do with you?" he asked.

"Hopefully just love me," I said in my sweetest voice.

He turned my head towards his. "I do love you, but I feel like you go out of your way to disrespect me." He held my chin firmly.

"I'm really sorry," I said, shivering.

"I love it when your body trembles for me." He kissed me. My body was shivering because I was naked wet and cold, but whatever he wanted to believe was fine with me. He ran his hand all over my body, stopping between my legs. "Why aren't you wet?" he asked, pulling his face away from mine.

Why would I be? "I just took a shower," I said innocently.

"Well, I want to fuck. Get the lube out," he said.

"Okay." I rolled over to my drawer.

"I'll be taking that ass tonight," he said, making me freeze.

"Babe…" I said, looking cautiously over my shoulder. "I don't want that."

"I don't really care. You owe me," he said, reaching for the bottle in my hand. "And you're lucky I'm using lube this time."

I guess he had a point. Normally he would just spit on me and rip me open while I cried in a pillow. Maybe this time I at least wouldn't bleed. I felt the wet cold liquid on my ass.

"You're just going straight there?" I asked, stalling.

"Shut the fuck up," he said, shoving my face down. He rolled me onto my side while he got behind me in a spoon position. There was no preparations, no foreplay to get me into it—it was pure punishment for my actions. This was for him, and the only thing I could do was try to zone out and be somewhere else while he did what he wanted.

The lube was a courtesy, but didn't get rid of the pain completely. I clinched my pillow and buried my face while he invaded me. "Oouch," I cried into the pillow.

"Relax…you're only making it harder on yourself," he whispered in my ear hungrily.

I cried as quietly as I could so he didn't get upset and waited for it to be over. As usual, it didn't take more than a few minutes, which was a blessing of its own.

When he was finished, he rolled away from me, allowing me to run to the bathroom. After I cleaned myself up, I curled up in the corner of my bathroom crying. I hated the way that made me feel; I hated the way *he* made me feel. What the hell was wrong with me?

Get over it, Savannah, I told myself. *It was only a few minutes, and it's over with now. Stop crying and move on.* I stood up and wiped off my face in the mirror. "You're stronger than this," I said to my reflection. I turned off the light and went to bed where Hector was already passed out.

CHAPTER EIGHT

Good Times

Being part of a motorcycle club requires traveling. *Lots* of traveling if you're as involved as Hector was. He would drag me all over the place, going to events in surrounding states. It was all about showing support. Every year, they have a huge event up in Philadelphia to kick off the beginning of riding season. Hector went every year, so of course, we were going. I was looking forward to it because instead of it just being him and me traveling, it was everyone.

The guys got on their bikes, and the ladies followed the pack in their vehicles. Gia has a pretty solid case of OCD, so she wanted to drive her own car. I was happy to let her and just relax in the back.

The "mother hen" of all the properties decided to ride with us, and we were happy to have her. Everyone called her Big Mama, and she was a delight to be around. She was a short, heavy-set black woman. She was so light-skinned that her husband, who is now the president of our chapter, would refer to the three of us as his "white women." He announced that every time we walked into the room, just in case we didn't stick out enough. Gia and I just loved them both. Big Mama was always kind to us. She tried to show us the ropes and keep us in line as properties. Even though we were loud and talked back more than we should, she seemed to genuinely look out for us.

This was Gia's and my first time making this trip. We planned to stop and stay for a night with Big Mama and the rest of our designated pack in her family's home in Virginia and then keep going. Gia, being the always-on-edge, angry road-rage driver she is, had us gripping our seats and even catching some air throughout the first half of the trip! Big Mama and I thought we were going to die a couple of times, but we managed. We had an awesome time. The three of us talked and laughed the whole way there.

When we got to Big Mama's family's house, she explained the rules to all of us: leave everything the way you found it and be respectful. The house had a reputation for being haunted, which Gia and I were both kind of excited and nervous about. The supposed ghosts were just a few friendly ancestors and possibly a dog. Big Mama told us that the ghosts didn't like anyone having sex in the house if they weren't married.

We laughed, and I said, "No sex. Got it."

We all hung out and had dinner together. When I took Hector's stuff upstairs, something fell out of his pocket. I picked it up, and to my surprise, realized what it was. I called for him angrily and confronted him immediately.

"Why the fuck did this bag of cocaine just fall out of your pocket?"

Reaching for the bag, he said, "Why are you going through my shit?"

"Wrong answer. Try again. I told you when you met me this shit is a deal breaker for me. Are you on drugs? Have you been lying to me this whole fucking time?!"

His tone changed completely. "Babe, don't be ridiculous! That's not even mine. My dad asked me to hold onto it for him."

"Why does your dad need you to hold his coke, Hector?"

"It was just a safety measure in case we got pulled over. He can't get caught with drugs, or he'll be in violation of his probation and go straight back to jail." He reached out gently and grabbed my hand.

"I love you, baby. Calm down. I understand why you're upset, and I'm sorry. I should have told you. I'll go give it to him right now." He kissed me on the forehead and went back downstairs.

Not wanting to ruin this trip when it had just started, I let it go and decided to believe him. He knew this was the one thing I wouldn't stick around for, so I convinced myself he was being honest. We all knew his dad was a cokehead, so at the time, it was believable.

As it grew later, all the ladies decided to be responsible and go to bed since we still had a long way to go the next day. Gia was sharing a room with Hector and me since there were two beds in it, so she and I went to our room.

The boys stayed outside talking until Big Mama finally went out and told them that it was 2 a.m. and they needed to get some rest.

I woke up to Hector ripping the covers off me and tearing off my pants. I asked him what he was doing, and he said, "Taking what's mine." He started preforming oral sex on me, which was odd because that didn't happen often. He wasn't good at it, so it didn't really bother me when he stopped.

I told him to stop and said that we needed to get some rest.

He sat up and said, "Gia! Gia, wake up!"

"What the hell are you doing? She's sleeping! Leave her alone!" I hissed at him, annoyed.

"I don't care. She needs to wake up and watch us." He began yelling again for her to wake up.

"Stop it, Hector. We aren't having sex. This is an old house, and everyone will hear us. Not to mention it's disrespectful."

"I want them to hear us. Shut up and open your legs."

"No!"

"Fine," he said and rolled me onto my stomach. He pulled my ass up and shoved himself inside me. Trying to be as quiet as possible, I just kept my face down in the pillow while he performed for himself. He still tried to wake Gia up, but she wasn't responding. Finally, he finished and rolled off of me. I gathered up my clothes put them on and went to the bathroom, praying I wouldn't run into anyone.

A little while later, I woke up to someone kicking the bed. I peeled back my eye mask to see an elderly black woman standing over me in disgust. I could tell that she was not human and that she was *not* happy with me. I screamed bloody murder and hid under the covers. I didn't know where Hector or Gia were. I was terrified! Why wasn't anyone with me?

I peeked out a minute later, and she was gone.

Gia came in, yelling, "What happened?! What happened?!"

I told her what I thought I had just seen, feeling like I was losing my mind, but she said, "Yep! She got me too! She jerked my arm out from propping my head up! Get your shit together—it's time to go!"

I never packed and got out of a building so fast in my life. Gia and I got outside as fast as we could. When we told them what had happened, the guys laughed. Big Mama said, "Now, I warned you not to have sex!"

Embarrassed and afraid, we waited outside until everyone was ready to go.

Back on the road and far less scared, the car was filled with our laughter and cackles. Big Mama thought our ghost story was hilarious. We told her that her ghosts were racist and only singled out the white people in the house.

"They singled out the room of fornication!" she said as we all laughed.

"I was an innocent bystander! I wasn't fornicating! Why was I singled out?" Gia yelled through her laughter.

We stopped for gas at some point, so I walked to the Walgreens next door to grab a few quick things. While there, I grabbed a big bag of wavy chips and spotted a cooler section with french onion dip. Chips and dip of any kind is my kryptonite, so before heading back to the car, I got them and a few other little things for us to munch on.

When traveling with the club they designate certain members to stay with the properties and make sure they get there safe. Somehow, though, we'd lost our escort.

We were stuck in the worst traffic I had ever seen. It was basically a six-lane parking lot. I decided to enjoy a little snack in the backseat. I popped open the chips and asked if anyone wanted any. They both declined, but that just meant more for me. When I opened the dip, Big Mama said, "That smells like a fart!"

Laughing I had to agree, but figured the odor was just the onions in it. The dip seemed plenty harmless, and I was hungry. Not two minutes later, the consequences of that decision made themselves apparent. My stomach started cramping horribly. I was hoping it would ease up, but it got rapidly worse. All of a sudden, I had to go to the bathroom…*Now*. In a panic, I asked if Gia could get off the highway and find a bathroom. She threw up her hands not knowing what an emergency it was and said, "Nobody's moving. Where am I supposed to go?"

My body started shaking as I tried to hold the demons in that were trying to escape, but I was quickly losing the battle.

Big Mama looked back from the passenger seat and said, "Oh shit girl! Are you okay? You're white as a corpse."

That got Gia's attention. "Oh okay. Hold on, hold on. Let me see if I can get out of here!" she said as she started to push her way through to at least the side of the road.

But it was too late.

I had to think quickly. This was happening *NOW!* I grabbed the bag of chips and dumped them out the window.

"What are you doing?" Gia said.

"Oh shit, here we go!" said Big Mama.

"*Not in my new car!*" Gia shrieked as I shamefully pulled down my pants and positioned the bag under myself.

"Girl, you better roll down these windows. This is happening!"

I locked eyes apologetically with Gia in the rearview mirror. She said, "*Fuck!* Okay, we got this! Just let it go!"

"*Stop looking at me!*" I screamed shamefully as the first wave hit the Lay's bag.

Big Mama sprang into action and started digging around in her bag. "I gotchu, boo! Do your thing! Get it all out!" She pulled out a pack of wet wipes and started pulling them out one by one while my hind end erupted like an angry volcano.

I prayed to God that I didn't make a mess in Gia's car. Thankfully, our escort had lost us so there were no other innocent bystanders. After what seemed like an eternity, I stopped having contractions. I threw the bag out the window, and it hit the pavement with a loud, wet *THUD.*

Big Mama handed me some wet wipes as traffic finally began to inch forward. I can only imagine what the cars around and behind us were thinking after witnessing my display through our open windows.

As I threw the wipes out while we drove along, I thanked God for the small miracle of a break in traffic. Round two was coming. I could feel it.

Gia pulled off and found a gas station in the nick of time. I was holding my butt closed while Big Mama barreled of me to clear my path to the bathroom before I shat myself. I practically dive-bombed that nasty gas station toilet.

While I destroyed the toilet, Big Mama said, "I'm going to go see if they have something for your stomach. Do you need anything else?"

"No, thank you," I said, defeated.

This went on for hours; we had to stop at almost every exit. When I started to break out in hives, Big Mama began to get really worried. She couldn't get ahold of any of the bros because they were all on their bikes. All of the stopping had put us way behind them. She made me take Benadryl and told me that if it didn't help, we'd need to find a hospital. Luckily, the Benadryl not only helped but knocked me out.

I woke up to Hector looking over my body. He looked not only concerned but furious. He was sweet and caring to me. "Hey babe, how are you feeling?" he asked with genuine concern. He helped me out of the car.

"I don't know," I answered honestly.

We were at a gas station less than an hour away from our destination. Big Mama was explaining to her husband what was going on. He didn't look happy. I knew someone was about to be in serious trouble. Her husband kindly asked me if I was feeling better and if I needed anything. Still groggy from the Benadryl, I said I didn't know. He instructed us to go inside so he could talk to his guys. Without hesitation, we did as we were told.

Inside, I realized that I was feeling much better. I saw how worried Gia and Big Mama were when I came out of the bathroom stall. "Sorry I shit in your car, Gia, but at least I didn't make a mess!"

We all burst out laughing. They were as relieved as I was that I was finally feeling better.

"Girl, we was about to take you to a hospital, for real!" Big Mama said.

"I'm sorry! I don't know what the hell happened! I was fine one minute, and then suddenly, I was sick as a dog," I said, ashamed.

"You're not allowed near any chips and dip for the remainder of this trip," Gia said.

Laughing uncomfortably, I agreed.

"Don't worry, girl. We're taking this story to the grave! Nobody needs to know the details," said Big Mama. Gia agreed and then they applauded my quick thinking.

"You handled that shit like a boss!" Gia said, laughing.

"Literally!" Big Mama added.

We went into the store area of the gas station and saw through the window that Hector was throwing a fit outside.

"Let's just do some shopping for a few minutes until we're cleared to go back to the car," Big Mama suggested delicately.

The rest of the weekend, I must say, was a blast. We all just partied and got along; there didn't seem to be any drama. The next day, we all got on the bikes and lined up. There were thousands of motorcycles of all kinds set up in formation to do the annual parade-style run. Even Gia hopped on the back of another member's bike. Nobody was left out. It was loud, but we had a really good time.

When we got back to the hotel, it was basically a huge party. Almost all the rooms were open, and everyone was having a good time. Hector didn't stay far from me, but he never actually seemed to be around. He would pop in from time to time to make sure I was okay, but he mostly stayed outside with his dad and a bunch of other people. We had a little property party in Hector's and my room. We talked and drank and laughed all night. People eventually started to trickle out, and doors began to close. It was getting late, and we had to head back the next day.

Gia and I said goodnight to each other around 2 a.m. I walked outside with her, and I noticed that Hector was with his dad and some chick I didn't know. She was flirting with him and was clearly all over him. Gia and I looked at each other, both seeing the same thing, and I just shrugged. I was used to all the little groupies. They were everywhere; patch-chasers we called them—always trying to be around the bros and do anything for attention.

Hector noticed me and came straight over to give me a kiss, the groupie trailing along. "Hey babe, are you okay?"

"Bye," Gia said, walking away while throwing daggers at the girl with her eyes. The girl seemed to realize that she wasn't getting anywhere with him and left.

"I'm tired, Hector. It's 2 a.m. Big Mama said that everyone has to be up by 7 and we ride out at 8. It's time to call it a night," I said.

"I'll be right in, babe. Let me just finish talking to my dad."

When he finally came to bed, he immediately started pawing at me.

"What the hell? It's 4 a.m. Where have you been?"

Still pulling my clothes off, he answered, "I was right outside, talking to my dad." He started kissing my stomach, trying to distract me.

"No, not tonight. I'm tired."

He stopped what he was doing and grabbed my throat. "I wasn't fucking asking. You are mine, and I will do with you as I damn well please." He planted a hard kiss on me, and I didn't like the way it tasted.

"Stop!"

He pinned my hands above my head.

"Hector stop!"

He ripped my panties off and stuffed them in my mouth. "That's your problem, babe. You don't know when to shut the fuck up."

He held my arms above my head and tried to position me where he wanted me. I bucked my hips, trying to get him off me, but that just seemed to turn him on more. He let go of my arms and grabbed my throat. "We can do this my way, or I can force you. But if I have to force you, I'm gonna fuck you in the ass. Stop fighting me."

I went limp. *Fine. Just get it over with.* He spat on my genitals and did his business. I quietly cried myself back to sleep after he was done. I couldn't wait to be back in the car with the ladies and away from him.

CHAPTER NINE

Cards on the Table

It was a rare occasion when Hector wanted to hang out with friends that weren't in the club, so it was kind of nice when he took me somewhere new.

One night he took me to a party at a friend's house. I didn't really know anyone there. When I walked into the garage, I saw Hector's father sitting on the couch with a beer in his hand. The man made my skin crawl. He was the most two-faced individual I had ever met. He could go from laughing and having a great time to pulling a knife on someone in an instant if he thought they'd disrespected him. He was an overweight, old Puerto Rican man who used a walker to get around. He was constantly in need of assistance when he wanted to be babied but could be on his feet and ready to kill you if you looked at him wrong. He always hit on me and said things like, "You know my son and I share women, right?" and "I have a bigger dick than Hector, you know." One time, I walked into the clubhouse and asked him how he was doing. He reached for a hug and said in my ear, "If he's not eating that pussy right, come to Daddy." Mostly I just brushed it off and tried to ignore him. It didn't seem like many people had anything good to say about the man. But he always had drugs, so he stayed surrounded. He would introduce me to new people as his daughter-in-law, and in the very next breath say, "Turn around so they can see that juicy ass!" So, he was by far my least favorite person. I blamed him for messing Hector up so much. I couldn't imagine my parents behaving like that, and it made me sick.

Hector started drinking and introduced me around. Everyone was very friendly, and I had met one of the men before. The man, Zack, was a very attractive young guy who lived near Myrtle Beach. He was kind of a pretty boy, so not at all my type, but he had a nice face and perfect smile. He was always very kind to me whenever he was around. He seemed to have a lot going for him, so I didn't really understand why he was friends with Hector; they seemed completely different. Zack was a bit sad the night of the party because his girlfriend had just dumped him and moved out of their apartment. Hector, of course, started giving him life and relationship advice, which I found ironic. As time passed, I seemed to be the only one not awake and full of energy. By 1 a.m., I told Hector that I was ready to go home. He pulled Zack over to talk to me and told me that he wasn't ready to leave yet and went inside the house. So I sat there talking to Zack and waited for him to come back out.

Finally, after I threatened to take my car and leave him there, Hector agreed that we could go. It was almost 3 a.m. Even after that, it \ took him another 30 minutes to get in the car. He seemed nervous.

When we got home, I took Rafiki outside to go potty and came back in, expecting to go straight to bed. But Hector was pacing in the living room with all the lights on, arguing with himself.

I asked him what was up. He didn't appear to have heard me, so I went around the section of the couch that formed an L shape and sat down. Something was coming. "Talk to me, babe. What's going on?"

"I want to tell you something," he said, "but I don't think I can." He looked terrified and on the verge of tears.

"Oh God, did you fucking cheat on me?" I asked.

"No! Nothing like that. I would never cheat on you," he said, avoiding eye contact.

"Just say it, for God's sake," I said as calmly as I could.

"I'm scared," he said as he finally looked at me and tears started streaming down his face.

"Scared of what?"

"I know you're going to leave me if I tell you, and I don't want to live without you."

"I doubt I'm going to leave you if you haven't cheated on me, so just tell me. It's obviously tearing you up inside."

He was still pacing in front of me and hitting himself in the head. Finally, he said, "Savannah, I'm a cokehead." He froze and stared at me as soon as the words were out.

Immediately, everything fell into place. It hit me like a ton of bricks. I felt so stupid. How had I missed this the whole time? I knew the signs of a junky; I had even found his little empty baggies before and thrown them away, not wanting to know where they had come from. I wanted to kick myself for being so purposely blind.

I sat back on the couch speechless.

"I'm sorry! I wanted to tell you; I hated lying to you. Everyone does it, so I didn't think you could be serious when you said you didn't. Until I realized that you really didn't. You always warned me that if I was doing that you would leave me."

He fell on his knees in front of me, almost weeping. He started breathing heavily and getting himself all upset. "You're going to leave me, aren't you? You're going to abandon me like everyone else! I'll kill myself! If you leave, *I'm going to kill myself!* I need you!"

I took his face in my hands and told him to calm down. "Why are you telling me this now?" I asked.

"You're the strongest person I know, and I need your help." With tears still streaming down his face, he told me that he knew he wasn't worthy of me. He told me that he had never known real love before and never felt worthy of it. He went on and on about how much he needed me and said that no one had ever cared enough about him to want him to quit. He never knew any different.

The more he talked and cried and broke down, the more I understood how hard this must have been to keep from me. I figured that if he were telling me now and asking for help, he must really mean it. I thought that moment was a huge turning point for us, so I agreed to stay and stick it out with him. But I didn't want any more lies. I told him that if he wanted me to stay, he had to be 100 percent honest from here on out.

He agreed that he could do that.

We went to bed, finally, and Hector wrapped himself around me tighter than he ever had. His whole body was shaking with vulnerability. He just wanted to be loved. It broke my heart to think of how hard it had been for him to carry on this lie the entire time. I could feel him crying as he was wrapped around me, so I rolled over to face him in the dark.

"Stop it, babe. I'm right here; I'm in your arms, and I'm not going anywhere," I whispered to him and kissed him lovingly.

He sobbed harder. "I'm so sorry for lying," he whimpered. "I love you so much. I can't be without you now that you've shown me what love is."

Just hearing those words fall from his lips melted my heart. It was working! I *was* having a positive effect on him! He still had a long way to go, but hearing him admit that made me feel closer to him.

"You *are* worth loving. I'm sorry you never got to experience that before me, but I'm not giving up on you," I said, wrapping my hand around the back of his head.

"I don't know what I would do without you, babe. I know I don't treat you right, but I want to. I want to be good enough for you. I just need your help," he said vulnerably.

"I know. That's why I'm still here."

"I love you," he whispered, climbing on top of me. "I need you," he whispered against my lips.

I could feel his erection. "Then show me," I whispered.

"How?" he whimpered.

"Get the help you need."

He kissed me passionately, shutting me up. He kissed down my body nibbling at my breasts before making his way delicately down between my thighs.

"I want you to come in my mouth," he said, putting his mouth on me hungrily.

I opened myself up to the rare experience. I felt so close to him in the moment. He finally had opened up to me in the most vulnerable, honest way possible. I thought about how hard that was for him and craved more. We made love for the first time in a very long time. It was passionate and raw; we were both hungry for each other in a way I had wanted us to be for a long time. I knew this was going to be a new beginning for us both.

The next evening, Gia came over. Hector was still on his best behavior even with her, but she could tell something was off with him. Eventually, he decided to go to the bedroom and watch TV while Gia and I enjoyed a couple glasses of wine.

As soon as he was settled in, she asked, "What's up with him? He's being awful nice."

I told her what had happened the night before and explained how exhausted we both were by the whole event.

As she was listening, she just kept saying, "Oh…" and playing with her hands.

Finally, I asked her, "Why do you look guilty right now? Did you know?"

She looked down at the table and quietly answered, "Yes."

"What the fuck, Gia?! You knew this whole time and didn't tell me? Everyone knows how I feel about this shit, and nobody said a word?!" I started getting upset. I felt like she betrayed me.

"Well I didn't know the *whole* time, no. But there was an incident at the clubhouse the night they told us they wanted us to be properties. I went to leave, and Hector walked me to my car. He pulled out some coke and started sniffing it off his keys right in front of me. I asked him what the hell he was doing, and he acted like he just forgot he wasn't supposed to do that in front of me." She went on to say that he had begged her to keep it between them. He assured her it wasn't a problem he just needed to "sober up" since we still had to get home on the bike.

"So, you agreed to lie to me for *him*?" I asked angrily.

"Well, not *lie* exactly—just not tell you," she said while she twisted her fingers. "I'm really sorry! Please don't be mad. I didn't want to stir things up; he and I were *finally* getting along. I knew that if I told you, he would know it had been me and then I would be the bad guy yet again."

My initial thought was why in the world she would call me her best friend but keep something like this from me upon *Hector's* request. He treated her like shit. He went out of his way to tell anyone with ears what a nasty whore he thought she was. But part of me understood why she hadn't told me. So, I just let it go. What difference did it make now? I still looked like an idiot to everyone since I was the only one in the dark.

She asked me what I was going to do. I told her I was going to stay and help him. He had confessed and asked for help, so the least I could do was try.

From having previous experience in my life dealing with addicts, I knew it wasn't going to be easy. But the main thing I expected was honesty. "That goes for you, too," I told her.

She nodded and agreed. "But there's no way he's going to get clean. If everyone is on it, and he's around it all the time, he won't be able to say no."

She was right. I had already been racking my brain about it all day. "I don't know what I'm going to do, Gia."

After she left and I went to the bedroom, I decided I was pissed off enough at him to say something about this.

"Hey babe," he said, nervously adjusting in the bed when I walked in.

"You made my fucking friend lie to me."

"What? What are you talking about?" he asked.

"The night you told us that we were going to be properties, you did coke in front of Gia and told her not to tell me," I said.

"So? Fuck that bitch."

"Now not only will I not trust *you*, but I know I can't fully trust *her* either, and it's your fault," I said.

"Well, you know now, so what's the big deal? I told you that bitch can't be trusted, so now you see I was right!" he said with a satisfied grin on his face. "Now maybe you'll listen to me when I tell you she isn't your friend. She just wants what you have, and she's jealous I didn't want her ass." He laughed and told me he'd had enough of this conversation and turned up the volume on the TV.

CHAPTER TEN

Well, That Got Weird

It had been some time since we'd seen Bessie. We still spoke regularly, but I hadn't invited her over.

One night, Hector wanted to go to dinner at this local restaurant and bar that we enjoyed. They had all-you-can-eat crab legs every Wednesday night, so we went there often, but tonight we felt like celebrating.

Hector's boss had offered to let him take over his small chimney-cleaning company to Hector's surprise. He was reluctant and nervous, unsure if he could handle it, but I encouraged him and told him I would help any way I could and support him however he needed me to. It had been in talk for about a month now, and Hector had already gone to Florida once to take the certification test. He hadn't passed, so he had to wait until the next one to try again.

John was eager to get things moving. He had started the company 30 years prior and had no kids or a wife, so he needed to either sell it to the highest bidder or offer it to someone he hoped would keep it alive. He was a very gentle man—tall and very skinny, almost frail. His skin was white and his short hair was even whiter. I had met him a few times, and he told me that he really liked the impact I was having on Hector. He mentioned several times that, prior to me coming into his life, there had been several occasions that he had considered firing him. He even said he felt afraid of him at times. I was happy to know that I was having a positive impact on Hector.

Bessie met us for dinner at the restaurant. She told us both that she was sorry for her outburst. She explained that she hadn't dealt with her feelings about the breakup and it all just came pouring out of her that night. We both understood—who hasn't gotten drunk and made a fool of themselves at least once, right?

We didn't dwell on it, and since we were there to have a good time, Hector started ordering drinks. It was nice to see Bessie enjoy herself and let loose a little. It was even nicer to see her and Hector getting along. The two of them started getting kind of flirty with each other, but that wasn't odd to me at all. Bessie always flirted with my boyfriends.

We decided we were sick of paying for drinks when we had a fully stocked bar at home, so we headed out. When we got back to the house, we stayed downstairs and had some more drinks. They continued flirting, and I continued not to care.

Finally, Hector suggested we all take a bath together. Apparently, we had enough alcohol because he talked us into it. While I started filling up the bath, he stripped naked immediately.

"Oh, you meant a *naked* bath?" I laughed.

"Of course!" he replied.

Bessie said, "Okay, let's get weird," and pulled off her shirt.

I was still trying to figure out if we were going to fit in the tub together when he jumped in. She was already naked, so she got in with him. I turned the water off, worried that the tub would overflow, and then realized that there was no way I was going to fit.

"Come on, babe," he said. "Take off your clothes and get in!"

They started kissing. I threw on some music. The silence seemed too loud for the moment. I took off my clothes and asked where I was supposed to sit.

"On my face," he said with his mischievous grin.

They each scooted as far over as they could and made some room for me. As I got in the tub, he carefully and slowly kissed every inch of my body as I stood in front of him. It was kind of nice. Later in our relationship, I'd come to understand that this was all a show for whover was involved or watching. He did his best work with an audience. But at the time, I was so starved for that connection with him that I just gave in and enjoyed it.

I ended up sitting in on their laps. It was a tight fit, but it was funny and kind of hot at the same time. I had my back to Bessie, so I didn't see much of anything going on behind me. I doubt there was very much happening back there since she probably couldn't move. I was squishing them both.

Finally, I said that we needed to get out. They both agreed because their legs were going numb.

We went into the bedroom and dried off. I told him I didn't want to have sex with Bessie, so I was hoping he wasn't going to force that.

He lay down on the bed and told me to sit on his face. "Bessie, come suck my dick," he commanded.

We looked at each other and did as we were told.

He seemed to be totally into me like he hadn't been in a long time. It was the first time in a long time that he made me feel sexy. He told me how sexy I looked from his angle and kept both hands all over me the whole time. I knew Bessie was behind me doing as she was told, and it sounded like they were both enjoying themselves. But I never actually looked back at her. My eyes stayed locked on him the whole time.

It didn't last more than a few minutes, and Bessie and I both walked away unsatisfied, but he seemed to have enjoyed himself. Once he was done, he said goodnight to her and told me that it was time for bed.

She got up and went to her room; I got under the covers, hoping he would finish the job he started on me. But he rolled over and went to sleep. The whole thing just felt weird. Once again, it was all about him and nobody else.

Disappointed, I rolled over and called Rafiki onto the bed. I kissed him on the snout in my favorite spot just under his eye and rubbed his floppy ears. "At least I have you, baby bear," I whispered softly. He snuggled up to me happily and settled in for the night.

Hector had decided to bring his little brother, Ricky, down from New York to visit for a while. He wasn't going to be here long—only about a week or two. I knew he was younger than Hector and had a different father, but that's about all I knew about him.

When he first walked into our home, I thought that there was no way they could be related. Not only was Ricky very thin and almost frail looking, but he had beautiful long, black hair. He had a baby face and a charming smile that could really get a young girl's attention. He looked like he wasn't even old enough to drink alcohol yet.

Ricky came in with a shy smile on his face and gave me a big hug. He told me he was excited to finally meet the woman who was having such a positive effect on his big brother. Equally happy to meet him, I asked how his trip down had been and if he needed anything to get settled in.

He was very polite and incredibly sweet. He didn't seem to have the temper Hector did, so that was a relief. He was very laid back and just enjoyed life.

Not wanting to waste time, Hector told me that they wanted to go out and have some brother time to catch up a bit. They got ready and headed out on the town.

Meanwhile, Bessie called me to see what I was doing. I told her that Hector and his brother were going out so I was just going to be at home watching a movie and eating snacks. She asked if she could join me, so I said sure. She and I sat around drinking wine and watching movies.

When Hector and Ricky got home, it wasn't incredibly late, so I was surprised that they were already back. I heard the garage door open and close and waited to see them coming up the stairs. It seemed like it took forever, so I got up and was going to head down and make sure everything was okay. Just as I got over to the top, I saw Hector climbing up the stairs with his little brother thrown over his shoulder. I started to giggle and asked how it had gone.

Ricky's head popped up, and he responded, "We had a great time Miss Savannah!"

Bessie and I laughed while Hector came in and put Ricky down gently on the couch beside Bessie.

"Are you okay here, or do you need me to take you into the bathroom to throw up some more?" Hector asked.

"No, I'm fine, big bro," Ricky answered.

I saw Bessie wiggle excitedly and readjust herself to throw a big, hungry grin at the new beautiful boy she hadn't met yet.

"Okay, keep an eye on him. I gotta piss," Hector said to us, walking down the hall.

"Oh, I'll take good care of him don't you worry," Bessie purred.

"Oh, hello ma'am!" Ricky said, just realizing that there was a new person sitting next to him.

"Ricky, this is my friend Bessie," I said.

"Nice to meet you," he said politely and held out his hand with an adorably intoxicated grin on his face. It looked like he was coming back to life.

I went and got him some water and handed it to him. Bessie was making small talk with him and staring at him like he was a steak. I just laughed and sat back down.

Hector came back out and said that they'd had a great time.

"Yeah, I can see that!" I said, laughing and gesturing to his brother.

Hector was smiling and happy until he looked over and realized Bessie wanted to pounce on Ricky like a lioness would a baby gazelle. He looked back at me and pulled me close to whisper in my ear, "That fat bitch better not fuck my brother."

Surprised by his immediate response to seeing them talking, I said, "So what if she does? He's grown and so is she. Let them make their own decisions."

"No, I'm serious. She better not touch him," he said. It was starting to sound more like jealousy than genuine concern for his brother.

"I'm not babysitting grownups. They're just talking—chill out."

We all sat in the living room and talked for a long time. The more we talked, the more sober Ricky became. We were all enjoying our conversation, but I was getting tired. I looked at the time and it was about 2:30 a.m.

"Okay, kids. Mama's off to bed. I need my beauty sleep," I said getting up from the couch. I asked if anyone needed anything before I went to lie down.

Hector stood up and looked at Bessie. "Your ass better be on that couch or in the other bedroom. Leave my little brother alone," he said, trying to sound lighthearted and playful.

"Worry about yourself, sir! He's a big boy—he doesn't need a daddy."

Knowing that infuriated him, I cringed.

"You need anything, bro?" Hector asked Ricky.

"No, I'm good. Thank you! Have a good night, Miss Savannah!" he yelled at me while I entered my room.

I brushed my teeth, took my contacts out, and got into bed. Hector was already under the covers with the lights off, so I was hoping we could just go to bed.

"If she fucks my brother, I'm gonna be pissed," he said before I could get settled in.

"I don't know why you care. He's grown. It's not like she can rape him. If he doesn't want to, I don't think you have anything to worry about."

"I don't want to think about her having had my brother's dick in her mouth next time she's giving me head," he said. I rolled over to face him.

"What makes you think there's going to be a next time?"

"Why wouldn't there be? You want to please me and keep me happy right?"

"You literally don't have *one* nice thing to say about her. You call her obese and fat and gross all the time, but you want to sleep with her?"

"No" he laughed. "I wouldn't fuck her. I just want her to suck my dick while you ride my face again." He started to roam his hands down my body.

"Ahh, I see. Well, a little word of advice, dear. If you want to be with two women at the same time, you should try to make sure they're having as much fun as you are," I spat out at him and tried to roll over.

He stopped me. "What the fuck does that mean?" he asked.

"Nobody likes a selfish lover," I said flatly.

"Whatever. Get naked. I want to fuck."

"I'm going to sleep. Goodnight," I said rolling onto my side.

"I said come ride this dick," he said with the tone of a teenager who was about to throw a tantrum.

I ignored him, irritated by his arrogance.

"Fine! I'll just fuck you in the ass," he said rolling towards me and trying to position himself.

"Stop it!" I slapped his hand and moved away from him.

He got up, pressed my face into the pillow, and was trying to mount me.

"*STOP!*" I yelled into the pillow.

"Then get up and ride my fucking dick like I told you to," he whispered hatefully, pushing himself off me with all of his force.

Irritated and aware of the fact that if I didn't do what he wanted, it was going to be worse for me, I did as he commanded. I was thankful it was so dark that he couldn't see the tears streaming down my face while I tried to complete the task so I could go to sleep. I was getting better at checking out in moments like these. I was there physically, of course, doing what I had to do, but mentally, I just had to go somewhere else. Otherwise it would become unbearable.

"Moan. I want them to hear us."

The next morning, it was obvious that Bessie and Ricky had slept together. She was swooning over him with dreamy stars in her eyes. He was just as sweet and polite as ever, and I thought it was hilarious. I knew Hector was pissed, but I didn't expect him to show it in front of them.

"You guys fucked, didn't you?" he said directly.

Everyone laughed uncomfortably.

"A lady doesn't kiss and tell," Bessie replied, turning red and giggling.

"You ain't no fucking lady," he spat back at her.

"Fuck you," she said playfully, enjoying all the attention.

"You know she sucked my dick a couple weeks ago, right?" he told his brother.

I was both shocked and mortified; Bessie was as well. Our jaws hit the floor at the same time, and Ricky looked both confused and uncomfortable, not really knowing how to respond.

"No, and why the fuck did you just say that?" Bessie asked.

"Why not? It's true." He shrugged, seeming satisfied by the uncomfortable moment he had created.

"Does anyone want breakfast?" I asked, trying to change the subject. Not wanting this to get any more uncomfortable for anyone, I asked Bessie if she wanted to help me whip something up in the kitchen.

Seeming grateful to be pulled out of the room, she got up and followed me. The boys went out to smoke on the back porch.

"What the fuck was that about?" she asked me as soon as it was safe. "Why is he acting like my jealous ex or something?"

Gathering the items, we needed for breakfast, I responded, "Fuck if I know. Ignore him—he's a child…So, how was it?" I asked, eager to talk about anything but what had just happened.

Her whole body language changed, and she was back to grinning from ear to ear. "It was fucking awesome!" she said. "Except for the fact that I'm on my period, and it got pretty messy. He handled it like a boss though." She went on to tell me the gory details about how they fucked all night and how they ended up having to do it in the shower because she was bleeding so badly.

"Did you at least use protection?" I asked.

"Well, it's not like we planned it, so, no we didn't have anything. I thought about asking you for one, but then we heard you guys in there already fucking, so we just went for it."

Not wanting to be reminded about *that* either, I just shrugged.

"It wouldn't have mattered though because we would have needed a whole box. We fucked all night—several times in several different ways. Girl, I needed that! He is amazing in bed; so sweet and generous yet firm and can manhandle me just enough! I like him!"

"Well, good. I'm glad you enjoyed yourself."

CHAPTER ELEVEN

Goodbye Baby Bear

The next week, I got up at 5 a.m. to get ready for work. I had agreed to do a job out in Douglassville, Georgia at one of the companies I used to work for full time. I went into the kitchen after I got ready to feed my fur babies, but I noticed that Rafiki was nowhere to be seen. He had grown attached to Ricky and had slept in his room with him the past few nights, so I knew where he was.

I went quietly down the hall and cracked the door open just enough for him to squeeze out happily. He ran down the stairs and waited at the front door, stretching his front paws up to the door handle ready for me to let him out. He didn't mess around too much when it came to potty time in the morning because he was looking forward to his breakfast.

He came back inside, wagging his tail, and walked back up the stairs to the kitchen. Gizmo, my cat, was already pacing and meowing impatiently at me. I got her food first since she was much less patient. Then I got Rafiki's food ready and even threw in an extra special treat. We had gone out to dinner at a Brazilian steak house recently and got a bunch of bones and fat for him; he was thrilled.

I gathered my things and got ready to leave. Rafiki came over to me to say goodbye, as usual, and I sat on the top stair to love on him.

"I'm starting to miss you baby bear. Mama needs her sweet snuggles," I said to him. "I'll be happy to have you to myself again when your new friend leaves." I laughed while he licked my face with his gross dog breath. "I love you, baby bear. I'll see you later. Be good!" I gave him a kiss on his snout just under his eye and another one on the top of his head. He walked me down the stairs to the garage and I patted him on the head one more time, thinking about how I really did miss having him in my bed. Then I closed the door and left for my hour-long commute to work.

I was in the middle of taping of the interior of a base cabinet when my phone rang later that day. It was Hector. Answering from my blue tooth headphones I had been jamming out with, I said, "Hey babe, what's up?"

"Hey, are you at work?" Hector asked, sounding nervous.

"Of course I am. Why, what's wrong?" I responded.

"Babe, I'm so sorry…Rafiki's dead," he said as if it was just an average phone call about the weather. There was no remorse in his voice—very monotone.

"That's not fucking funny, Hector," I snapped while my heart dropped to my stomach.

"I'm not kidding. He just got hit by a truck. I didn't know he was outside. We heard a dog get hit, and the guys went running to see what had happened. He was already dead. I'm so sorry."

My hands started shaking, and my knees began to buckle. I started to panic. I didn't know what do. How could this happen?! He was just loving on me and eating breakfast. He was only 4 years old! He was my baby! My everything!

I ran out front, not wanting anyone to see me lose my shit. I lit a Newport and screamed at Hector, "Take him to the vet right now! What are you waiting for?! He's not dead!"

"He's gone babe. He got hit right in the middle of his head and the truck was speeding. There was a guy who saw the whole thing. He didn't feel anything. He's gone. There's nothing more to do. The guys are digging a hole. We wrapped him in a towel and laid him down in the garage. You need to come home."

I fell to my knees in the gravel, unable to stand any longer. I dropped my phone, put my head in my hands and started screaming. My boss, Jack, was pulling into the driveway at the time and saw me. He pulled up in front of me and hopped out of his truck running to my side as fast as he could. At about the same time, one of the guys who heard me screaming came running out to help. I couldn't stand and I couldn't talk. All I could do was scream and cry. So, they knelt on the ground and tried to console me.

"I need to go home," I managed to say between sobs.

"Okay, that's fine. But I need you to calm down for me. I can't let you drive that far like this," Jack said, rubbing my back. "What in the world happened?" he asked Eddie who was in just as much shock as Jack.

"I don't know! I saw her rushing out of the building on the phone, and I just thought she was trying to get better reception. Then I heard her scream, so I ran out after her."

"My dog got hit by a truck," I sobbed and fell into Eddie's arms. "He's dead, and I wasn't there!" I started crying even harder and clung to Eddie's shirt like if I let go, somehow, I would fall into a bottomless pit.

Jack and Eddie both shook their heads and told me how sorry they were to hear that. They had met Rafiki a few times. I would bring him to with me if I just had to come by and pick something up or drop something off. They knew how attached we were to each other.

My phone wouldn't stop ringing. Apparently, I forgotten to hang up with Hector, so all he'd heard was me screaming bloody murder and some of the commotion that had followed.

After a few minutes of sitting there with Jack and Eddie, I was able to convince them that I was good to drive. I had to see my baby one last time. I got in the car and started driving. My first call was to Gia. I knew she was at work and her coworkers hated her, so I wasn't sure she would be allowed to answer or not, but I didn't want to talk to Hector, and Gia knew what Rafiki meant to me.

"Hello? What's wrong?" Gia answered. I *never* call her, especially at work, so she knew right away that something was wrong.

"Rafiki's dead!" I said much louder than I intended to and started bawling again.

"*What?! Oh my God, what happened?!*"

I told her what Hector had told me and said that I was heading home to bury my baby.

She said, "Okay, well, you don't sound like you should be driving right now, but I understand. I will be over when I get off work. I'm so sorry, Savannah," she said, on the verge of tears herself.

Hector wouldn't stop calling, so I finally answered. "I'm on my way," I said. "Don't bury him yet; I need to see him. I need to hold him and say goodbye." Then I hung up the phone. I didn't want to hear anything else from Hector.

I called my mom to talk me through the rest of the drive. She and my stepfather are animal-lovers themselves, so they understood how devastating it was for me. They both stayed on the phone with me until I pulled into my garage.

"If you need anything, I'm here," my mother whispered softly, not knowing what else could be said. "I love you," she said.

"I love you too, Mom," I responded, hanging up the phone.

I didn't see anyone, so I didn't know where the boys were. All I saw was the towel and my baby's paws sticking out the bottom. I fell on my knees again and crawled over to his already stiffening body. "I'm here, baby bear," I whispered, "Mommy's *so sorry.*" Then I let out an indescribable scream. It was the most terrifying sound I had ever heard myself make. I hadn't ever had to deal with a loss like this until now, and I couldn't control what was happening to my body. I heard what sounded like shovels dropping and feet running towards the suffering sound I had just made as I laid my head on the towel that now held the most beloved thing in my entire world.

"No, no, no. I got her. Give us a minute," I heard Hector say from outside. He rushed in and planted himself right next to me, hugging me and trying to pull me away.

"Get the fuck off of me!" I spat at him. For some reason, I lifted the towel to see the damage. Although he wasn't bleeding anywhere or torn apart by the accident, the sight of him was more than I could bear. His eyes were wide open and lifeless. I could see the point of impact very clearly due to the giant bulge in my angel's head. I screamed again, this time jumping into Hector's embrace.

"I'm so sorry, babe. I'm so sorry." That's all he could say.

"Please cover him back up," I wept into Hector's shoulder.

He did as requested and said, "Okay, go inside. We can bury him. The hole is ready; we just waited for you."

"NO!" I shouted, pushing him away from me and turning back to the lifeless corpse. "I'm not ready. Leave me alone for a minute; I need to say goodbye."

Reluctantly, he got up and walked back out of the garage.

I moved the towel so I could see his snout. I noticed there was a trail of ants already disturbing him, and I started frantically swept them away. I told him again how sorry I was and how much I loved him, knowing he couldn't hear me. I prayed for him to wake up and for this to all be a bad dream, but he didn't. The innocent, precious creature I loved most in this world was gone. The finality of it was heartbreaking. Finally, I leaned down and kissed him on his snout just under his eye for the final time. He didn't smell the same; he didn't feel the same. I knew it was time.

I called out for Hector, and he and the two boys appeared at the same time. His brother was still staying with us for a couple more days, and Hector had one of his employees with him, as well. He was a sweet guy, I had only met him recently, but he was always very polite. They were looking down, waiting for me to say something.

"It's time, but I want to bury his bone and his toys with him," I said, still kneeling by my baby's body and rubbing his cold paw.

"I'll go get them," Ricky said, ready to be of some help. He ran inside and was back out in no time.

Hector picked up the body and carried him out back. They had a little hole ready for him just off our back porch. Hector laid him in gently with the towel still wrapped around him while I wept.

Ricky came running out with all the toys and bones he could find and handed them to me. I put them in the hole.

Then, suddenly stricken with panic, I said, "Wait! I want his collar!"

"Okay, I'll get it," Hector said. He retrieved his collar and handed it to me. "Go inside, babe. We can do this."

I grabbed a shovel and put the first scoop of dirt on him—that's all I could handle. I handed over the shovel and went inside. I went to the kitchen and sat on the floor next to Rafiki's dog bowl. Again, I started crying.

Immediately, my fluffy Gizmo appeared and got into my lap, purring. She was a grouchy old cat who hated almost everyone, but she and I were meant for each other. I rescued her after her mommy had died when she was just two weeks old. I'd fed her with an eye-dropper and kept her for my own. She loved me and I loved her, so that's all that mattered. She wasn't a fan of me getting a puppy when I first brought Rafiki home, but they grew to love each other. It was as if she knew what had just happened and that my heart was forever broken. She just lay in my lap, purring and fluffing my clothes with her paws. I hugged her and cried into her fur, and she just allowed whatever I needed to do in the moment.

Eventually, Hector came upstairs and told me that it was done. "I'm sorry, babe, but I'm not leaving you here alone, and I have to go to work, so you're coming with me," he said.

I laughed and rolled my eyes. "No way in hell," I responded.

"I can't leave you here alone—not like this. Get yourself together, and get in the van please," he said.

I got up and looked him dead in the eye. "I don't care where you go or what you have to do. My fucking dog was just killed. I'm not going anywhere. Go to work. I'm going to take a bath." I walked past him and headed to the bedroom. I heard him outside, yelling at the guys and trying to figure out what to do.

I was sitting in the tub, wanting to be left alone when he came in. "They're going to go do what I needed to do, and Titi is on her way," he said.

"Why?" I just wanted to be alone.

Nervously he responded, "Well, partly to bring me some paperwork and partly to be here for you. She's bringing you a surprise to make you feel better."

"Can you please leave me alone right now? I just need to be alone," I begged.

"I'll sit in the living room until she gets here," he said as he walked out.

What seemed like only a few minutes later, he came back in. "Titi's here, babe," he said as she walked into the bathroom behind him. "I figured it was okay since you're both girls," he said nervously.

"Hey Savannah," she said sweetly. "I am *so* sorry about Rafiki. I know how much you loved him. He lived a really good life."

Tearing up and still staring out the window, I said, "Thank you."

"Do you want a glass of wine, babe?" Hector asked, wanting to be helpful.

"No, I want a bottle of wine," I responded.

He laughed uncomfortably and left.

"I don't know if this is the right time, but I brought you something," Titi said, sitting on the edge of the tub.

I finally looked over and her and, in her hands, she held a very tiny kitten. It looked almost sickly. Normally, I wouldn't mind taking in a stray. I loved animals. But this was not the time. "I don't even want to look at that thing right now," I said, looking back out the window.

Understanding how I felt, she went on to explain how she had found the little creature at the shop and couldn't find its mommy so she wanted to see if I wanted to take it.

"No, thank you," I said as politely as I could. I just wanted it away from me. I never wanted to feel like this again so why on earth would I want another pet? That was my feeling at the time.

Unbeknownst to me, Hector had called and reached out to everyone, so for the rest of the evening, my house was full of people coming in and out to say they were sorry for my loss. I appreciated all the love but all was to be left *alone*. I kept asking him to make people leave, but he didn't want me to be alone. At the time, I didn't realize that it was actually because he didn't want to be alone with *me*. He felt responsible for the death of my dog and my greatest heartbreak, and he wasn't sure how I was going to react.

Suddenly, it started to pour down rain out of nowhere.

"Oh my God! Rafiki's out in the rain!" I said, bringing on another wave of uncontrollable grief. I realized by the look on everyone's faces that this was not only ridiculous but heartbreaking for them to watch.

"Rafiki is gone, baby. He's in heaven right now, playing with all the little kids and getting treats and snacks," Bessie said. She had gotten there shortly after Titi and was going to stay the night.

I got up and excused myself politely. I went to my bedroom and flopped facedown onto my bed. Finally, a moment alone to cry. I cried it out for about 15 or 20 minutes when I heard a slight knock on the door. Assuming it was Hector, I just ignored it. The door opened and someone sat on the bed and covered me with their body.

"I know," she said, rubbing my back. It was Gia. "I know, honey," she said again and let me cry a little longer.

CHAPTER TWELVE

Beginning of the End

The next morning, I woke up with puffy eyes and a pounding head. I decided I wanted to do anything but be smothered by Hector all day, so I got up and texted Jack that I was going to come in for work. He was hesitant to let me after what had just happened, but he knew he wouldn't be able to talk me out of it.

"Just get here when you can, there's no rush. And if you decide to stay home, that's fine too," he texted back lovingly.

I went to the kitchen, and as usual, Gizmo was screaming her meow of starvation, so I went ahead and fed her. Out of habit, after I fed her, I went to grab Rafiki's bowl to feed him. My heart sank when it was nowhere in sight. I started to panic and frantically started looking for his things, but they were all gone—even his little dog crate with his bed in it. There was no sign of my baby bear anywhere. Even the dog food was missing. Livid and ready to smash someone's face in for daring to touch his things, I started crying and frantically searching my house. Finally, I found them. Some ass-clown had the audacity to hide all of his things downstairs in the room that Hector wanted to turn into a dungeon. I gathered his leash and his bed and sat against the wall bawling my eyes out, wondering how I was ever going to get through this. My best friend in the whole world had been taken from me.

Just then, Bessie stepped reluctantly in the room. Obviously, she had heard the commotion as I lost my shit, searching for any trace of my dog. She had a very troubled look on her face from seeing me cowering and sobbing in the corner, smelling his bed.

"That fucking asshole!" I screamed as loud as I could. "How fucking dare *he* move *my* dog's stuff?! He didn't even love him! He died because *he* was too fucking stupid and irresponsible to close the fucking door! I fucking *hate* him!" I prayed Hector would hear me. I wanted him to know how much I hated him in that moment. What kind of irreversible pain he had caused. I dropped my head back down in Rafiki's squishy dog bed and sobbed.

Bessie sat in front of me on the floor and said, "Oh honey, I'm so sorry. But Hector didn't move his things. I did."

I looked up at her in anger and confusion. "What the fuck? Why would you fucking do that?" I spat at her, still crying and now trying to control my temper. I wanted to kick her face through the wall. I had never been so mad in my whole life!

"I'm fucking stupid," she responded, both catching me off guard and calming me down instantly. "For some stupid reason I thought it would be too hard for you to see his things this morning. I am *so* sorry. I should have never touched anything. Gizmo scratched the shit out of me and was yelling at me the whole time. She followed me around, attacking me, trying to tell me not to mess with anything, but I didn't listen. Your cat's a thug."

I busted out in the most uncomfortable laughter. As mad and distraught as I was less than a minute ago, I now understood. I knew my cat was a badass, and the way she had worded that was hilarious and much needed in the moment.

She, too, thought I was crazy for going too work.

"I can't be around him right now," I explained. "He's smothering me to death, and I don't even want to see him."

"Yeah, well, obviously he's freaking out. He thinks you're going to leave him now. He knows he was irresponsible and that you have every right to blame him. He's terrified that this is going to break you two up," she said matter-of-factly.

"Did he say that?"

"Yeah, that's why he called everyone over yesterday. He was so scared, and he didn't know what to do."

"How am I going to go to Puerto Ricco with this man in three days?" I asked. "I don't want to leave Rafiki." He was the reason my whole life was falling apart. My heart was so broken over the loss of my baby bear—such a completely avoidable death. It made me sick to my stomach to imagine pretending to be happy for a 'romantic' five-day trip with the person who had caused this pain.

"Well, it's already been paid for and set up for weeks, so I doubt he's going to postpone it. But I understand how you feel. Maybe it will be good to get away from here for a few days," she said, trying to be encouraging.

"Maybe." I thanked Bessie for being honest and making me laugh, wiped away my tears, and went off to work.

When I got home, Ricky was there alone. I had stopped on my way home to get a big box wine to drink my feelings away.

"Let me get that, please!" He jumped up and took it out of my hands. "Is there anything else you need me to carry in?" he asked politely while he took the box to the kitchen.

"No, that's it. But thank you."

"Would you like me to pour you a glass?" he asked, poking his head out from around the kitchen wall.

"That would be fantastic, actually. Thank you. I'll be right back," I said, heading to my bedroom. When I came back out, he had already poured my big beautiful glass of wine and handed it to me with pride.

"I don't know how you drink this stuff—it smells awful!" he said with a silly face to make me smile.

"This is a grown-up drink, dear," I answered with a smile, trying to be playful.

"Aye! At least I got you to smile!" he grinned and winked at me.

"Want to go smoke a cigarette?" I didn't allow smoking in the house, so we went on the back porch, overlooking my dog's fresh grave.

"I feel so bad about yesterday, Savannah," he said, shaking his head and looking down and the freshly dug dirt mound. "He was the coolest dog; I understand how heartbroken you are, believe me."

I started to tear up but was trying with everything inside me not to cry again. I was exhausted and sick of crying.

"But you're a strong-ass woman—I can see that already only knowing you a couple of weeks. You have had a real positive impact on my big brother. He seems so different with you," he said smiling at me in a hopeful way.

"I used to be strong," I responded and took a sip of my chardonnay.

"Nah, you're just having a hard moment right now, Ma. But you strong as hell. It's a beautiful thing. My brother loves you so much, and I see why. He'd be a fool not to." He grinned.

"Did he tell you to say that so I wouldn't be upset with him?" I asked, half joking.

"No, nothing like that. I can just see it. He's never been like he is with you. I'm happy for you guys."

We continued to talk on the back porch until Hector got home. It was nice to sit and chat with Ricky for a while since he was leaving to go home the next day. He told me that he'd enjoyed his visit and couldn't wait to come back one day and bring his little girl.

"You're always welcome," I told him.

Shortly after Hector got home and had settled in, he brought up the upcoming trip. "We're still going to Puerto Rico, right? Everything's all set up, so I can't change it."

"Yes, I know." Whether I fought it or not, he would still make me go.

"Good, it will be good for us to get out of here—just me and you," he said.

"I'm going to go take a bath. Obviously, I won't be cooking tonight, so if you boys want something to eat, you're on your own," I said, heading to the kitchen to refill my class before disappearing for about an hour into my safe haven.

When I came out, Bessie was there to spend the last night with her new boytoy. We all sat around talking and enjoying each other's company until I couldn't keep my swollen eyes open any longer and said my final goodbye to Ricky. I knew I wouldn't see him before he left the next day since I had to get up and leave so early. He gave me a big hug and thanked me once again for everything.

On the morning of our trip, my dad offered to take us to the airport. It was 4 a.m. when he picked us up. It felt good to be with him. I never felt safer than when my dad or brother were around me. He was as heartbroken as I was about Rafiki, but we both tried to avoid talking too much about it so we wouldn't cry.

Hector and I were in the airport waiting to board our flight when a woman walked by us with a couple of dogs—one looked just like Rafiki. I immediately started to tear up, and Hector turned my head to face him. "Enough. You're not going to ruin this trip for me with this crying shit. I'm sorry he's gone, but I don't want you to think about it, talk about it, or cry about it while we're there, so stop it now," he said sternly.

"It hasn't even been five days," I replied, shocked that he could expect me to move on that quickly and pretend I was happy while my heart was shattered.

"I don't fucking care. I paid a lot for this trip, and you won't ruin it for me. We're supposed to be having fun," he said, looking away from me. He smiled at the lady checking our tickets before we entered the gate to board our fight.

I knew then that this trip was going to be difficult for me.

The flight didn't seem that long really. I did as I was instructed and tried to paint on a happy face. I didn't want to invoke his evil while I was so far from home, so I decided to play along and please him.

When we landed, there was a little confusion about how to get to our hotel, but eventually we found a taxi and made it there safely. We put our stuff in the room and decided to go next door to a local restaurant and bar. They had someone there making balloon hats for all the customers. It was a funny little gag that I thought was a good way to grab people's attention and keep the atmosphere light and friendly.

We had a pretty good time the first day we were there. The scenery was amazing; the food was amazing. We ended up at the bar and restaurant next to our hotel for the final half of the evening. The drinks started flowing, and we were chatting with people coming off the cruise ships and having a really good time. I even thought to myself at one point that he had the potential to be a really good boyfriend. He could be very fun and charming, especially when anyone was around that he wanted to put on a show for. But as we ended the evening I was quickly reminded that things were never going to change.

We walked back to our hotel room and started making out. I loved when he would seem so eager to have his hands on me like this, and I wanted to keep feeling good. But then he stopped kissing me suddenly and grabbed his cell phone out of his back pocket, drunkenly dropping it on the floor. I thought he was going to fall over trying to pick it up. I had already started to realize that if he was drinking without cocaine he was easily intoxicated. But he wouldn't stop himself from getting sloppy drunk and throwing up everywhere.

He handed me his phone and started pulling off his clothes. "Take pictures of me," he commanded.

Not thinking anything of it, I did as he asked. But after about the fourth pose he struck, trying to look like some sex god, naked and shitfaced, it dawned on me that he was probably making me take these so he could send them to other women. "Why am I taking these on your phone?" I asked.

"Because I told you to. Do I look sexy? Does my dick look big from this angle?" he asked, not wanting to be bothered by my questions.

"It looks like it always does," I answered, not really sure how to respond.

"Whatever. Take your fucking clothes off," he barked at me.

"Fine, but I don't want any pictures of me, if you don't mind," I said as nicely as possible.

"I don't care. I want some. Lie on the bed," he said, annoyed.

"Babe, I'm serious. Put the phone away," I said.

"If you don't shut the fuck up, I'm going to punch you in the face. Lie down and open your legs. You belong to me, and I will do whatever the fuck I want," he said as sternly as he could sound while slurring his words.

I lay on my back and let him take his stupid pictures.

Then he started recording. "Open your legs. I want to record my dick going in your pussy," he said trying to sound sexy for the camera.

I sat up, keeping my legs together. "I am not doing that. I asked you nicely, now please stop." I wrapped my arms around my knees.

He stopped the camera and threw his phone at me. "Why the fuck you gotta ruin everything with that fucking mouth of yours?" he yelled in my face.

I didn't move or respond at all. He smacked the left side of my head, then the right. Luckily, he was so drunk that it really didn't hurt, but I didn't want to escalate the situation so I just closed my eyes and tucked my head into my knees covering my ears from the pathetic blows.

"Get on your knees and suck my dick, you fucking whore," he spat at me.

I didn't move. I didn't want him to see the tears in my eyes.

He grabbed my hair and pulled my head up clutching my throat with his other hands. "What the fuck is your problem? Why are you trying to ruin this trip? Don't you know how much I love you?" he said and started to cry. He sat on the bed next to me. "I brought you here to have a romantic trip and be alone with you. Why are you making me feel like you don't want me, babe?"

For whatever reason, the shocking turn in his demeanor made me feel bad for him. That sad little boy that just wanted to be loved popped back out, and I fell for it once again. Readjusting myself I turned my body towards him and grabbed his hand. "I'm sorry babe, I didn't mean to make you feel that way. We've been eating and drinking all day, and I feel bloated, so I just didn't want to be on camera tonight, that's all," I lied.

He turned towards me and started kissing me gently. He climbed on top of me, trying to steady himself.

"Are you okay?" I asked.

"Yeah, I'm good," he said, poking at me in all the wrong spots with his dick.

"Babe, why don't you let me get on top?" I asked, not wanting this to go on any longer than it had to.

"Good idea," he said, rolling onto his back.

I did my chore and lay down next to him when he was finished.

"I really do love you," he said, looking at me like he was broken-hearted.

"I know. Let's go to sleep," I said, pulling down my side of the covers and turning off the light.

The rest of the trip was the same. The mornings I enjoyed because he wanted to sleep until noon, so I got a little alone time. I went to the pool on the roof of the hotel and got some swimming and tanning in until he got up. He wasn't a fan of me doing it, but I left a sweet note every morning on his pillow and acted like I was thrilled to see him as soon as he came to the pool. I enjoyed going around the island and checking out the little castles and the rain forest. He was always too hung over and grumpy to enjoy it, but then when we started drinking, he came to life again. The nights all played out relatively the same as the first night. He got to drunk and wanted to be an ass. I just gave in and gave him what he wanted. We were there five *long* days, so I was glad to be heading home when the time came.

It made me sad to come back to the house without being greeted by my dog. I picked up my grief right where I left it. I went to take a bath in the tub I had been missing. It was about 8 o'clock at night, so I wanted to settle in for the night and relax, but Hector had other plans.

When I came out, he had music going and was getting things together to make drinks. "What are you doing? Go get dressed," he said, noticing that I was in my bedtime gear. "Ceelo and Chocolate are coming over to party."

"What? We just got home, and I'm exhausted! I don't feel like partying."

"Oh, well they're already on the way. Go get dressed. If they see you in what you're wearing, they're gonna want to fuck you. But hey, I'm down for a foursome!" he laughed.

I rolled my eyes and walked back to the bedroom.

Ceelo and Chocolate arrived shortly after. They were a fun couple; they were always friendly to me, and I enjoyed seeing them from time to time.

The first time I met them was at Hector's birthday party at the clubhouse. Hector decided to do a body shot off of me on the bar, so then a few more people did their own body shots off of each other. But when Ceelo put Chocolate on the bar and pulled up her sundress she was completely naked underneath—neither of them cared. She opened her legs, and he put his tongue in her crotch while Hector poured liquor down her body. I, like most people there, was shocked. But they were swingers and did stuff like that all the time, so it was nothing to them. It became common knowledge that, whenever they were around, at some point you were going to see Chocolate's vagina.

We went down to the party room and had some drinks. Hours went by, and I was getting really tired. I went upstairs to use the bathroom and realized it was already 2:30 in the morning. I went back downstairs to discover Ceelo performing oral sex on Chocolate while Hector held her chair, watching intently. Nobody stopped what they were doing when they saw me, and I didn't really know what to do, so I awkwardly sat in the corner, waiting for them to finish. Luckily, they picked up on my discomfort and stopped. I was getting really tired, so I told Hector it was time for us to call it a night. I didn't want them staying over after what I just walked in on; I wasn't about to just go to bed while my man had a threesome in my house. Ceelo agreed it was getting late, so he collected his wife and left. *Finally*, I could go to bed.

Hector stayed up all night. When he finally came to bed, I had already gotten up and showered for the day.

"So you invited them over to bring you coke?" I said, towel-drying my hair.

"No," he responded flatly with his back to me.

"I told you I would stay and help you get clean, but I will start packing my shit right now if you feel like lying to me is going to work," I snapped.

"They had it, so I did a little. I'm sorry babe," he said, turning to face me.

"I don't want that shit in my house, Hector. Can you at least respect *that?*" I asked.

"Yes. I'm sorry. I won't bring it in the house again, I promise."

By now I was growing sicker of his promises. I went to the back porch and my phone rang. It was Bruce, my ex-boyfriend that Hector hated for me to talk to. I knew Hector was in bed for the day, and I honestly didn't care. I needed a friend. So, I sat down and lit a cigarette as I answered my phone.

"Is this fuckboy putting his hands on you?" was the first thing he said.

My heart sank into my stomach. *Where the hell did that come from?* "What?"

"One of your little friends reached out to me and told me they were worried about you—said you're acting like you're scared of him and there are marks on your body all the time. Tell me the fucking truth Savannah—*now*."

Having known Bruce as long as I had, I knew he wasn't going to let this slide, but I also knew he could tell when I lied. I didn't know what to do so I just started crying.

"Where is he? I want to meet this bitch-ass motherfucker," he said, obviously getting upset.

"No, it's not that bad—I promise! Who called you?" I asked.

"None of your fucking business who called me! The fact that you're in a situation that requires me to be notified because people are concerned for your fucking *safety* is a goddamn problem!" Bruce was never one to be very delicate to say the least. He was from the streets, and he taught me a lot about them. But he didn't play when it came to this kind of shit, and I didn't want any problems. I calmed him down the best I could and told him it wasn't like that. Unsatisfied with my answers and excuses, he ended the conversation with, "Fine, but if I catch this nigga out anywhere, it's over," and hung up.

Sitting there alone after that conversation and looking down on Rafiki's grave, I realized at that moment that I couldn't do this much longer. I was tired of being miserable. But I didn't know what to do. I still cared about Hector; I didn't want to hurt him, and I didn't want anyone else to hurt him. But mostly I didn't want Hector to feel abandoned again. I hated what he had allowed to happen to Rafiki. I hated his dark side and his drug problem. But that little broken boy was still in there, pulling at my heartstrings. I couldn't leave him, but I couldn't keep doing this to myself. I was stuck.

CHAPTER THIRTEEN

A Losing Battle

For my birthday in August, Hector surprised me by whisking me away for the night to a beautiful winery and hotel in Braselton, Georgia. The day we left, we had popped open a bottle of champagne and were dancing lovingly in our bedroom. Then he said that we had to leave and not to ask questions. I noticed when I went into the bathroom that my box of makeup and my toothbrush were missing, so I got excited to find out where he was taking me and what we were doing. I thought it was adorable that he was planning something because he seemed so excited about it.

It wasn't the first time he'd surprised me with a really sweet, thoughtful moment. Previously that year, he had flowers and a stuffed animal delivered to me at work. When I called him to thank him, he said he was sending me an address and that I was to just go there. When I arrived, it was my favorite salon. He met me there and told all the ladies to give me whatever I wanted. So I got my hair, nails, and a pedicure done. He paid for it and told me to meet him at the house. When I got home, he made a beautiful dinner and had wine and candles. It was very romantic and unexpected. However, it was the day *after* Valentine's Day. He had ruined Valentine's Day completely and was trying to scramble to make up for it. He had gotten so coked up the night before he mostly slept through it, then was an irritable jerk the rest of the night. He always had a motive when he was being sweet.

When we pulled into the winery and I finally saw where we were, I got really excited. I had been there before to do the wine tasting tour, but it had been years, and I had never stayed at the hotel. It was beautiful. When we pulled up to the valet I said, "Babe, I don't have any clothes."

"Don't worry—everything is taken care of. This is for you, babe."

When he opened the trunk for the gentleman to get our things, I was surprised to see a big suitcase. He really had thought of everything. We went inside and the lounge was even more gorgeous than the outside. When we got up to our room it was fantastic! Big beautiful bed with rose petals laid out into the shape of a heart; two fresh white robes to lounge around in and a pool view; a note that said happy birthday sat on the bed. He was quite proud of himself.

"Here open your gifts, babe, we're on a schedule," he said nervously.

My first gift was a beautiful black dress. It fit perfectly and was shaped just for my curves. After it was on, he handed me another box. It was another dress; this one was a beautiful blue color. It reminded me of the color of the ocean in advertisements for the Bahamas. Finally, the last gift was a gorgeous necklace. It was called a forever necklace and had little diamonds and an infinity symbol. It was beautiful. I put it on immediately.

* * *

"We have to go down for dinner in a few minutes, and after that, we are booked for a painting class with all-you-can-drink wine!" he squeaked out excitedly.

"Wow, babe! You really went all out this time!" I said impressed.

"Well, I really love you, and I want us both to be happy. I know I'm a jerk most of the time, but I've never had a woman like you, and I want to keep you forever," he said sincerely. "Do you know how to tie a tie?" He asked with a nervous grin.

Laughing, I responded, "I sure don't, but I'm sure there's a video on YouTube."

Eventually we were able to get him all dressed up in his suit for dinner and went down to the dining area of the hotel. It was an all-you-can-eat seafood buffet! I was thrilled. They had steak options as well, but I love seafood. The waiter brought over a wine menu and some sort of bread.

I asked for a water with my wine and he said, "Sparkling or flat?"

I'd never been asked that question before and was feeling fancy, so I said, "You know what? Sparkling sounds fantastic!"

I was having a great time.

"Time to go to our painting class," Hector said excitedly.

"Shouldn't we go change first?" I asked, not wanting to get anything on my new dress.

"Nah, we're at a fancy place—I want to stay fancy," he said, grabbing my hand to help me out of my chair. He was being so sweet and charming; I felt like I was in a fairytale.

If only he were like this all the time, I thought to myself.

We walked over to the building where they were doing the painting class. It was a lot bigger than I'd expected. There were at least 30 other couples in there with us. They had a wine spread that you could just walk up to and pick what kind you wanted, and they kept filling your glass. It was fantastic! Neither of us had ever done anything like that before so we were a little bit nervous. I paint cabinets all day, but I am by no means an artist. We were both relieved to see how easy it was to do. Everyone painted the same picture, but no two looked the same. I was sad when the class was over but thrilled to have my new trophy of a hand-painted wine bottle and wine glass.

There was a big tub in our bathroom, so when we got back, Hector started filling it so we could take a bath together and relax. It was nice to just have a little one-on-one time—no cell phones or people to impress; just us, a hot bath, and some music. When we moved to the bed, he broke out a box of sex toys.

"Oh wow, so it's going to be *this* kind of night?" I laughed.

Hector thought of himself as a dom so it wasn't completely uncommon to want to tie me up and flog me. I didn't mind usually. Ironically, he never did anything that hurt me when we were playing. It was all very sensual. He tied up my wrists and went to work.

I was just starting to get into it when he stopped and said, "Oh shit, babe, you're bleeding everywhere!"

I wasn't expecting my period for another week, so I was shocked. I asked him to untie me so I could run to the shower. He came with me. He was trying to continue but there was nothing in the shower for me to grab or steady myself with—it was just a glass box with a showerhead in it. So, he told me to clean myself up and bend over the tub. For some reason, the blood was almost gushing out of me. I couldn't believe it. I wasn't a heavy bleeder, so I had never experienced anything so dramatic. I told him we had to stop, and he got upset.

"Why can't you ever just do as I ask you to do and fucking please me!" he yelled as he pulled my head back by the root of my hair. He shoved himself off me with all of his might, and I fell forward into the tub. As punishment for getting my period at this most inconvenient time, he made me wash his privates off in the shower before I was allowed to clean myself up. While doing so, he decided that it was time to degrade me verbally.

"You fucking ruin everything. I put all this money and effort into this for you and look what you've done." He went on and on the rest of the night about how horrible I was as a person. At one point he even said "You're not even the most beautiful girl I've been with. I've had bitches with *way* better bodies—that's for sure."

I was more than ready for him to just pass out drunk and let me do the same. The day had gone from a fairytale to a nightmare. As I lay there quietly weeping after he'd finally passed out, I thought to myself, *At least he didn't hit me this time.*

Then next morning, we woke up and he acted like nothing had happened. He ordered room service for breakfast and we sat in our hotel robes, eating and drinking orange juice. I was so happy we were back to being happy that I had completely put the night before out of my mind.

When it was time for checkout, I assumed we were going home, but we went to Atlanta instead. We walked around the city holding hands and stopped for lunch at a restaurant we hadn't been to before. Then he asked if I wanted to go get my hair done on the way home.

"Sure, that sounds good," I said.

We went to the salon, and I noticed him looking at his phone a lot. He stepped out to have a phone call here and there while I was getting my hair done. I figured he had something else up his sleeve. When we got in the car to head home, I told him how tired I was.

"Lay the seat back and close your eyes for the ride home then. We have other plans, so there's no time for a nap, young lady!" he said playfully.

When we got home, he didn't park in the garage because Gia's car was there. When I looked around there were about 20 cars parked all around my house, so the surprise was already blown. Hector was livid.

"That stupid fucking bitch," he said, gritting his teeth and clenching his hands. "Well your fat ass ho of a friend ruined the whole surprise. Happy fucking birthday," he said, getting out of the car.

"I'm still surprised, babe!" I said, trying to lighten his mood before we went in.

"I fucking hate that cunt."

I walked around the front of the car to head in through the garage and stopped him. "Babe, I love you, and I'm so grateful you did all this for me. Please don't ruin the party because of this. It's not a big deal!" I kissed him and made him promise to be nice.

We walked in the house and up the stairs to the living room.

"*Surprise!*" everyone yelled, and to my surprise my mother popped out and gave me a big hug! My mom lived in Florida at the time, and I had no idea she was here. I was so happy to see her and to see everyone.

"Mom! How did you get here?" I asked.

"Hector," she said, gesturing to him.

"You brought my mom up for my birthday?" I asked shocked.

"Yeah, well at least I was able to surprise you with something," he laughed nervously.

I looked around and my house had been transformed into a beautiful wine country. The cake alone was insane. I couldn't believe how gorgeous everything was. There was food, different wines, and all the people I loved. I couldn't be happier. I excused myself to go change and came back out in a more comfortable dress.

There were so many people there that I didn't know where to start, so I walked over to see my cake.

"Yeah, that cake was $500, just so you know," Hector said loudly enough for everyone to hear.

"Why would you spend $500 on a cake? I don't even like cake that much."

Everyone laughed.

"I just wanted everything to be perfect for you," he said sweetly and grabbed my hands and kissed me. "Happy birthday, baby," he said while everyone watched and went *Aww*.

I noticed Gia behind him with her arms crossed angrily, rolling her eyes in disgust. I wondered what that was about, but then my nephew asked me to cut the cake, so I was sidetracked.

I passed out cake and opened my gifts happily before making my rounds the best I could, wanting to say hello and thank everyone for showing up. After a while, I went out onto the back porch and Gia was out there smoking a cigarette amongst a few other guests. I made my way over to her to see why she was so crabby.

"Happy birthday," she said, giving me a kiss on the cheek.

"Thank you. What the hell's wrong with you? You look mad as hell. Did I miss something?"

"You know this was all me, right?" she said.

"What do you mean?"

"Everything—I planned everything. I suggested he take you to the winery and booked the room and the class for you guys. I bought the two dresses for you that he gave you. I did all the food and put the decorations up and even ordered the cake. I bet he didn't tell you *that* did he?" she said, hatefully taking a drag off her cigarette. "And then he's cussing me out and being an asshole all fucking day over the phone!"

"I didn't know any of that. Did he at least pay for everything?" I asked.

"Yeah, of course. He gave me money and told me to get it done, but then gives me *none* of the credit when I did all the work!"

"Well, I'm very sorry. I know he's an ass sometimes. But don't let is spoil your mood. Let's have a nice evening," I said.

"Yeah you're right," she said. "I don't want to spoil your party. I'll shut up."

When I went back inside, my mom came over and told me that she was going to go stay at my brother's house with my nephew, and that she was going to head home with them. So I said my goodbyes to my family, and they were one of the first groups to leave.

I went down the hall to go to my bathroom, but the bedroom door was locked. Knowing that it wasn't mounted correctly, I pushed it in and discovered Hector quickly hiding something in his pocket. His friend from Myrtle Beach was in there with him and they both looked at me like they'd just got caught. I immediately knew what was going on.

"Are you fucking kidding me right now?" I said, almost hissing at him. His little friend got up and ran off somewhere, not wanting to feel my wrath. "After you *promised* me you wouldn't bring that shit in this house anymore, you're doing it at *my birthday party*?!" I took a step towards him.

"I'm sorry, babe, but it's not just me who wanted it. Everyone's doing it pretty much and most of these people are your friends! What do you want me to do?"

I was so mad I was shaking. "So, what? You threw me a big cocaine party for my birthday knowing that it's the shit I don't want around me? Or *you* for that matter. You're supposed to be getting off that shit!" I said. I couldn't believe he was trying to rationalize this.

"Babe, it's not like that. Don't be so fucking dramatic. It's not that big a deal. After everything I did to show you how much I love you, you really want to ruin this weekend over this?"

I stormed out of the room, disgusted.

When I reentered the living room, Bessie grabbed me to tell me something, and she knew immediately that something was wrong. "Come on," she said, pulling me into the room she always stayed in at my house. "What's wrong?" she asked.

I told her what I'd just discovered, and she shook her head.

"Are you really surprised? Everything he does is for him, not you. I'm just glad he didn't propose. We were all worried that that's what all this was leading up to," she laughed.

"Yeah, I kind of got that feeling too. I mean, he went above and beyond to make this weekend romantic, but I'm glad he didn't do that!" I said, honestly relieved.

"Look, it's your party, your birthday, your house. If you really want to, you can shut it all down and make everyone leave and have a big fight. Or you can shake it off and try to enjoy the night. How much trouble can he really get into? He's at home surrounded by your friends."

She had a point. Everyone was enjoying themselves, so I decided to do the same. I let it go and went back to my party. I actually did wind up having a good time. As long as I avoided Hector, I was fine; I was still pissed at him. But every time he disappeared, I knew what he was doing, and it made my skin crawl. Eventually, I couldn't take anymore. I was so tired that I didn't care what anyone else was doing I had to go to bed. I said my goodnights to the coke crew and thanked them for coming.

The next morning, I was the only one awake. Hector had only come to bed an hour before I'd gotten up, so I assumed everyone else had as well. To my surprise though, Bessie seemed to be the only one that stayed the night. She got up a little while after I did and came into the living room.

"How was the rest of the party?" I asked.

"It was fine, I guess. I went to bed before some of the others left. Then I was woken up twice by your boyfriend trying to get me to suck his dick," she said. She seemed annoyed but said it extremely casual like that was a normal thing.

"What? Did he really?"

She yawned and stretched, nodding her head. "Yeah I just played dead and he finally went away. He did feel the need, though, to announce to the party that I had sucked his dick. I don't know why, but everyone knows now."

After a moment of quiet, she changed the subject. "Should we make breakfast or go to Waffle House?"

"I don't care." I didn't like what she was telling me. Why would he try to go behind my back like that—and at my birthday party, in my own house?

I found out a year or so after that party that Hector had also dragged one of my best girlfriends into my shop downstairs that evening, asking her to show him her breasts for a line of coke. He apparently did this to several of my friends while I was asleep after the party.

So much for Prince Charming and the fairytale.

CHAPTER FOURTEEN

Was That Necessary?

Hector had a friend I didn't really know who worked on motorcycles. Chris was a nice enough guy. We went to his house once or twice. He rode, but I don't believe he was affiliated with any clubs, or if he was, I don't remember.

One Saturday night, we were getting ready to go to the clubhouse when Hector said, "Can you drive separate and meet me there, babe? I want to go meet up with Chris and ride in together so he can look at my bike."

Not thinking anything of it, I told him that was fine. Gia was already headed up there, so I grabbed my vest and gave him a quick kiss on the way out the door. Gia and I always managed to have our own fun even when it was dry and boring at the clubhouse.

We were sitting together and chatting with everyone at the clubhouse when Hector called me a little while later.

"Hey, I think I ran out of gas or something. Can you go get some gas and bring it to me?"

I told him to text me his location, and Gia and I got up to leave.

After we bought a gas can and some gas, we went to find him, but I couldn't find them anywhere. He called me wondering where I was. He was getting pissed off at me, so I put him on speakerphone so Gia could hear and hopefully get a better understanding of where he was. She knew the area well, and I was completely unfamiliar with it.

Finally, we spotted them. I could tell he was mad when he walked up to my car, shaking his head in disgust. "Jesus Christ you need to learn how to take directions," he said, grabbing the gas can.

"And you need to learn how to put gas in your vehicle like a grownup," I snapped back at him.

"Watch your fucking mouth," he spat.

"All right you two—enough. Let's just get this done so we can go," Gia said.

We waited in the car for further instruction.

"I don't know how much longer I can do this," I said with tears welling up in my eyes. "I'm so fucking miserable." I started confessing to Gia just how shitty this relationship was and how shitty he made me feel.

"I get it, he's an ass!" She said. "What are you going to do? Eventually, this shit is going to blow."

"I know. I feel stuck."

Finally, Hector got his bike going and told us to go on ahead. We went back to the clubhouse to meet them as instructed. When they got there, Hector took Chris around to introduce him to everyone. They grabbed a beer and chatted a bit, and then Hector, Chris, and Hector's cousin, Jimmy, all went to the back of the clubhouse where the bathroom and three other rooms were and closed the door.

After having a couple of beers, I had to pee, so I got up to go to the bathroom. The door I had to walk through to get to the bathroom was closed, but it was unlocked, so I went in. I saw the three gentlemen sitting at a long table; Hector was getting ready to snort the little pile of cocaine he had on the tip of one of his keys. He immediately tried to hide it underneath the table when he saw me coming through the door.

Pissed and disgusted, I crossed my arms and told him, "Go ahead. I already see you. Snort away, you fucking junkie."

Not knowing how to react, he nervously tried to put the cocaine back in the bag and the bag in his pocket. "Don't fucking talk to me like that," he said.

I started thinking about my birthday party a few weeks back and got even more pissed off. "I'm done with the lies, Hector. If you're going to be a junkie, at least be honest about it when I walk in and physically see you doing it."

Embarrassed and upset, he got up from his chair. "I already told you to watch your fucking mouth! You aren't gonna talk to me like this," he said, grabbing my vest and pushing me into a room, closing the doors behind us.

"Don't fucking touch me," I said, trying to shrug him off.

"Take off your rags. You aren't going to disrespect me in *my* clubhouse, wearing *my* name." He slammed me up against the wall.

"Fuck you."

He slammed me again and said, "*Take off the rags.*"

"Why are you doing this?" I asked. "Why are you constantly lying to me and risking our relationship when you said you wanted to get clean?" I gripped both of his wrists, desperate to understand.

"Why can't you learn to shut the fuck up?" He still had me pinned against the wall.

Then—*Bam!*—he headbutted me right in the face. I could taste blood in my mouth, but it didn't appear to be gushing or anything. I tried to knee him in the balls but missed and stomped on his foot instead, which did nothing since he was wearing riding boots.

"That's it—take off the vest, now!"

"Who's gonna make me? I don't see a man in this room," I said as hatefully as I could.

Now it was on—a full-blown fist fight. He wouldn't let go of my vest and had a pretty firm grip on my right shoulder, which was making it difficult to hit him back with that hand. So, I started kicking him.

That's when I noticed that he had a knife. I went into full defense mode. He kept coming at me with the knife, so I threw my hands up to protect my face and head. He swung me to my left, almost knocking the TV stand off the wall and bringing me to the ground while cutting the shoulder of my vest in half. He got on top of me with the knife, accidently slicing my left arm.

"*Stop it!* You're going to fucking stab me!" I yelled. I started crying and screaming for help. Nobody could hear me over the music, so I was on my own. "Please, babe, why are you doing this? I love you!" I yelled, begging him stop.

I wasn't scared or in fear for my life, surprisingly. I didn't feel anything; I was completely numb at this point and just wanted this to be over.

He hit me just above my ear with his knife hand and told me, "Stop fighting me! Nobody's going to help you here, you stupid fucking bitch. You should have kept your fucking mouth shut!" He pushed himself up, put his knee on my head, and started cutting the vest off my body. Not wanting to get stabbed, I gave up and let him do it.

When he was done, he stood up and kicked me in the stomach. I went into the fetal position and rolled over away from him. "Now maybe you'll learn to keep your fucking mouth shut," he said. Then he left the room with the knife and shredded vest in his hand.

I lay there on the nasty floor crying.

"Oh my God," I heard Gia say just above a whisper. She obviously hadn't known that this type of thing was happening.

Hearing the shock and concern in her voice, I tried to get up and stumbled.

"Okay, hold on. I've got you." She wrapped an arm around me and putt my right arm over her shoulder to brace me. "We're going to go to the bathroom so we can get you cleaned up, okay?"

"Get me out of here," I whimpered like a wounded animal, tears streaming down my face.

"I will. I just need to get a good look at you," she said, leading me to the bathroom. Nobody was around; they were all up front, completely clueless to what was going on.

When she turned the light on and closed the door, she propped me against the wall. Tears started to well up in her eyes, and she looked genuinely heartbroken.

"Oh my God, Savannah. That motherfucker!"

She wet a towel and cleaned me up the best she could, looking me over to see if I needed to go to the hospital. The only open wound I had was the scratch on my left arm from the knife and some blood in my mouth from my teeth cutting my lips, neither of which were very bad.

"Okay, we have to get you out of here. I can't do anything here; we just need to go or it's only going to get worse."

I wanted nothing more than to leave, so that was fine with me. "I can't walk through there like this. Can we go out the back door?"

"Yes, absolutely." She went to grab our purses and told one of the bros that we were leaving out the back door. She came back to get me and helped me out.

As the back door was opening, I heard one of the bros say, "Hey, is everything okay? What's wrong?" I looked back at him and his whole face changed. He was shocked.

"No, everything is *not* fine, and she is *not* okay. We are leaving now." Gia escorted me to my car. "Are you okay to drive?"

"Yes, thank you. I'll call you when I'm home," I said, falling into my car seat.

"Do we need to take you to the hospital?"

"No, they'll file a police report. I can't get the club involved," I said. She nodded in understanding.

I made it home safe and couldn't get any farther than my staircase. I broke down in tears and sat in the middle of my steps. A little bit later, my phone rang.

"Are you home?" Gia asked when I answered. "Do you need me to come there?"

I told her that I was home and I'd be fine.

"You're not fine, Savannah! You just got the shit kicked out of you by your fucking boyfriend! When your dad and brother find out, he's a dead man!" she yelled, finally able to react the way she wanted to.

"Don't you dare tell them, Gia!" I snapped into protection mode.

"What the fuck?! Why on Earth would you want to protect *him*? When I walked into that room and saw you like that…" she choked up and started to cry. "That motherfucker!"

"I know…this time was bad."

"*This time?* What the fuck?! So, there's been other times?!"

That was so stupid. Why had I said that? "Look, I'm fine. You have to promise not to say anything! They will literally kill him, Gia. Please!" I begged.

"You need to figure out what you're going to do. You can't stay there. You're miserable and apparently a punching bag!"

"I can't leave, Rafiki's here. I can't just leave him," I said, bursting into tears.

"Oh, Savannah. He's not there—it's just a body," she said delicately.

"Not to me." I was sobbing. "Thank you for getting me out of there, but I need to go lie down."

"Okay, well I talked to Hector briefly before I left, and he already knew he'd fucked up big time, so he won't be coming home tonight. At least you can relax a little bit."

That was the best news I'd heard all week. "You talked to him?"

"Yeah he was outside when I went to get in my car."

"What happened?"

"He came up to me, and I told him he was an asshole and that he fucked up big time. He agreed and told me that he lost control. He said that he didn't mean to hurt you. I told him that he was lucky we were at the clubhouse when it happened because it would have turned out differently if we weren't," she said.

"Well, I'm relieved he won't be coming home tonight. Have a good night," I said.

"Yeah right, goodnight, but you need to do some serious thinking right now. This can't happen again," she said before hanging up.

Gizmo was already in my lap, purring to comfort me. I moved her and went to the bedroom. She jumped up on the bed with me after I had taken off my torn clothes and put on an oversized nightshirt. I wrapped my body around her and scratched her fluffy neck while sobbing.

Why did I have to open my mouth? Why did I challenge him like that? I'd known he wouldn't react well. I wasn't supposed to be like that towards him, especially not at the clubhouse. And why had I slipped and let Gia know that this wasn't the first time? She wouldn't understand. Nobody would.

Why do I stay here? Is he even capable of getting clean? Does he even really want to get clean? What if he had stabbed me in the face? Even if it had been an accident, I could have lost an eye or been killed. Why would he do that? Doesn't he know how much I loved him? Doesn't he see how many sacrifices I've made for him? Why do I have to say things to him that embarrass him? I know how insecure he is and yet I keep making it worse.

My thoughts were running wild as I finally drifted off into a restless sleep.

The next morning, I woke up with swollen puffy eyes from crying all night and finally realized how sore my body was. I slowly got up to use the bathroom and check the damage. I obviously had some bumps and bruises, but the thing that upset me the most was seeing the sadness in my own face. I was losing who I was; I couldn't even recognize myself anymore.

I had started to draw a bath in hopes of relaxing and taking some of the soreness out of my body when I heard my phone vibrating. It was Gia.

"How you feeling?" she asked.

"How do you think?"

"Have you heard from stupid yet?" she asked, making me chuckle. I pulled the phone away from my face and saw that I'd missed about 20 texts throughout the night.

"Apparently, but I just got up and haven't read anything yet."

I grabbed the Epsom salt and poured it into the running water. I read the texts out loud to her while I waited for the tub to fill. They were all very apologetic. He sounded like a scared child who didn't want his mommy to stop loving him. He always got more emotional when he was high, so I wasn't surprised.

"Well, he messaged me this morning as well. I'll send everything to you. I told him he fucked this all up, and he's an idiot," she said matter-of-factly.

"No argument here," I replied.

"Have you thought about what you're going to do?"

"Not really. I went to bed as soon as I got home, and I just woke up. I really just need some time."

"I understand. I'll send you the conversation I had with him this morning. Let me know if you need anything," she said.

"Thank you."

I hung up and finally slid into the tub. The water felt good on my skin as I sank in further. Enjoying a brief moment of quiet and relief, I asked God, "Why am I here, Lord? Where do *you* want me to be?"

I needed something—a sign, some clarity, some understanding of some sort. Feeling disappointed in the lack of response, I went back to feeling sorry for myself.

After a few minutes, my phone started to buzz repeatedly, and I took a deep breath. "Here we go…"

I read through the conversation they had first. Gia put him in his place. I could tell how angry she was. He pathetically asked her for help at one point, saying, "What do I need to do?"

"GET OFF THE COKE," she responded. "And don't ever put your hands on her again." She went on to tell him what an idiot he was and how I had already been unhappy, so she was sure this was going to be the final straw.

Finally, I went to check my personal messages. He'd gone on all night with them. "What have I done? I'm so sorry babe. I don't deserve you." Those were first. He would go from telling me what a piece of shit he was and how he knew I was too good for him to begging me to let him come home and make it up to me. He said he was scared to come home to an empty house because he couldn't live without me. He was terrified that I was already gone.

I read through everything, but I wasn't sure if I was ready to talk to him yet, so I set my phone down and tried to relax.

When my phone buzzed again, it was Hector's cousin, Jose, calling me. Jose worked for Hector, so I was getting to know him quite well. He was responsible for picking up Hector in the mornings and bringing him home after work so he could use the company van. He would even eat dinner with us if it was already made. I liked him a lot; he was always very nice to me. He had a very street vibe to him, being from the Bronx. He wasn't bad looking, bald like Hector, and he was fun once you got to know him a little bit. He was married to a very sweet woman named Frankie, and they had two kids. I liked Frankie a lot; she would always volunteer to help cook or clean up after we had a party.

I picked up the phone and Jose said, "Hey, what the hell is going on? Are you okay?" I could tell that he was genuinely concern.

"I'll be fine—why?"

"Hector just called me, crying. He said he did something terrible to you last night, and he's afraid to come home to an empty house. Did you leave him?" he asked.

"No, I didn't leave him. I'm home."

"What the hell happened? Do I need to kick his ass?"

I went through what happened and he said, "I mean he has a history of putting his hands on women, so I'm not surprised; it was only a matter of time I guess. I don't know why he won't get off that coke shit though— that shit fucks with your head bad. He's just like his fucking father." He sounded disappointed. "So, what you gonna do? He's waiting on me to call him back, so what should I tell him?"

I paused for a moment, not sure what to say. "Tell him whatever you want. I don't care," I finally said.

"All right, you need anything?"

"No, I just want to be alone."

Less than 10 minutes later, Hector was messaging me again: "Now that I've learned how unhappy you've been, I can see that the best thing for you is for me to leave. I'm sorry I hurt you; I wish I could take it back. You were the best thing that ever happened to me and I fucked it all up. I love you."

That message broke my heart. I thought to myself, *What am I doing? I can't let this be the end. It would destroy him.* I didn't want to be the reason he flew off the deep end.

Finally, I responded to him: "I love you too, and I'm sorry I embarrassed you, but I can't stand seeing you like that. You're better than that, and you told me you were going to stop. I can't keep doing this. But I don't want you to leave either."

We texted back and forth for about an hour and finally he asked if he could come home.

"Yes, of course," I responded.

He was home in less than 30 minutes. He came up the stairs to the living room where I was sitting on the couch with Gizmo. He looked like he had been crying as much as I had. He dropped to his knees and put his head in my lap, wrapping his arms around my hips.

"I'm so fucking sorry, babe," he said and started to cry in my lap. I lifted his head to look at me and told him to stop crying.

I told him that I was sorry too but we both needed to try harder.

He agreed and said, "I was so scared you were leaving. I don't know what I would do without you. I just wanted to kill myself." He put his face back in my lap and sobbed.

"I'm still here, but this can't happen again. And the coke has to stop," I said sternly.

He looked up and said, "I love you so much. Thank you for not leaving me." With tears in his eyes, he continued, "I know I deserved it, but I'd rather die than not have you." He sat up and kissed me, tasting like stale cigarettes and old beer.

I pushed him back and said playfully, "Yeah, that's all good, but go brush your teeth and take a shower—you stink."

He chuckled, "Yeah, I stayed the night at the clubhouse."

Then he began trying to remove my pants.

"What are you doing? I just said you were gross." I tried to squirm away.

"I can still make you feel good," he said, kissing my inner thighs and lower stomach.

CHAPTER FIFTEEN

When Will I Learn?

For the first couple of weeks after the incident at the clubhouse, he was very sweet, almost submissive. He was passionate and loving, communicated with me more instead of watching TV all the time.

One of his friends, Victor, invited us out to their house for a wine tasting party he was hosting with his wives. Yes, *wives*. The threesome lived about an hour away from us in a big beautiful home they had designed together and built from the ground up. It was gorgeous. They had an outdoor hot tub that was perfectly placed. The whole house was perfect.

I love wine tasting, so I was happy to attend. I was aware that Victor and his wives were all swingers, and that Hector had played with them before with his ex-wife. They had a charm about them that made you feel very comfortable. As the day turned into night, everyone was getting to know each other and just having a really good time. There was a strange sexual atmosphere in the air. Victor suggested to those of us who remained that we should take a dip in the hot tub. Nobody was prepared for that, but they clearly did this all the time. They had plenty of bathing suit options for both men and women. Having had plenty of wine throughout the day, I felt like this was a great idea.

We all jumped in together. It was actually plenty of room for all of us. It was Victor and his two wives, Hector and me, and one other couple. I can't remember their names, but they were both very attractive and friendly. We all sat there talking for about 20 minutes, having more wine and sharing stories.

Then one of Victor's wives said she was getting hot, so she took off her bikini top. That led to everyone eventually getting completely naked. I hadn't really been in a situation like this before, but I was drunk enough to just roll with it. One of the wives started kissing me and that was it—everyone was hands on.

Hector was all over me, enjoying watching everything happen. He was running his hands up and down my body while I made out with Victor's first wife. Victor asked if he could taste me, and Hector put me up on the side of the hot tub allowing him access to me. I was a little nervous, but there was something exhilarating about the whole thing. Victor clearly had more experience in this area. He looked up at me hungrily while enjoying his time between my legs. He moved slow and steady, unlike Hector who would just eagerly peck at random places. Victor seemed to be enjoying the moment even more than I was.

Eventually, Hector pushed Victor to the side and put himself in Victor's place when he saw that I was enjoying myself. I was disappointed, honestly. Victor had me on the edge of climax, and Hector taking over made me lose it. I was hoping he would have learned something by watching Victor, but clearly, he did not.

Everyone was having some form of sex with someone at this point, so it didn't feel shameful or dirty. The blond woman from the other couple was sitting on the edge of the hot tub next to me, making out with her boyfriend who was standing up behind her on the ground, feeling her breasts. Victor's wives were going back and forth with her, pleasing her orally. It felt sexy and hot to have so many people around me having sex.

Hector gave up on his pecking between my legs, realizing it was getting me nowhere. "Come here," he said, guiding me back into the hot tub. He went over to Victor who was watching his wives play with the blond-haired lady.

"Suck his dick," Hector demanded, telling Victor to stand up out of the water. "I want to watch."

Knowing how jealous Hector was all the time, I was hesitant. Victor stood up in front of me, already erect.

"Come on," Hector said, grabbing the back of my head. He gripped Victor's cock with his left hand and pushed my head towards it with his right, sitting eye level. "Lick the tip, and look up at him like you do," Hector growled hungrily still holding Victor's member in his left hand.

I found it strange and a little uncomfortable that he was doing this, but I didn't want to be the party killer, so I did as commanded. Hector never moved his hand from Victor and stayed eye level to the action the whole time. I locked eyes with Victor who seemed to be enjoying himself and tried to forget about the fact that my boyfriend was holding his friend's dick in my mouth.

"Okay, that's enough," he said, pulling my head back. He kissed me deeply and whispered, "I need to fuck you" against my lips.

I climbed on his lap, and he slid inside me.

"I want to play with her," I heard Victor's other wife say.

"Hell yeah," Hector said, pushing me off him. "Bend over and eat her pussy, babe," he commanded.

"I wanted to eat hers," she replied.

"Well, I need to fuck while this is happening, so unless I'm allowed to fuck you, she's going down on you while I fuck her," he said.

"I don't mind you fucking me, but you need to put a condom on," she replied.

"Yeah, bend over, babe," Hector said, pushing me over.

I went to my task as he commanded and let him have his fun. It didn't last more than two minutes.

Eventually, when the sex part was over, it was just me, Hector, and Victor left standing. Everyone else had gone to pass out somewhere. I went to dry off and put clothes on, and I heard Hector asking Victor for another line.

Drunk and pissed I approached them. "Are you fucking kidding me?" I said, catching him red-handed.

We got into another verbal altercation, but I realized I was drunk and just wanted to lie down. I remember Hector coming to bed shortly after and needing to have sex again. I was really drunk and tired, but I let him do what he wanted, not having the energy to fight.

When I woke up the next morning I was hung over. Hector wasn't in bed with me. So, I went to find him. Everyone was on the porch surrounding the hot tub, eating breakfast. They happily welcomed me and offered me food and orange juice. I sat in one of the chairs, happy with just water for the time being. Hector was the only one sitting in the hot tub, taking selfies on his phone. He didn't seem upset. When he got out, he sat next to me and we all started talking.

Somehow, relationships were brought up, and Hector told them we were having some problems. So, we discussed it a bit with them and they gave us some advice.

"Well, in my experience if one or both people are secretly miserable, the relationship will eventually fail," Victor said, picking up on how I was feeling. "That being said, I think you two are a beautiful couple, and I hope it works out for you both. I can see how Hector has changed. He seems very happy with you." His wives agreed.

We had to go home and get ready to go to Six Flags for his aunt's birthday. When we got in the car Hector changed completely. "You fucking embarrassed me again last night," he said, pulling out of the driveway.

"As did you," I replied dryly.

"I am a grown-ass man. If I want to do a little blow at a party, I will. I'm sick of you hounding me about it," he said flatly.

"Okay," I said, staring out the window, not really listening to him.

"And why are you trying to act like you aren't happy in front of my friends? I fucking give you everything you want! Yeah, I have a temper and I like to party, but I also take you on trips and surprise you and try to make you feel special, so stop making me out to be such a monster."

"Okay," was my reply once again.

"I'm fucking talking to you."

I stared out the window unresponsive.

"Hey!" He backhanded me, knocking my head into the window. "I'm fucking talking to you, bitch."

"Don't fucking touch me, Hector," I snapped at him.

"Oh, shut up. That didn't hurt," he responded, waving away my reaction.

"You want to know why I'm miserable? Because you're fucking psychotic. You're Dr. Jekyll and Mr. Hyde. One week you're fine, the next, you're beating the shit out of me. I fucking *hate* you," I said, meaning every word.

"You hate me? Okay, fine. Fuck it! It's over," he said matter-of-factly.

"Fine by me."

"You can get the fuck out of my house this weekend," he said, getting upset.

"It's our house—both of our names are on it, and all the furniture is mine. My dog that you let die is buried in the backyard. I'm not going anywhere. You want to leave? Fine. But you aren't kicking me out," I said calmly.

"Yeah, we'll see," he said.

When we got to the house, I asked for my car keys. I knew he was going to Six Flags, but he wasn't about to take my car.

"Fuck you," he laughed when I asked for them.

"You aren't taking my car. You just broke up with me, remember?" I reminded him with my hand out.

"Go your ass upstairs and get dressed. We have somewhere to be."

Not wanting to be around him or fake being happy any longer, I told him that I wasn't going.

"Yes the fuck you are! Now get your fat ass upstairs and get the fuck dressed!" he screamed, getting out of the car and coming to my side to open the door.

"Why do I have to go? You just said you were done with me!" I said while he opened the door.

He grabbed my hair and the shoulder of my dress and dragged me out of the car. He pulled me into the house by my hair and threw me into the steps. "Go get ready. You have 10 minutes. If I have to come get you I will break your fucking face," he said, walking back out through the garage.

He was serious? Why on Earth did I have to go? I just wanted to be away from him, but I didn't want it to go any further and I realized that my phone was in the car so I couldn't call for help, so I just did what he wanted.

When I got back in the car, he didn't say a word; he just drove. It was a 45-minute drive, and we didn't say a word to each other the whole way. I sat quietly staring out the window, fighting off tears.

When we got there, he parked and said to me, "I don't want you anymore, but if you embarrass me in front of my family, I'll kill you. Stop pouting and be happy—*now*."

I followed him as he got out of the car. That's basically all I did all night— follow him around quietly. They could all see something was wrong, but nobody pushed it.

When we were finally leaving, he said, "Let's go to the clubhouse."

"No," I protested, "I'm exhausted and need to lie down."

"I don't really fucking care what you want," he spat.

"What the hell is your problem?" Titi spoke up. "If she wants to go home, let her go home. Don't talk to her like that," she said.

At her defense of me, he shot my way that said that I had just crossed a line. "Fine," he said, throwing my keys at me and walking away. "Go the fuck home then."

"Wow, I'm sorry, Savannah," Titi said when he was out of earshot. "I warned you he was a fucking asshole. Go home—we'll take him with us."

Honestly relieved to get away from him, I went to my car happy and alone.

The next morning, he texted me to say that he was coming to get his wallet but he didn't want to see me. It had started to sink in that maybe he was serious about breaking up. For some stupid reason, that hurt my feelings. *He* wanted to leave *me*?

When he walked in, I asked if we could talk.

"I told you I didn't want to see you," he said, walking past me.

"So, that's it? We're really done?" I said sadly.

"I guess so. I don't want to make you miserable, and I don't want to be controlled," he said.

The hypocrisy of that statement didn't escape me. "*You* don't want to be controlled? You just forced me to endure an entire day at Six Flags with your family after supposedly breaking up with me. You threatened to break my face, and then told me to smile and look pretty so I didn't embarrass you!"

He just looked at me stupidly, not knowing what to say.

"I thought we were going to try harder and work on things," I said trying to calm down. "Two weeks ago, you were begging me not to leave you. We agreed to work on things, and you agreed to stop doing coke. Now look at us. I bust you doing coke again and you just want to run?"

Hector's uncle was waiting for him in the car, so Hector sent him away so we could sit down and have an actual conversation. We, again, agreed that we didn't want to break up, but we needed figure out how to compromise. It wasn't some sweet passionate makeup like the other times. It was just like 'okay, we'll stay. What's for dinner?'

He turned on the TV and I went to the kitchen like nothing had happened.

CHAPTER SIXTEEN

New Orleans

Two weeks later, Hector decided we needed to get away for the weekend to reconnect, so he rented a car and we drove to Louisiana.

He had rented a room at a bed and breakfast in New Orleans just a few blocks from Bourbon Street. The inn was in an old Victorian house painted such a bright pink that it looked like Pepto Bismol. There was some history there. They still had the original poles in the ground with little horse head statues on the top where the original owners parked their horse and carriages. The posts were painted the same hideous pink as the house.

When we walked inside, the inn smelled old and musty but it was cozy. Our room was a good size, but the bathroom was tiny. It was cute, though, and we were only spending two nights, so it would be just fine for us.

"I didn't want to just get a hotel like we always do, so I thought this would be a nice change," he said insecurely.

"It's fine, babe! What more could we need?"

We asked the man behind the front desk where the best places to eat were, and he gave us copious amounts of information. I could tell that his bed and breakfast wasn't as busy as he wanted because he seemed to want to sit there and chat all night.

I ordered an Uber and set it to take us to Bourbon Street since I was starving and didn't want to waste time walking. The diver was nice and took us to one of the places where he liked to eat on the strip. We got out of the car, and immediately, the smell hit me. The whole area has a foul musty odor I wasn't expecting. You could still see the flood line on the buildings from Hurricane Katrina years ago.

"Don't worry, you get used to the smell," the driver said, smiling and bidding us a good night. He had told us how to get the rest of the way there because he could only take us so far since they would only allow cars in certain areas.

I instantly fell in love with the place as we started walking. There was so much life here; so much excitement! I wanted to see everything and try everything. After we ate, we walked around, trying out different bars and looking in all the shops.

We eventually stumbled upon a strip club, and I wanted to go in. It was dark and quiet for a strip club—nothing like the ones in Atlanta. They didn't get fully naked here, and they didn't seem to be as acrobatic either. But it was entertaining enough to sit back and watch the few people that were in there enjoying themselves. There was a bride-to-be and her bachelorette entourage right up front, getting loud and rowdy. It was pretty early still so we hadn't gotten to that level yet. I decided it was boring in there, so we made our way out. That's when I realized there were several more adult clubs there on the strip.

"Well," I said, grabbing Hector's hand. "Might as well see them all!" I laughed, dragging him into the next one.

He wasn't a big fan of strip clubs, but I always liked going, so he obliged since we were there to experience everything. The night went on and the drinks were flowing.

"Look babe," he said, pointing over to a male strip club, laughing.

Thinking he was pointing it out so we could try that one too, I started to cross the street towards it. But suddenly, his hands were in my hair as he pulled me back to the sidewalk, slamming me into a wall. I scraped my elbow and grabbed it with my right hand.

"Don't you go acting like a fucking ho!" he yelled at me, causing people to stop and look at us.

Embarrassed, I said quietly, "I'm sorry babe, I just thought we were going to all of them."

Noticing everyone now looking at us, he stormed off down the sidewalk.

"Are you okay, ma'am?" a young man with a group of people asked.

"Do you need some help?" his friend asked.

Panicked, I answered, "No, I'm fine. I'm just clumsy. Thank you, though," and darted towards the direction Hector had gone. I didn't know this town, and I didn't know the name of the inn where we were staying, so I didn't want him to just leave me behind. I finally caught up to him as he was turning down a side street.

"Babe!" I yelled as I approached him, half jogging.

He turned around, checking to see if anyone was around then turned around and slammed me into another wall. "Why would you do that?!" he growled. He let go of me, walking away.

"I'm sorry, I honestly thought it was just another strip club to see. Why did you point it out?" I said.

He turned around and grabbed me again, slamming me once more into the wall, this time hitting the back of my head hard. "I didn't bring you here to be a whore and fuck other guys! Leave me alone, go fuck someone else," he said, pushing himself off me.

I was shocked and confused. I reached up to feel where my head had hit the wall, but I didn't see any blood on my hand. Following him, I said, "What are you talking about? I don't want to fuck anyone! Where did that come from?"

He ignored me and kept walking. Quietly, I followed him back to the place we were staying.

When we reached out room, he sat down on the bed. There was no TV in the room, so it was very quiet. I went to the bathroom and brushed my teeth. When I came out the lights were off, and he was lying on the bed. I pulled my clothes off, knowing that I had to make up for whatever I had done to set him off. He was obviously feeling insecure, so I had to assure him that I didn't want anyone else.

I climbed into bed and wrapped my left arm around him trying to cuddle. "I'm sorry for upsetting you, babe. What can I do to fix this?" I asked, kissing the side of his head.

"Stop being a whore."

"I wasn't. I don't know why you feel like that, but I'm sorry."

He rolled over to face me. "I saw your face when Victor was eating your pussy in the hot tub. You don't make that face for me," he said.

Okay, I thought, *here's the* real *reason he's mad.* "Babe you let him do that to me—it turned you on at the time. Isn't that what you're into? The whole swinging thing?" I asked.

"You don't make that face when I do it. What—you like him better?"

"I didn't do this to you when Bessie sucked your dick, so why are you tripping?"

"That's different" he snapped.

"How so?"

"You know I love you," he said as if he were unsure that my love for him was genuine.

"You asked me to go with it and enjoy myself. I didn't fuck anyone, so what the hell?" I said, rolling onto my back in defeat.

"But you wanted to, didn't you? You wanted him to fuck you right?" He asked me accusingly.

"No, Hector, I only want you," I said, reaching up to pull his head down and kiss me.

"Prove it," he said, climbing on top of me. "Let me get you pregnant."

"What?" I said, shocked. *Where the hell did that come from?* I thought to myself.

"I want you to have my baby. I want you to marry me and be mine forever," he said passionately before devouring me.

Then next morning, we woke up and both wanted to go get some breakfast. We ordered another Uber and asked the driver where we could go for brunch. He recommended a place called Ruby Slipper—they specialized in a brunch menu, so we decided to go check it out. We didn't expect to have to wait an hour to be seated, but the place was packed, so we figured it would be worth the wait.

We finally got seated at the bar and ordered some mimosas while looking over the menu. Hector was very quiet so far, but it didn't seem like he was in a bad mood—more like something was on his mind. I decided not to bother asking since I was so hungry, and we still had one more night there. I just wanted to try and enjoy it and hopefully not fight.

After breakfast, we decided to walk around and do some exploring. This was our only full day there, so we decided to experience everything possible.

We did some window-shopping and then discovered a casino. I had never been to one before but was happy to check it out, even though I was scared to gamble. It wasn't very busy at the time, but I figured it was too early in the afternoon for everyone to be out partying. We sat at a machine, and Hector started pushing buttons. He ordered us drinks right there from the machines we were playing on, and they were free! I followed him around while he played a few games until he got sick of not winning anything big.

We kept moving and decided to stop at a restaurant and grab a snack. We had been walking around all day, so we really just wanted to sit down for a bit.

On the way to find a place, we walked past a psychic reading place. I had heard that these were popular here and thought it would be fun to try, so we went in. Hector was reluctant to participate at first, but I was totally on board. It was only $35—what's the harm?

I paid the lady, and she went behind a curtain to tell the woman who does the readings. She came back out and asked Hector to leave.

Looking at each other in confusion, we said, "What?"

She explained that they wouldn't do readings for couples because it often creates unwanted stress. So, to avoid any conflicts, they would ask the spouses to separate for the readings. She directed him right around the corner to go sit down and enjoy a drink and some nachos.

Reluctantly, he agreed and kissed me goodbye. "Don't you go running away from me now," he laughed nervously.

"I'll be right there as soon as I'm done. It's going to be fun—don't worry!" I assured him.

"Come on back," I heard an elderly lady say from behind the curtain.

The other lady who ran the front store escorted me to the reading room. It was plain; I'd been expecting crystal balls or something all flashy like the rest of the city was, but it was just an older, slouched lady sitting at a white table with two white chairs. The psychic wasn't exactly friendly—not rude, just very to the point. I could tell she took what she did very seriously, and she meant business.

"Sit down, dear," she said gesturing towards the empty chair. "Are you sure you want to do this? This is no joke like they make it out to be in the movies. What happens here is real, and once I start, whatever *they* want you to know will be said, whether you want to hear it or not," she said, looking at me while unwrapping her tarot cards from the white cloth they were folded in.

"I'm sure," I said, excited.

"It's not usually good news. Everyone comes in wanting to hear about the money or love they are about to find. Don't expect anything, okay," she said, locking eyes with me.

"Yes ma'am." I was getting nervous.

"Let's begin. Give me your hands," she said, reaching out to me. She grabbed my hands and closed her eyes, not saying anything. It almost looked like she was praying.

"Wow, you have an old soul," she said, letting go of me. "I saw your purple aura when you came in the door. It was shining through the curtain."

"Oh," I said, sliding forward in my seat. "Is that a good thing?"

She chuckled and said, "It's a rare thing—most people's auras are barely visible, and some don't glow at all. Purple is the color I see the least. You're a diamond in the rough—one of a kind," she said, seeming pleased.

She had me pick the deck of cards up and cut them. I stacked them back up and placed them back on the table in front of her.

"You aren't where you need to be," she began. "But you'll find your way soon. I see money, but you don't work for a company. You're starting your own business." She was still looking at the cards.

She officially had my attention.

"You will be very successful, but not where you are. There's going to be a man coming into your life. He will be the one who helps you get to where God wants you."

Still not looking up at me at all, she continued, "You are very strong—a leader. You will set an example for many people. You shine like your aura. That's why people love you like they do. But something dark is trying to overpower you, trying to dim your light and keep you hidden," she said shaking her head. "You aren't happy—not at all. I see you taking care of someone like a mother would a wounded animal she thinks of as her child, but you can't fix it. You won't fix it."

My jaw fell open. I honestly didn't expect this to be so real.

"This animal means to destroy what's beautiful about you. You can't let it. You play a much bigger role in this world. You have to let it go if you want to move forward."

I started to tear up.

"This man who comes into your life isn't coming in as a love interest. He's going to show up exactly when he needs to. He is going to help you find your way pure of heart. Let him lead you. This will change your life forever," she said, wrapping up the reading.

Finally looking at me, she grabbed my hand. "You are a rare, beautiful, dying breed. Take care of yourself; you have more to do—much more."

I nodded my head and thanked her for the reading. I was relieved it was over but excited that it had been mostly good. I expected this to be a fun conversational topic. But she described my relationship with Hector better than I could at the time.

Feeling good about my experience I went to find Hector. The place really was just around the corner, so he was easy to locate. He sat there nervously with a beer watching something on one of the TVs.

"How did it go?" he asked, sitting up in the booth. "Did she tell you to leave me?" he asked nervously.

Surprised by the question, I said, "It was actually really good, babe. You should go do it. It was a fun experience."

"I don't know about that," he said, leaning back on the wall of the booth. "Tell me about yours."

I told him about her starting out with me starting my own business, that I would eventually be successful and that I had a really bright purple aura that she seemed to enjoy. I didn't go into much more detail than that because I didn't want him getting anymore insecure than he already was.

"Go try it babe; I'll wait here." I grabbed some cash out of my wallet and gave it to him. "Here, I'll even pay. Go on! Don't be a chicken—we're here to experience everything," I said, urging him to get out of his comfort zone.

"Fine, if you say so." He guzzled what was left of his beer and stood up. "Don't flirt with any guy's while I'm gone."

"Have fun!"

When he came back, his face was red, and his eyes were watering. He looked like he had been crying.

"Oh my God, babe, what happened?" I asked.

"I shouldn't have listened to you," he snapped at me, holding back tears. He was wearing a necklace he didn't have on before and had a bag with something in it.

"What's all this?"

"Well, apparently I have a bunch of demons attached to me," he said looking at me wide-eyed. "This necklace is supposed to help protect me, and they sold me soap to wash them away and help repel them from being attached to me. She said I was going to destroy this." A tear fell as he looked down at the table. "I told you I wasn't good enough for you and now I have confirmation."

I didn't know what to say. "Let's get out of here and walk around. We can head back to the room and put our things away. I want to shower before we hit the strip again tonight anyway."

He nodded his head looking scared and alone. My heart ached for him. I grabbed his hand, and we continued our walk.

We stumbled across a vampire boutique. Hector immediately perked up. "We gotta go in here, babe!" he said, dragging me inside.

They went all out to make it spooky. It was vampire everything you can imagine—even clothing to dress the part. And these weren't cheap costumes you would find at a Halloween store. These were heavy cloth cloaks with the pointed hoods. They had handmade leather journals there with ink and quills.

Hector noticed a back-room area labeled "Vampire Fangs". He asked the man in the store about it and learned that you could get custom fangs made and installed in your teeth.

"How does it work?" he asked excitedly.

It was a simple process. The man who does them wasn't there, but we could put a deposit down and make an appointment. "Can we do it today? We leave tomorrow morning," Hector asked.

"Let me call him and find out." After a quick phone call the man said he could be there at 6:30 PM.

Hector put down the $100 deposit and eagerly made the appointment. We had just enough time to walk back to the room, shower and change, and catch an Uber back. We got there just in time.

The guy who did the fangs was an interesting personality. It didn't seem like he saw this as a novelty, which I guess was good because for $250 cash these things had to be amazing—that's how I felt anyway.

It didn't actually take long considering he was physically making teeth. The whole process took about an hour, but the man was very good at what he did. I couldn't believe how real they looked when he was finished.

"You're all set. Try not to eat with them in because they will pop off and you will most likely swallow them," he said half joking. "But they stay on pretty snug, so drinking is fine." He told Hector how to store and care for them and then sent us on our way.

Now we were walking Bourbon Street for the rest of the night—me and my vampire boyfriend. We didn't get many strange looks. There were a few, but considering where we were, he didn't stick out like a sore thumb. We were having an awesome night so far—no fighting, just having fun. We walked down one side of the street the night before, exploring that, so now we wanted to check the other side.

We found some drinks that were in a plastic fish tank. They had a lanyard attached so you could hang them from your neck. I thought it was hilarious, so we each had one.

We found a place with a bunch of empty seating outside in the back, so we sat down back there for a little while to catch our breath.

"I know that woman was right today," Hector said suddenly. "I know I have demons, and I don't know how to fix it. But I don't want to destroy this. I want to keep us." He sounded so vulnerable.

I grabbed his hand, trying to comfort him. "I know, babe."

Even though we were having a good time tonight, I just had this eerie feeling this was our last trip together—like it was a big 'goodbye' trip or something. I didn't know why; it wasn't because of what the psychic had told him or what she had told me, for that matter. I just felt something stirring inside me.

When we'd finished our fish tanks, we got up and walked down a little further. "Oh shit, look! It's a gay bar," he laughed, pointing at it.

I laughed. "Do you want to go in?" I asked.

I wasn't expecting him to say yes, but he did, so off we went. The bar had a go-go dancer feel to it—neon lights and techno music, and half-naked men dancing on the bars and stages with glow-in-the-dark wristbands and neck-laces. They wore garters around their thighs so you could put a dollar in.

"Here, go give that guy a dollar," Hector said, handing me a five-dollar bill. He pointed out the biggest guy up on the bar. He was beautiful and had a body to die for. I assumed he was gay, so I politely asked him if I could put the money in not sure how to behave here just yet.

"Of course," he said, pulling the garter away from his leg enough for me to slide the bill in. "Thanks!" he said, jumping down from the bar still dancing. "You're gorgeous," he said. "Are you here with friends?" he asked.

"No!" I yelled over the music. "That's my boyfriend!" I pointed over to Hector.

"Oh, too bad. He's cute though," he said smiling and waving at Hector, who made his way over. "Do you want to take a picture of us?" the almost-naked man asked Hector.

"Yeah sure," he said, pulling out his phone.

"Is it okay if I pick her up?" he asked Hector respectfully.

"Yeah," Hector laughed, "do whatever you want with her!" He laughed and readied his camera. The man swept me off my feet and held me like a baby while I stuck one leg up and stretched my left arm out for the picture.

He put me down and thanked us both. "I'd better get back to work—you two have a good time!" he said to us before hopping back up on the bar. He had a fantastic backside, I must admit; when I looked over at Hector, he noticed me looking a little too long at it. Hoping I wasn't in trouble I asked what he wanted to do.

"Let's just walk around. I'm sure we'll see something entertaining," he yelled over the music.

The place was really big. We went into a room to our right and there were people dancing everywhere. Everything looked normal, people dancing and having a good time. All the men working were mostly naked. They all just wore boxer briefs or a speedo. There was one with a thong on and glitter all over his body getting a lot of attention.

Hector noticed there were people above us looking down on the dance floor. "How do we get up there?" he asked one of the men running by with a drink order. The guy directed him and Hector pulled me, leading the way. We climbed some stairs and got to the upper level. The floor had a perfectly sized hole cut into it with railings, making a kind of walkway area that wrapped around the lower dance floor; it was great for people watching.

We went into the room with the bar and happily ordered a couple of drinks. That area had a small outside balcony where you could look down at the party people on Bourbon Street. We went out there for a little while to smoke a cigarette and check out the scenery; it was nice.

"Come on, let's go watch the gay dudes grind on each other," Hector said, dragging me inside.

I laughed. I would have never expected him to want to go into a gay bar to begin with, but he seemed to really be enjoying himself. He clung to me the whole time so everyone knew he was with me, but that didn't stop the male attention. One after another kept coming up to say how cute he was; I could tell he liked the attention.

We were in the back corner of the top level looking down on the party below, and Hector was behind me with his arms wrapped around my waist when he growled "I want to fuck you," in my ear.

"Okay," I laughed, "I guess it's time to leave then?"

"No, I'm going to fuck you right here, right now."

I looked around, and although it was much less crowded than downstairs, there were still plenty of people around.

"Um, that's not gonna happen right here," I said, nervously making eye contact with the people directly across from us on the other side of the opening.

"My dick's already out. Just bend over and lean on the railing." He pushed me forward.

"Babe," I said looking back at him, "what if we get caught?"

"Just let me stick it in. I just need to feel you," he said, licking his fingers to prep me.

I was scared. I felt like everyone was watching us, and we were about to get arrested. Then he entered me, letting out a sigh of relief.

"Yes, that's what I want," he said.

I just tried to keep my eyes down at the crowd and not look guilty. Suddenly, he stopped what he was doing and told me to pull my skirt back down.

"We're leaving." He zipped up his pants and grabbed my hand, leading me out. I noticed a group that had just come up to that area that seemed to be suspicious of what we were doing. We hightailed it out of there and went back to the room where he could finally finish what he started.

While lying there afterwards, he got emotional again. I reassured him that everything was fine, even though my gut told me otherwise. The next morning, he was too hungover to drive, so I drove us most of the way. It's about an eight- or nine-hour drive back to Atlanta, but he slept and I was enjoying the peace and quiet that allowed me to think a little bit and listen to whatever music I wanted to.

When we got to the rental car place to drop our car off, Hector decided we were going up to the bar to meet up with his uncle and Cousin Jimmy. I just wanted to go home, but I had a feeling he needed to get high again since he just had to be cocaine free for the past two days.

I wasn't bothered by it. Something had changed during this trip. I knew this wasn't the path I was going to be on forever, so why bother fighting it? I just knew what I was dealing with at this point, so I needed to stop being so upset about it.

One way or another, things were bound to change. I didn't know when or how, but I could feel it coming.

CHAPTER SEVENTEEN

Here We Go

The week after we got back from New Orleans, Hector got news that his cousin in New York had died in a motorcycle accident. I didn't know him, but his sister, Barb, had stayed with us earlier that year. Hector went out to meet up with his family and asked me not to come. I respected his wish; I knew everyone grieved differently.

When he finally came home, I heard the garage door open but he never came upstairs. I heard him talking and yelling, so I went down to check on him. He was lying on the pool table, talking to someone on the phone crying. I let him finish his conversation and then came to sit with him. "Do you need anything?"

"No," he snapped.

"Do you want to be alone?"

"I think I made that pretty fucking clear," he said hatefully.

Saying nothing, I walked back upstairs and went back to bed.

He joined me some time after I had fallen asleep. He wrapped his arms around me crying and apologizing. "I'm sorry I was mean to you. I just don't want to be close to anyone anymore; everyone I love dies."

"It's okay. I'm here for you," I said rolling over to face him.

"I gotta fly up to New York in a day or two. I need to be there for my family right now. Victor and Titi can take care of the shop," he said. "Please don't ever leave me, Savannah." He squeezed me tightly.

"I won't, babe," I said trying to comfort him.

While he was gone for a week, Bessie spent a lot of her free time at my house. We kept preparing for the Halloween masquerade we had been planning for weeks.

To cheer Hector up, I decided to paint our unused downstairs room blood-red with black trim and a black door, turning it into the BDSM playroom he always wanted. He and his cousin had already constructed a St. Andrew's cross that he was anxious to chain me to. I painted that black as well and set it up along with his floggers and some other dungeon-type things we had. I was sure it was going to be a fun surprise when he got back.

The day before he was supposed to return, he let me know that he would be bringing his uncle down with him to stay with us for a while. "His son just died—I have to help him," he said.

They were going to fly in an hour before our guests were going to arrive to the party, so one of my other good friends offered to pick them up for me so I wouldn't have to change the party arrangements.

When Hector, his uncle, and my friend finally got there, they went upstairs so they could change into their costumes for the party. When they came back down, Hector introduced him to everyone. Joe was tall and bald, just like Hector. He had a nice build and seemed polite. He also had the New York accent, so I saw Bessie eyeballing him already.

I pulled Hector aside and said that I had a surprise for him. I took him to the room and opened the door.

"Oh, wow! So this is what you've been up to?!" he laughed, kissing me.

"Yup, I'm sneaky."

"I love it, babe! I can't wait to get you in here!"

Everyone came in, of course, and checked it out. It was a highlight of the party.

The party went fine—everyone had a good time. I was relieved when it was over, though. It had been a crazy few weeks, and I was really tired. After most of the guests had left, we changed into more comfortable clothes and sat in the living room talking. It was just Bessie, Hector, his uncle Joe, and me.

Joe talked about the passing of his son, and we told him how sorry we were for his loss. He said that he was looking forward to being down here and away from everything.

When I got up to go to bed, Hector told me to tell Bessie not to fuck his uncle.

Here we go again, I thought.

"No, I'm serious," he said, seeing my expression. "He has hepatitis. He can't even share razors or anything like that with people."

"How did he get that?" I asked.

"Sticking needles in his arms. He shoots heroin."

"What?! Why didn't you tell me that before you brought him into our home?"

"Relax, he's clean now—I promise."

I started to go give Bessie a heads up, but he said, "No, you ain't going back out there. Lie down."

"But you just told me to warn her."

"Fuck that. If she wants to be a ho, she gets what she gets. He ain't gonna fuck that fat bitch anyway."

The next day, we all hung out at the house; it was Sunday, and everyone had to work Monday. Hector mentioned that Titi was pissed at him—Joe was her brother, and they didn't get along. She didn't want Joe around and was furious that Hector had brought him here. They had some confrontation back and forth, but Hector told her to shut up and know her place like he did to everyone.

The next day when Jose came to pick them up for work, he had already heard about it from Titi. Hector told him that she would get over it, and they left for work.

About an hour later he called me. Bessie had Monday and Tuesdays off, so she was still with me. "I need your help," he said.

"Oh God, what happened?"

Titi had come in, put the books and work phone back, and cleared out all her personal things. He was screwed.

"Okay, we'll head up and do what we can," I said.

When we got there, we didn't really know what to do, but once I started answering the phone and talking to customers, it was easy enough to manage. Hector had already put out an ad for a new office worker. He had one lady there, but she did a separate job; she was actually a mutual friend of Gia's and mine. We got through the day as best we could and agreed to come in the following day to help out.

Hector said that he had a lady coming in for an interview the next day. When this little girl showed up for her interview, she was dressed like a stripper—stilettos and all. She was beautiful and young and had a nice body but wasn't professional by any means. He, of course, hired her on the spot because of her looks and the fact that none of the women liked her.

I was irritated. "I thought you were looking for someone with experience. This girl has no experience. You only hired her to look at."

"So?" he laughed.

I stood up, grabbing my purse. "Come on, Bessie." She grabbed her things, and we walked out.

"What? You jealous?" He seemed pleased by the idea.

"I get the feeling that's what you're looking for, but I'm more irritated that you wasted our time the past two days."

"Right," Bessie said, agreeing. "The second a little ho walks in looking for a job she knows nothing about, you give it to her just because she's hot!"

"You went out of your way to piss off the one woman who was running your business for you, and now you're going out of your way to piss off the woman you live with," I said, disgusted by his adolescent behavior. "I'll see you at home. Goodbye, boys, and good fucking luck," I said over my shoulder.

"He literally hired that bitch just to piss you off," Bessie said as we walked out.

"I know. But that's okay. When his business fails because he's a fucking child, I won't be there to take care of his stupid ass."

When we got back to my house, Bessie left; she'd had enough of Hector for a while.

On Wednesday, I had a touch-up job close by his shop, so I decided to pop in and see how it was going. This little tramp was half-naked. She was wearing a nude jumpsuit that hugged her body and had her ass cheeks hanging out the bottom of the shorts, and the front was unbuttoned all the way down to her navel exposing her bra. And don't even get me started on the camel toe.

Hector saw the look on my face when I walked in and immediately took me to the warehouse to let me say what I wanted so I wouldn't embarrass him. I took note of the six-pack of Coronas that was sitting there and the open one he and his uncle both had in their hands. It wasn't even lunchtime yet.

"What the   *actual* fuck?" I spat as soon as we got to the back.

"I know, I already told her she can't dress like that and gave her a couple of company shirts," he said, trying to make me be quiet. "

Then why the fuck isn't she wearing it? And why can I see her vagina?"

He laughed uncomfortably. "Yeah, it's a bit much," he agreed.

"Well that's what you get when you hire the first little ho that prances in here looking for a job and a come up," I said with fury in my eyes.

"Deadass," his cousin, Jose, chimed in. "Bitches like that do this shit on purpose to set dumb niggas like you up! They come in looking sexy and as soon as you hit on them or sleep with them, you have a lawsuit for sexual harassment. That bitch will take everything you have if you're dumb enough to let her," he laughed.

Hector's attitude changed immediately. "Shut the fuck up, both of you. This in *my* company, and I'll hire whoever I want to hire. If you don't like it, take your jealous ass home!" He shoved me through the door.

"You can have your company. I don't want to be anywhere near this shitshow. You're going to lose all of this shit if you keep acting like a douchebag," I said, walking back out. "And don't come running to me to fix it next time, you fucking dick," I said over my shoulder.

When I got home, I called Bessie and told her what had happened.

"He's fucking stupid," she said. "Let him fall on his face and then remind him that it was *his* company and you weren't at all involved."

"Why are men so stupid?" I asked.

"That I can't answer, but yours is extra stupid for some reason. When are you gonna leave his ass?"

"Good question," I sighed.

"I'm serious, Savannah. He's a piece of shit, and you deserve someone way better than him. I hate what he's turning you into. It's hard to watch." She was being honest but not in a hurtful way.

"I know. I hate who I'm becoming. I'm *not* happy, and I just need to re-mind myself how much I *don't* need him."

"That's the fucking truth! He really isn't shit! He's a fucking loser," she said.

Later that afternoon, Jose's wife, Frankie, texted me, saying that the guys wanted us to meet them for all-you-can-eat crab legs at a local pub. I wasn't surprised; we did this often on Wednesday nights. I *was* surprised, how-ever, that Hector didn't say anything to me.

When I got there Frankie was arriving at the same time. "What the hell is going on?" she asked as we sat down at a table. "Jose said something about a new girl getting hired and you and Hector fighting over it. Do I need to worry?"

I filled her in on the past two days and told her that it wasn't a big deal.

Everything seemed okay at dinner, but Hector barely spoke to me—he didn't even sit next to me or look at me. Ironically, *he* was still mad at *me*.

When we got home, I took the liberty of going to the bedroom. I was hoping Hector would stay out in the living room with his uncle a bit longer, but he came in shortly after me. I was lying in bed on my cell phone and noticed that my boyfriend had a new Facebook friend…it was the ho from work.

"Why are you friends with your work whore on Facebook already? You must really want her attention." I was fed up with him.

"Why don't you mind your own fucking business and not worry about what the fuck I do before I remove *you* from all my social media and block you so you can't fucking see shit."

"If you do that, you may as well pack your shit, because we won't be together anymore, buddy." I looked back down at my phone.

"That's not sounding like such a bad thing, but you'll be the one leaving. This is my house."

Here we go again, I thought to myself. "First of all," I said sitting up. "This is *our* house, and the way you're managing things at your little company, you won't be able to afford it soon, boo."

"Fuck you, bitch," he yelled while throwing one of his boots at me.

I caught it and shouted, "No, bitch, fuck *you!*" I threw it back at him.

He swatted it away and looked at me like I had lost my mind. "You're really this jealous because I hired a chick that's hotter than you?"

"Did you really just ask me that and then wonder why I would feel insecure?"

"Well, you better get used to her because I already invited her to the club-house," he said with a smug look on his face.

"Why on Earth would you do that? You don't know shit about this little girl!" I was shocked.

"I know she's hot, and the bros would like her," he laughed. "And you can get the fuck over it because it's *my* clubhouse and my club, and you don't dictate what the fuck I do."

"That's fine. Maybe I'll see if Bruce is free that night."

He looked up at me with fury in his eyes. "See? I knew you were a fucking ho!" he said, his eyes blackening.

"I'm not a ho. But two can play this game, and I promise I'll win."

He grabbed his phone charger and went across the hall into the guest room.

As I lay there fuming, I soon realized that I'd crossed a line; I shouldn't have stooped to his level. I know the mention of Bruce made his blood boil. Why was I behaving like this? Acting crazy and jealous was clearly what he wanted, so why give it to him? After about 30 minutes, I decided I needed to go apologize.

I walked out and noticed that all the lights were still on in the living room and the TV was on softly—his uncle was still up. I went into the guest room and turned on the light.

"Turn the fucking light off and get out," he said, staring up at the ceiling. He was lying on his back with his arms folded behind his head.

"I can't let things go like this babe," I said, sitting next to him. "I know I crossed a line. I'm sorry I said that."

"Yeah, well... I knew you were a whore, so no big deal," he snapped with his eyes still fixed on the ceiling.

"Please stop calling me that. I have never been a whore. Can we just stop this? I'm tired, and I love you, and I don't want to fight. I'll take all the blame, and I'll apologize. Just come to bed."

He didn't say anything.

"Babe, I'm sorry," I said, reaching for his arm.

He slapped my hand away.

"Okay, you don't have to do all that," I said, putting my hand in my lap.

"No, apparently I do," he said sitting up. He got out of the bed and slapped me hard in the back of the head.

I thought that maybe this time I would take a different approach; maybe if I didn't fight back he would just stop.

He slapped me again in the same spot, causing my hair to come up over my head and be in my face. Moving the hair aside, I looked over at him and asked him to stop. "I'm not hitting you back. You have no reason to keep hitting me, babe. Please stop and calm down," I begged, keeping my hands planted firmly in my lap.

He grabbed my hair and threw me on the floor in front of him.

"*Stop!*" I yelled loud enough for his uncle to hear.

He kicked me in the back and told me to get up and leave.

I lay there, trying not to react, but he grabbed my hair again and started dragging me out of the room by my hair. I only had a tank top and panties on, so I immediately started getting rug burn on my thigh.

"Get the fuck out, you stupid bitch. Pack your shit! You're leaving," he said, dragging me into the hall.

"Let go of my hair, you fucking pussy!" I yelled.

His uncle was definitely listening because the TV had gone silent.

"Pussy?" Hector yelled, not believing I had the audacity to call him that.

"You heard me right, you fucking pussy! You fight like a fucking female. Let go of my hair, you little bitch!" I'd finally had enough. Not fighting back was clearly a horrible strategy.

He let go of my hair and threw my head into the bedroom doorframe when he let go. "Go live on the streets, you fucking whore!" Then he went back into the guest room and locked the door.

For a brief moment I looked over to see if maybe his uncle was going to come see if I needed help, but of course, he didn't do anything; nobody ever did. I was on my own once again.

I went into beast mode; I wasn't raised to be a punching bag. I stood up, went into my bedroom, and got a running start, slamming through the guest bedroom door, smashing the entire door to pieces. As he stood there like a deer in headlights, I knocked him backwards as hard as I could. The window was open and he went flying through the blinds and the screen.

"Don't you ever fucking touch me again," I said, looking down on him struggling to get back inside. I turned around and opened what was left of the door I had just bulldozed and started walking back into the hallway.

Next thing I knew, he had me by my hair again. He slammed my head into the wall a few times and got me down on the floor, mounting me. He held me down with one hand and began punching me repeatedly with the other while I screamed and bucked, trying to get him off me. After a few good punches, I started to give up. I could already feel the swelling in my head, and it was starting to hurt.

"Stop it, babe, please!" I screamed now, starting to cry.

"Oh, now you wanna stop? You're the one that started all this shit with your fucking mouth! I want you out of my fucking house!" he said, standing up. He kicked me in the back again, so I swung my body out of the fetal position and leaned against the wall.

"*Stop fucking kicking me!*"

"I'm gonna do a lot more than that if you don't get out of my house! I'm done with you!" He kicked me again in my outer left thigh and then squatted down to get in my face.

"Oh, the feeling is mutual, honey," I spat back at him, rubbing my leg and trying to catch my breath.

"Oh yeah? Okay then, time to go!" he said, grabbing my hair again with both hands. He started dragging me down the hall by my hair.

"*Help!*" I screamed at the top of my lungs, knowing that motherfucker was sitting in *my* living room on *my* couch letting *his* nephew do this shit to me. "*Stop it!*" I begged when I saw the top of the stairs. "*Please stop!*"

I saw his worthless uncle finally stand up and look right at us. *Do something you piece of shit!* I thought to myself.

"Yo, Hector," he said putting his hands up like he didn't want any trouble.

"Yeah, I'm almost done," Hector said. He yanked my hair and dragged me down the stairs to the front door. As my body hit each step, I could feel it on the same spot on my leg where he had just kicked me. By the third or fourth step, I was screaming louder than I ever had and praying it would stop. If felt like I was getting kicked in the same spot over and over by someone who had sandpaper on their shoes. I could feel my skin being ripped open the further down we went.

Finally reaching the door, he unlocked it. "Now you can get the fuck out and go find Bruce! Go live with his ass!" He pulled me out the front door and onto the concrete steps.

"Fine! At least he knows how to fuck!" I yelled, wanting to hurt him somehow.

"What the fuck did you just say?" Hector said, pulling my head back so I could say it to his face. He had his fist clenched and raised. He was clearly prepared to knock my teeth out tonight.

"All right, Hector," his uncle said from behind us. "That's enough, man, come on! You want the neighbors to call the fucking cops? Think. This is gone far enough, now stop!"

Standing there, holding my hair, still catching his breath halfway out the front door, Hector looked down at me and said, "Fuck it. *I'll* leave," and slammed my head down into the doorframe. He kicked my ribs and added, "Get out the fucking way, you fat whore." He said it as if I were a dog in the street, begging for food. He stepped over me and went back up the stairs.

His uncle came to my aid and helped me sit up. "Are you okay, honey?" he asked.

"I'll live," I responded, not very happy with him but still grateful that it was over nonetheless.

"Can you try to walk?" he asked.

"My leg is on fire."

He looked down at my raw thigh. "Yeah, it's going to look like hell tomorrow." He helped me up the stairs and sat me on the couch. "Just stay here until he's gone, okay? Don't need to make anything worse."

At the time, I agreed with him, but I was also thinking about what a coward he was for letting this go on for as long as it had. "Would you mind going to get my phone for me?" I asked.

"Nah, I can't do that. You don't need to call anyone. Just let him leave, okay?" He looked at me, almost pleading.

"I'm calling the cops," I said matter-of-factly. "He's going to learn it's not okay to do this to women."

I heard Hector storming down the hall towards us. "You're calling the cops? Then call the fucking cops, bitch! You hit me too! We can both go to jail, you stupid cunt!" He slapped me upside the head one final time as he walked behind me. "I'm out of here. Fuck this shit." As he left he said to his uncle, "I'll make sure Jose picks you up for work in the morning."

"Don't call the cops," his uncle said after we heard the garage door open and close. "I've seen this happen a million times and nothing ever gets done. You want to just piss him off even more?" He asked me.

"No, but you can't possibly think this is right."

"I didn't say it was right, I just said it's not going to go the way you think it will. Do you love him?"

I broke into tears. "Of course I do."

"Then just give him some time. He'll come around eventually. He ain't leaving you. He'll be back."

The fact that this man really thought *that* was what I was worried about in this moment showed me that he wasn't who I should be bothering to talk to. My head was pounding and so were my leg and my ribs.

"Let me go get you some ice," he said as I laid my head in my hands.

I sat there with ice on my head and ice on my leg for a few minutes, but I didn't want to be around Joe any longer. "I'm going to bed," I said, trying to get up.

"Let me help you," he said, rushing over to me. He didn't have a shirt on; he never did, but I became uncomfortably aware of how naked I was as well.

"I've got it, thank you."

"Are you sure?"

"Positive, thank you."

I tucked myself in with my ice packs placed where I needed them and tried to go to sleep. All I could do was cry. *What the hell is wrong with me?* I thought. *How far would that have gone if his uncle didn't finally step in? Why am I sticking around for this? Why am I not enough for him? Does he even like me? I'm pretty sure this isn't how love is supposed to feel. Why can't I control my mouth?*

The next morning, I got up early and left for work. I had agreed to help out another cabinet company in Jonesboro, Georgia. Honestly, I was glad to get out of the house. I didn't want to deal with Hector's uncle. I tried to cover the bruising on my face, which had already started turning purple. The swelling was so severe in my head that it was draining down into my eyes. Even though I didn't remember him hitting me in the face, both of my eyes were swelling. I hoped nobody would notice, but as the day went on, the color kept getting darker.

One of the men working there asked me if I was okay.

"I'm fine," was all I could muster.

By the time I got home both of my eyes were black. I was glad to have the house to myself to shower and think. I was so scared that Hector would come home. I didn't want to see him yet. I needed some time. I hoped that wherever he was he would keep his uncle with him. I didn't know this man nor did I think very highly of him.

I called Gia, hoping to get out of the house until I knew whether Hector was coming home or not.

"Hi!" She answered excitedly.

"What are you doing tonight?" I asked.

"Nothing, why?"

"Do you want to meet up for dinner and beers? I need a friend."

"Where's stupid? Are you allowed out the house?"

"Yeah, he's gone. I'll explain when I get there. The tavern has wing specials on Thursday nights—want to meet there?" I asked, trying to move things along.

"Yeah that sounds good. What time?"

"I'll head over as soon as I get my face on. I just got out of the shower."

"Okay, sounds good. See you then!"

I hung up the phone and looked in the mirror. Holy shit, how was I going to cover this up? The swelling had gotten worse; makeup can't cover that. I did what I could and tried to cover my eyes up as much as possible. I dug out a big pair of sunglasses and left for dinner.

It was a nice day out so I asked if we could sit on the porch. I wanted to keep my sunglasses on during dinner, so she didn't notice. Gia talked for a bit about her day and the people at work she hated. But it wasn't long before she said, "What are you trying to cover up with those sunglasses?"

Well crap, I thought. *Busted already.* Why lie? I took a deep breath and pushed the sunglasses up on my head.

"Oh my God, Savannah!" she said bringing her hand up to her mouth. "What the fuck happened?"

About the time I got through with the story of what happened my phone rang. It was Hector's cousin, Jose.

"Hey are you home? We need to get in the house. Hector needs some of his things, and Joe doesn't have a key."

I was glad Hector wasn't coming home. "I'm at dinner, just finishing up. Are you taking Joe back to Hector? I don't feel comfortable with him staying there with me alone," I said.

"Well, I don't either but Hector doesn't want him at the hotel with him, so he's here," Jose said.

"I really don't want him there. Can you take him with you?"

"I don't know this nigga. We ain't related, he ain't my problem. Sorry. Tell Hector to take him."

"Whatever," I sighed. "I'll be there in 20 minutes."

"I'm coming with you," Gia said as I hung up. "You aren't about to go into this shit alone."

I was relieved. At least I'd have a witness to stand up for me if something happened.

When we got there, the boys were already in the house to my surprise. Gia and I came up the stairs through the garage and the two of them were sitting on my couch.

"How did you get in?" I asked them.

Jose jumped up to give me a hug and said, "Your guest bedroom window was wide open and the screen was popped out. Let me look at you." He looked shocked when I removed my sunglasses. "Jesus Christ Savannah, and that's *with* makeup?"

"Yeah, you should see the rest of me," I said sharply.

"Go take your makeup off. I want to take a picture of your face so his bitch ass can see what the fuck he did to his girl." He was more upset than I expected him to be.

"I took pictures," I said opening my phone so he could see them.

"Send these to me, please. Jesus Christ, is that your leg?" he said, coming across the pictures of my thigh.

"It sure is. I imagine this will all only look worse as I heal," I said.

"This is fucked up. You're a good girl. You don't deserve this," he said shaking his head.

"I fought back, and you know I got a mouth on me. It is what it is." I shrugged…always making excuses.

"Man, whatever. He better pray to God your brother and dad don't see this shit. I know they're crazy for real."

"I think it's about time for them to know the truth!" Gia said from the couch.

"Let's all just calm down," I said. "I don't know what to do just yet. What does Hector need, Jose?"

He told me what he'd asked for, and I went to pack him a bag. "Can you help me?" I asked Jose, wanting to discuss this Joe situation more seriously. "Why the fuck am I being stuck with this guy? I didn't bring him here, and he's not my problem," I whispered to him.

"I don't know. I tried to get Hector to take him. I told him this shit is going to be a recipe for disaster; that nigga's a drunk. What if he tries to come at you in the middle of the night or something?" That was exactly one of the things I feared myself. "I wouldn't leave any man alone like that with *my* wife. He's crazy."

"Look, I have no interest in seeing or speaking to Hector right now, so can you *please* tell him that he needs to take his uncle?" I pleaded.

"I did try. He said if you didn't like it you could leave and give him his house. I told him he was being stupid but that nigga don't listen for shit."

"Oh, I see! Now it makes sense. He couldn't drag me out, so he's trying to make me uncomfortable so I'll leave. Well, fuck him. Here's his shit." I handed him the black carry-on-sized suitcase.

"Look, I'm sorry. This shit is so fucked up. He's an idiot, but he'll be crawling back in no time. Trust me. You're the best thing that ever happened to his ass."

"I don't know if I even want him to come back this time," I said, tearing up. "I can't do this anymore."

He wrapped his arms around me in a big hug. "I know, and you shouldn't have to. Look, I'll stick around as long as I can tonight to watch this nigga.

There's something off about him that I don't like. But eventually I gotta go home, so can your girl stay here with you tonight?" he asked.

"I'm sure she has to work in the morning, but if I feel uncomfortable so, maybe she will stay."

We went back into the living room, where Gia and Joe were talking. Joe had taken the liberty of grabbing a bottle of whiskey from our bar for himself. He was the only one drinking it. Gia and I had a glass of wine while we all sat there talking about how shitty Hector was. Joe got drunk and started telling his side of the story. How he felt bad for not stepping in earlier, but he didn't know what to do since he's here because of Hector and he would be stranded without a way home if he decided to kick him out. At one point he grabbed my leg wanting to see how bad it was and started rubbing my calf.

"I'll be fine," I said taking, my leg back. Eventually Jose stood up and said he had to go.

"I'll be staying here tonight," Gia said. Jose and I were both relieved to hear that. Gia and I made our way back to my bedroom at about 9 p.m., saying our goodnights to Joe.

It was about 2 o'clock in the morning when my bedroom door burst open, waking us both up. In the doorway stood Joe wearing only boxer briefs; in his hand he held a can of cheese dip.

"Hey ladies, what's up?" he said drunkenly.

"We're sleeping; it's time for you to go to bed," Gia said sternly.

"What?" he said swaying back and forth.

"It's time for you to go to bed," Gia said.

"You want me to come to bed?"

"No, you have a bed in the room across the hall. Go to that room and go to bed," she said.

"Behind you," I finished her sentence.

"Oh okay," he said and turned around, closing the door. Both Gia and I breathed a sigh of nervous relief.

"Thank God I stayed with you," she said, lying back in the bed.

"Yeah that's what I was afraid of. One of his first nights here he got so drunk he crawled into bed next to me and Hector. I was scared so I pushed him out and he fell on the floor. I told him he was in the wrong room and he apologized," I told her.

"Are you kidding?"

"No, Hector just thought it was funny, but I was completely naked, so I didn't find it amusing."

"You need get that door fixed properly."

"I did, and then he broke through it again. I can't call my brother back to fix it."

"Well you're gonna have to get someone to replace the other door across the hall now." She said, laughing.

"I know, my life's a mess."

CHAPTER EIGHTEEN

Make a Plan

The next morning Gia and I both got up early to go to work. I thanked her for staying and said I would keep her posted. She had already told me she wasn't letting me stay there alone with him any longer. So, if I couldn't get rid of him then she would come to stay with me until this was all sorted out. I was relieved that she was so adamant about it. After he barged in my bedroom in the middle of the night for the second time I was done putting up with him. On the way to work I called Hector's cousin Jose. I told him what had occurred the night before and begged him to talk to Hector and make him take his uncle to wherever he was.

"Hell yeah I'm making him get rid of this nigga, he could have fucking raped you!" Jose said sounding genuinely upset. "Don't even worry about it, ma, I'm on the way to pick him up and I'll tell him just bring all his shit with him, so they don't have a fucking choice. This is bullshit," he said angrily.

"Thank you so much for helping me through this. Can I ask one more favor?"

"Anything, I got you," he responded.

"Can you replace that guest bedroom door and do a couple patches and repairs this weekend? I can't ask my brother again or he'll catch on."

"He damn sure will, yeah it's no problem."

"But, shit. It might not be such a bad idea to tell your brother and dad. Hector needs his ass whopped for this shit."

"They won't just beat his ass, Jose, they'll go to prison for murder. I can't be responsible for that," I said softly.

"Yeah I hear you. I'll do the door."

"Thank you so much. I'll pay you, just let me know what you want for it."

"Actually, instead of paying me why don't you owe me a night of babysitting so I can take my wife out to a nice dinner?"

"That's fine too! She would love that, absolutely."

"It's a deal," he said.

"You're the best!" I said before getting off the phone.

I went home and was relieved that my house was empty. We were getting into a routine of Hector picking fights with me on Friday after work so he could storm out and disappear all weekend to get high or do whatever he was doing. So, I was assuming this weekend would be no different since he had the things he needed and a hotel room. I wanted a glass of wine for my nerves, as I was pouring it my phone rang. It was Jose.

"Hey," I answered.

"Check this shit out!" he said. I knew I was in for more drama, so I grabbed my glass of wine and went to the back porch, lighting a cigarette. Joe had told Jose that he had a threesome with Gia and I the night before!

"*What!*?" I yelled.

"Wait, it gets better. He said you guys were licking cheese dip off each other and shit." I burst into laughter.

"I told you he had cheese dip with him when he came into my room! This motherfucker is crazy!" I said laughing.

"Yeah, I know, but I wanted to see how far he was gonna take this shit, he didn't know I had already gotten a phone call from you this morning," he went on. "I told him I didn't believe him and that it sounded like he needs to stop getting so drunk. I told him I knew you and you are a good girl so you would never do that, *especially* with a family member of Hector's in his own house."

"Well thank you for sticking up for me," I said, genuinely grateful. "But if he tells Hector that, he's actually going to believe him since he's so fucking insecure," I said, realizing that this lie could ruin my life. Now I see why Titi didn't want him around.

"He told me not to tell Hector, because he didn't want to get stranded in Georgia but, he couldn't resist you. He went on and on about your ass and all the shit he had been waiting to do to you this whole time. Talked about what he wanted to do when you were sitting on the couch in your panties after he made Hector get off you and leave when he was beating your ass. He's *sick* for real!" Chills went up my spine and I got a little queasy.

"That actually makes me extremely uncomfortable. Did he get all his shit out of my house?" I said, standing up to walk back to the guest room he was staying in. "I don't want him back here."

"I think so, I told him he was going to stay at the hotel so he should have," he answered as I was opening the door to the bedroom. It smelled like dirty feet and stale ass. The bed was made, but the bedding was a dark burgundy color and now had strange streaks of something all over it.

"I don't know what the hell he got all over my bedding in here, but I don't think I want to know," I said. I propped the phone between my ear and my left shoulder and carefully started to remove the bedding.

"He was probably in there jacking his dick thinking he was having a threesome!" he burst into laughter.

"That's disgusting, I wouldn't fuck him with someone else's pussy," I responded, moving around to the other side of the bed. My foot kicked something, and I looked down to see what it was. It was the empty cheese dip.

"Oh my god, I just found the empty cheese dip jar, and it looks like it was licked clean," I told him.

"It probably was, that nigga is dead ass crazy." I started removing pillowcases and discovered a pair of *my* used panties hidden behind the headboard. I was completely disgusted.

"Throw those out for real. He probably nutted in them or something," Jose said. I felt like I was going to throw up.

"This shit has me sick," I said to him. "It should, this dude is obsessed with you, and your man just fucking left you with him." I took the panties and cheese dip and threw them both in the garbage. I would deal with the bedding later.

"Did you actually talk to Hector about any of this?" I asked.

"Oh yea, I told him that I didn't like the way his uncle was toward you when he wasn't there, I told him your friend stayed the night because she wasn't happy with it and that he barged in your room in the middle of the night. He *still* didn't want me to leave his uncle Joe with him, but I told him that if this guy raped you your family would kill everyone and it's not a situation that needs to happen. He said he was fine with whatever happened as long as you finally left his house." Tears welled up in my eyes.

"Wow," is all I could muster. "I told him he was an ass and in three days he's gonna be begging you to come back so just chill." I thanked him once again and he said he would come by the next day to fix up the house.

"Okay I'll see you tomorrow," I said, hanging up the phone. I sat there staring at Rafiki's grave silently with tears streaming down my face. *I have to start making plans,* I thought to myself, while petting my new white lab puppy. Her name was Halo and I adopted her a few weeks prior. She was a rambunctious little thing. She chewed on everything and wanted to go potty in the house since she was raised in a cage. So, she was a handful. She and Hector didn't get along well. She wasn't exactly filling the Rafiki void, but it was nice to have her right now.

I woke up the next morning, alone. It was nice to be alone and have a quiet peaceful house. I knew I didn't want to leave the house, but I also didn't want to be with Hector anymore. I was done being treated like this. I went to the bathroom and saw my reflection. The swelling hadn't gone down much in my eyes and now they were both alarmingly blackened. I sighed and said to my reflection, "Well I guess you aren't going anywhere today." I started the shower and began to undress. With my pale white skin every mark now showed. My body was bruised all over. It didn't hurt as much physically anymore, but the sight of me like this was too much to bear. I started to sob. Why would someone who claims to love me do something like this? I thought about how this would break the hearts of my family and friends to see this. I couldn't bare it. I thought about taking more pictures, but I didn't know if I really wanted the evidence. How had things gotten this terrible?

After my shower I got a text from Jose saying he would be by in about an hour and take me to Home Depot with him to get the stuff he needed. Just after I responded "Okay," my phone rang. It was Titi, I hadn't spoken to her since before Hector came back from N.Y. and she walked out on her job at his company.

"Hello?" I answered.

"Savannah, how are you?" she asked cautiously.

"I'm okay, how are you?"

"Jose told me what happed and what's been going on. I saw the pictures of your eyes," she said gently. I didn't know what to say. "Let me start off by saying that piece of shit deserves an ass beating like I can't even imaging. Nobody deserves what he did to you, it was wrong and I'm sorry to be related to him." She spat out as if it tasted like vinegar to even discuss her nephew.

"It's not your fault, and I'll be fine," I told her.

"It is my understanding that this all started when I quit, and he hired some tramp to try and take my place. So, I'm sorry for what happened after I left, but I'm not sorry I left. Fuck Hector." She went on to tell me about how she hated her brother Joe and he was a heroin junkie and alcoholic. She didn't trust him, and he didn't need to be around. Since she had gone to New York also in October, to attend the funeral of his son, which I didn't know, she told me that she and Hector had had a big fight up there. She told me that she knew for a fact that Hector was high right along with Joe. She said she warned him that she wouldn't return to work if he brought Joe back and she did what she said she would do.

"I think it might be time to tell your dad and brother," she said softly.

"I can't do that. They'll go to prison over this, I can't let them throw their lives away because I was stupid," I said.

"I understand that honey, but you have to see this can't continue right?" she said gently.

"I know. I don't know what to do, but I don't want to leave, I love this house. I just don't want Hector if he's not going to get help. I can't do this anymore." We talked for a little while and then I heard Jose at the door so I told her I needed to go. She told me to call her anytime and I thanked her.

Bessie called me when she got off work and asked if I wanted her to come over. I was nervous to let her, just because I hadn't come clean with her yet, and as soon as she looked at me it would have to come out. But she mentioned wanting to go to church the next morning and that actually pulled at me, so I knew I needed to do this.

"Okay, I'll tell you about everything when you get here. Hector is gone and so is his uncle," I said.

"Okay, I'll be there soon," she said, suspicious of what was going on. I took the liberty of redoing my makeup, and then I decided maybe I needed to go get some more wine. I ran to the closest grocery store and picked up a box, knowing how uncomfortable my night was going to be. I noticed I was getting looks from people around me, so I was anxious to get out of there. I grabbed a block of our favorite cheese and some crackers and made my way to the checkout line. The cashier was very friendly and was smiling and happily talking with the woman in front of me. As I stepped up for my turn, I saw the look on her face change. It went from happy and approachable to sad, shocked, and worried. Dammit, I needed to learn how to cover this better. She politely rang me up and was still very friendly, but it was in a way that you would treat a wounded animal you didn't want to scare off. I didn't like people being able to see my pain. I had gotten fairly good at hiding it. But this, I couldn't seem to cover enough.

When Bessie arrived, I opened the front door to let her in.

"Hi!" she said happily; she was looking down at her dog yelling for him to come in. She always brought her dog with her since she lived alone.

"Get inside," she yelled at him while holding all her bags.

"Here let me take that," I said grabbing some of her things so she could focus on him. I took them upstairs and dropped them on the guest bed in the room that now had a brand-new door. She followed looking strangely at the unpainted new door.

"What happened here?" she asked, looking over at me and finally seeing my face.

"Oh my God," she said dropping her other bag on the bed. "Where is he!? I'm calling your brother right now!" she said, making me nervous.

"No! Don't do that, Bessie, please!" I pleaded with her.

"Look at your fucking face Savannah! Where is that motherfucker!? Enough is enough!" I understood her reaction completely. There wouldn't be much that could stop *me* from reacting the way she wanted to if the shoe was on the other foot, so I know how hard this was going to be.

"I'll tell you everything, just please don't get involved! I know I have to get out. I know I do; I just need to do it in the smartest way possible," I said holding both of her hands.

"Come on, we have all night, I'll get us some wine and I'll tell you what happened." Wanting to know the truth, she agreed to hear me out.

After a glass of wine each and a long conversation, she wanted to see the rest of me.

"Strip. I need to see how bad it is," she said. Not really wanting to, but understanding again how she felt, I obliged. She was the first and only person to see the damage to my body up close. She sat there quietly, not responding much at all verbally. She wasn't an overly emotional person, so she didn't often cry. But I could see her hands were in fists and her foot was tapping while she ground her teeth, thinking of what to say or do.

"I knew he was fucking hitting you, why didn't you tell me all this sooner?" she asked calmly.

"Because I thought I was handling it. I didn't want anyone to hurt him. It's my fault," I said.

"What exactly is your fault? This motherfucker does *not* have the right to hit you *ever*!" she said forcefully.

"I know, but it's not like I didn't hit him back," I said, trying to defend Hector.

"Plus, you know I'm mouthy; I need to learn when to keep my lips closed," I said laughing uncomfortably trying to lighten the mood a little.

"None of this is funny, this is heartbreaking and infuriating, scary even, but not funny," she said with tears welling up in her eyes. "How am I supposed to keep this from your family? When this all comes out, and it *will* come out, don't you think they're going to be a little upset that I didn't tell them?" she asked.

"Well Gia knows too so it's not just you," I said not knowing what else to say.

"I don't think that's going to make things better," she said. "I don't know what to do, but I need to make plans, I can't just walk away. This house is in both of our names, and *all* the utilities are in *my* name. So, I need to think about what I really want and figure out a plan to achieve it."

"I understand that, and I'll give you time to do that. I won't bring anything up to your family, but if they ask, I won't lie. And if he touches you again, I'm going to tell everyone. I'll shout it from the fucking roof tops until everyone in Georgia knows what a piece of shit woman beating asshole he is, and I won't care how you feel about it." She said sternly.

"That's fair." What more could I really ask for? I just needed some time.

The next day, we got up and went to church. Since she had errands to run afterward, we took separate cars. I opened the garage door when I pulled into the driveway, I saw Hector's motorcycle, and my heart sank. I walked in with my head held high and found him and his disgusting uncle in the living room. Joe was playing with Halo on the floor, and Hector was sitting there with his feet up watching TV.

"Where were you?" he asked.

"I could ask the same question," I said walking to the dining room table to put down my purse.

"None of your fucking business," he said.

"Hector, come on man, don't start this shit, please. I leave tomorrow, and I don't want any more drama," his uncle Joe spoke up. I was relieved to know he was about to be gone from our lives.

"You're leaving tomorrow?" I asked Joe. "Yeah, so this is the last time you'll see me. Hector's taking me to the bus station in the morning," he said sounding disappointed.

"Should we try talking?" I asked Hector, not knowing what was going through his head.

"Not now, we have a dinner to go to this evening and I don't want to fight, we can talk later," he said not looking at me.

"Okay, well are you home? Or are you just getting more stuff and going back to the hotel?"

"That's up to how you behave at dinner," he responded.

"Oh, I'm going with you?" I asked, confused.

"Well, obviously," he said, as if I had asked a stupid question.

"If you don't mind, I'd rather not, I don't want anyone seeing my face right now," I said sadly. He looked over at me.

"It will be dark. Use makeup, you're going," he said, turning his head back to the TV.

"What time do I need to be ready?" I asked defeated.

"We're going to meet a couple people at about 7 p.m.," he said, laying back in the recliner part of the couch. "Now go away; we're tired and need to rest."

I happily obliged. I grabbed my purse and went to hide in my bedroom. Why does he want me to go to dinner? And why come back home and then not want to talk things through? I wish he would just leave for good.

At dinner Hector acted like nothing had happened. He sat next to me and talked, laughed, ordered me wine and beers for him and his bros.

"What's up with you?" one of his bro's asked me midway through the evening.

"Yeah, why are you acting all quiet and shy?" Hector asked. He nudged me with his elbow and painted on his charming smile.

"Cheer up babe," he said giving me a kiss. "I love you," he said, putting on a show for his audience. It turned my stomach. I wanted to stand up and scream. I wanted out of this. I didn't understand what he was doing right now, but it felt like a game. Instead, I painted on a smile and tried to be more present in the conversation without bringing too much attention to myself. Luckily, they were all so self-involved they never even noticed my face. Or didn't mention it if they had noticed. Either way, I was glad the topic never came up.

Dinner ended, and we went home. I said goodnight and Hector said he would be in shortly, so I went to my bedroom. I got ready for bed and made sure to wash my face. I wanted him to see exactly what he had done to me. When he came to bed the light was still on. He looked right at me and just laughed shaking his head.

"Is something funny?" I asked.

"Were you hoping for some dramatic apology? I see you took off your makeup," he said, closing the door behind him and going to the bathroom. When he came back out, he turned off the light and crawled into bed.

"I thought we were going to talk," I said, confused.

"I'm tired, there's nothing to talk about, just keep your fucking mouth shut and it won't happen again." I was blown away. After missing in action for four days without a word, *that's* all he had to say to me? I laid back in my bed in disbelief. I rolled over with my back facing him and closed my tear-filled eyes, praying that God would show me what he wanted me to do. I wept silently for a long time before finally falling asleep.

The next morning, I was working from home, which I was grateful for because it seemed like my eyes and bruises got even blacker. I didn't want to see Joe, but I had to let the dog out and feed the animals, so I did end up seeing him one more time before the guys left. Jose had arrived to pick them up and asked me if everything was okay. I told him we'd talk later and he nodded.

"I see you got the door fixed," Hector said, coming down the hall. "Who did that?" he asked as he approached Jose and me.

"I did," Jose said. "She didn't want her brother to see the damage, so I told her I'd fix it," he said flatly.

"Yeah I bet you did. What else did she ask you to fix?" he said his gaze now on me.

"Shut the fuck up nigga; let's go," Jose said. "Oh, by the way, can I cash in my night of babysitting this Friday? I want to take Frankie out." he asked.

"Yes, of course, I look forward to it."

"Why aren't you working?" Hector asked me.

"I'm working downstairs this week. I have a delivery coming later this morning."

"Oh okay, I'll let you know what I want for dinner before I head home," he said walking down the stairs. *What a complete psycho*, I thought to myself. He didn't even talk things out or try to apologize to me. Now I'm supposed to pretend to be happy and move forward?

That whole week was very uncomfortable for me. Hector still didn't want to talk about anything with me. On Thursday night we were invited to go to dinner with my ex-sister-in-law for her birthday. While we were at dinner the waiter asked if we wanted another glass of wine. We all said yes, but then Hector said, "That's your last glass for the night."

Feeling challenged by the demand, I told him he didn't get to tell me what to do just like I didn't get to tell him what to do.

"Well you pop off at the mouth more when you drink too much, and we don't want a repeat of *last* Thursday, do we?" he said arrogantly. I froze. Of course, he waits until we're in front of people to bring that up.

"Besides, I'm starting to wonder if you need to quit drinking for a while so we can get you pregnant," he said looking over at my nephew. "You want a cousin, right?" he said rubbing the top of his head. My stomach was knotted so tightly I thought I was going to throw up on the table. Why the hell would he say something like that? My sister-in-law's eyes widened.

"What? You guys are trying to get pregnant!?" she asked excitedly.

"No," I said quickly. He looked at me with daggers.

"Yes we are. We talked about this in New Orleans." My mind flashed back to him saying he wanted me to get pregnant while we were making love, but I hadn't thought about it since then. Especially with how everything had been going lately. Not wanting this conversation to continue I put the focus back on the birthday girl and shut it down.

When we got home that evening, I started a bath. While it was filling and I was lighting, some candles Hector came into the bathroom. Wanting him to see what he had done to me I disrobed while he watched me. I saw him look over my body and cringe at the sight of each mark and bruise that was still there. He reached out and touched the biggest one on my left thigh. That one was still a little tender, so I moved away when he touched it.

"Please don't touch me," I said, turning off the light and stepping into the tub. To my surprise he sat on the edge of the tub and put his head in his hands.

"I hate myself, you know," he said, so low I almost didn't hear him. "I don't want to talk about it because I hate myself for what I did." I lay back deeper in the water, stretching out my legs.

"Look at me when you say that please," I requested.

"I can't," he said shamefully.

"I need to see some sincerity in you Hector, or I don't know how long this can continue," I said flatly.

He turned to face me looking like that scared child I thought I would have seen when he came home Sunday.

"Please don't leave me babe, I need you." He whimpered with tears pooling in his eyes.

"Why did it take you so long to apologize?"

"Because I was embarrassed, I was certain you would leave me, and I was scared. But I didn't want anyone to know how scared I was, so I just acted like I didn't care," he said, shaking his head. He got on his knees beside the tub close to my face.

"I *do* love you, and I see now that you really don't want to leave me." He kissed me softly stroking the side of my face. "Jose told me about what my uncle did and said, and that made me feel even worse," he said, cringing. "He didn't tell me until after I dropped him off at the bus station, because he knew I would have beaten his ass," he continued. "But when I called and confronted him, I could tell he was lying. I'm so sorry," he said laying his head on his arm that rested on the tub.

"Thank you for apologizing finally. I'm sorry too." He lifted his head and kissed me again a little harder this time. He dipped his hand down in the tub and slid his fingers inside me. I wanted to make up; I wanted to make him feel how much I loved him.

"Can I get in the tub?" he asked, barely pulling his lips away from mine and continuing to explore me with his fingers.

"Yes," I said in a whisper.

"Better yet, why don't you get out?" he said, standing up and grabbing my hand. He grabbed my towel and gently dried off my body. He grabbed some of my favorite lotion and led me to the bed.

"Lay down on your stomach," he said. He climbed on the bed and started to give me a massage. It was a nice effort. It was dark except for the candle-light that spilled out from the open bathroom door.

"I'm going to make this up to you babe, I swear," he said opening my legs. He lifted my hips off the bed, almost bringing me up to my knees. He lay on his stomach and held up my hips with his hands. Kissing my ass and the insides of my legs, he kept talking to me which was turning me on.

"I do want you to have my baby," he would kiss me a few more times. "I want you to be mine forever," again kissing me, followed by a light nibble. While he was teasing me, he started to rub me with his thumb. He *never* took his time on me like this. It was always about him. So, this kind of thing hadn't happened since we first started having sex.

"Can you forgive me?" he asked with his lips touching my most intimate parts. I was putty in his hands; I wanted his mouth on me so bad I couldn't even think to respond.

"Say it," he said.

"Yes," I whimpered, opening myself up for him a little more.

"Yes what?" he said in a stern sexy voice, his lips barely brushing me where I wanted him to be.

"I forgive you," I said my body starting to shake in anticipation.

"Do you love me?" he said still teasing me.

"Yes!" I said loudly.

"And you won't ever leave me, right?" he asked.

I was about to explode if he didn't get in there, "Yes for God's sake baby *please*!" I said sounding like a mad woman.

"Good girl," he whispered happily and then dove in. After I was given my sweet release, we made love. It was passionate and explosive. Rough yet tender. It was everything you want to feel when you're really making love to someone.

The next morning, I woke up when Hector's alarm went off. Hearing Halo whining in her crate, I went to go take her outside. I was in the kitchen getting the food ready for her and Gizmo and Hector stormed in and kicked my puppy. Yelping, she went flying across the kitchen floor and scurrying away.

"What the fuck?" I yelled, getting in front of him. He tried to chase after her, but I slammed him into the fridge.

"Don't fucking touch her!" I growled in his face, ready to take this as far as I needed to.

"You need to find her a new home," he said shoving me off him.

"What happened?" I asked. He showed me his glasses that had been chewed up.

"She fucking destroys everything! She's chewed up my wallet my charger and now my glasses!?"

"Where were they? Why was she able to get to them?"

"That's not the fucking point, get rid of her or I'll put her out in the fucking street and let traffic sort it out." I instantly became aggressive.

"Are you fucking kidding me? After what you let happen to Rafiki you have the audacity to say that to me?" I'm now screeching.

"Whatever, find her a new fucking home. She's out of here one way or another," he said, walking away from me. Halo was in the living room cowering behind the sofa; he walked over and dragged her out by the back of her neck, showing her his glasses.

"You see that? That's bad!" He yelled and punched her.

I lunged at him, tackling him into the hallway. I mounted him and screamed at him, "Don't you *ever* fucking touch her like that again you piece of shit!" I pushed myself off him.

"Get the fuck out and go to work," I barked at him.

"Gladly," he said. "But you're gonna wish you didn't do that," he said.

"Fuck off! I don't give a shit about your little threats anymore, and I won't let you hurt an innocent animal." I felt powerful in the moment. I heard

Jose pull in to pick up Hector and was happy he was here to break up the moment. I searched for Halo who was now hiding in her crate shaking and scared.

"Oh baby, I'm so sorry," I said, reaching in gently to pet her. I got her food and showed it to her. She reluctantly came out and started eating. She was jumpy, but who could blame her?

"I'm sorry I got you into this situation, sweet girl," I whispered, petting her while she ate her food. Jose came in and said good morning.

"We still on for you babysitting tonight?" he asked, smiling.

"Of course, what time?"

"I think like maybe 7 or 8 p.m. Frankie said she wanted to do it a little later so the baby would just sleep through it and you wouldn't have to do anything."

I laughed, "Well I'm good with whatever time, I don't mind at all." Hector came out, obviously irritated.

"What's up with you?" Jose asked.

"The fucking dog chewed up my shit," he said like a grumpy teenager whose parents told him to take out the trash. Jose laughed. They left, and the house was mine. I didn't have any work to do, so I was planning on lounging around all day.

CHAPTER NINETEEN

Blast from the Past

I was lying on the couch looking through random videos and ran across one that made me think of a guy I used to date years ago. He was a sweet fun guy, but he had a heavy drinking problem that I didn't really like. He was always a gentleman. He brought me pretty flowers and planned dates for us to go on. Our first date was to Taco Mac, then the Atlanta Aquarium. We ended up at a bar just down the street from the aquarium and sat next to a couple with the same names as us. His name was Giovanni; he was a tall friendly Italian man with a strong Jersey accent and beautiful blue eyes. He had light brown hair and a perfect smile. We'd met on a dating site years ago and only dated for a couple of months. I liked to think of myself as not being ready for a man like him in my life. He had a way of making me feel like I would never be good enough for him. Not that he meant to; he and I just came from two different worlds.

So, after not speaking to this man for the past four or five years, I decided to send him this stupid video. It was some machine for making alcoholic beverages. I have no idea what possessed me to send this, but I'm happy I did because it sparked a conversation. I had forgotten how easy it was to talk to him. It had been years since we spoke. He sent me a message after Rafiki passed but I could barely read it before Hector grabbed my phone and deleted it. But now he seemed receptive of chatting with me, so we talked all day. He told me he bought a house near the apartment I had lived in when he met me. He and I dated before Hector ever entered the picture. I jokingly told him he should get a dog, but then an idea popped into my head. Maybe he would take Halo! I sent him pictures of her, and although he agreed she was cute, he wanted to get a Rottweiler.

After hours of messaging back and forth, I lost track of time. Hector had sent me a message that he was going to his dad's that night to pick him up and take him to the clubhouse. Even though I knew what that actually meant, I was relieved. I knew I didn't have to be home until 7 p.m. to babysit, so I asked Giovanni if he wanted to hang out for a bit and grab some a beer. I was nervous after I sent the message. Was I being too forward? I didn't want to get him involved in my drama. But it would be nice to see a fresh friendly face that I didn't have to lie to or hide from.

"Sure, what did you have in mind?" he responded. I got butterflies in my stomach and actually squealed like a little girl. I told him where to meet me and that I was getting ready now. He said he'd be there. So off I went to the bathroom to get myself together. Damn these bruises, I said to myself. They were starting to fade a little so I thought maybe this would be fine.

"Just need a little makeup," I said to my reflection.

When I arrived at the Tavern, I was happy to see that Giovanni was already there. I got out of the car and gave him a hug hello. We went inside and started catching up. We ordered a couple of beers and some cheese dip and enjoyed each other's company. We were so busy talking that we actually never even ordered food. He told me about his house-buying experience and that he actually closed on his house on *my* birthday, which I thought that was funny.

Then finally he said, "So are you going to tell me about those bruised eyes you have?" I didn't know how to respond. I didn't expect him to notice, let alone call me out on it. I tried to conjure up some lie, but the question made me emotional. I fumbled my words a little bit in a panic trying to figure out what to say.

"No, tell me the truth," he said calmly. I took a deep breath and started my confession. I told him everything. He was the first person I was actually honest with about it all. I didn't really try to make excuses for Hector; I just told someone for the first time ever what was actually happening. It felt good to get it all off my chest, but it made me feel vulnerable as well. I had barely known this man years ago, we literally just started communicating again hours ago, and now I'm spilling my guts to him? What was wrong with me? I didn't want him involved in this mess. He's the nicest guy I had met, and now I look weak and stupid. The last thing I wanted him to see me as was some victim.

We decided to go sit on the patio outside and finish our beers so we could smoke a cigarette. Time was ticking away, and I still had to be home by 7 p.m. to babysit for Jose and Frankie.

When I was finally done filling him in on everything he asked, "So what are you going to do? You don't want to stay with this guy, do you?"

I told him I didn't want to stay with him if he was going to continue being this way. But I didn't know what to do. I was worried about my new puppy now, and I didn't know where to start.

"Okay, so I'll take the dog, for now at least. My brother lives with me; he's home all day, so he can potty train her. She'll have a big fenced in yard and everything," he said.

"Really?" I asked, hoping he was serious.

"Yeah, we'll try it out. Then at least you can start to plan how you're going to get out." I was so relieved. He said I could come visit her whenever I wanted. He had already told me he had Fridays off so I could go there during the day since Hector would be at work.

"Can I bring her this weekend?"

"Yeah that's fine," he said as if it was no big deal. To me this was huge.

"Sunday after church? I can bring Bessie with me to help me." He already knew Bessie from us dating years ago. His work friends referred to her as "cock block" because she used to be around any time we went out. I preferred the term "safety blanket" personally, but to each his own.

"Why are you being so nice to me?" I finally asked. He laughed and smiled.

"Have you ever seen the movie *Hot Tub Time Machine*?" he asked, still smiling.

"No why?"

"Well, I think of you as my 'great white buffalo,'" he said.

"Is that a fat joke? Or a white joke?" I asked, not knowing what that meant.

He laughed and said, "No, neither of those things. It's actually a very good thing. I talk about you a lot, actually," he said.

"You do?"

"Yeah my neighbor is kind of my 'bestie,' and we talk all the time. I actually told her I was coming to meet you today, so she's probably dying to hear all about this when I get home," he said, still smiling that beautiful smile.

"Well she'll be interested to hear you're taking my dog then," I laughed.

"Is she single?" I asked, being nosy.

"No, she's married. She and her husband have been living in that house forever; she's Southern so she's very social. She knows all the neighbors in the cul-de-sac," he answered.

"Oh, that's nice," I said, satisfied with his response. *Wait a minute,* I thought to myself. *What do I care? It's not my business if he's seeing someone.*

"Well, I have to go. I have to get home to babysit," I said, not wanting to leave. I was having a good conversation with a good guy. The last thing I wanted to do was go home. We stood up and he walked me to my car.

"It was really nice to see you," he said, giving me a hug goodbye. He smelled fantastic.

"Same here. I'll see you again Sunday unless you change your mind!" I said smiling.

"Yeah Sunday's fine. I guess I need to go get some stuff," he said.

"Well I'll bring all her things. I have food, toys, potty-training pads and everything to get started."

"Okay, that's a good start then. See you Sunday," he said as we went our separate ways.

On the way home I called Bessie. "Hey, I was with you tonight if Hector say's anything when he sees you," I said, making sure to cover my bases.

"Okay," she said with curiosity in her voice. "And where were we?" she asked.

"We went to dinner. But since you usually come over on Saturdays, I thought I'd cover my bases before tomorrow." I said.

"So, do I get to know who you were actually with? Was it Bruce?" she asked, giggling mischievously.

I rolled my eyes, "No it was not Bruce. If I went to see him it wouldn't be for dinner," I laughed.

"Oh I know!" she responded, laughing as well.

"So?" she said.

"I actually was with Giovanni," I said.

"The guy you dated back in your old apartment? The one we went to Florida with?"

"That's the one."

"How did that happen? I didn't think you guys stayed in contact."

"We didn't, but I sent him a stupid video today on Facebook and we were chatting all day. So, I decided I wanted to see him."

"Good for you! Maybe he'll sweep you off your feet and rescue you from that asshole," she said, her tone changing.

"Bitch, I don't need a rescue," I said laughing. "I'm pulling in at the house, and Jose will be here any minute to drop off the kids, so I'll fill you in tomorrow," I said, getting off the phone.

"You'd better! Love you, bye!"

I was home long enough to change and brush my teeth before the doorbell rang.

"Hey guys," I said, answering the door happily. They came in and their son, who was 12 years old at the time, greeted me with a big hug. He was a good kid.

"I can help with my sister," he said.

"Well that's awesome. I couldn't do it without you buddy," I replied ruffling his hair.

"She has a clean diaper and just had a bottle so you should just be able to leave her in her car seat. She should go to sleep pretty soon and just stay asleep so you shouldn't have any problems," Frankie said nervously.

"We will be fine," I assured her, taking the diaper bag. "Go have fun with your husband, enjoy a little one-on-one time for a change."

"Call us if you need anything or have questions, we'll be right down the street," she said, still nervous.

"She already knows all that. Let's go!" Jose yelled, already back down the stairs. "Thank you, Savannah," he said on his way out.

"Not a problem, you two kids have fun!"

The baby was sitting quietly in her car seat on the couch with her big brother next to her.

"What do you want to do?"

He shrugged and asked if he could pick out a movie to watch.

"Of course, do you want snacks or something to drink?"

"Yes please," he responded politely while flipping through Netflix. I brought everything out and he asked if we could watch *Zootopia*.

"Sure, whatever you want."

"My sister will fall asleep soon so this will be a good one for her to watch until then," he said matter-of-factly. He started the movie and I sat on the other section of the couch.

"Do you need anything else?"

"No thank you." The baby was already zoned in on the movie, looking happy and comfortable.

"Should I take her out of that thing?"

"No, she likes being in it," he answered.

"Okay then." I sat back on the couch. For some reason it hit me that I was *really* tired. I had been lethargic lately, and I didn't know why. I messaged Giovanni that I made it home safe and thanked him for meeting up with me. He was happy to hear from me, but I suspected he was filling his neighbor in, so I didn't want to interrupt. I said good night to him and deleted all of our messages from the day. Put my phone down and looked over at the kids. The baby was already out like a light.

I decided to stretch out, so I lied down on the couch. I didn't know why I was so tired; I only had a couple of beers. I felt like I hadn't slept in days, I couldn't keep my eyes open. I tried to focus on the movie and keep awake, but the next thing I knew I heard Jose standing over me.

"I told you not to worry, they all passed out. They were fine!" he said to his wife.

"Oh hi!" I said quietly trying not to wake the baby. We had all been sleeping so long there wasn't anything on the TV screen anymore.

"How was it?" I asked yawning.

"It was great, but she was worried about the kids the whole time," he said, annoyed.

"Well this was all we did," I said sitting up. "I know I worry too much, I'm just not used to having a babysitter as you can tell. Were they good?" she asked.

"They were perfect. I didn't even do anything," I answered laughing.

"Thanks again," she said getting her son's coat on him.

"Anytime," I answered.

"Where's your man?" Jose asked me.

"With his dad I think," I said, not really caring where he was.

"Oh God, that's a terrible duo," he said, shaking his head.

"Not my problem when I'm not there!" I said happily. They left and I still felt like I needed to sleep. I went straight to bed and passed out as soon as my head hit the pillow.

Hector showed up at some point in the early hours of the next morning. He smelled like cigarette smoke and arm pits. I knew he was getting high all night; I could smell it in his sweat as he wrapped his arms around me.

"If you're going to stay out all night and come home smelling like that, could you at *least* take a shower before you get in the bed?" I asked, already annoyed at his existence. I realized after I said it how snappy I sounded. *Hmm what is going on with me?* I thought to myself.

"Sorry babe," he said, sounding like a small boy who didn't want to upset his parents. He got back out of bed and started to take his clothes off.

"I didn't know I smelled," he said.

"Why wouldn't you know that? You went straight to partying after working all day. Clearly you snorted enough coke to kill a fucking horse. I can smell it in your sweat," I snapped, again realizing that I was being ridiculous. Shut up Savannah, I was saying in my head. Looking at me like a dog who was just kicked he apologized again and went to the bathroom. I laid there thinking I must be about to have my period. I was clearly hormonal. When he came back to bed the sun was nearly up.

"Is that better?" he asked.

"Yes, thank you. I'm sorry, I didn't mean to snap at you," I said rolling on my side to face him. "I'm probably PMS-ing," I said.

"It's fine, I know you hate when I stay out all night. But I texted you a bunch, and you didn't respond," he said.

"Oh, I was so tired I went straight to bed after your cousin picked up his kids. I even passed out on the couch when I was watching them," I said chuckling.

"I don't know why I'm so tired lately." I said.

"Did you have a good night?" he asked sleepily. Giovanni popped into my head.

"I had a great night actually." I responded, smiling. He popped his head up.

"What the fuck does that mean?" he said, now suspicious.

"I just had a good night."

"What did you do?" he asked propping his head up on his hand.

"I went to dinner with Bessie is all," I said, trying to sound innocent.

"Do you have a receipt?" he asked. Nervously I remembered Giovanni got the check.

"No, she actually paid for a change," I said quickly. He looked at me scrunching his face in confusion.

"That bitch never pays for shit, now I know your lying."

"Whatever Hector, ask her yourself. She'll be here tonight," I answered rolling out of the bed. I had to get out of this conversation.

"Why does she have to come over every Saturday?" he asked.

"Because I like going to church on Sunday and she likes to go. Why? Are you going to start coming with me?" I answered with sass.

"Yeah fuck that," he said, lying on his back.

"Where are you going, I want to cuddle," he said.

"I have to pee, is that okay, master?" I asked snapping again.

"Whatever, hurry back."

I took a few extra minutes in the bathroom, hoping he would just be asleep when I came back out. I was in luck. He was passed out cold. I snuck past him and headed for the door.

"I said come back to bed," he said angrily. Dammit, I was so close.

"I thought you fell asleep. I was going to go feed the animals and let Halo out."

"No, I'm horny come ride my dick." Ugh…that was the last thing I wanted to do.

"I need to let Halo out."

"I'm not going to ask you again," he said, his eyes darkening.

"Why do I have to jump on your dick every time you come home from partying all fucking night? You never actually make *me* come, so why the fuck should I keep doing this exactly?" It came out of my mouth before I could stop it. *Shut up Savannah*, I was screaming to myself inside. He sat up.

"What the fuck is wrong with you? Don't talk to me like that," he said.

"Oh right, sorry don't beat my ass again. I'm still healing from your last hissy fit," I said, walking out into the living room. I heard him follow after me and expected to be hit, or grabbed, or shoved.

"Why are you trying to make me feel like shit?" he said almost sounding sad.

"I don't know," I answered honestly. "I guess I woke up on the wrong side of the bed this morning," I said rubbing my head.

"You know when you say dumb shit like that it makes me want to kill myself right?" *Oh God*, I thought to myself. *I am so sick of hearing that shit from his ass.*

"If you're going to kill yourself just do it already, I'm sick of you threatening me with suicide to control me." I said to him, unexpectant of what he was going to do next...As he stormed off to the back bedroom, I took a deep breath of relief thinking I had won. I had finally shut his stupid tantrum down and got away with standing up for myself without even a backhand or being shoved in a wall or through a door! A small victory, but a victory none the less...or so I believed. Less than 30 seconds later he came back out with MY 45-caliber handgun. I always kept it in my purse, and my purse was in the bedroom, where he had gone.

Not knowing what was about to happen, but fully aware of the fact that my gun was loaded...and I had just told this man to kill himself. I knew two things right then. 1.) I didn't want to die. 2.) I didn't want to watch anyone kill themselves. Especially with MY gun after what I just said. He came over to me, grabbed my hair at the roots in the back of my head just above my neck and pulled me onto the floor.

He said, "You want me dead bitch? You're coming with me." Then he put his head against mine, and my gun to his head.

"Babe, don't," I said. I didn't go into panic mode like you think you might with a gun to your head. I was surprisingly calm.

"Why not?" At this point I knew he wasn't going to shoot us. Being a gun owner and knowing several others, I feel like if you actually get me to the point of pulling out my gun, the conversation part is over. I would only pull it out if I fully intended to shoot someone in self-defense. But, I knew I had get myself out of this.

"Fine, if you go, I go," I said.

"Then we would be together forever," he whispered.

"We'll be together forever regardless," I said. "Do what you want to do, but I love you."

"I want you to want me like I want you," he said, loosening his grip on me and putting the hand that held the gun down by his side. I turned and grabbed his face with both hands. He was looking at the floor.

"I do want you babe. I'm sorry. I picked a fight; it's my fault," I said, reaching slowly for my gun while we sat on the floor. He snatched it away from me and put it in his other hand.

"Don't ever say that to me again or I'll really do it," he said, looking up at me.

"I won't. I'm sorry," I said, kissing him.

"Let me put the gun away please," I said, still calm.

"I'll put it back," he said, standing up.

He walked down the hall and I finally took a deep breath. Holy shit, I thought to myself. I started thinking about if he actually pulled the trigger. Who would find us? I thought of Bessie walking in to discover us both dead on the floor since she was coming over later. I thought of her having to call my parents and tell them. I thought of how crazy my brother would react. How mad everyone would be at me for keeping this all a secret. How broken hearted my parents would be. So many things went through my mind right then in a matter of a minute. I started shaking. Hector came back out to the living room.

"I put the gun away. But Jesus Christ did that make my dick hard." He got on the floor again where I still was. He was only wearing his boxer briefs, so I could see his arousal. Before I could say anything, he was kissing me and pushing me on my back on the floor.

"I need to fuck you," he said tearing off my panties. "I need to feel you," he growled. He leaned back on his knees and spat on me. He rubbed it in and then spat on me again. Satisfied with his preparation he mounted me and slowly plunged inside me. My body was still shaking.

"I like it when your body trembles for me," he said. *He actually thought I was turned on right now?* I was shaking from what just happened yes, but it was far from arousal. All I could think about was how dangerous this relationship had become. How I needed to be smarter. I didn't know what he was capable of at this point.

"Go bend over the couch. I want to see that ass," he said getting off me. I snapped back into what was actually happening. *Oh right, I'm supposed to be sexy right now.* I did as instructed, and he mounted me again.

"Do you love me?" he asked.

"Yes, of course," I answered robotically.

"Nobody's ever gonna fuck you like I do, right?" he said, going faster. I knew he was getting closer to finishing.

"Nope, you're the best," I said, trying to sound convincing.

"Look at me," he growled. I looked back at him. I had tears in my eyes that I could no longer hide.

"Why are you crying?" he asked slowing his pace. Shit, what do I say?

"I just love you so much," I spat out as fast as I thought of it. He stopped and turned me to face him sitting me on the couch. He remained on his knees but brought my head down to meet his. He kissed me passionately.

"I love you too babe," he said, kissing me. "Open your fucking legs I need to nut in you." He said, grabbing my ass and moving me forward on the couch. I did as he asked once again and leaned my back against the couch, letting him get what he wanted. When he finished, he laid his head on my chest, still inside me, panting. "That was amazing," he said, breathing heavily. I rolled my eyes, knowing he couldn't see my face.

"Yup," I said. "I need to go to bed now," he said, biting one of my nipples while he got up.

"I'll be in to take a shower after I feed the animals," I said.

"You better put some fucking pants on before you take that dog out." I forgot he ripped off my underwear; I looked over at the floor and saw it shredded.

"Yes, of course," I said, standing up. At least this was over now. While I was in the shower, I decided that I could never breathe a word of what just happened. If anyone found out, I knew they would go to my father and brother. Luckily, I had a few hours to get my thoughts together before Bessie arrived. But while I was in the shower, I had another breakdown. I sat against the shower wall, holding my knees and crying while the water ran. I pictured my brother freaking out as he got to my house, wanting to come inside and fighting the police who were stopping him from seeing the gruesome scene. I imagined my father being so overwhelmed with emotion that he had another heart attack on my lawn just behind the crime scene tape. I could see my mother falling to her knees, wailing uncontrollably when she got the call of my murder. I cried until the water went cold. I thanked God for letting me be calm in that situation and avoiding what could have happened. I asked him to show me where he wanted me to be and help me get there. If I stayed much longer, I would die. One way or another, he was going to kill me.

CHAPTER TWENTY

Really? Now?

When Bessie arrived, she was dying to hear about my 'date' the night before, as she called it. I obviously couldn't talk about it when Hector was there. After what had transpired earlier that morning, I needed to be more careful. Luckily for us, he wanted to go to the clubhouse after he woke up. He slept all day, so he woke up at 5:30 p.m., grumpy from coming down off his cocaine bender the night before.

"Why is this bitch here again?" he asked me angrily when she went to put her stuff in her room.

"I told you babe; we have church in the morning," I said as sweet as possible.

"Can I make you something to eat?" I asked, trying to keep him happy.

"No, I'm not hungry," he snapped. Bessie came into the living room talking about her day at work. I could tell Hector was beyond annoyed. "Fuck this. I'm going to the clubhouse," he said at about 7 p.m. "I assume you aren't coming with me?" he asked me.

"We have church in the morning, babe. I don't want to be out all night drinking and smelling like cigarettes if you don't mind," I answered innocently.

"What is this church thing about all of a sudden?" he asked, irritated.

"We love Jesus," Bessie replied shortly. He shot her an angry look.

"You're welcome to join us anytime," she said with a smug smile on her face.

Not wanting this to escalate, I said, "There's no harm in it babe, it's not like we're going out to the bar or something. Bessie and I used to go all the time back in the day."

"You better not be going out to a fucking bar," he said angrily.

"We aren't, we'll be right here all night. Go have fun, we'll be fine."

"Fine maybe Bessie can suck my dick again tonight when I get back." She rolled her eyes.

"What time are you supposed to be there?" I asked.

"I'm going to go get ready now," he said, walking past the couch to go to our bedroom.

"Hurry the fuck up," Bessie whispered softly so only she and I could hear.

When he finally left for the night, we celebrated. He was so overbearing that it was like a breath of fresh air any time he left the house now. I had been walking on eggshells all day trying not to disturb him even though he was sleeping all day. Waiting for him to wake up and see what kind of mood he would be in was a different level of stress. Since I had just had a gun to my head and an emotional breakdown in the shower that day, I was extra relieved to see him go out for the night.

"Tell me everything," Bessie said excitedly.

"You want some wine?" I asked.

"Duh," she said, rolling her eyes. She followed me to the kitchen. I told her about the day of texting and that I'd just really had the urge to see Giovanni again, so I did.

"How did you get away with that with the warden watching your every move?"

"Easy, he never came home."

"He went to pick up his dad and take him to the clubhouse. I could smell the cocaine coming out in his sweat this morning when he came home," I said disgustedly.

"No surprise there. I'm sure he's rushing to get some more as we speak," she said, sipping her wine. "At least he's out of our hair for the night!"

"So, here's the thing," I said. "Oh, there's something more!" she said, setting her wine down.

"There was a situation yesterday morning with Hector kicking and punching Halo." Her whole face turned angry.

"What? After what happened to Rafiki? Are you fucking kidding me?" She shook her head and called Halo over to take a look at her.

"No, I'm most certainly *not* kidding, and he threatened to put her out in traffic even," I said, getting upset.

"You need to put *his* ass out in traffic and do the world a fucking favor," she spat angrily.

"How are you still here? How is this still what you want to do?"

"Oh, it's not, trust me. And after all that and this morning, I am fully aware that I need to get out as soon as possible," I said, not thinking.

"Why, what happened this morning?"

"Oh," I said, again searching for the right thing to say. "I just have no patience for him so I got mouthy and picked a fight," I said, not wanting to elaborate.

"Did he fucking hit you again?" she asked. "No, but I know it's only a matter of time. Even if he doesn't hit me, he always thinks of some form of punishment. Then he makes me have sex with him, and I always feel like a urinal," I said sadly.

"That's because you're being raped all the time," Bessie said.

"What? How can you be raped by your spouse? That's not even a thing." I never thought of it like that. I just looked at it as something I had to let him do to not upset him.

"Do you say no?" she asked.

"I do sometimes," I said honestly.

"Does he stop?" she asked. "No, obviously he always gets what he wants," I answered shamefully. "That's the very definition of rape. Nonconsensual sex," she said flatly.

"But I sometimes enjoy having sex with him," I said, getting more confused.

"Yeah, those are the consensual times," she said. Not wanting to continue this uncomfortable conversation, I changed the subject.

"Anyway, Giovanni agreed to take Halo off my hands for a while." She leaned back on the couch.

"Oh, did he?" she said, making a strange, satisfied face.

"Yeah, so if you don't mind, we are going to take her over there tomorrow right after church."

"Okay," she said still grinning.

"What?" I asked unsure of her expression.

"He's a smart man. What better way to get you to come around, than take in your wounded puppy," she said, visibly impressed.

"I don't think he's thinking of it like that. He's a nice guy. I told him the truth about everything, and he just wanted to help," I said.

"He did call me a white buffalo or something though. Do you know what that means?"

"Like from *Hot Tub Time Machine*?" she asked, laughing.

"Yeah, what is this movie? Am I the only one that hasn't seen it?"

"It's stupid funny, you would like it if you were stoned maybe. But it's not worth watching the whole movie," she said pulling her phone out from her bra. "Hold on." She looked up the movie scene and handed me the phone.

"Watch that." In the scene, one of the men in the car was describing his "great white buffalo" as basically "the one that got away."

"Ohhh," I said, now understanding its meaning.

"See, he's smart," she said taking her phone back.

"Well I'm sure after everything I told him last night, he's not going to think of me as a love interest right now. I'm a fucking mess," I said shaking my head.

"Be that as it may, he really likes you if that's how he thinks of you."

"I'm sure I've ruined that," I said laughing at the ridiculousness of the whole thing. "He's too good for me anyway."

"See," she said sitting up. "That comment right there, that's *not* the Savannah I know." She had a point. I had a mostly positive self-image years ago. Not now. Now I was constantly feeling ashamed, embarrassed or insecure.

The next day we got up and went to church. Hector wasn't even back home yet. I was hoping he would stay gone so I didn't have to explain where I was taking Halo. I needed to get her out and explain later. After church we went back to my house to get ready for the drop off. My anxiety was extra high, but when we saw that Hector was home, we both started to get nervous.

"Okay, let's just get in and get out as quickly and quietly as we can," I said. He was out all night so I assumed he would be passed out cold. I messaged Giovanni to see if he was still okay with this and he sent me his address. We loaded up all of Halo's things first. Then Bessie carried her to the car. I grabbed my purse and headed for the stairs.

"Babe," I heard from the back bedroom. Shit!

"Yes?" I said lovingly.

"Come here when I call you," he demanded. "What the hell are you bitches up to?" he asked as I entered the room.

"We just got back from church. I found an old friend that wanted Halo, so we are taking her to drop her off. Then Bessie and I are going to the salon to get our nails done. I figured you would want to sleep," I said, trying not to sound scared.

"You're getting rid of our dog?" he asked, surprised.

"Well, you were really upset the other morning and I don't want you hurting her," I said, not thinking about what was coming out of my mouth.

"Plus, she's not doing well with potty training, so I'm ready to get rid of her," I said trying to recover. I couldn't make it *his* fault or he would never allow it. "I think it was too soon for me to get a dog after Rafiki, and I found her a good home with a fenced-in yard and everything. I think she will be very happy," I said.

"Whatever. Bring me back some food when you come home," He said, settling into the bed.

"Okay babe, I'll call you to see what you want before I head home." I went to walk away.

"Excuse me," he said. "No kiss?" I rolled my eyes before turning around and went in to give him a kiss.

"Love you," I said backing away from his smell.

"Love you."

I got in the car.

"About time, what took so long?"

"He woke up," I replied.

"Oh shit, are we already in trouble?" Bessie asked.

"Surprisingly, no." I started the car and got out of there before he decided to change his mind. When we pulled in the driveway and hopped out, Giovanni came outside to greet us. I introduced him to Halo.

"What can I grab?" he asked. We got all of her belongings in the house and asked where he wanted the crate set up. His living room was large and full of sunlight. I immediately noticed he had done some work either on the chimney or just replacing sheet rock. The wall facing me didn't have paint on it, and you could see exactly where he had repaired it.

"Doing renovations?" I asked, pointing at the wall.

"Oh no, there was a leak, so I had to fix it," he said.

"You want to take her outside so she can see her new backyard?" he asked politely.

"Yeah that would be awesome." He opened the French door that led to the back deck. We stepped out and were impressed with the size of the yard. It was plenty big enough, and he had a big in-ground pool.

"Guess we know where we'll be this summer," Bessie said, putting Halo down. "That's a bigger pool than I thought it would be." It was covered up now, but I was hoping to see it in all its glory one day.

He gave us a quick tour of his house. For a bachelor's place, it wasn't terribly dirty. But it seemed empty. Way more house than a single man would need. But it was nice. He introduced us to his gray cat named Douche. Yes, that was his real name. Douche was living a great life. He had the whole downstairs to himself, cat toys, and a cat tree. He looked like the cat that played Church in the original *Pet Sematary* movie by Stephen King. He also didn't look pleased that I just brought in a new rambunctious puppy. Giovanni's brother Gabriel came down from his bedroom to introduce himself. He was even taller than Giovanni, black hair, heavy build. He had a shy smile and seemed to be an introvert; he didn't speak other than saying hello and shaking our hands. But he lay on the couch and let Halo come love on him. Everything seemed like it was going to work out okay. We hung out for a little bit on the back porch talking. I asked if it would be okay to come over and see her on Fridays.

"Yeah that's fine, you can see her whenever you want," he said.

"Well I make my own schedule so I'll just move everything around as I can, so I don't have to explain where I'm going every Friday." Bessie was starving so we got up to leave. "Thank you again, I really appreciate this," I said, giving Giovanni another hug.

"It's no problem," he said. I gave Halo hugs and kisses goodbye and went to my car. When I got in the car and drove away, that's when it hit me. I started crying. I didn't want to get rid of my new puppy, but I knew I had to.

"It was the best thing for her, and you can see her whenever you want," Bessie said as I sat at the stop sign wanting to turn around. I was overwhelmed with emotion.

"She's okay; she's with a nice man."

"Where do you want to eat?" I asked.

"Mexican," she said quickly.

"There's a place on the way to the salon," I said.

"Perfect."

When we got to the restaurant, I realized I was starving. Bessie ordered a small pitcher of margaritas for us while I ordered spinach queso dip to go with our free chips. While we were looking over the menu, I must have eaten half a basket of chips with salsa. I never eat salsa, but my hunger was so urgent and angry I had to have something.

"Dang lady, are you okay?" she asked when she realized how much I had already eaten before the queso came.

"I am a level of hungry I cannot describe," I replied, still eagerly shoveling chips in my face. We started discussing what the next steps for my escape plan should be after we ordered our food.

"You could always just stay on my couch until you save up some money to get your own place again," Bessie offered.

"I don't want to live with anyone if I can avoid it. Maybe I can just pick up some extra jobs and start saving more money and get out slowly. I really wish I could keep the house. I love that house. Maybe I can just try to have a calm adult breakup and convince him to leave," I said. "You would have to be dealing with an adult for that to work," Bessie responded, rolling her eyes. When the queso got there, I just went harder.

"Can we get more chips please?" I asked the gentleman who brought our cheese dip. My food order was even outside of the normal order I would place. Then a light bulb came on in my head. When was my period supposed to start? I had an app on my phone to keep track of it since I wasn't on birth control. Reaching for my phone Bessie must have seen a strange look on my face.

"You okay?" she asked, concerned.

I opened the app and realized I was five days late. That wasn't normal for me. I was usually right on schedule—a day late, maybe two, but *never* five days. I could feel the blood drain out of my face as I went pale.

"What is wrong?" Bessie said, now sounding concerned.

"I'm five days late." She took a long sip of her mango margarita.

"Well, I'm sure it's just stress, I mean look at you. You're *still* healing from the last fight. You just had to give up your new puppy to save her from being abused and now you're trying to escape a horrible situation all while hiding the truth from everyone," she said, making some good points.

"Yeah you're probably right." I said, taking a sip of my margarita. "But what if I'm pregnant?" I said taking another sip.

Bessie put her hand up, "No! You aren't pregnant; don't even say that out loud," she said, staring at me wide eyed. "If we have to stop and get a test on the way to the salon and make you take it to clear your mind then we will. That might help you relax."

CHAPTER TWENTY: REALLY? NOW?

"That's not a bad idea. Publix is right across the street, maybe I'll do that," I said, relaxing a little bit. "It would be one less thing to stress over."

After lunch we did just that. I grabbed the most expensive test they had thinking that the more expensive, the more trustworthy.

"Good, now you can pee on this real quick and relax for some pampering," Bessie said, getting into my car.

"Yeah, hopefully," I said, getting nervous.

"You'll be fine. There's no way you're pregnant. Your luck could not possibly be that shitty," she said, laughing.

"I sure hope not," I laughed nervously. We got to the salon and said hello to all the ladies who worked there. It was a small, family-owned establishment that we had been going to religiously for years, so we knew everyone there.

"What do you need done today?" one of the women asked.

"I need nails and toes, she's just getting a pedicure, and eyebrow wax for both of us," Bessie said.

"Okay right this way," the woman said.

"I'm going to use your restroom really quick," I said heading towards the back of the salon.

"Okay, come to the first chair when you come out," she said sweetly.

"Yes ma'am," I said, anxious to get this test over with. I went in, opened the box, and read the directions. It said to pee on it for 5 seconds and let it lay flat for 3 minutes to get the results. It had two windows on it: The big window would tell me whether or not I was pregnant, and the small one would show a line to signify the test was working. I got into position and started to urinate. Before I could even count to five, I could already see the positive sign.

In disbelief, I pulled the stick out and looked at it closer. Yup, I'm pregnant. "What the fuck?" I said just above a whisper, still urinating. I put the cap back on the test and grabbed the directions. "No, this can't be right, God please no!" I started shaking. I must have done something wrong. *This can* not *be happening.* I started to tear up. *Really? Now? I just started to implement my escape! Now he's never going to let me leave.* I pulled my pants up and rushed out of the bathroom, not even washing my hands. I ran over to Bessie who was already getting her nails worked on and shoved the test in her face.

"I'm fucking pregnant," I yelled. Everyone turned to look at me.

"Let me see that," she said grabbing the directions and looking at the test.

"No, I don't except that. You must have done something wrong," she said in denial.

"Let me see," the woman who was doing her nails said. I showed her the test.

"Congratulations! You're gonna be a mommy!" she said, smiling.

"No, she's not," Bessie said still in disbelief. One of the other workers came over and confirmed it was positive.

"Congratulations!" she said, smiling and giving me a big hug. They had seen Hector in there with me a few times, just to pay to get things done for me and put on a show like he was an awesome boyfriend. They had no idea what was actually happening. I started to cry immediately.

"Oh, it's okay," the woman said, "You're going to be a good mommy!" she said, trying to comfort me. "Come sit, relax," she said, ushering me to the pedicure chair. *This can't be real; I must have done something wrong. What am I going to do with a baby?* His *baby?* The thought of it had me weeping. What if he was abusive to our child? What if he abused me in front of our child? I couldn't be *that* mom. But how am I going to leave him now? He'll never allow it. I'll never get out. I needed to talk to someone, so I took a picture of the positive test and sent it to my mom.

"Does that say you're pregnant?!" she texted me back. I called her.

"Oh my God you're pregnant! I'm gonna have another grandbaby!" I interrupted her celebration with my sobbing.

"Hey, are you okay?" she asked, realizing this was no happy moment.

"Mom," was all I could muster. I couldn't form words. Here I sit in the middle of a relatively busy salon with a woman scrubbing my feet while I sob like some grieving widow.

"Calm down," my mother said gently. "Why are you so upset? This is a blessing!"

"Oh mom, this isn't a blessing at all. I was going to leave him! I literally just dropped Halo off to her new home, and Bessie and I were making plans an hour ago about how to leave." I continued crying.

"You're leaving Hector? Why, what's going on? I mean I knew you guys were having problems, but is there something I don't know?" she asked. I took a deep breath and decided I better shut my big mouth before I said something, I wasn't ready to say.

"No, it's fine, I'm just really overwhelmed right now, I just took the test in the bathroom at the salon." I said trying to distract her.

"So does Hector know yet?" she asked. "No, the only people that know are in this salon," I said, slowing down my uncontrollable sobs.

"Bessie is here with me."

"Okay, just take a little time to relax and let it sink in. This is a blessing, I swear! It's always scary finding out when you weren't planning it, but you are going to be an *amazing* mommy! And I am *so* excited!" she said, beaming.

"Thanks mom, I'm going to let you go now. Thanks for calming me down," I said taking deep breaths.

"Anytime, I love you *so* much! I wish I could be there with you!" *I wish I could tell you the truth*, I said in my head. I hadn't wanted to curl up in my mom's lap and cry while she ran her fingers through my hair comforting me in years, but I did right now.

"I love you too, Mom," I said hanging, up the phone.

I realized I had three messages while I was on the phone with my mother. "Where the hell are you?" was the first one. "You better be on your fucking way home," was the second one, and "Stop and get me a steak I'm starving since you didn't feel it was important to feed your man today," was the last. I put my phone down and started to cry again. Do I even love this man? I asked myself. If I loved him so much, shouldn't I be happy on some level? I felt nothing but fear. I had really made a mess out of my life, but that was okay because it was just me. Now I'm going to be responsible for an innocent defenseless person? I got another text: "Hello? I'm talking to you." Finally, I responded.

"I'm almost done at the salon; I'm not going to get steak, but I'll get you some wings on the way home," I said.

"That's not what I asked for," he responded quickly. "I'm about sick of you spending time with that fat whore, you always chose your slutty friends over me," he said.

"I really am not about to fight with you right now," I responded.

"I want steak," he said.

"Then go get it," I replied.

"Watch your fucking mouth," he said.

"I'm trying to get home; we need to talk," I said.

"Yeah we need to talk about your fucking mouth" he responded.

"PLEASE stop. I can't do this right now." I said, hoping my phone would stop chiming.

"You will do what I tell you to do, I'm your man." Sick of the back and forth I sent him the picture of the pregnancy test.

"I'm fucking pregnant, I just found out and I'm freaking out. STOP FUCKING TEXTING ME," I replied. Silence…Finally.

When we got back to my house, Bessie jumped in her car and left. I grabbed my grocery bag of tests. I bought a two pack so I could be sure. I was sure he was going to make me take the other one now. I came in the bedroom and handed him the repulsive smelling wings he loved so much and then the positive pregnancy test.

"How am I supposed to know that's yours?" he asked, opening his wings.

"I have another one, I will go take it now."

"Let me see it," he said taking, a bite of a wing. He was laid back in my bed with his legs crossed watching some superhero movie.

"See the test I haven't taken?" I asked confused.

"Yes." I pulled out the box and tried to hand it to him.

"You see my hands are dirty and I'm eating, don't be stupid. Pull it out," he said, chewing away like a barn animal. I did as he asked, seeming satisfied that it was still in its individual wrapper and sealed, he nodded. "Let me see the directions," he said, still looking at the TV. Rolling my eyes, I opened the paper and held it for him so he could read it.

"Would you like me to read them to you as well?" I said, annoyed.

He finally looked up at me over his Coca Cola bottle glasses, "I'm not gonna tell you to watch that mouth of yours again," he said calmly whilst picking up another wing.

"Can I go take this now?" I asked still holding the directions.

"Leave the bathroom door open."

I turned toward our bathroom. I took the tip off and assumed the position. Once again, it was positive before I could get done urinating. I shook my head and started crying again.

"Bring it out here," he barked with a mouth full of food. I put the cap back on and pulled up my pants. With tears streaming down my face I showed him the second test. I couldn't even look at him. He put the wings to the side and sucked off his fingers before grabbing the test. He uncrossed his legs and turned to sit up with his feet touching the floor. He grabbed the other test and compared them.

"We're having a baby," he said in disbelief. I started crying harder. "You're pregnant with *my* baby!" he said, looking up at me excitedly. He smiled bigger than I had ever seen him smile. He was genuinely happy? What the hell would he be happy for? He hated me. He stood up and wrapped his arms around me.

"Why are you crying babe? This is amazing! We're finally going to be a family!" he said, putting his hand on my lower stomach.

"Why are you happy about this?" I blurted out. He let go of me and sat on the bed, looking up at me confused.

"What do you mean? This is everything I ever wanted." I sat on the bed next to him and put my head in my hands, sobbing uncontrollably.

"But you hate me!" I said much louder than I'd intended to. He laughed and put his arm around my back, using his other hand to lift my head and face him. I could no longer get air through my nose I was so swollen and puffy from crying.

"Babe, I don't hate you at all. I know we've been going through a hard time lately, but now that I know why you've been acting so crazy, I completely forgive you! You're pregnant! I can deal with hormones now that I know what it is!" he said in celebration. I was so confused I literally stopped crying.

"Look at my face! I still have two black eyes! I just found out you beat the shit out of me and drug me out of the house by my HAIR while I was pregnant! And you think that's something I should be happy about?" I asked.

"Well, had I known you were already pregnant I wouldn't have done that," he said waving away my concerns as if they were irrelevant.

"Oh, so you *can* control your temper? You just *don't*. Let me make something *very* clear right now. If you *ever* touch me again, I am leaving. I will *not* raise a child in a toxic environment. And you are going to have to go to rehab, the cocaine has to go," I said.

"I know, a baby is all I've ever wanted! I will do whatever it takes to be a good dad," he said seeming to really want to mean that statement. "I don't want my child to ever have to feel like I did growing up. And *you* are going to be an awesome mom!" he said grabbing my hands and kissing me.

"Clean yourself up; we have to start making some phone calls!" he said, pulling out his phone.

"No, we should wait, I don't think we should tell people just yet," I said, not wanting to spread this terrifying news yet.

"Well that fat slut knew before I even did, so I want to tell some people." He started to video dial his cousin Jose. He and his wife were excited and happy to hear the news. Then he called one of his brothers, his mom, two of his sisters, and finally my dad and brother. They were shocked to say the least. I could tell they didn't want to be on a video chat; it was an awkward reaction. They never really like Hector to begin with, my brother especially. They just tolerated him for me. After getting done with all that, I just wanted to take a bath and escape. I just wanted to be alone. But Hector wanted to be glued to me now. He insisted on taking a bath with me to help me relax. He wouldn't shut up the whole time.

"We need to get you to the clinic this week so you can get healthcare. You need to apply for WIC, and we can probably get food stamps!" he said excitedly.

"You own your own company; I doubt we're going to get food stamps," I said wishing he would go away.

"Yeah but we aren't married yet, and Frankie is good at playing the system, so she can probably show you how to do it." He rambled on like a giddy schoolboy who just found out he was going to Disneyland.

"I need to go lay down, babe," I said getting out of the tub.

"Okay, I'll dry you off," he said grabbing my towel. *Oh, now he's going to be my caretaker all of a sudden?* I thought to myself. I let him towel me off and then went to the bed. It was only about 7 p.m. by this time, but I had a day from hell. So, I was ready for bed.

"Can I get you anything?" Hector asked me, coming out of the bathroom.

"I'm good, I'm just exhausted." I said, closing my eyes.

"That's because you're growing my baby inside you!" he said happily. "I'm going to go smoke and make some more phone calls okay?" he said, seeming to care about me again.

"Okay but babe, please don't say anything on social media. It's bad luck," I said.

"Yeah it's too early for that," he agreed. I closed my eyes and passed out.

I woke up to Hector's alarm going off. He was wrapped around me so tight I could barely move. It reminded me of a boa constrictor keeping its prey from escaping. *He's never going to let me leave*, I thought to myself, defeated.

"Wake up babe, your alarm is going off," I said, making him roll off me. He mumbled and grumbled like he always did in the mornings. I went to the bathroom and then to feed the animals.

"Get up babe, Jose will be here any minute," I yelled on the way to the kitchen. Then I realized I didn't have Halo anymore. Gizmo squawked her normal starvation song from the kitchen counter where she was pacing. I had gotten so caught up in the shock of the pregnancy that I had completely forgotten Halo. Oh my God, what is Giovanni going to think of me now? I thought.

My doorbell rang. Jose was here to pick up Hector. I let him in, and he gave me a hug and patted my tummy.

"Congratulations," he said to me, smiling. "Now *this* will finally calm Hector's ass down!" he said, sounding hopeful.

"It's gonna have to," I laughed nervously. He came out of the room beaming with pride.

"Good morning baby mama," he said, smiling as he wrapped his arms around me giving me a kiss.

"Don't call me that. I'm going to go to the clinic today when I get done with work and find out what's next," I said.

He slapped me on the ass. "Good! We need to get you looked at."

I arrived at the clinic at about 1 o'clock in the afternoon. It didn't take long at all to get called in.

"Pee in this cup please," the woman barked at me staring at her clipboard while handing me a cup. "Then bring it back in here with you when you're done," she said and walked out the room. I was slightly hopeful they would test negative. Maybe I got a bad box of tests and I was all upset for nothing. I came back in the room and waited with my cup of urine on the counter.

"Yup, you're pregnant," she said, writing something down on her clipboard. Shit, this was real.

Taking deep breaths to trying and remain calm, I asked, "So now what do I do?" She threw everything away and took off her gloves. She handed me the paper she wrote on.

"Take this to the exit window and they'll tell you what to do," she said, not ever looking at me.

"Thank you," I yelled at her on her way out. The lady at the exit window wasn't much more pleasant but at least answered my questions.

"Take this to the WIC office; you can apply for emergency Medicaid at the same place. Once you get approved, you'll need to see an OBGYN as soon as you can. They will provide you with a list of the ones that are covered," She said almost robotically.

"Anything else?" she asked, handing me the paperwork I needed.

"Where is the WIC office?" I asked. I had never had to do this before, and I was by myself and scared.

"The address is on the top of your paperwork," she said, annoyed that I hadn't looked at it.

"Okay, thank you so much, I hope you have a blessed day," I told her, trying to sound sweet. She turned her chair to the person next to her and they picked up whatever conversation they were having.

I drove to the address provided and found my way around. I was able to apply for the Medicaid with what I had but I needed to come back with more for WIC. I didn't expect to do all this in one day, so I didn't have proof of income or anything like that on me. I turned down the street where I lived and got pulled over. The cops had a speed trap set up at the bottom of the hill, and I was in such a hurry to be home I was going almost 15 miles an hour over the posted limit. I explained to the officer why I was speeding, I showed him the paperwork proving my case. I apologized and told him I lived just down the street and begged him to give me a warning.

"I can't do that ma'am, but I will drop the speed down, so you won't get any points on your license," he said with a stick up his ass. I sighed,

"Okay, thanks for that at least," I said. He went to write up my ticket and came back a few minutes later.

"Here you go ma'am, here is your court date, here is the number you can call in three days to find out how much your fine is," he leaned in a little closer. "I'm sorry, if my supervisor wasn't out here with me right now, I'd let you go," he said. *Oh, that makes sense*, I thought.

"I understand. You guys are just doing your job. I appreciate it," I said, forgiving him instantly. He let me go and I was home in less than a minute. It was already almost 4 p.m. I went inside to start dinner, when my phone rang. It was Hector.

"Hey babe! How are you feeling?" he asked. This was strange, but I went with it.

"Tired and a little irritated, I just got a speeding ticket one minute from the house," I said.

"Are you serious?"

"Yeah they have a speed trap set up so be careful coming home."

"Okay, did you go to the clinic?"

"Yeah, they gave me the paperwork to file for Medicaid and WIC. I filled the Medicaid already, but I didn't have what I needed for WIC."

"That's okay; the Medicaid is more important right now. What do you want for dinner? Any cravings?" he asked. Okay now *that* was rare.

"No cravings, what do you want me to make? I just got home."

"Nothing, I'll pick something up. You just relax. I love you; I'll see you soon," he said.

"Okay," I said not knowing who this new Hector was. "Love you too," I said, hanging up the phone. Maybe this IS going to be a good thing.

CHAPTER TWENTY-ONE

False Hope

I didn't want to tell anyone else I was pregnant until I went to an OBGYN and found out how far along I was. I scheduled an appointment as soon as I got approved for Medicaid. Hector went with me to make sure he wasn't left out of anything. Hearing the heartbeat for the first time was emotional for us both. Happy tears filled our scared eyes.

"We have a heartbeat!" my doctor said happily while she slid her hand-held device over my stomach.

"Let's get you into the ultrasound room and see how far along you are," she said.

"Today?"

"Yeah, just go back to the waiting room for a few minutes and we'll call you back in when it's ready," she said sweetly. They called us back less than 10 minutes later.

"Since we want to get an accurate measurement, we are going to insert this wand in your vagina that has a little camera on it," the ultrasound technician said. "Then we can be sure how big your little one is. You ready?" she asked me.

"I guess." She slid in the cold wand and turned the monitor so we could see what she was seeing.

"Oh, hold on a second," she said moving it around in every direction she could. "Okay, sorry it almost looked like two for a second!" she giggled.

"What?" Hector said, wide-eyed.

"Don't worry, there's only one!" She said smiling. Relieved, I looked at the screen.

"There it is!" the lady said pointing at a tiny peanut shape blip on the black and white radar.

"That's it?" I said with my lip quivering, trying to hold back my emotions.

"It's so small," I said, a tear falling down my cheek.

"That tiny thing is making you crazy," Hector said jokingly while grabbing my hand. I looked up at him and he was crying.

"Looks like you are six weeks and two days along," she said examining the peanut on the screen.

"Wow, you can tell down to the day?" I asked.

"Not exactly every time, but pretty close usually. So according to this your due date is July 12, 2017," she said printing out some images for us to take home. "Do you have any questions?" she asked nicely. I couldn't think. I'm sure I had a hundred questions, but I didn't know what they were right now.

"No, I don't think so," I said.

"Okay, I'll get these to the doctor and give you a minute to get dressed," she said, standing up.

"Thank you," I said. Before we left, I got a prescription for prenatal vitamins and scheduled my next doctor visit. This was real, this is actually happening, I thought to myself.

The next day I went out to Douglassville again for work. I decided at the end of the day that it was time for me to tell Jack, my old boss. He congratulated me and told me that as long as my doctors were okay with me working, he would always have work for me. It was a relief. My doctors didn't love what I do for a living, but cleared me to continue if I agreed to wear a respirator and gloves all day and stay completely covered. The fumes I work around all day are very dangerous, but I was happy to do what I needed to do. I called the supervisor in Jonesboro to let them know. His wife didn't feel comfortable having me around the fumes while carrying. I understood her thinking. They had been doing in vitro for over a year and couldn't seem to get pregnant. So, I wasn't shocked when they told me they wouldn't be able to work me until after I had the baby.

It was already December, so I wanted to put up the Christmas tree and decorate my house. Bessie came over to help me. Hector even helped put the tree up. He had been treating me like a queen for the past few weeks. But it was a Saturday, and he wanted to go do his club thing. I was fine with it; he had been under me so much since we found out that I was starting to crave some space. He left to go to the clubhouse around 7 p.m. while Bessie and I settled in with some Christmas movies and snacks.

"So, have you told Giovanni yet?" she asked.

"No, at first I was waiting to go to the doctor, but we went to the doctor yesterday and I still haven't told him. I'm nervous to tell him, to be honest," I said.

"Why?" she asked.

"I don't know really; I just feel like he's going to think horribly of me."

"Well, it's not like you meant to get knocked up."

"Yeah obviously," I said, laughing uncomfortably. "Plus, Hector has been up my ass since the moment he found out. I don't really want to text Giovanni when Hector's looking over my shoulder."

"Yeah that's drama you don't need," she said.

That night Bessie and I went to bed about 10 p.m. Hector rolled in at about 5 a.m. He had clearly been back to his old ways. I could smell it all over him. It made me nauseous.

"Hey babe," he said crawling into bed.

"I see you had a good time," I said annoyed that he was high again.

"Yeah I ran into that Weasel dude from the other club, the one that knows your ex-boyfriend Bruce," he said.

"That guy's a fucking douchebag; don't trust him," I said.

"Yeah, he said the same about you," he responded. I sat up.

"He doesn't even know me," I said, annoyed.

"Well he said Bruce told him all about your relationship. He said he's still in love with you and that you two talk all the time." I could tell by his tone this wasn't going to go well no matter what I said.

"You know every time I talk to him. I tell you, and it's not that often."

"Do you know he's still in love with you?" he asked accusingly. I sighed.

"He'll never *not* love me, Hector. He's known me since I was 18. He knows my whole family; my dad still talks to him sometimes. What do you want me to do about it?" I said, already tired of this conversation.

"Are you still in love with him?" he asked.

"No," I answered without hesitation.

"I will always love Bruce; he was my best friend for years. He is always going to look out for me if I need him to, and he's someone I know I can rely on for anything. I don't see him; I haven't seen him since before I met you. I've only spoken to him a few times here and there when he calls. That's it. But don't fool yourself. Anyone can do blow with you all night, that doesn't mean he's a good person to hang around," I said.

"Well we exchanged numbers, so he'll be coming around more. I think I'm going to put him in my club," he said.

"Why on earth do you want to do that?" I asked. "Because I can," he said.

"Fine, do what you want with your club, but I don't like that him, so don't bring him to this house. I mean it," I said.

"This is my house; I'll do what the fuck I want," he said laying back and crossing his legs. "Come ride my dick." I rolled my eyes and rolled back over facing my back to him.

"Good night, Hector."

"Better yet, go wake up your fat ass friend and have her suck my dick again while you ride my face," he said, rolling over to grope me.

"I'm not in the mood, go to sleep."

"Fine, then I'll just jack off on you," he said, pulling his dick out. I got up and went into the bathroom to brush my teeth. It was morning, anyway, may as well let him have the bedroom.

"Do what you want, I'm up now, enjoy yourself," I said.

"Really? You aren't going to fuck me?" I walked over to the door and looked back at him.

"Sorry, I'm pregnant and your smell is making me nauseous. I have to think about the baby," I said sarcastically and walked out. I closed the door behind me, but I heard him yell for me to wake Bessie up and send her in. I just ignored him and went to the living room. I was so sick of him at this point I didn't even care if he fucked the universe. Anything to keep his attention off me was fine. I just wanted him to leave me the hell alone.

The following week Giovanni finally reached out to me, suspecting something was wrong since he hadn't heard from me. Reluctantly I fessed up and told him about the pregnancy. He was shocked of course, but he handled the news well. I told him that I would come by Friday to see Halo if that was okay with him. I bought a stocking for her for Christmas with dog toys and treats that I wanted to give her. He of course said that was fine. I felt relieved that he knew. I didn't know how he really felt of course, but he wasn't a jerk to me when I told him. He just asked me how I felt about it and listened. Didn't offer any unwanted advice or suggestions. Friday morning, I woke up when Hector's alarm went off. I told Hector I was off for the day, so I might do some shopping. I was honest with him about wanting to go visit with Halo. He surprisingly didn't seem to care. I waited until 9 a.m. to bother Giovanni. I figured he would be sleeping in since he was off. Plus, I didn't want him to think I was anxiously awaiting coming over. He got back to me about 30 minutes later and said I could come over whenever I wanted. So, I told him I could be there in 30 minutes.

Halo was excited to see me. I opened her Christmas stocking for her and let her go crazy with all her fun toys and yummy treats.

"You don't have a Christmas tree up yet?" I asked Giovanni.

He laughed and responded, "No, I don't decorate." He told me his neighbors went all out for every holiday, and the next time I came over it would be a Christmas wonderland next door.

"I am going to make some Christmas cookies today though," he said.

"Oh?" I said. He smiled.

"Do you want some?" he asked.

"Obviously I want all the food ever," I said rubbing my belly. We talked a little bit about the pregnancy. He asked me again how I felt about it and how Hector was taking the news. I told him everything. It was so easy to talk to him. He was the only person I could tell everything to. I didn't feel like I had to hide the truth from him at all, so it was a huge relief. I quickly became addicted to our conversations.

He got up to go start the cookies in the kitchen. I got up to watch.

"It's a delicate process," he said. He sounded like a professor giving a lecture in a college room. "You have to have a certain finesse to achieve this level of greatness," he said, making me laugh. The first batch was finally done and smelled amazing when he pulled them out and popped the next batch in. The peanut inside me eagerly desired a taste. They were some kind of sugar cookie with a jelly in the middle. Not normally the kind of thing I would want. I didn't have a sweet tooth much at all. I don't know if it was the pregnancy or if the cookies were actually mind blowing. But I could have eaten the entire pan right there. I was shoving another cookie in my face when I felt something wet in my pants.

"Can I use your bathroom?" I asked.

"Yeah of course, there's one downstairs and two upstairs. Take your pick," he said, still working. I went to the bathroom and was surprised to see I was bleeding. I came back out and told Giovanni.

"Like, a lot of blood? Or a spot of blood?" he asked.

"More than a spot less than a lot. I think I better call my doctor." I picked up the phone. When the nurse I spoke with told me to head to the E.R. I started to get a little nervous.

"Your doctor will meet you there, she's on call in the hospital today," the nurse said politely.

"Okay, thank you," I said, hanging up the phone. I told Giovanni what they said.

"Are you okay going there alone?" he asked calmly. "I'll have to call Hector. I'm sure he'll want to come, but I can call my dad and have him meet me there, he lives right by the hospital."

I called my dad on the way and asked me if he would meet me at the emergency room.

"Yeah I'll be there in 10 minutes," he said nervously. I called Hector next and told him my dad would be there with me, hoping that would keep him at work.

"I'm on my way."

"Babe, I'm sure everything is fine, don't worry about it, I can just keep you posted," I said praying he would stay at work.

"I'm on my way, I'll see you shortly," he said hanging up the phone. My dad was already there when I got there. I went in and told the lady at the desk what was happening, and the doctor was supposed to meet me here. They got me right in. They asked me what seemed like a hundred questions over and over while checking my vitals. Finally, they put me in a room hooked up to a monitor and waited for the doctor. Hector arrived, visibly concerned, and put on a display of love and affection since my dad was in the room. A male doctor walked in and introduced himself.

"Dr. Johnson has been called into a birthing room, so she won't be able to make it. She did have your file sent over and you'll need to schedule a follow up visit for next week with her." He was a tall thin man with black hair that had some silver showing through in spots.

"You have a negative blood type," he stated matter-of-factly.

"Yes," I said.

"I'm sure your doctor gave you a shot your first checkup?" he asked flipping through the folder.

"Yes, I have a card in my wallet with the date that it was administered," I said reaching for my bag. I pulled it out and showed I to him.

"Good. Well, the baby looks to be fine from what we can tell. There's still a heartbeat which means you aren't miscarrying," he explained. "Because you have a negative blood type your body will want to naturally dispose of the child if the fetus has a blood type that is different, especially if it's a positive blood type. That is the reason you have to get the RhoGAM shots throughout your pregnancy. It helps protect the fetus from your antibodies," he said.

"Okay, so I'm fine?" I asked, not really understanding what he was talking about.

"Well, the baby is fine for now, and you may experience some light bleeding off and on throughout your pregnancy, but you are high risk. You need to be mindful of how much rest you are getting and maybe even need to cut back on work," he said.

"Does she need to quit her job?" Hector asked.

"No, that's not necessary. But you do need to follow up with Dr. Johnson on Monday and let her do another ultrasound. Just to take a peek and know everything is fine. Other than that, you are free to go. The nurse will bring some paperwork for you to sign before you leave. Take it easy this weekend," he said.

"Oh, she will," Hector stood up and shook his hand.

"Do you have any questions?" the doctor said before leaving.

"No, I don't think so." I was just so relieved that I wasn't having a miscarriage that I couldn't think much further than that. My dad stood up and said that he was going to head home but he was glad I was okay.

"Hector, can I talk to you outside?" he said. Hector got up and followed along. I was wondering what that was about but quickly distracted myself. Wait, why was I so relieved that this wasn't a miscarriage? A week ago, I was crying my eyes out and praying it wasn't real. Am I already attached to this kid? When did that happen? All I knew was I wanted to keep this baby alive and growing. My mama bear instincts were developing rapidly.

Hector took me home. He had been dropped off at the hospital, so he insisted on driving me. I expected him to hover over me all weekend. He did for the rest of the day. But then he invited all his bros to hang out at our house instead of going to the clubhouse Saturday night. I didn't feel like socializing, so I used the baby as an excuse to stay in my room and watch movies. They all stayed downstairs drinking and playing pool. Hector would check on me every so often, seeming more and more intoxicated each time he checked on me. I was grateful for being able to stay away from it all. I didn't want to be around anyone. Eventually I drifted off to a deep sleep. When I opened my eyes, it was already morning. I rolled over and noticed Hector wasn't in bed. I got up and went to the bathroom. To my relief the bleeding had already stopped. I brushed my teeth and went to find Hector to report the news. I was surprised to see he and two others were still downstairs listening to music. They were standing outside with the door opened smoking.

"Wow, stayed up all night again?" I said. They turned to look at me. Hector, just realizing that it was already morning, looked startled and nervous.

"Oh, hey babe, how are you feeling?" he came inside to give me a kiss. The smell of him in my face made me want to vomit. I turned my head letting him kiss my cheek and then backed away from him.

"Well, the bleeding stopped! But I'm pretty hungry," I said rubbing my tummy.

"Do you want some eggs or something?" he asked.

"I want Greek food." Everyone laughed.

"Here come the cravings!" one of them yelled from outside.

"The mall opens in an hour and you're taking me to my favorite Greek place. Sorry to break up the party boys, but Hector needs to get ready to go, you don't have to go home but you can't stay here," I said lightly.

"Say goodbye to your friends and get rid of all this garbage please, I'm going to take a shower." I went to kiss Hector on the cheek and had to hold my breath. How could he not smell himself? I was irritated that he was obviously down here doing coke and partying all night in my house, but too hungry to fight about it.

When we got to the restaurant, he didn't even order food. He was too high to eat. I ordered all the things I wanted and waited happily for my food. Hector hadn't said anything the whole time and I noticed he looked like he was upset. He was staring at his hands in his lap and his lip started to quiver.

"What's wrong?" I asked. He just shook his head and tears started to fall out of his eyes.

"Why are you crying?" He just shook his head again not wanting to respond.

"Look at me," I commanded. He looked up from his hands with tears streaming down his face.

"What the hell is wrong with you?" I asked.

"I'm scared," he said barely loud enough for me to hear him.

"Scared of what? The bleeding stopped." He shook his head and looked back down at his hands.

"No, I'm scared you're going to leave me," he said, crying harder. He started to breathe heavily and panic. "I don't want you to leave me, but I know I'm a piece of shit," he said. I was getting annoyed by the whole pathetic display. I knew none of this was authentic. He was just too high and getting himself all worked up. "I'm always worried about it," he said. I handed him a napkin.

"Wipe your face please. We are in a public place and now is not the time for you to be having a meltdown. The doctor wants me to take it easy this weekend and you are stressing me out. Sit up, take some deep breaths, and stop fucking crying," I growled at him. I had zero sympathy for this little scene. My patience had worn thin and I was ready to leave him there. "You're acting like a child right now. It's not at all cute. Stop fucking crying," I said harshly. Normally something like this would pull at my heart strings and make me feel sorry for him. But for some reason, it had the opposite effect on me now. I had bigger things to worry about then patting him on the butt when he turned into a crying baby. I was more concerned with the new baby growing inside me.

The waiter brought me my appetizer and set it down on the table. "Thank you!" I said excitedly. "Could we possibly get some more napkins when you get a chance?" I asked politely.

"Of course, anything else?" he asked looking over at Hector, realizing he was crying.

"No, we're fine, thank you." He smiled politely and walked away.

"Can you please stop?" I asked Hector. He just cried harder. "You are embarrassing me, if you can't stop go wait in the fucking car please," I barked at him, completely annoyed. He got up and handed me his wallet.

"I'm sorry babe," he said, sobbing.

"Go away. I'll be out when I'm done," I said snatching his wallet. "I'll be driving us home," I said looking up at him. He nodded while he wept and walked out with his head hanging. *If he thinks I'm going to console him every time he gets high and emotional, he's got me all wrong*, I thought to myself. I hated him when he was high. I hated when he lied, I hated how he treated me. But mostly I hated the thought of my innocent child having to live like this. It wasn't fair; I wouldn't allow it. He made so many promises but never held up his end of the bargain. I couldn't keep telling myself he would change. He hadn't hit me since we found out I was pregnant. So that was something I told myself in his defense. Finally, my food came, and I was happy to have it all to myself. I took my time eating and asked for a box for what was left. When I got out to the car Hector was lying down in the passenger seat passed out. I drove him home in silence with the windows cracked enough to not smell him.

The next day I followed up with my OBGYN and was told everything looked normal. She did remind me that I was considered high risk and to try and avoid stress if I could. I laughed when she said that. I was almost always stressed. I was happy to hear that the baby was still doing well, and since the bleeding had stopped already, she didn't see the need to order another ultrasound yet. Relieved, I left and went back home to plan the rest of my week since I was cleared to work. I had a touch up job in Atlanta that Friday. I got done around 11 a.m. and was close to Bessie's job, so I called her to see if I could stop by. She said she was working on her last dog, so once she got done then maybe we could go do lunch. I told her I would be there shortly. She was a dog groomer, so her job was either laid back or completely overwhelming. I walked in and went up the hair-covered stairs to her station. She was working on a little dog, and in the corner of the same room Sergio was working on another dog. It was good to see him, and he gave me a happy smile and asked how I was. I hadn't seen him or talked to him since he and Juan moved out of my apartment. He always worked with Bessie, that's how I originally met him and Juan. It was nice to see him.

I was standing there watching Bessie groom the dog she had on her table talking when suddenly I felt a gush of fluid. It was almost like I urinated on myself, but I couldn't control it or make it stop.

"Oh my god," I said looking down at my wet pants.

"What's happening?" I yelled. Bessie looked over at me and said

"Okay calm down, follow me to the bathroom," she got up and Sergio ran over to her table to be with the dog she was working on since he was already done. She took me downstairs to the bathroom and gave me a pad.

"Let me go see if I can get someone to take this dog and I'll take you to the hospital," she said.

"I need to call my doctor first." I sat on the toilet. The fluid coming out of me wasn't just blood. It was like a watered-down bloody mixture. But the amount that kept coming was what worried me. I picked up the phone and called my OBGYN. I explained what was going on and what had already happened the week before and asked if I should go to the emergency room again.

"Hold on a minute; let me go ask your doctor," the woman said. She put me on hold, and two minutes later a different woman picked up. She was a nurse.

"Can you describe the fluid to me sweetie? How much is coming out and if it's slowed down at all." I went through my description again.

"Can you come in now?" she asked.

"I'm in Atlanta, but I could be there in 40 minutes. Is that okay or should I just go to the hospital near where I am?" I asked shaking nervously.

"No, we want you here if you can come now," she said, trying to sound calm.

"I'm on my way," I said, hanging up.

I came out of the bathroom and told Bessie I was leaving. I explained that they wanted me to go there instead of the hospital, but I had to go now. She understood and told me to let her know as soon as I knew anything because she couldn't leave yet. When I got in the car, I picked up the phone and called Hector. As soon as he answered the phone I started crying.

"What's wrong?"

I tried to tell him what was going on, but I was sobbing so hard he couldn't understand me.

"Babe, please calm down, take a deep breath and tell me what's going on." I told him what was going on.

"Okay, I am at a customer's house in Atlanta, but I will be there as soon as I can. I promise." I told him that was fine and got off the phone. Since my pants were wet and I didn't want to walk in there looking like this I stopped at home to change. I was a complete mess and it was still coming out but had slowed down extensively. I got back in the car and was at the OBGYN office in less than five minutes.

I walked in and told the lady who I was and what was happening. She stood up.

"Yes, honey, we've been waiting for you, go over to the door and I'll let you right in." I did as she instructed and followed her straight back to an exam room. The nurse that I had spoken on the phone with came in and gave me a gown to put on.

"The doctor needs to examine you vaginally and she may order an ultrasound," she said calmly. She left the room so I could change but she and the doctor were back very quickly. The doctor asked me to lay back and put my feet up. She pulled out the handheld heart monitor while the nurse applied some jelly to my stomach. She put it on and started gliding it around. Almost immediately, we heard the heartbeat.

"We have a heartbeat," the doctor said, smiling. I started weeping. "So, let's see if we can figure out what is going on," she said, going to sit in her stool. During the examination she asked me several questions and I went over everything with her again.

"I stopped to change my pants on the way over, they were soaked through completely," I said. She got up and said everything looked fine, but she wanted an ultrasound done immediately.

"There is still some light bleeding, but nothing that would normally alarm me. But we need to make sure your water didn't break, and you don't have a tear or leak. Let me go see how backed up the ultrasound room is. You just sit tight," she said.

"Thank you," I said, still worried that something serious could still be wrong. A few minutes later the nurse came back in and told me it would be about 20 minutes before they could get me in for the ultrasound.

"Go ahead and get dressed. Also, there is a man here that wants to come back. I believe his name is Hector. Is that okay?" she asked gently.

"Yes, that's fine, he's my boyfriend." I said, relieved that he was there.

"I'll bring him back." When he came in the room, I was putting on my shoes. He rushed over to me and kissed me.

"What's happening? Are you okay?" he asked, concerned.

"So far yes, and they found a heartbeat, so the baby is still alive," I said tearing up again.

"Thank God!" The nurse came to get us and took us back to get the ultrasound. Seeing our little peanut on that screen made me so happy and so emotional.

"So, what's wrong? Is the baby okay?" Hector asked anxiously.

"Well, we are going to look at every angle and then I'll consult with the doctor and she will answer your questions," she said politely. She seemed to be taking images of everything. She was very thorough. Finally, she got up and ripped the printed images off.

"I will be back with the doctor so she can go over everything with you," she said, leaving the room. I cleaned off the jelly on my stomach and sat up.

"Why the fuck aren't they telling us anything?" Hector asked, getting irritated.

"Calm down, she has to wait for the doctor." The two women finally came back in and told us that everything looked fine. There didn't appear to be any obstructions, or tears or leaks that they could find, so they couldn't explain the rush of fluid. But the doctor told me I was going to have to quit working.

"Is she on bed rest?" Hector asked.

"No, but she doesn't need to be exerting herself at all. At this point she is very high risk and I am referring you to a specialist for closer care," she said.

"So, when do I have to quit working?" I asked.

"Today, and you need to try and avoid any stress as well," she said.

Hector walked me to my car and told me to follow him home.

"I'm buying a car, so I need you to take me, but we have to drop the van off at home first," he said.

"Wait, what? You're buying a car today? Didn't you just hear what they said? I'm supposed to go home and get some rest," I said, irritated.

"Yeah, and you will, after you take me to buy this car. I'm not arguing about it. Do what I asked you to do," he said, opening my car door. I did as he asked and followed him home. I went inside to use the bathroom and clean myself up a little.

"Come on, the guy's waiting for me and I don't want to miss out," Hector yelled up the stairs.

I came down irritated with him and got in the passenger side of my car since he was already in the driver's seat. We drove 10 minutes down the road and went into this small buy here pay here office.

"Can I just drop you off? I really want to go lay down."

"No, you can come in and wait until I tell you that you can leave," he said getting out of the car. I felt like he was being ridiculously selfish. I followed him in the building and sat down while he discussed the purchase with the man he had apparently been dealing with all day. About 30 minutes went by and he asked if we wanted to test drive it. I personally didn't care; I just wanted to go home and lay down. But of course, Hector made me go. He decided he liked it and wrote him a check on the spot.

"Can I please go home now? I am exhausted."

"Yeah, I'll follow you," he said. We finally got home, and I went straight up to the bedroom. I just wanted to lie down. Hector came in after he got off the phone with someone.

"So," he said standing at the doorway. "Since you have to lay here and rest, I'm going to go out. I want to show off my new car." It was Friday afternoon; I knew why he wanted to leave. It didn't have much to do with the car.

"Whatever, that's fine." He went to the bathroom and turned on the shower.

"I don't know how late I'll be, so don't wait up," he yelled as he threw his clothes on the floor. When he got in the shower, I was curious about who he was so eager to go see, so I got up and unlocked his phone. He was always changing the password, but I happened to glance over while he was putting it in when he was intoxicated so he didn't know I knew how to get into it. I pulled up the call log to see who he had just spoken to. It was Weasel, my ex boyfriends' "friend" who seemed to be around way more than I wanted him to be. I knew he was a major cokehead and a terrible influence on Hector. I didn't want to say anything to him, or he would know I got into his phone. Not wanting to discover anything else, I put the phone down and went back to bed. When he came out, he shaved, got dressed, and even put on cologne.

"Who are you getting all dressed up for?" I asked, annoyed. He never put in any effort to look or smell good for me anymore.

"Nobody, I just feel good and want to look good." He gave me a kiss and told me he would check in at some point. When he left, I called my mom. I told her what had happened throughout the day and what the doctor had said. I told her about having to go with Hector to buy a car as I left the doctor's office and that he was already gone for the night. It was still early, not even 7 o'clock. Christmas was right around the corner, but, luckily, I had already gotten done Christmas shopping, since I was no longer allowed to work. My mom and stepdad were coming next week to stay with us for Christmas. So, I was excited to see them and have someone here for me.

At around 4 a.m. I was woken up by the sound of the garage door opening beneath me. After it closed, I was expecting Hector to appear, but he never did. I got up and went out to see where he was and none of the lights were on. I started to go down the stairs and saw a light on underneath the door to the little office we never used. I tried to open it and it was locked.

"What are you doing?" I asked, knocking on the door. He opened the door and was pulling his pants up. He was fumbling with his phone.

"What the fuck are you doing down here? Are you having phone sex with some bitch?"

He laughed uncomfortably and said, "No, nothing like that I swear, I was just horny and didn't want to bother you since you're bleeding, and I didn't want to hurt the baby." I could smell the cocaine seeping out of him again.

"So, you're hiding down here to jack your dick?"

"Yeah basically," he laughed uncomfortably.

"Then why were you on the phone?" He opened his phone to show me, it was a porn website.

"See I'm just masturbating; I'm not talking to anyone." I turned around and went back upstairs. By the time I was able to fall asleep again I woke up to him crawling into be with me.

He wrapped his arm around me and placed his erection against my ass.

"I can't come," he whispered.

"Then stop doing so much coke," I said, annoyed that he was bothering me again.

"Will you suck my dick?"

"Are you fucking kidding me? You told me you would stop doing this shit, and now you want me to reward your disgusting behavior with a blow job? Get off me," I said, pushing his hand away. He let out a sigh and started pulling at himself again shaking the whole bed. Then he was back on me.

"I need to come," he growled in my ear.

"That's not something I'll be helping you with. Leave me alone." He sat up on his knees and pulled my ass towards him moving my panties to the side. I tried to roll over, but he lay on top of me pinning me down.

"What the fuck are you doing? I'm still bleeding you aren't doing this! I could lose the baby!" I wiggled and struggled but it got me nowhere.

"Relax, I'm not touching your pussy," he said, spitting his fingers and rubbing in on my ass.

"Oh, hell no!" I yelled bucking underneath him.

"I said relax. Damn, you're only going to make this worse for yourself," he said, spitting on his fingers again. "Relax, trust me it won't take long," he said, poking at me with his erection. I was *not* ready for this, nor did I want any of this.

"Please stop!"

"Shhhh I need this," he said trying to put himself inside me.

"Stop it, that hurts!"

He pushed himself up laying all his weight into the one hand he had me pinned down with. He used his other hand to line himself up better and tried to enter me. I started to cry, I knew he wouldn't stop, I knew the more I fought the worse it would be. I just went numb and checked out of my body. I felt him enter me more forcefully than I thought he would. It *really* hurt. I started sobbing into the pillow begging for it to end. I tried to leave my body again, but the pain wouldn't let me. I could feel my ass tearing open with every stroke.

"Are you crying?" he asked, not stopping what he was doing. He loosened his grip on me and asked me again.

"Just get it over with," I cried into the pillow. He stopped what he was doing and pulled himself out of me.

"Are you done?" I asked, lifting my head from the pillow. He let go of me and rolled on his back. Before he could touch me again, I got up and ran to the bathroom. I closed and locked both doors behind me and sat on the toilet. I was crying and I couldn't control it. I got up and went into the shower, both to clean myself up and mask the sound of my sobs. It took a while for me to calm myself down.

Finally, I calmed down enough. I went back out to the bed and laid down quietly hoping he was asleep.

"Why did you do that?" he said in an unfamiliar tone.

"Do what?" I asked cautiously.

"Why did you make me feel like I was raping you?"

"You were babe, I begged you to stop."

"It's not possible to rape you. You belong to me; I can do whatever I want with you. But don't ever try to make me feel bad about it again." He rolled over with his back facing me signifying the end of the conversation. I could see the faint light of the sun trying to come up and decided I didn't want to be next to him anymore. I grabbed my phone and walked out closing the door. I went to the kitchen and fed Gizmo. I lost all the strength I had, and my knees buckled so I sat on the floor in the kitchen with my back against my sink base cabinet. I pulled my knees up to my chest and started to cry again. I started to ask God how I could get out of this. I felt like a caged animal trapped in a prison. I didn't want to raise a baby with him. I didn't want to be with him. But how was I supposed to do anything now? I couldn't work, so I had to depend on him to provide for me until I could work again. Eventually I calmed down, got up and went into the living room. I was grateful that he would probably be sleeping all day.

CHAPTER TWENTY-TWO

Okay, Now What?

It was the week of Christmas, and I was excited to see my family. My mother and stepdad arrived on Christmas Eve. We helped them bring things in and get settled. My stepdad always seems to have errands to run, so shortly after he got there, he left to go do what he needed to do. My mom and I talked on the couch for a little while she sipped tea. Hector and one of his longtime friends showed up, and my mom decided to go lay down for a while. She has health issues, so it wasn't uncommon for her to be tired after traveling. We were sitting in the living room talking and his friend asked me how I was feeling. We started talking about the pregnancy and how I was officially pulled from work.

"Oh man that sucks, good thing your man has a company and can afford to take care of you!" he said, pushing Hector's knee.

"Yeah, I'll take care of the house, but she's going to have to get rid of her car," he said laughing uncomfortably.

"What?" I asked surprised. This was the first time he mentioned anything like this about the car, so I was a surprised. Gia had put the car I had in her name while I went through bankruptcy a year ago. I couldn't just stop paying on it, or she would get screwed.

"What are you talking about? I can't get rid of my car; Gia's credit will be ruined," I said.

"Yeah, fuck that fat bitch, I'll buy you a new car," he said.

"That doesn't make any sense." He stood up and started yelling. "I'm not doing anything to help that fat whore! She isn't your fucking friend! It's in her name; let her pay for it. I'm not paying a fucking dime on that car and that's final!" he said.

Embarrassed that this was happening in front of someone I barely knew, and loud enough that I was certain my mother could hear, I said, "We can talk about this later. You need to calm down."

"No, there's nothing to talk about. It's done. Drop the car off to Gia and tell her fuck you and goodbye," he said still pacing.

"I am *not* doing that. I will get a job somewhere else part time if I have to. It's Christmas eve, why are you picking a fight right now?"

"I'm not fighting, I'm just telling you how it is." He said picking up his phone from the end table.

"Fuck this, I'm out of here, come on," he said to his friend. They walked down the stairs together and I heard the garage door open. I listened as the car doors closed and the garage door started to go down. I sat there, shocked.

I started crying and picked up the phone to call Gia. I told her everything he just said and that I didn't know what I was going to do but I wouldn't let him do this to us.

"I swear to God, Savannah, if you fuck me over on this car, I will never speak to you again," she said.

"Really? I just told you I would get it paid no matter what." I said defensively. I didn't call for her to make me even more upset. I just wanted a friend to vent to.

"I'm just saying, you'd better figure it out!" She said loudly.

"I'll figure out something, I just have to get it cleared with my doctor. She told me I needed to be resting and free of stress or I could lose the baby. So far I haven't been able to do either," I said.

"That's because you got pregnant by an idiot," she snapped.

"I'll talk to you later," I said, hanging up the phone and feeling worse than before I called her.

"Are you okay?" I heard my mom ask softly. I looked up and she was standing in the hallway cautiously peeking into the living room.

"I heard everything," she said as she came all the way into the living room.

"I don't know what I'm going to do, Mom," I said, starting to cry. I've never had to rely on anyone before, so that was a very uncomfortable feeling in itself. But fighting with Hector and Gia being a total ass to me just had me feeling even worse. I sat there and talked to my mom about all of it for hours. Finally, my stepdad came back and asked what was going on. We caught him up on the situation, and he asked where Hector was.

"I don't know."

I looked at the time and it was already 9 p.m. I decided to text him and see if he planned on coming home. My whole family was coming over the next morning to open gifts for Christmas, so I expected him to be there. He finally texted me back and told me he was at his dad's house. Oh great, I thought. He's probably shit-faced.

"Why can't you at least *try* to not do this shit when my family is here? You start a fight with me and run off *every* weekend lately so you can get high. Tomorrow is Christmas! Get your ass home!" I messaged him.

"I know, I'm sorry, I won't be out late."

I finally gave up on waiting for him and went to bed about 11 o'clock. He crept in about 3 o'clock in the morning smelling of his poison. I was not happy, but I didn't want to start a fight. It was Christmas and I needed to get through this with a happy appearance. I didn't want my family to have a bad time.

When I got up in the morning, my mother was already in the kitchen petting Gizmo while she waited for her tea water to boil.

"Merry Christmas!" she said warmly and gave me a big hug.

"Merry Christmas," I said back. "Is Hector home? I didn't hear him come in last night," she said.

"Yeah, he didn't stroll in until about 3 a.m."

"Wow, that's late. Does he do that a lot?"

"More and more as of late."

"Is he just trying to get it all out of his system before the baby arrives?" she asked, trying to find an answer.

"I hope so," I said not wanting to talk about it any further.

"What time is everyone coming over?" I asked.

"I don't know. I haven't heard from anyone yet," she said, taking the screaming tea kettle off the stove.

"I'll text dad," I said grabbing my phone. Everyone came over by 9 a.m.: my dad, my brother and his girlfriend and her two children. Then my nephew's mom dropped him off so he could open gifts with us as well. One of the kids passed out all the gifts to everyone. I was sitting on the couch next to Hector when a very heavy gift was dropped into my lap. It wasn't wrapped with the wrapping paper we had, but it said it was from Hector.

"Who wrapped this?" I asked, always suspicious of him.

"I did," he said.

"Where did you get the wrapping paper?"

He paused.

"The dollar store," he said, grinning.

"Yeah, whatever," I said, getting the wrapping off.

"She's gonna need a knife for this one. Do you have a knife?" he asked my brother while nervously adjusting on the couch. He moved a box in front of him and started fidgeting.

"Why are you nervous?" I asked.

"I'm not nervous," he laughed uncomfortably.

"I just want to see if you like it." I cut the box open and saw packing popcorn. I scooped it aside and saw something dark grey. I pulled it out.

"What is this?"

My nephew yelled, "It's coal!"

While everyone joked about me getting a lump of coal for Christmas, I asked, "Are you serious?"

"You have to open it up," he said grinning.

"How do I do that?" I turned it over and there was a little hidden door. I opened it and a little wad of paper fell out with something in it.

"Oh, there's a little present!" I said still not understanding what all this was about. I opened the waded-up paper and there was a huge gaudy ring. *Oh no*, I thought, *he's not doing this right now is he?* I read the note that said, "Do you still want to marry my pain in the ass?"

"Oh my God," I said out loud.

"Are you serious?" I asked, stunned.

"Yeah," he said, waiting for my answer.

"Then get down on your knee," I said still not believing this was an actual proposal.

"Oh fuck, are you kidding me?" he laughed.

"No, you need to ask me," I said.

My mom yelled happily from somewhere in the background "We want to hear it!"

"Do you still want to marry me?" he asked.

"Yes," I said, knowing there was no other way to move through this situation without starting world war three.

"Good," he said relieved. I handed the ring to him and told him to put it on.

"Aww it fits babe, is this real?" I asked not believing the ring I was looking at was an engagement ring. It looked more like gaudy costume jewelry to me. It was 3.5 carats of clusters of diamonds.

"No, it's fucking fake," he said sarcastically.

"Okay one more kiss," my dad said.

We kissed for the camera and Hector said, "You didn't even read the note, did you?"

"Yes, I did," I said.

"Will you still marry me? I'm a pain in the ass," I said not wording it exactly how it was written. Everyone laughed and I held up the note to the camera my dad was recording this on.

"She's so shocked," my mom said, laughing.

"Yeah, I don't even know how to behave right now," I said nervously.

"Now do you see why I was so anxious yesterday?" Hector said.

"I see. All that shit you be talking," I said locking eyes with him while he grinned.

"Okay," I said, nodding.

We finished up gift time and my brother and dad packed up all the kids and their gifts to take them back home. They were all coming back later for Christmas dinner. Hector went to go sleep off his hangover and I sat in the living room with my mom.

"Are you excited?" she asked me.

"Um, yeah I was just really not expecting this. I mean you heard our fight yesterday, and then he didn't come home until this morning. It just feels like a weird time to get engaged," I said honestly.

"Yeah, and we all knew he was going to do it. He's been planning it for weeks."

Confused, I asked, "Are you serious?"

"Oh yeah, he went to your father and brother and asked for their blessing and everything. He showed them the ring, so he already had it," she said, sipping her tea. "I'm not going to lie; his behavior yesterday was confusing. But I think he really loves you and is just scared. There's a lot going on right now. You're expecting your first child, and you can't work so he has to provide for you. Maybe he's just feeling overwhelmed," she said.

"Yeah maybe, I'm overwhelmed too," I said. I wanted to tell her everything. I wanted to tell her that I would never marry this monster and why. But I couldn't. I just had to roll with the punches. We still had to get through Christmas dinner.

My stepdad had to go back to Florida after Christmas, but my mom stayed behind to spend time with my nephew. She was going to be keeping him at my house until he had to go back to school. On New Year's Eve, he decided he was going to some big party with his club. I had no interest in going whatsoever, but I was a little irritated that he didn't want to spend the holiday with me, so he decided to take me to dinner before he went out. He invited his cousin Jose and his wife and kids, and we all met at the local place we went to for crab legs. He decided he wanted to announce our pregnancy on social media finally. With the help of Frankie and Jose, we wrote up two signs. Mine said something clever like "28 more weeks sober," and his said "Drinking for two!" We put a baby bottle full of milk between us and took a few pictures.

It was a big hit for our social media sites. So, announcing it was fun. When we got home, we showed my mom the post and how much response we were getting. Somehow, she delicately brought up the car situation. It started to be an argument, but eventually Hector agreed to pay the upcoming bill in January.

"That's it; don't ever bring it up to me again. I'd rather just buy you another car than benefit that fat bitch in anyway," he said.

Not wanting to argue in front of my mother I simply responded, "Fine babe, thank you."

It was still early for New Year's Eve, about 9 o'clock. But after the long talk with my mother, he was eager to leave.

"Don't wait up," he yelled over his shoulder on his way down the stairs.

"I never do," I yelled back.

"You don't want to go out with him?" my mom asked.

"No, he's going to the clubhouse. That's the last place I want to be right now. The cigarette smoke makes me nauseous." Plus, I knew he would be high in less than an hour and most likely not want to come home until the sun was coming up. But I couldn't tell her that.

I sat and watched the countdown live from New York with my mom. We were even able to see some fireworks going off from the neighbors. It was nice and peaceful.

My mom said to me at one point, "I'm worried about you stressing out over the car, and I hate how Hector is behaving about it. He doesn't seem to understand how important it is for you to be low stress right now. You could lose the baby."

Nodding my head in agreement, I said, "Yeah, he doesn't seem to see that as a priority. But I'll make something happen," I assured her.

"I wish I had the money to pay for it every month. I would do it," she said genuinely.

"I know you would, Mom." We finally went to bed sometime around 12:30 a.m., and I passed right out. I expected Hector to come home and wake me up at some point, but when I woke up the next morning he was still out. I came out of the room and my mom was already in the kitchen making breakfast for my nephew.

"Good morning," she said warmly.

"Good morning, what time is it?" I asked.

"It's 8 o'clock. What time did Hector get home? I didn't hear him," she asked casually.

"He isn't home," I answered flatly.

"Oh wow, I hope everything is okay," she answered, concerned.

"I'm sure he's fine." I went to check my phone and see if he left me any messages. Nothing; not a word. I picked up the phone and called him. It went straight to voicemail.

"Are you fucking kidding me? You go off on a drug binge and go missing a week after you ask me to marry you, *while* my mother is staying with us! Call me back," I said angrily to his voicemail box. I went out to the living room and sat on the couch.

"Everything okay?" my mother asked putting a plate in front of my nephew.

"I don't know, his phone is off or dead. I left him a message," I said, irritated.

"Are you hungry?" she asked.

"No not right now, thank you though." I got on Facebook and saw a video one of his friends posted at the clubhouse of everyone passed out in chairs and couches. Hector was amongst the bodies.

"I found him," I said, showing my mother.

"Wow," she said unimpressed. "I hope he gets his shit together soon; this isn't father behavior. Hell, this isn't even husband behavior," she said shaking her head.

Finally, sometime in the afternoon we heard the garage door open. Seeing the pissed off look on my face, my mom said to my nephew, "Let's go play in the bedroom with your new toys," and ushered him down the hall quickly. When Hector walked in the house, I could smell him before I saw him.

"Look who found his way home."

"Before you start, I wasn't doing anything wrong. I passed out at the club-house and my phone was dead when I woke up," he said reaching to top of the stairs.

"I know; I saw a video of it on Facebook."

"I'm sorry," he said pitifully.

"I don't know if you ever get tired of saying that, but I am beyond tired of hearing it," I said, rubbing my temples. I could feel a migraine coming on.

"Can we go in the bedroom and talk please?"

"No, I have nothing to say to you anymore."

"Babe, I know you're mad, come to the bedroom please," he said walking around the couch to come towards me.

"Don't," I said, putting my hand up. "I know what you were doing all night, I can smell you from here. Not only am I disgusted, but I'm com-pletely embarrassed. Go sleep it off, we'll talk later," I said, getting up from the couch and walking away from him toward the kitchen. He didn't say anything else; I heard my bedroom door close.

CHAPTER TWENTY-THREE

Here for the Sex

I decided that I wanted to do a gender reveal party. When we went for the ultrasound, the lady put the images in a sealed envelope, and I went straight to the bakery to order the cake. The plan was to cut open the cake to reveal either blue or pink cake telling us what we were having. Everyone wanted to be involved. We even planned to go live on Facebook so everyone who lived out of town could share the moment with us. Bessie and I went to Party City and got everything we needed. The plan was to do the party on the last Saturday in January, since another girlfriend of mine was doing one the Saturday before. We got blue and pink everything, from napkins and plates to food and beverage choices. We were so excited for it.

We attended my friend's party first. She was the one who had worked for Hector in his office when Titi quit and that tramp started working there. Even though she quit shortly after because she got pregnant a week after I did, she still invited everyone. It was good to see Titi, she and Hector had worked out their issues enough for her to come back to work for him. But, like me and everyone else, she wasn't impressed with the tramp. Titi brought her husband, so he texted Hector to come up there so he wouldn't be alone. Us girls were standing around the cake talking when the door opened and Hector walked in, with his arm wrapped around the tramp.

"Why did you invite *her*?" Titi asked.

"I was just trying to be nice; I didn't think she would actually come," said my friend.

"Did she come with Hector?" Titi asked.

"She better not have," I said. An older Spanish woman walked in behind her. They all walked over to where we were standing, and she said hello.

"Did you come with her?" I whispered to Hector.

"What? No, don't start your shit," he said walking away and shaking his head in annoyance.

I took a deep breath and let it go. I knew my hormones were raging so I didn't want to overreact and cause drama at my friend's party. We went outside to watch the happy pregnant couple find out what they were having. They popped a balloon and blue confetti poured out. We all clapped and cheered and celebrated. Hector came over to me and said he and his uncle were going to leave. I saw his uncle discussing something with Titi, she seemed irritated.

"Where are you going?"

"Out," he said rudely. I noticed the tramp standing there watching, she could hear everything so of course he was going to be a dick to me to put on a show for her.

"Out where?"

"What does it matter? I don't need your fucking permission," he said looking at the tramp who looked away uncomfortably.

"Okay, your little whore is gone, nobody to show out for anymore. So, where are you going?" I asked again, annoyed.

"We're going out for some beers, it's no big deal," he said, trying to get his uncles attention.

"Just the two of you? It's only 3 o'clock in the afternoon."

"Not that it's any of your fucking business, but we're going to meet up with Weasel. Don't wait up," he said, turning to walk off. I grabbed his arm.

"Why are you talking to me like this?"

"Because I know you have something slick to say about me hanging out with Weasel, and I don't want to hear it. He's my friend."

I laughed, "Oh honey, he's nobody's friend. You're only saying that because he likes to do coke with you and talk shit about my ex. He's a fuckboy," I said letting go of his arm. "You keep choosing him and partying over me and I'll be leaving soon, y'all can have each other."

"See that's why I don't tell you shit, because you got a smart mouth."

"I have a real mouth," I shot back at him. "When the fuck are you going to quit this shit? Do you think I'll actually stick around and raise my kid like this? You've lost your fucking mind if you think that's the case. You're digging your own grave here, buddy. I'm about fucking *done*."

I went to go inside when he grabbed my arm and pulled me close to him whispering in my ear "*You* don't tell *me* what to do. Your ass is broke and jobless and can't work right now so you ain't going nowhere. Put on a smile, and walk the fuck away," he said, squeezing the back of my arm as hard as he could. "I will be home when I fucking feel like it, and there's nothing you are going to do about it." He let me go and walked off towards his uncle. I felt like I was about to cry. *Why is he being such a dumb ass?* He was obviously never going to change; he just kept getting worse. But he was right; where was I going to go? I had no money.

When I got home, to my surprise, Hector was there. He and his uncle were drinking beers. I could tell they were antsy and Hector didn't want me there.

"I thought you guys were going out," I said coming up the stairs.

"Yes ma'am we are, we're just waiting on his friend to be off work," his uncle said standing up to give me a hug. "That bitch is *not* his friend. He's a junky fucking loser," I said walking casually into the kitchen.

"I told you to watch your fucking mouth!" Hector yelled from the living room. "I'm not gonna let you talk about my friends like that."

I laughed "Why? That's how you talk about *all* of my friends!" I yelled. "Fat bitch, fat whore, fat slut, dirty cunt: those are the words you use to describe my two BEST friends on a daily basis," I said, walking into the living room with my water.

"If you can do it, I can do it." I could see the fury in his eyes.

"Fuck this, let's just go. We don't have to listen to this stupid bitch," Hector said.

"Hey, don't call her that," his uncle said grabbing his beer. "She's the mother of your child, she's hormonal, just let it go."

Hector looked at me like he wanted to punch me in the face, so I blew him a kiss.

"Bye babe, have fun!" I said, pissing him off even more.

"Bye miss lady," his uncle said shaking his head and grinning.

I sat on the couch, relieved that I most likely wouldn't have to see Hector the rest of the weekend. I messaged Bessie to see if she was coming over and she was. I realized I hadn't spoken to Giovanni since the Christmas engagement, so I went to message him. I could tell his tone was different while we were talking, so I got curious and looked at his profile. He had removed me from his friends list on Facebook.

"Oh God, he's probably pissed," I said out loud. I felt like I had to explain to him that I had no intention on marrying this monster. I just didn't know what to do in the moment. He seemed to loosen up a little throughout our conversation. I asked if I could come by and see Halo, but really, I just wanted to come talk to him. For some reason I didn't want him thinking bad of me. He said I could come anytime I wanted, and I knew Hector would probably not come home tonight, so he would either be missing all weekend, or sleeping all day, so I told him I would come over after church on Sunday.

When Bessie got there, I told her about how Hector had spoken to me and that he and his uncle were gone. She rolled her eyes and shook her head.

"He's such a fucking infant," she said with disgust.

"I am *so* fucking miserable," I said, tearing up.

"Of course, you are! I've never met such a douchebag in my life! Do you want to move in with me? I'm here now; he's gone; let's pack up what you need and just fucking *go!*" she begged. "It's only a matter of time before he puts his hands on you again."

"I can't leave right now, I have the gender reveal next Saturday, it's all set up. I already paid for the cake," I said weakly.

"So, we can just do it at my apartment," she said.

"Where am I going to stay in your apartment? On the couch? And then what? What happens when I give birth?" I asked.

"We'll figure it all out, I just want you out of here!" she said.

"I know, I just have to wait for the right time," I said.

"He's never going to let you leave once that baby is here," she said flatly.

"You think it's bad now? Assholes like him get even worse once they have a kid in the picture. He'll just use it to control you more." She had a point.

Maybe it would be easier to get out if I left before the baby was born. But what was I going to do to support myself?

The next day I got up and Bessie and I went to church as usual. She had to go to her parents' afterwards, and I went straight to Giovanni's house. Hector hadn't come home yet, and I hadn't bothered to try to reach him; I just wanted to be somewhere far away from him. I was happy to see Giovanni; I could tell there was still an uncomfortable awkwardness in the room. But he busted out his bottle of Fireball so I knew he would loosen up soon.

"So, you took me off Facebook?" I laughed uncomfortably.

"Yeah, I saw that video on Christmas and raged," he said waving his hand in the air while he paced back and forth.

"I don't know what that even means," I laughed.

"That means I was ready to throw my computer out the window," he laughed still pacing.

"I get it," I said.

"No, you don't. I drug Gabriel out of his room to watch it while I cussed you out, then I went next door and made Leah come watch it. I was livid," he said honestly.

"I understand, I didn't expect that at all. l was completely shocked. I won't marry him, I can't," I said, looking down at the ridiculously gawdy ring on my finger.

"Well that's a relief," Giovanni said. I caught him up on everything that had been going on within my life. I told him that Bessie offered me refuge and I was actually considering it since I was so desperate to leave now before I had the baby.

"Gia wouldn't stop sending me job applications and openings, so I applied to be an Uber driver. I think I should be able to do that, and I need to get her off my ass about the car. She stresses me out as much as Hector does," I said, defeated.

"Well that's not cool. The goal is for you to be *less* stressed," he said, slamming a shot of Fireball.

"Yeah, it just seems to get worse. Ever since the doctor told me I couldn't work, Hector has changed. He's so mean to me all the time. I feel like I'm walking on eggshells at home when he's there. But then my hormones get the best of me from time to time and I find myself saying really hateful things to him," I said.

"Well, you're under a lot of stress. I don't think moving in with Bessie is the right move though if he knows where she lives. He isn't going to take it well when you leave, so you need to go somewhere he won't find you." I didn't think of that, but he was right. When I leave, he's going to go crazy. I started getting nervous thinking about it.

"Well, then I'm fucked. He knows where everyone lives." I felt like giving up. I didn't want to go to some battered women's shelter, but it was looking like that may be my best way out. But then my family would know. Then they would go after Hector. *Oh God, what can I do?!* I thought to myself.

"He doesn't know where I live," Giovanni said.

I laughed, "No he sure doesn't." He sat back on the couch.

"I have a whole extra bedroom. I have a bunch of room downstairs that I don't even use, extra bathroom, and everything you need," he said.

"You can't be serious. I don't want to get you involved in this shit show. I would hate myself if anything happened to you because of me," I said.

"Well, I'm serious. The offer is there, if you need somewhere to go, you are more than welcome. At least you would be safe and not have to worry about supporting yourself right now," he said.

"Why are you so nice to me? I'm a fucking mess," I laughed uncomfortably.

"You're not a mess; you're in a messy situation. I can help," he said gently. His phone rang, and it was work. He stepped outside to take the call while I gently pet Halo, who was chewing on a bone on the couch next to me.

Giovanni came back in and said, "Well, I just got called into work."

"Right now?" I asked, disappointed

"Yeah, they don't have any power in the yard, so the trains can't keep their schedules. I have to go," he said. Giovanni worked as an electrician for the railroad.

"Oh okay, well we are doing the gender reveal next Saturday, so if you want to tune in, we're going live on Facebook. But I'll come over on Friday if you want," I said.

"Yeah okay, Friday sounds good."

"Thank you for everything" I said, giving him a hug.

"No problem, I'm sorry I got called into work."

"Are you okay to drive?" I asked.

"Oh yeah! I'm a professional," he responded. I laughed shaking my head as I walked out the door.

When I got home, Hector still wasn't home. It was about 2 p.m. now, so I must have really made him mad. I didn't want to give him the satisfaction of contacting him, so I decided to take a bath and try to relax. The warm relaxing cocoon of water was my only form of relaxation. I took a deep breath and started thinking. What if Giovanni was serious? I didn't want to leave my house; I imagined raising my child there. But he was right about me needing to find somewhere to hide. He made me feel safe; I liked that. But I knew he liked me, and I didn't want him to just help me hoping I would fall for him. I couldn't even think about anything like that right now. All I could think about and focus on was this life growing inside me. I hoped it was a boy. I thought Hector would be a better father to a boy. I didn't want a girl with him. He treated women terribly. I didn't know how he would be raising a girl, but I didn't even want to imagine it. I was overthinking everything when Giovanni messaged me that he made it to work safe and was already done and headed home.

"Wow that was fast." I told him Hector still hadn't come home, nor had I heard from him.

"Maybe that's a good thing." It was a great thing for ME, but I was starting to worry about him now.

I finally messaged Hector to see if he was alive.

"Yes," was all he responded. *Okay*, I thought to myself, *fuck you too, then*. I put my phone on the nightstand next to my bed and laid down to watch a movie. I fell asleep of course and woke up to the garage door opening. I sat up to look at my phone, it was 8 o'clock in the evening. I could smell him coming down the hall. When he entered the room, he looked like a zombie. Dark circles under his eyes like he hadn't slept in two days, he smelled of his weekend and looked dirty.

"Don't fucking say anything to me," he said, lying in bed next to me.

"No problem," I said, getting up. I grabbed the things I needed and let him have the room. I went out to the living room and watched some TV until about 9:30 and decided I wanted to sleep in one of the guest rooms. I snuck in my bathroom quietly and grabbed my toothbrush and contact case, grabbed my phone charger, and went into one of the rooms. For the following week, I remained in the guest room. Hector was furious about it, but I told him it helped my back to sleep on that bed. I got the job with Uber, so against his will, I started doing some driving. He wouldn't allow me to work at night at all. I could work when he was working and that was it. If I didn't answer my phone because I had a customer in the car, he would call repeatedly.

"There has to be a way I can see your profile while you're working. I want to know where you are and who is in the car with you at all times," he said.

"If there is a way to do that, I am not aware of it," I would say honestly. He was so mad at me for working that it just created more of a wedge between us. Finally, Friday came. I went to see Giovanni as promised. I told him about everything that had been going on. I told him that Hector was getting more and more upset with me by the day. How I was sleeping in another room and was extremely restricted on how much I could work during the week.

"He won't even let me work on the weekends at all, but if he goes missing, how can he stop me?"

Giovanni thought the whole thing was ridiculous. "If he would just pay the car note, you wouldn't have to work," he said.

"Yeah, tell *him* that. At least the gender reveal is tomorrow," I said excitedly.

"Are you going to tune in?" I asked.

"Yeah, I'm interested in seeing what you're having. I think it's a girl," he said.

"No, I want a boy," I said laughing.

"No, you don't. He would never let you go if you give him a son," he said matter-of-factly.

"I don't think he'll let me go either way," I said rolling my eyes.

"It will be worse if it's a boy, trust me."

Bessie was coming to stay the night so she could help me set up and decorate. Gia wouldn't be there; she had to work. Which I didn't mind because she and Hector stressed me out anytime they were around each other.

When Hector came home, Bessie hadn't gotten there yet. He and his cousin Jose came inside, and Jose told me his wife Frankie was making a baby carriage centerpiece out of a watermelon. I thought that was a cute idea.

"I'm going to my dad's in a little bit," Hector said, coming out of the kitchen with a Corona in his hand.

"Tonight? But the party is tomorrow," I said.

"Yeah, I know, my dad wants to come so I'm just going to bring him home tonight with me." I hated his father, he was disgusting.

"So, you're just going to pick him up and come back?" I asked already knowing that wouldn't be the case.

"No," he laughed as if that was a stupid question.

"Well, try to be home *before* the sun comes up for a change please," I said.

"Shut the fuck up," he snapped at me. "How many times do I have to tell you to watch your fucking mouth."

"I'm sorry, I just put a lot into this party for us, and I'm excited and nervous to find out what we're having. You have been gone every weekend since November, and I'm sick of feeling like I'm doing all this alone," I said tears welling in my eyes.

He didn't say anything; he just shook his head and rolled his eyes.

"You've been sleeping in the guest room for a week!" he exploded. "When are you going to act like I'm your fucking man?"

Jose went to sit on the couch, getting out of the line of fire.

"It helps my back, I told you that. But I also can't stand your smell when you come home after you fucking drug benders," I snapped.

"You *will* be in our bed tonight, and I won't tell you again."

"Fine, then try not to smell like a soggy bag of cocaine and an ash tray when you come to bed. Bessie will be in that bed anyway."

"Why is she coming over? I hate that fat bitch."

"You don't seem to hate telling everyone she's sucked your dick, though, do you? She's coming to help me set up, which I would clearly be doing alone if she didn't offer, so run along now. Enjoy you fucking evening," I spat over my shoulder before sitting on the couch.

Jose stood up and said he had to go. Hector went back to the bedroom to get ready for his night of getting intoxicated. He didn't say a word, just walked out and left after he showered and changed. Bessie showed up shortly afterward, and I told her what happened.

"Oh, great so his dad's going to be here all night? I'm locking my fucking door," she said.

"Can't blame you there."

We chatted and put up decorations while discussing the game plan for the following day. Finally, at about 10:30 p.m., we decided to call it a night. Eventually, the garage door opened. I looked at my phone; it was 12:30 a.m. I hadn't slept a wink yet; I heard the loud grunts and groans of Hector's father trying to climb the steps.

Hector crawled into bed and wrapped himself around me. He was naked and I could feel his erection.

"I'm glad to see you listened for a change," he said rubbing himself against me while his hands started roaming.

"I guess I could say the same to you," I said. He laughed while rolling me onto my back and kissed me hard. I couldn't remember the last time I enjoyed him touching me. But my body came to life. It had been a while since we were together, so I gave in to feeling the need deep in my belly for release. He continued kissing me passionately and put his hand between my legs.

"God, I miss you," he whispered against my lips. "I need to have you," he said. He started kissing his way down my body covering every inch of me. "I love you so much babe, I can't wait for you to have my baby," he said consuming me with his mouth.

I don't know why it was so hot, maybe the hormones and the fact that we hadn't been together since he forced himself in my ass, but I climaxed within 2 minutes. It was an orgasm I had never felt before. My whole body exploded with pleasure. My back arched, my toes curled, and I gripped my sheets like I would fly away if I let them go.

"Holy shit," I said when it ended, still shaking. I had heard that pregnancy orgasms were the best, but I didn't know until now. "My God, that was insane," I said laughing while he got on top of me.

"That was different," he said. "I've never seen you come like that."

"I never have."

"Well let's see if you can do it again, I want to see your face this time." Even sliding himself inside me was amplified. I had never been more sensitive in my life. Everything he did felt amazing. It didn't take long for me to climax for the second time, and it was even better than the first. He leaned back on his knees, forcing himself deeper while I arched and flailed around on him. It was more than he could take, he exploded with me. This was the first time in a long time that I enjoyed him like this. When he rolled off me and laid down, I knew we were both drained. My body felt so good. I laid down and was finally able to relax and fall asleep.

The next morning, Bessie and I got started on preparations for the party. The first thing we did was go pick up the cake. It was adorable. It was a white cake with "We're here for the sex" written on it. It had a pair of little pink and blue footprints on each side and was covered in little pink and blue dots of icing. Bessie helped me make a sign for people to vote on boy or girl. We had a name suggestion clothesline going across the dining room where everyone would write a name down on a paper onesie and pin it to the clothesline. I went all out.

Bessie and I made all the food. We split the table in half, one side was pink the other blue. I had a pink lemonade and a blue Hawaiian Punch in clear containers, all the food we colored pink or blue. The cake was of course in the middle. The place was picture perfect, and guests were already starting to arrive. Since my brother couldn't make it because he had to work, I asked my ex-sister-in-law to bring my nephew. She was excited to be invited, and I was excited to have my nephew by my side.

I brought up the Facebook live and got one on my friends to record it for us. I brought my nephew to stand next to me while we cut the cake.

"Is everyone ready?" I yelled.

"Yes!" they all yelled. I picked up the knife and Hector put his hand over mine.

"I'm nervous now, I haven't been nervous the whole time, but now I'm shaking," he said. We all laughed, waiting for the results.

"Okay here we go! Let's cut the corner babe," I said directing the knife. I had a dream that night that it was a pink cake and I started crying in front of everyone. I had my heart set on a boy.

"It's fucking pink isn't it?" he said after we cut in the first time.

"I can't tell," I said, moving the knife to cut the corner of the cake off.

"What is it?" someone yelled from the back. We pulled the cake out and to my surprise it was pink!

"It's a fucking girl," Hector said, laughing uncomfortably and dropping to his knees dramatically. I was shocked to say the least. I pulled out a plate and lifted the slice in the air for everyone to see. The crowd roared and clapped in celebration. I was incredibly nervous when I found out I was having a girl.

Hector stood back up, laughing and said "Titi where are you? This is all your mother fucking fault!"

"Actually, it's the male that determines the sex of the baby," said my pregnant friend, "so it's *your* fault." I scooped off some icing and smushed it in his face playfully. Everyone laughed and gathered around for cake and congratulations. I gave my nephew the piece we cut and kept cutting slice after slice.

"Where's the envelope? I want to make sure they got it right," Hector said. Bessie went to retrieve the images, and they confirmed without a shadow of a doubt that we were indeed having a girl. I could have cried. The thought of raising a daughter around him made me sick to my stomach. What would I be teaching her? I want to teach her what love really is, how to be strong, independent and kind. I didn't want her to have a weak mother. I smiled my way through the party while panicking in my head.

As the party went on, everyone ate, suggested names, and had a good time. I went downstairs to see if Hector was down there, since I couldn't find him, and he was, along with his uncle and a few other guys.

"What's wrong babe?" he got up with a concerned look on his face.

"Nothing," I said, noticing his eyes were dilated and there was a white residue on the table they sat at. I looked down at it and locked eyes with him. "Really? Today?" I said.

"What?" he asked guiltily. I walked away and went back upstairs. Some of the guests were leaving, so it was starting to die down. I sat at the dining room table with Bessie, Titi, and Frankie.

"What's wrong?" Titi said noticing the disappointed look on my face. "You're not excited to be having a girl?" she asked smiling.

"I'm not excited to be having anything with *him* right now."

"How have things been?" Titi asked me gently.

Bessie rolled her eyes "The same old bullshit," she said.

"Maybe this will change him," Titi said softly.

"I don't know that it will. Things have only gotten worse. He's gone every weekend out partying. He's awful to me most of the time," I said, fed up.

"She's been sleeping in the guest room," Bessie said.

"Really?" Titi said surprised.

"Yeah, it's been bad. All he wants to do is drugs and party." We talked about it until the guys came upstairs. Eventually, everyone was ready to go. Bessie stayed behind to help clean up and get my house back in order. Hector decided to stay home for a change that night.

"You aren't going to the club house?" I asked.

"No, I'm tired and I didn't think you would want me to," he said.

Bessie was the only one left. The three of us sat on the couch talking about how we couldn't believe we were having a girl. He started getting emotional and said, "All the womanizing I do, and God gives me a daughter." He laughed uncomfortably.

"Well, maybe this is the time for you to step up and change your ways. Be the man you want your daughter to date," I said.

"I don't ever want her to date."

"You know what I mean. You have *got* to stop all this crap, I mean it. Eventually I *will* put what's best for her in front of you," I said rubbing my little belly.

"I know you will, that's why I love you," he said grabbing my hand.

"I'm going to take a bath, and then I'll be going to bed." I stood up and thanked Bessie for all her help.

CHAPTER TWENTY-FOUR

Final Days

In the two weeks following the gender reveal, nothing changed in Hector's behavior towards me. If anything, he was getting worse. He went out of his way to bully me every chance he could get. On Thursday, February 9, 2017, I went to a Valentine's dance with my nephew at his school. My brother came along and brought his girlfriend's daughter. We got all dressed up and fancy and made a date out of it.

Hector said he was going to go out for dinner while I was gone. My brother picked me up with the kids, and we went on about our evening. I hadn't been to a school dance like this with him before, but I was thrilled that he asked me. We went in, and the music was already bumping. There were kids and parents everywhere, but nobody was dancing. It was still early, so we were hoping they would get more into it as the night went on. Eventually, they danced so hard that they came up to us with wet hair and looking for water. We called it a night and gathered the kids up to head home. I was tired, but it was still early. When my brother dropped me off, I noticed there were no lights on in the house. It was 8:30 p.m., so I figured Hector found somewhere else to be. I went inside and changed into something more comfortable. I called Hector to see where he was, and he didn't answer. He texted me immediately.

"I can't hear I'm at the bar." It was Thursday night. So that was unusual.

"Well I'm home, when are you coming back?"

"I don't know, I ran into Weasel and we decided to go out for a drink."

He didn't "run into him." He had this planned.

"I told you I didn't like you hanging out with him. So, I would like it if you came home," I said irritated.

"I'm not doing anything wrong babe I won't be out late, just go to bed."

I didn't understand what the hell he kept doing this for. I felt like I was at the end of my rope. I didn't want this for my daughter. I wouldn't allow it. I went in his nightstand drawer, being nosy to see what else he was hiding. I found a pack of condoms, which were opened. We didn't use condoms, so I was furious already. I dug deeper and found several empty cellophane wraps from his cigarette packs that had left over white residue in them. My heart was pounding. How long had I allowed myself to be blinded by this man? I'm a complete idiot. I sat on the bed and started to cry, putting my head in my hands. I knew he was a junkie, but I didn't think he was cheating on me. I pulled the condom box out and looked at the count. It said there were three magnums included. I laughed, because he was ridiculous for thinking he would need a magnum. I pulled out the condoms and there were all three there. Okay, maybe he didn't cheat on me. But he bought condoms for a reason, so he was thinking about cheating at least. I took everything out of his drawer and left it all for him to see on top of the nightstand. I hated feeling like this all the time. Everything this man did made me feel horrible about myself. I didn't ever want my daughter to see this as a normal life. I had to do something soon.

Finally, the garage door opened around 2 a.m. I sat up and turned on the light, ready to confront him. He walked in the bedroom, surprised to see me awake.

"Hey," he said nervously. He looked over at his nightstand and immediately got defensive.

"You went through my things?"

"I sure as fuck did," I said, crossing my arms. "You want to explain to me why you have an open pack of condoms in your nightstand?"

He laughed.

"I bought them after we had a few threesomes type situations. I thought maybe I would need them one day, even though you don't let me fuck anyone," he said annoyed.

"Then explain to me why there are 16 empty cellophanes in your drawer that *all* have a clear drug residue in them."

"Man, you don't need to be going through my shit," he said, pushing everything back in his drawer.

"You don't need to be lying to me all the fucking time!" I yelled.

"I have to lie to you, or you flip out and say mean shit when I tell you even half of the truth!" he yelled back at me.

"You need to go to rehab!" He laughed and shook his head.

"No I don't."

"Yes, Hector, you do. For the *last time*, I will *not* raise our daughter with you like this!"

"Let *me* make something clear," he said, his eyes darkening.

"You don't tell me what to do. I'm a grown ass man. And if you ever threaten to take my kid away from me, I fucking kill you as soon as you give birth. I will take my daughter and run, don't fucking try me!"

I felt all the blood rush from my face and my stomach tightening.

"Did you just threaten to kill me and take my baby?" I asked, shocked.

"It wasn't a threat," he said, turning off the light and climbing into bed.

"I won't warn you again," he said.

I sat back quietly shaking. Would he really kill me? Silent tears of terror started to slide down my face. He rolled over to face my direction and pulled at my panties.

"Take these off, I need to nut," he said as if I were a sperm collection cup.

"Don't touch me," I said, moving his hand away and throwing my legs off the side of the bed. I went to stand up and he grabbed the back of my head by my hair.

"I'm beginning to think you like it like this since you just can't do what you're told," he growled, pulling me down on the bed. He got on his knees and shoved his erection in my face. "Suck it," he said holding my head down by my hair. I clenched my jaw shut and said through my teeth

"I will bite that fucking thing off," meaning it. He slapped me in the face.

"If you bite my dick, I'll break your fucking neck. Open your fucking mouth!"

He slammed my head against the bed, repeatedly trying to get me to do what he wanted.

"Fine, you stubborn cunt," he said rolling me on my stomach and getting on his feet behind me. I was bent over the bed, and he tore my underwear off halfway, granting himself access. I started crying.

"You just threatened to kill me and now you want to fuck me?" I wept. He put my arms behind my back and pinned me down with one hand.

"I'll do what the fuck I want with you," he said spitting on me. He rubbed the spit up and down with the tip of his penis. "Which hole do I want tonight," he said. He put pressure on my asshole first, and I clenched up, putting my face down in the mattress.

"Please don't," I said, crying.

"Fine," he said flatly and shoved himself inside my vagina. This was fine, I could always check out when he did this. I left all the feeling in my body. He pumped away for a few minutes and finally finished. He slapped me on the ass and told me to go clean myself up before I came back to bed. I shamefully grabbed another outfit to wear to bed out of my drawer on the way to the bathroom while he climbed in, peacefully relieved. I closed the door and turned on the light. My tank top had been ripped at some point during the struggle and what was left of my underwear hung off my left thigh. My hair was a mess. Looking at my reflection like this I started weeping. I turned on the shower to wash the shame off. I cried until the shower no longer had hot water, like I normally did. I put my pajamas on and quietly opened the door. He was snoring, out cold. I quietly went into the guest room. I cried myself to sleep with my arms wrapped protectively around my stomach.

"I'm sorry peanut," I whispered to my unborn child. "I'm so sorry I got you into this. Mommy's going to make things right, I promise."

The next morning, Hector came bursting into the guest room.

"Okay, so you really gonna sleep in here forever? Why even be together if we don't sleep in the same fucking bed?" he asked, overly upset.

"I told you it feels better on my back," I lied.

"What the fuck ever," he said, slamming the door shut. I heard him getting ready for work. I didn't want to see him or deal with his drama, so I hid in the room. He didn't say anything else to me; he just left. Once I heard the garage door close, I knew he was gone. I called my dad to see if he was working and asked if I could come out there and go to lunch with him and some old coworkers I used to work with. He said of course, so I got up and showered. I did a few Uber rides before I met up with him to kill time and earn some cash. I had just dropped off my last customer when my phone rang. It was my ex, Bruce.

When I picked up the phone, Bruce said, "I don't know what the fuck your little fuckboy ass boyfriend's problem is, but you can give his bitch ass my number if he has something to say to me! I'll meet him anywhere anytime!"

Confused, I asked, "What? Where did that come from?"

"Last night he was at the bar with *my* supposed friend Weasel. They ordered some product from my other boy Drake. When Drake went up there to give them the shit, they were talking all kinds of shit about me." Confirming my suspicions that Hector and Weasel were high last night, I was already irritated.

"Now I know Weasel is my problem and believe me I'm gonna handle his bitch ass, I know that nigga *very* well. I know where his baby mama stays, I bought him clothes, gave him an opportunity to make money, even helped put him in a vehicle. *That* nigga is trash, and he already knows we're gonna thump when I run up on his ass over this shit," he said angrily. "But tell me *why* Drake was listening to them plot on me?" he continued.

"Plot on you how Bruce? I know nothing about this conversation. I tell Hector all the time not to fuck with Weasel."

"Drake said Weasel was up there bragging about all the work I put him on and all this shit I've had him do. Number one, they don't need to be talking about me or any of my business in public for real. I could go to fucking prison over these junkies and their loose lips. And number two, suddenly now Hector said he wants to meet me! He and Weasel were trying to put together a 'business plan' to propose to me! Like what *fuck* would ever make that nigga think him and I would *ever* be cool? I know he's putting his hands on you, so I may just jump on him before he even speaks," he said.

"Wait a minute. So now Hector thinks Weasel is going to hook the two of you up so he can sell for you?" I asked lividly.

"Yes!" he responded. "I already learned my lesson not to put these snorters out in the streets as workers. They snort up all the product and then I have to deal with *that* accordingly. But he wants to get his club involved and shit, I don't want *nothing* to do with his fuck ass!" he said. I took a deep, disappointed breath at the red light I stopped for.

"He's really just getting worse! He said he would get off this shit and get it together before our daughter comes in July," I said with tears welling up in my eyes. "But he's trying to get in deeper."

I was disgusted. He was *worse* than his shitty father. At least you knew what to expect with that piece of shit. But Hector was trying to live two lives, and he was failing miserably at it. I didn't know if I was more disappointed in how far gone he was or how blind I had allowed myself to be. He was never planning on getting help, he wasn't interested in getting clean and sober. Hell, it didn't even seem like he was interested in becoming a father.

"You're having a girl?" Bruce changed the subject, hearing how upset I was.

"Yeah, can you believe it?" I said.

"Of course I can. You're going to be an amazing mother, Savannah."

He and I had known each other since I was 18 years old. Years before we were lovers, we were the best of friends. So even though we were no longer lovers, we still loved and cared about each other genuinely.

"Now what I *don't* understand, is how *you*, one of the strongest women I have *ever* known, are still with this junkie ass bitch!" he said as lightly as he could.

"Yeah, that's the burning question isn't it. I want to leave so bad! I hate him! I'm trying, but I can't work, and I have no money until after I give birth, so I don't know what to do." I started crying.

"Okay, don't cry. Take a deep breath. I'm sorry I got you upset," he said, changing his entire tone. "Look, if you need to leave, I will put you up somewhere if I have to. You know I will always look out for you," he said.

"I can't ask you to do that," I said. "I made my own mess. Besides, when I leave, you'll be one of the first people he suspects I'm with," I said, laughing. "He's convinced we're having an affair even though we never see each other. I don't know what you want me to do here; as soon as I tell him you called me, it's going to be a huge fight. He gets insane at the mention of your name."

"Well, he's clearly obsessed with me, but let him know I don't like boys, I fuck women. So, he can jump off my dick," he said jokingly.

"I doubt I'll quote you on that," I said laughing. "You don't have to say shit to him, give me his number and I'll handle it. Or, better yet, give me your address, and I'll be sitting on his couch with his girl when he gets home," he growled.

"Well, that's a terrible non-option. I'll talk to him when I see him. But, it's Friday. If he comes home, it's long enough to shower, change, and start a giant fight so he can walk out angry to make himself feel better about bailing on me for drugs and fuckboys," I said.

"If you don't want to get involved, that's fine. I've been blowing up Weasel's phone all day; he won't even answer. But I'll be taking this up with him for sure," he said.

"Okay, well I'm pulling up to dad's work, so I'll let you go."

"Okay, tell your dad I said hello," he said politely.

"I will, have a good day."

"You do the same, and I'm serious. If you need to leave in a hurry or make a plan, I'm here for whatever you need," he said firmly.

"Thanks." Bruce was a long part of my history. I learned a lot from him, and I loved him as a person and a friend. But I couldn't go down that road again. I didn't need to get addicted to him. I had to figure this out myself.

I went to a nice lunch at a local pizza place with my dad and a couple of coworkers. It was nice to be around friendly safe people. I told my dad about the conversation I just had with Bruce on the way over and as much as I could about what had been going on with Hector and the drugs. If I was going to leave anyway, I may as well start leaking the truth a little bit at a time so it wasn't a surprise when I didn't want Hector to find me. Obviously, my father was displeased by my story. He wanted to call Bruce himself and tell him where he could find Hector.

"We never liked that fucker, but when he came to ask your brother and I for our blessings to marry you, he seemed genuine. He put on a good show, I'll give him that," he said, shaking his head. His fists were clenched, and his face was getting red, I could see I had upset him enough for one day.

"Well, I'll figure it out eventually," I said trying to comfort my father.

"I don't like this one bit. Why do I feel like you aren't telling me something?" he asked.

"It's fine, I'm sure it will get better when the baby arrives," I said.

"You know if he harms you or that granddaughter of mine, we'll kill him, right?" he said seriously.

"I'm fine, Dad," I said trying to defuse the uncomfortable moment.

I did some more Uber driving on the way back home, but I was tired, so I decided to lay on the couch and take a nap. I woke up to the garage door opening and slowly sat up. In walked Hector, Jose, and their uncle. All holding tall beers they had clearly already started drinking on the way home. As usual Jose and their uncle were a ball of fun. They always seemed to be lighthearted about things and give Hector a hard time, so I liked them both.

"You didn't go home with Titi today?" I asked their uncle.

"No, it's guy's night out," he said, holding up his beer. He had been helping Hector at work since he quit his job a couple months ago. Hector's phone chimed. He looked down at it and immediately got enraged.

He looked up at me and said, "So you called Bruce today?" *Must be Weasel finally had his ass chewed out*, I thought to myself.

"No, he called me though."

"You are lying, you fucking whore!" Hector yelled, standing up.

"I just got a text from Weasel and he said *you* called *Bruce* and told him we were out last night. Weasel's pissed at you!" he said.

"First of all, I couldn't give *any* fucks about that dumb bitch being mad at *me* for shit. He's a worthless lying junkie. Second of all, I was going to talk to you about the conversation when I got a chance. But I didn't want to embarrass you in front of your company," I said.

"Embarrass me how? By letting them see what a lying whore you really are?" He yelled now pacing behind the section of the couch he was just sitting in.

His uncle stayed seated with Hector pacing angrily behind him. "Come on guys, let's calm down. This is going to go nowhere good," he said. Jose got up off the couch and went towards the kitchen, getting out of the way.

"Fuck this. You want Bruce's dick so bad, go fucking be with him!" he said walking towards the bedroom. We all sat there uncomfortably shaking our heads for a few seconds.

"Why did he call you?" Jose asked.

"He called me because Weasel and Hector were buying drugs last night off one of his workers and talking all kinds of shit about him. Then in the next breath wanted to pitch some sort of business idea to him. Evidently this Drake guy, who was the one there selling them a bag of coke, played nice and stuck around to see what they said and reported it all back to Bruce. So he thought I should know that my fiancé and father of my child was trying to be some dope boy." I said loud enough for Hector to hear.

Both men shook their heads, looking down.

"I told him to quit that shit," said Jose softly.

"Well, he never will with Weasel around pretending to be the badass that Hector wants to be," I said flatly. I heard Hector storming down the hall. When he got to the end of the hallway he picked up one of my lamps that was sitting on the end table and pulled the chord out of the wall. He threw it toward me as hard as he could, barely giving me enough time to turn my head before it smashed in the back of my skull. There were glass shards everywhere.

"I told you to keep your fucking mouth shut, you stupid bitch!" he screamed at me. I sat there, checking my head with my hands to see if there was any bleeding and make sure there was no glass stuck anywhere.

"Where is my phone?" I asked standing up. "Congratulations, you stupid fuck! You're about to go to jail!"

"I fucking *dare* you to call the cops, bitch," he said, walking back to the bedroom. I found my phone and started to dial 9-1-1.

"Don't do that," his uncle said calmly.

"We will take him out of here. Please don't call the cops," he said.

I looked up from my phone and noticed Jose trying to pick up the glass smashed all over the place.

"So, you two are covering for this pussy? You saw what the fuck he just did to me! Did you raise him to beat on women? To treat the mother of his child like this!?" I screamed at him.

"Hell no, but let us deal with him, I'm begging you," his uncle said. Hector came back into eyesight in completely different clothes and with a bag.

"I want your ass out of my house before I get home," he said pointing at me.

"And I want *you* to stop being a junkie fucking loser, but we don't always get what we want do we doll?" I said holding up my phone that I just needed to hit call on. The two men ushered him out and down the stairs even though he tried to run at me after that comment. Jose ran over to give me a kiss on the cheek and check my head while his uncle pulled Hector down the second flight of steps.

"You're a tough broad, ma," he said, looking in my hair and picking out glass.

"Don't call the cops. Call your dad," he whispered in my ear. "I'll catch up with you later, but it may be time to go." I understood that they had to try to do what they could to seem like they were on his side. They were all family, and they all worked for him. But I know if Titi were sitting there when that happened, it would have gone much differently. She wasn't afraid of him. She didn't enable him like everyone else did.

When I heard the garage door open, I paced around the living room. I picked up my phone and called Bruce.

"What the fuck did you say to Weasel? I just caught a fucking lamp to the back of my head from across the room!" I said, crying.

"What the fuck?" Bruce said shocked. "I *just* spoke with that nigga like 10 minutes ago!"

"I know. He texted Hector and told him I called you. It set him off," I cried.

"Okay, first, calm down, you don't need to be stressing like this. Hold on, I'll call Weasel on my other phone and put him on speaker phone so you can hear it." I heard a phone ringing and his grimy voice answer the phone.

"What the fuck did you just say to your little Hector boyfriend?" Bruce asked in an angry voice.

"Nothing why?" he said.

"Because whatever your lying ass said just started some shit. I already had this conversation with you earlier, but I can see I need to roll up on you and see you face to face for you to understand how out of line your bitch ass is," he said.

"I don't know what you're talking about." Weasel whined like a little girl who didn't want daddy to give her a spanking.

"I told you I don't even fuck with that nigga; I just snort up all his shit. He likes to show out since he has his little company, so hey, if you want to pay for me to party all the time, I'll use you," he said, laughing.

"I don't give a fuck what you doing with this nigga, but you *will* take *my* fucking name *and Savannah's* name out your bitch ass mouth! You know me enough to know I'm *not* fucking playing anymore," he growled.

"I don't even know that bitch, she just doesn't like me," Weasel said. Not knowing he couldn't hear me; here I go with my mouth.

"Your mama's a bitch, you fucking loser! I bet you're sucking my man's dick for all those extras you're getting! Fuck you! I hope Bruce beats the shit out of you!" I screamed into the phone. Clearly, I wasn't on speaker phone, but Bruce chuckled.

"Don't you EVER call her a bitch. I would go to war over her, and I promise you don't want that," Bruce said flatly.

"Man whatever, I'm just saying. I don't ever see her, so she doesn't know anything about what Hector and I talk about," he said, sounding defeated and defiant in the same breath.

"Well, since I'm sure you'll be running into your little fuck buddy tonight, let him know I'm coming for him if I catch wind of where his bitch ass is," Bruce said.

"Man, it doesn't even need to be like that. He hasn't done anything to you," he said, trying to protect his new bride.

"He knows exactly what the fuck he did, and I'll be sure to remind him when I see his ass. And if you're with him, you can get it too," he said and hung up the phone.

"You know he couldn't hear you, right?" Bruce asked, chuckling.

"I realized that eventually," I said.

"I told you he's a bitch," he said. "Yeah, he's worse than that. He's using, lying, and taking advantage of everyone. I hate people like that," I said.

"So, what are you going to do? You can't stay there anymore," he said.

"I know," I said, still unsure.

"Do you need me to come get you?" Bruce asked.

"No, that's only going to make things worse. I'll figure it out," I said.

"Let me know what you decide, then," he said.

"I will. Thank you," I said.

"You know I'd do anything for you, so just let me know."

I was pacing everywhere. My heart pounded; I chewed on my lip, bit my nails, pulled on my eye lashes. I went downstairs, not looking for anything, just searching for an answer. I went back upstairs and got a sick feeling when I saw the area where the lamp broke on my head. Jose had picked up some of it but the lamp busted lamp shade and broken glass were still evident. Tears formed in my eyes again, I walked back to my bedroom. His drawers were open and in disarray, his closet door open with the lights on. He was clearly in a rush when he ran out of here. I messaged Giovanni and told him what happened as I sat on the edge of my bed.

"Just come here. Bring what you can and just get out of there."

I put the phone down next to me and slid off my bed, dropping to my knees on the floor. I prayed to God all the time, but I had never heard him speak to me before. I never felt like it was really getting me anywhere. But I had to give it a try. I locked my hands together with desperately clinched, intertwined fingers.

"What do I do, Lord? Help me!" I cried. "What do *you* want me to do?" I may have said those words before, but I never imagined where God wanted me to be would be different then where I wanted to be for some reason. I just asked him for things I thought I wanted. But this time, he answered me immediately. I heard a loud and clear voice in my head that said, *Call your dad.* Honestly, I couldn't believe I was hearing anything. *Maybe I'm losing my mind*, I thought to myself. *But I can't do this anymore.*

I reached for my phone and got off my knees, leaning back against my bed on my bottom and pulling my knees up to my chest as far as I could comfortably. I took a deep shaky breath and dialed. My whole body was shaking. It kept ringing and finally went to voicemail. I hung up and called my brother. They still lived together, so I figured one of them would answer.

"Hey Schmoo!" my brother said happily. Schmoo was the nickname my dad and brother both called me for years.

"Hey, is Dad there?" I asked nervously.

"Yeah, what's wrong?" I took a deep breath again and said to God in my head, *Tell me what to say, Lord.* I opened my mouth and responded.

"I need you to listen to me very carefully and please do as I ask." I couldn't have sounded any calmer if I tried. It was like a whole new voice speaking through me.

"Okay, what the fuck is going on?" my brother asked, realizing this was serious.

"I need you and Dad to come get me. I'm at home, and I need to leave. I need both of you to come and bring both vehicles so I can get whatever I can throw into garbage bags. And I need you to not ask any questions please," I said.

"Where's Hector?"

"He's gone, I don't want him to come back before I'm gone, so please stop asking questions and come now," I said.

"Okay, we'll be there in 10 minutes."

"Thank you," I said and hung up the phone.

I messaged Giovanni and told him what I had just done. I asked if he was 100 percent certain I could come there.

"Yes, come, I'll be waiting." I popped up off the floor, ran to the kitchen, and grabbed the whole box of garbage bags out of the cabinet. I ran down to open the garage doors and unlock the front door, so my dad and brother could just come in. I started throwing everything I could into garbage bags. I had two full bags already thrown down to the front door ready to load and was loading the third when I heard my dad's and brother's voices.

"Schmoo!" they yelled together. I was so relieved that they were there that I immediately started to cry.

"I'm back here," I yelled from the closet in my bedroom.

"What the fuck is all this?" I heard my brother say. I knew already he was looking at the mess from the lamp. My dad appeared in the doorway.

"What is going on? Did that fucker hurt you?" I looked up at him, still crying with my face all red and puffy.

"Dad, please just get me out of here before he gets back. I promise I will tell you everything later, but I just need to get out of here," I said, desperate not to have this conversation right now.

"Okay, what do you want me to do?"

"I need help packing. I only have garbage bags, and I have to get whatever I can now," I said, going back to shoving what was left of my clothes into my third bag.

"Okay, where is your computer, your files, anything important?" he asked.

"Down in the office. I need the cat carrier out of the storage cubby as well." He walked out to look for what I needed.

I came out and dragged the last bag of clothes I had to join the other two. My brother was standing over the broken lamp, inspecting it.

"What happened here?" he asked with a terrifying look on his face. He was always aggressively protective of me, so I knew the truth was going to upset him.

"These bags are ready to load. Dad's grabbing stuff from downstairs. I have some stuff I've gotten for the baby in the back guestroom that also needs to come with me," I said, ignoring his question and walking back to the bedroom.

I heard some commotion outside and my dad and brother both clearly yelling "Fuck Hector!" I got scared and froze. Was he here? Did he come back? *Oh no, this is going to get violent* very *quickly.* I heard them coming back in the front door muttering "Fuck that pussy bitch, I wish he would show up right now." Cautiously, I came out of the bedroom.

"What happened?" I asked, shaking.

"Jose just drove up and we asked where Hector was," he said.

"He wasn't with him?" I asked.

"No, he asked if we were getting you out of here. We told him to tell Hector we are looking for him and fuck him," my dad said.

"Yeah, *that* part I heard." I breathed a small sigh of relief. "Did he leave?"

"Yeah he's gone, he didn't say why he was here," my brother said. "We're running out of room in the cars, and we still have to put Gizmo and her kitty litter box in. Is there anything else that's important to have tonight?"

"No, I just want my bedding and pillows, but everything else will have to wait," I said, anxious to leave.

"Well we only have room for so much at the house," my brother said.

Oh, right, of course they think I'm going with them. I hadn't mentioned Giovanni yet.

"I'm not going to your house," I said over my shoulder walking into my bedroom to strip my bed.

"Where are you going then? Gia's or Bessie's?" my dad asked.

"Neither actually, I am going to stay with Giovanni. He offered me safety and a spare room all to myself," I said, pulling off my pillows and throwing them towards my brother who caught them. They looked at each other confused.

"What?" my dad asked.

"Who the hell is Giovanni?" my brother asked, confused.

"We used to date years ago, remember? I went to Florida with him and everything. We dated before I ever met Hector," I said.

"The democrat?" my brother asked. I had to laugh.

"Yes, the democrat," I said.

"He's the one who has Halo now," my dad said, catching him up.

"Oh, well, I would rather you come stay with us," my brother said.

"Where?" I asked. "Your house is so full, you are already stepping on each other. It's smarter to go somewhere he can't find me. Your place, Gia's, even Bessie's, he knows where everyone is," I said. They looked at each other again still uncomfortably, but eventually shrugged.

"Well, I would like to know why you need to be somewhere safe. What makes you so afraid of this douchebag?" my dad asked.

"Yeah, tell us what the fuck happened out there," my brother said. I folded up my fitted sheet as best I could and grabbed the last pile of sheets and my comforter.

"He threw the lamp at me and hit me in the back of my head in front of his uncle and cousin. They didn't let me call the cops and ushered him out," I said, not able to look at them when I said it. I was staring at my naked mattress waiting for the response.

"Are you fucking kidding me?!" my brother said, getting so angry he started to pace back and forth.

"That pussy motherfucker! Is that the first time?!" my dad yelled.

"No, and it wasn't even the worst, but it IS the last time. I'll tell you everything later. Can we please just go?" I asked.

"What do you mean they wouldn't let you call the police?" my dad asked. "They don't strike me as the kind of men to just sit there and watch that," he said in disbelief. My dad and brother had grown to like Hector's family members. They had spent some time with them on several occasions.

"They asked me not to, but Jose knows something more he isn't telling me, we've been talking more frequently because he was here to see the damage done to me a few times and isn't happy about it. He told me to call you guys on several occasions, everyone did. I was scared and didn't want you to hurt him, so I swore everyone that even suspected anything to secrecy. His cousin and uncle work for him, so I understand their position," I said, walking towards them with my pile of stuff. My dad took it off my hands. "Can you guys load that up? I want to look in the kitchen and get some food. I don't want to just show up empty handed." They did as I asked, and I messaged Giovanni that we would be there shortly.

"Okay, I'll be looking for you," he said.

"We have three carloads and I'm digging through my pantry and fridge now to bring some food with me."

"Don't worry about any of that, just get out of there!"

I grabbed all the cat food and a few things I wanted, and my brother took them down to the car for me. I took one final walk through the house to see if there was anything I needed. I shut off all the lights, locked the doors, and left. With the two cars following me, I put on my headphones to make calls on the drive. The first call was Gia. She was working that night at the mall, but I figured she would be leaving by now.

"Hello?" she answered the phone in a worried voice.

"I'm headed to Giovanni's house now. My dad and brother are both following me in their cars. All three are full of whatever shit we could grab," I said.

"Okay, what happened?"

"He threw a lamp at my head," I said.

"*What?*"

"Yeah, I'll tell you all about it later, but it's over. I'm gone, and now I'll be safe."

"Okay, well, I just got off work. Do you need me to come help unload or anything?"

"No, but the good news is you'll only live 5 minutes away from me now!"

My next call was to Bessie, it went almost exactly the same as the call to Gia.

"So they finally know the truth?" she asked.

"Not all of it, but enough to know I need to get away from him."

"Do you need me to come?"

"Not tonight, I'm so tired I just want to lie down somewhere and pass out."

"I'll see you tomorrow then," she said.

"Okay," I said, hanging up the phone as I pulled into the driveway of my new home.

The front door opened, and Giovanni stumbled out smelling like cinnamon. He had clearly been drinking his Fireball while he waited on our arrival. He and his brother Gabriel helped my dad and brother unload everything and took it up to my new room. I didn't have a bed, because I couldn't take it with me at the time. But at least I had a roof over my head, safe people around me, and my fluffy cat. Plus, I was back with Halo, which I was happy about. I came down and plopped myself on Giovanni's couch. My dad and brother asked if he was really okay taking me in.

"Yeah, it's no problem," he slurred.

"Okay, well, if you need anything, you call us," my dad said. "I can take you to get an air mattress or something tomorrow if you want, Schmoo," he said lovingly.

"Okay, thanks you guys, I love you," I said, giving them both a hug from the couch. Giovanni sat on the coffee table in front of me.

"So, do you want to talk about it?" he asked, swaying.

"Not really, I'm exhausted and my whole life just changed," I said with tears pooling in my eyes.

"Okay, that's understandable."

"Thank you so much for taking me in. I don't know how to repay you for everything, but I am *so* grateful," I said genuinely.

"I told you, we'll figure it all out as it comes. The biggest step is already done. You left; you are out. That's all that matters right now," he said.

"Yeah, you're right. Is it okay if I go try to get some sleep? My body hurts," I said.

"You don't have to ask for permission to do anything here," he said, laughing.

"If you need anything, let me know. I'll be down here playing video games with my friends," he said, smiling and gesturing towards his computer.

"Oh, okay, well have fun, and good night," I said.

"Good night," he said, walking towards his desk and putting his headphones on. I noticed he had a bottle of Fireball and a shot glass sitting on his desk. It was already half empty, no wonder he was so drunk. I made sure to lock my bedroom door just to be safe. These were sweet guys, but I knew how different people became when they were intoxicated, and I understandably wasn't interested in taking any chances. I had never stayed there before, so it made sense to be cautious.

The first night was the worst. I got no sleep. I couldn't get comfortable on the floor to save my life; Gizmo was smothering me to death. Giovanni was laughing and yelling and talking shit on his headphones all night. It was funny to hear a one-sided conversation. Then at some point I guess Gabriel got on the same game because they were both talking to each other through the headphones. It was freezing in that room; I was fully dressed and bundled up, but I couldn't seem to get warm. Eventually all the chatter stopped and all I could hear was snoring. Good Lord, the snoring vibrated the house. I hadn't heard anything like it since before my dad got a CPAP machine for his sleep apnea.

Eventually, laying there in the cold empty room on the floor, it all hit me. I just left Hector. There was no going back. *I'm still pregnant and going to have a baby in 5 months, I don't have any money and can't really work. How am I going to get through this?* I still had my engagement ring; I didn't even think about it being on my finger until that moment. I got up and dug around to find my safe. I unlocked it and found that I still had the receipt and the boxes for both rings. He had paid $5,600 for this thing! Maybe I could sell it back to the store and have the money to get my own place after I had the baby. I decided then that I wasn't giving this thing back to him. He could take me to court if he wanted, but as far as I was concerned, this was my nest egg for getting back on my feet and providing a home for my baby.

CHAPTER TWENTY-FIVE

New Life.

The first morning, I waited until the snoring stopped to come out of my room. Giovanni was up and out on the back porch smoking a cigarette.

"Good morning," he said, smiling at me from the doorway when I came down.

"Good morning, how are you up already?" I asked, laughing.

"I don't ever really sleep in."

"If I drank like that, I would have to sleep all day to recover."

"Nah, I'm fine. I'm a professional. Did you get any sleep?" he asked.

"Not at all," I said, sitting on the couch. "I'm so tired, but between being on the floor and freezing and my mind going a mile a minute, I had no chance," I said.

"Why were you on the floor?" he asked confused.

"Why wouldn't I be? I couldn't bring my bed," I said.

"Oh, I thought you were sleeping in my bed. That's why I slept on the couch," he said.

"Oh, I didn't realize that. You never told me to sleep in there. Not that I would have, you've already gone above and beyond for me," I said.

"Well, I don't want you sleeping on the floor. What kind of ass would I be to allow that, you're pregnant for God's sake," he said, closing the French door and coming inside.

"Well my dad is going to get me an air mattress today, so hopefully that will be better."

"Yeah I guess that's better, but if you want, we can just go get your shit," he said.

"I'm scared to go to the house right now. I haven't heard anything from Hector or about him, so I'll just give it a few days and see what my next move is," I said.

"That's fine. Are you hungry?" he asked.

"No, not really," I said, not wanting to be a burden.

"Well you'll have to eat eventually. So, help yourself to whatever you want."

"Thank you."

We sat there talking for a while, I told him he snored so loud the house shook. He laughed and said he has a CPAP machine upstairs, so, luckily, he wouldn't be snoring anymore. My dad called me and asked what I was doing. I told him we were just hanging out.

"Well, I want to take you to get a blow-up mattress and maybe go to lunch. Does that sound good?" he asked. It was almost 11 a.m., so that sounded great.

"Okay, I'll be over in a few. Ask Giovanni if he'd like to join us."

"Okay, thanks Dad." I told Giovanni, and he agreed to join us, so he went upstairs to change, as did I. I was going to have to figure out what to do with my clothes, since digging through garbage bags was already no fun. My dad came in and chatted with us a little. Giovanni took him out back to see the pool since it was so dark the night before. He showed him around the house, putting my dad's mind at ease.

"What are you going to do with all your clothes?" my dad asked me, looking at the garbage bag mess.

"Well, I don't know, but I can hang some stuff up in this little closet, I said.

"Do you want a dresser?" Giovanni asked.

"Do you just have an extra one laying around?" I asked laughing.

"Yeah, I do. There's two in Gabriel's room. He doesn't use them both. We'll move that in here after we get back from lunch if you want," he said.

"That would be awesome, thank you," I said.

"See, I told you we would figure everything out as it came." He smiled sweetly.

We went to Walmart first and picked out a full-size blow-up mattress that had a built-in pump. I was so excited to finally try and get some sleep later. By the time we decided where to eat, I was starving. We sat down at a table in a Mexican Restaurant just down the street from where Giovanni lived.

"So, any word from Hector yet?" my dad asked, dipping a chip into the queso.

"No, nothing."

"Well he posted a post on Facebook last night that your brother and I wanted to respond to," he said with a mouth full of chips.

"Oh? I guess I didn't see it." I went on Facebook and discovered he had unfriended me and put me on "restriction" from seeing anything on his profile that I wasn't tagged in. "Wow, he removed me from Facebook."

"Are you serious?" Giovanni said. I handed him my phone.

"Wow, he sure did," he said, looking through it.

"Why didn't he remove me and your brother then?" my dad asked, pulling out his phone. He pulled up his post from last night: "Oh, so it's fuck me huh? Well fuck you too, say it to my face!" I rolled my eyes handing it to Giovanni.

"Yeah we can't *wait* to say it to his face! That fucking pussy motherfucker!" my dad said, turning red with rage.

"Calm down old man, you'll give yourself another heart attack," I said, trying to lighten the mood. "I still want to know the whole truth. But also, I'm scared to know," he said sadly.

"I know, just give me a little time to process everything and get my thoughts in order." He nodded in agreement. Lunch was fantastic, and my belly was stuffed.

"Well, let's go put your bed up!" My dad said.

"Sounds good to me!"

We got back to the house and he and Giovanni went to work on getting the bed going. Gabriel finally came out of his room, sleepy-eyed.

"Hey, we need to move one of those dressers in here for her. So, make sure one is cleaned out," Giovanni said to his brother, who was headed to the bathroom.

"Okay, no problem. I just have to pee." When he came back out, my dad was already blowing up the bed.

"Which dresser do you want?" Gabriel asked me.

"Whatever one you aren't using." I followed Giovanni into the bedroom where Gabriel stayed and there was a shorter wider one and a taller thinner one. Both the same color, but I chose the short wide one since it looked like it would hold more. They moved it in to my room, and now I had a bed to sleep on and somewhere to put all my clothes. Things were already coming together on day one!

"Well, looks like you're all set, so I'll leave you to it," my dad said, standing up. He reached for Giovanni's hand and shook it.

"Thanks man, you don't know how grateful we all are for this. You're a good man," he said.

"It's no problem, she's welcome as long as she wants to stay," he said, letting go of my dad's hand.

"Well, thank you again," he said walking down the stairs.

"What about your car payment for this month? I don't know if I'll be able to come up with all of it, but I can probably help if you need it," my dad said.

"I have half of it already, I can work some shifts and try to get the rest."

"Well, I don't love you doing that Uber thing in your condition. I wish I had the money to just pay it off, so you didn't have that to stress about right now," he said shaking his head.

"I know, Dad. I'll find a way. I always do," I said, reassuring him and myself.

When he left, I sat on the couch to take a breath. Everything seemed so overwhelming right now. I was so riddled with anxiety; every time my phone made a noise I was stricken with worry. I didn't want to hear from Hector, but also was wondering why I hadn't yet. Had I done the right thing? Is he going to try to hurt me? What if he finds out where I am? What if he tries to hurt Giovanni? What if my dad or brother finds him?

"You okay?" Giovanni asked, coming back inside from a smoke break.

"Yeah, I'm as good as I can be. I think I'm just in shock or something," I said.

"Yeah, this is a lot." Suddenly his doorbell rang.

"Oh, here comes Leah. I know she's dying to meet you," he said heading towards the door. He opened the door, and in walked a short woman with skinny little legs, a little round belly, and dark hair. She had a pair of reading glasses hanging off the front of her shirt and was holding two gift bags. She was really pleasant. She had a big welcoming smile on her face and greeted me with open arms.

"Hey! I'm sorry to intrude, but I wanted to meet you and introduce myself! I'm Leah," she said, giving me her hand to shake.

"You must be Savannah! I have heard *so* much about you!" she said.

"Is that a good thing?" I responded laughing. "Oh yes! Giovanni just adores you!"

I could tell she was a born and raised Southern woman. She had a Southern accent. She surely had a Southern hospitality vibe to her.

"I brought you a couple of things. I know you're pregnant and I just had these laying around, so I thought you may like them," she said, handing me the gift bags she came in with.

"Oh my gosh how sweet! I wasn't expecting gifts!" I looked up at Giovanni, smiling. "I like her already," I said.

"Yeah that's how she is. Plus, she's a hoarder, so if you ever need some random ass thing, just go to Leah's house, she has it, I guarantee you," he said. She smiled and shot him a look.

"Excuse me sir, but I am *not* a hoarder. I just shop sales and stock up on things," she said, laughing.

"Oh please," he said, rolling his eyes. "You should see this woman's garage! You couldn't park a bicycle in there, it's so full of shit," he said, walking around the living room. I liked the back and forth between them. It was entertaining to watch. Like a reality show where people who are nothing alike are forced to be in the same space and try to get along. I could tell they had a genuine friendship. Having her there put me at ease a little. There was something comfortable about her. Motherly almost, welcoming for sure.

I opened the bags, and she had given me two beautiful photo books. "If you're anything like I was, you're going to want to take pictures of *everything* when that baby comes," she said sweetly.

"Oh, I have no doubt I will! Thank you so much Leah, that was very thoughtful of you," I said.

"Oh, it's no big thang," she said with her Southern drawl. "So, how are you feeling?" she asked, getting to the real reason she came by. "Giovanni said you were here to stay; is that right?"

"If he doesn't get sick of my shit and kick me out," I said jokingly.

"Oh, he won't do that, trust me," she laughed.

"So, what happened?" she asked. I told her about what had occurred the night before and how I ended up here in such a hurry.

"So, you weren't able to get any of your furniture?" she asked.

"No," I said. "But my dad just bought me a blow-up mattress and Giovanni had an extra dresser, so at least I have somewhere to sleep and put my clothes. The rest I can figure out later. I haven't even heard from Hector yet," I said, looking at my phone.

"Really? Is that like him?" she asked.

"I honestly don't know; I've never left him before. But he already took me off Facebook. So, we are definitely broken up," I told her.

"Oh wow, I would have thought you would have heard from him by now," she said.

"Oh, she'll hear from him eventually," Giovanni said. "He's just trying to bandage his wounded pride right now, so he doesn't know what his next move should be." He opened the back door to have a cigarette.

"Yeah, that makes sense," she said. We sat there and chatted for a little bit longer and then Leah got up and said she had to get home. "I just wanted to come by and meet you finally," she said. I stood up to give her a hug and thanked her once again.

"Oh, no problem at all. If you need anything, I'm right next door." She reminded me of myself a lot. I was usually the sweet hostess running around trying to make everyone feel good and taking care of people. It was indescribably uncomfortable to be the one being taken care of. But God had put me in a place where everyone was just genuinely nice. For no hidden reason. It was a big change from where I came from.

I grabbed my gift bags from Leah and walked upstairs. Just as I got all my clothes where I wanted them my phone rang. It was Jose. I answered and sat on my air mattress.

"Hello?" I said.

"Yo, Hector is buggin' out. Where are you?" he asked.

"I'm safe."

"Tell me you didn't go back with your ex," he said.

"What?"

"This nigga thinks you back with that Bruce dude. He swears you've been cheating with him this whole time."

I laughed and laid back on the bed. "That's funny."

"So, you're not with him?"

"Yeah I moved in with Bruce and his *wife* and their *three* children last night. We're all sharing the same bed," I answered sarcastically.

"Wait, he's married?"

"Yes, he is married with three children."

"He never mentioned that."

"I bet he didn't," I said rolling my eyes.

"I'm not with Bruce, I'm not seeing Bruce and I have *never* cheated on Hector. Why is he so insecure?"

"Shit, he's always been like that. So, where are you at then? You at Gia's house? Or that other big girl with the purple hair?"

"No, I'm not where anyone is going to find me. I'm in a safe place and that's all anyone needs to know right now until things cool down a little."

"Well, he wants the ring back and he's threatening to cut off your phone. I told him he couldn't do that; he has to support you while you're pregnant. If he doesn't, it isn't gonna look good on him in court. And he gave you that ring on Christmas Day, so no judge is going to make you give it back."

"Well, he's not getting the ring. I have them both and the receipts and intend on selling them back to the store after I have the baby. I'll be able to get my own apartment with that money. And as far as the phone goes, he can do whatever he wants, I don't care," I said.

"No, he can't!" Jose said. "I told him he needs to support you financially even if you aren't together. He's going to have to pay child support anyway so he may as well get used to it if he wants you to let him see his kid," he said, speaking from his own experience.

"I heard you saw Pops and my brother loading me up last night, why were you there?"

"Hector sent me to get some of his shit. He got drunk and emotional and wanted to teach you a lesson. I told him I would go so he stayed at my house. But I wasn't trying to go in there with all that going on. I'm glad you called them though, you needed to get out of there. He's never gonna change. But if he does, this will do it," he said.

"What do you mean?" I asked.

"You leaving. All that nigga has talked about wanting for years is a kid of his own. Now he finally has one on the way and he fucked it up so bad you left mid pregnancy. If he doesn't wake up now, he's a lost fucking cause," he said.

"Yeah, well it doesn't seem like he even cares about me, so, whether he changes or not, it's over. I'll never go back to him after all this," I said genuinely.

"I think he knows that; that's why he's bugging out right now. He knows he fucked everything up for good," he said.

"Did you guys say anything to him about throwing a lamp at my face?" I asked.

"Of course, he said it was an accident! I'm like nigga we were there! You 'accidentally' pulled the lamp out the wall and threw it with perfect aim at your baby mama's face? I told you he's bugging," he said with his Bronx accent.

"Wow, he's never at fault, is he?" I said.

"Hell no, he thinks he's right about everything," he went on to vent about all the things going on at work and how everyone hated working for him, how they all had to walk on eggshells to even get along with him.

"He's going to kill this business if he doesn't chill. He cussed out a couple of customers and even started threatening them like he was gonna roll up on them and beat their ass," he said.

"Are you serious?"

"Dead ass. He's tweaked the fuck out all the time. He's a total junkie anymore," he said. "Well that's the truth."

"I slept on the floor last night freezing my ass off, but Pops just brought me a blow-up mattress until I can get my bed," I said.

"Well, you may have to wait until he's out of town or something one weekend, cause if you go back over there anytime soon, it's not going to be pretty."

"Yeah, I know, but everything in that house is *mine*; he didn't have shit when I met him. He only owns that pool table and the dining room table. That's it," I said.

"Oh, I know. He should be a fucking man and let you have the house. What kind of scum bag lets his pregnant girl sleep on a floor alone in some house somewhere after he beats on her?" he said, seeming genuinely upset. "He ain't shit, but I'll keep working on him. He'll come around eventually, he has to, he's losing everything he ever wanted for fucking drugs and wanting to pretend to be a badass."

"Yeah, well it seems to me that everyone enables him. Nobody ever wants to upset him, so they quietly move out of the way and let him throw his fits like an angry toddler who isn't getting to eat cookies for dinner," I said.

"Well, it's hard because we have our own families to feed. If he gets pissed and fires me, where do I go then?" he said.

"I don't mean just you guys. His club buddies, his friends, everyone. Nobody stands up to him," I said. "Myself included." He laughed.

"Are you fucking kidding? You *do* stand up to him. You're one of the only ones that says the real shit everyone else is thinking to him! That's why he's so insecure with you. You make him feel like shit," he said.

"Well, I don't want to make him feel like shit," I said sadly.

"I know that, but when you hear the truth about yourself and you're a shitty person, then it makes you feel like shit." I couldn't argue with that. But I didn't like being responsible for hurting someone. He was broken when I met him, I never intended on making him worse.

"Well I need to lay down and take a nap. Thanks for checking on me."

"I'll keep you posted. Don't worry; you're going to be fine," he said, hanging up the phone.

I went back down to the living room. Giovanni was playing on his computer, but he didn't have any headphones on, so I decided to pick his brain about what had just occurred.

"Well, it sounds like he tried awful hard to get you to tell him where you are. Do you think Hector asked him to do that?"

"I don't actually know. Jose is pretty good to me. It's not the first time he's been there for me when I needed a friend," I said.

"Why is that?" he asked.

"What do you mean?"

"Well, he's Hector's cousin, right?"

"Yeah."

"So, don't you think it's a little strange that he would be trying to show loyalty to *you*? I mean, he's literally betraying Hector by doing that, if he is doing it without being told to by Hector. And he works for Hector and has a family to support, so why risk his livelihood?"

"Yeah, I don't know, I guess because he's sick of Hector bullying everyone."

"That could be," Giovanni said, nodding his head.

"Or he's trying to gain your trust, so you'll be comfortable around him."

"What do you mean? I am comfortable around him," I said.

"Well let me ask you this, has he ever tried to make a move on you?" I laughed.

"No, never. He's not that kind of guy."

"Well, From the outside looking in, it sounds like he wants to fuck you," he said matter-of-factly.

"No, he doesn't. I know his wife and kids. They are very happy together. He's never even flirted with me or anyone else for that matter," I said, defending Jose.

"Okay, just an outside perspective," Giovanni said calmly.

After a few days had gone by, I was starting to wonder if I would hear from Hector at all. It was Tuesday morning, February 14, and it had been four days since I left. I had an early morning appointment with the specialist to get another ultrasound done. I knew Hector had it on his calendar, and since he was adamant about being there for all of my doctor appointments, I figured maybe he would show up. But I didn't want to call or text him since he hadn't reached out to me at all. On my way to the doctor I got a call from Jose.

"Hello?"

"Hey, Hector wants to know where the specialist is and what time to be there."

"Well, he should have asked *me* that earlier. The appointment is in 15 minutes and I'm almost there. Why didn't he just ask?" I said, already annoyed with how childish he was being.

"Because he's an idiot. You know he has to cause drama however he can," he said.

"Well, I haven't heard a word from him since I left, so I had no idea he planned on coming."

"Well, he said he's going whether you want him there or not."

It was unnecessary comments like *that* that irritated me. If he had been man enough to contact me the night before, I would have been happy to tell him when and where. I wanted him to be a father, I wanted him to care about the growth of our daughter. But, why did he have to always be such a controlling ass?

"Well, the appointment is at 9 a.m. It's in the same hospital as the OBGYN and the maternity ward I'll be giving birth in. If he wants to come that's fine, but if he's mean to me or threatens me in any way, he won't be allowed into the room with me," I said knowing that I had full control over *all* of my and my daughter's care. He wasn't my husband, so by law he didn't have any rights. I didn't know if he was going to come, so when I got there, I told the lady at the front desk that he may be coming. I told her very quietly that I had just left him four days prior due to domestic violence and I just wanted someone to be aware of it since I wasn't feeling completely comfortable around him.

"Oh, I see," she said with a look of concern. She called over one of her colleagues and they both talked with me for a few minutes.

"You don't have to let him back there if you don't want to. But if you do, we can make sure you're never left alone with him in the room."

"That would be fantastic," I said relieved. I didn't like feeling like some victim of abuse that people had to look out for. But I just wanted to do whatever I could from here on out to avoid any other situation. As long as I had gone hiding this, it felt strange to be telling people openly about such shameful truths. But there was also something freeing about it.

"Nobody is going to say anything to him, though right? If he knows I told you it will just get me into trouble when I leave."

"No, absolutely not, and if you are uncomfortable leaving at the same time, I can happily have security walk you to your car." I liked this lady.

"But you should let your doctor know what's going on as well if she doesn't already know. Any time you have to encounter him in any way, make sure someone is aware of it. This isn't something to mess around about," she said, genuinely concerned.

"Yes, ma'am I will."

I went and sat down nervously. I was messaging Giovanni telling him about my morning so far when a nurse called me back.

"I'm just going to check you out really quick and then you'll wait in the waiting room again until the specialist is ready," she said putting me on the scale.

"Okay, thank you."

"Are you nervous?"

"A little."

"Don't be, we all know your situation, we'll take care of you here," she said squeezing my arm. It was comforting. I felt like I had a band of warrior women surrounding me. They didn't know me, never met me, but the minute I told them what was going on, it didn't matter. They weren't going to let anything happen to me on their watch. I was back in the waiting room messaging Giovanni when the door opened to the small waiting room. It was Hector. He looked awful. He had his work clothes on, but he looked like he hadn't showered in days. He smelled horrible. His face was overgrown, and his clothes looked dirty.

"Hello," I said, trying to break the tension.

"Hey." He laid back in the chair and put his dirty boots up on the chair in front of him. I noticed the lady at the desk taking note of his already rude behavior. She shook her head and pointed at him with her pen showing her colleague. I was already embarrassed.

"Can you please take your dirty boots off the chair? This is a nice place, and you're being rude already," I said in a whisper. He looked at me like he wished I would die and sat up.

"You're not my fucking mother."

"That's the truth, if I had raised you, you wouldn't be such a jerk," I said going back to my phone.

"What the fuck did you just say to me?" The door to the back area opened and I heard the young lady call my name. I got up and walked towards her hearing Hector's boots scrape the ground lazily behind me as he followed.

We went into an exam room full of fancy equipment and monitors everywhere. It was dark, but enough light to see where I was going.

"I'm going to leave the door open so you can have enough light to get settled in," she said while I sat on the table. "The doctor will be in shortly. Do you need anything?" she asked, looking directly at me.

"We're fine," Hector said answering for me.

"If *you* need anything Mrs. Savannah, please let me know," she said, keeping her eyes on me.

"Thank you," I responded smiling sweetly. I laid back on the table, waiting to see the doctor. Hector stayed on his phone. We didn't say a word to each other. It was extremely uncomfortable.

"So, how are you?" I asked trying to break the awkward silence. He just shot me an "are you fucking serious" look and shook his head while rolling his eyes. He looked down at my hand and noticed I was still wearing my ring. I thought for sure he was going to ask for it back, but he didn't. I had it on my right hand now, but I still hadn't taken it off. I'm not sure why, I didn't really like the ring, but I didn't know what was going to happen yet. He didn't say anything but the look on his face softened. At least he didn't look like he wanted to murder me now. The doctor walked in with her assistant nurse smiling happily and shaking my hand. She briefly nodded at Hector, being polite, but kept the conversation toward me the whole time. She pumped a handful of sanitizer into her palm and rubbed her hands together while the nurse read off a few details from my file. "Okay, so have you had any bleeding since you were last seen?" she asked.

"No ma'am," I answered. "Great! Let's see if we can find something to hopefully put your mind at ease then."

She asked me to pull my shirt up and put the jelly on my little tummy. With all the stress I had been under I had been losing weight. So I wasn't really showing much yet. She moved the device around on my stomach and told us we could see what she was seeing in the big flat screens above her head. There she was, my sweet baby! She was growing like a weed! She had gotten so big since I last saw her. Seeing her up there moving around just melted my heart. I loved her *so* much already. I started tearing up. She had no idea what kind of sacrifices I had already made for her. How much I wanted her to be happy and safe and live a great life. Tears were streaming down my face when I heard Hector sniffle. I looked over and he and I were on the same emotional page. It broke my heart. I could see the pain I had caused him all over his face. I didn't want to hurt him. I just needed him to stop hurting me. Plus, I couldn't allow him to hurt our daughter. I was responsible for another life now.

"Well, she's stubborn, I'll say that," the doctor said laughing.

"Yeah, that's not surprising," I said. "I'm trying to get her to move or roll over so I can get images of everything but the more I nudge her, the less she wants to give me," she said. Finally, she had to give up.

"Well, we got enough to make sure there are no rips or tears anywhere that are leaking fluid. She's at a great measurement, so she looks perfectly healthy. I don't see any cause for concern right now, but, given your recent history, I would like you to remain taking it easy and trying to avoid stress. You're still high risk, and we will still be monitoring you throughout your pregnancy along with your OBGYN just to make sure. But so far, she's doing great," she said, smiling. "Do you have any questions?" She took off her gloves.

"Can I keep some of the images?" I asked, hopeful.

"Of course!" she said. "Here you are, have your next appointment scheduled for two weeks from now at the front desk on your way out," she said sweetly.

"Thank you!"

We went out front and I scheduled my next appointment. Hector stood there with me putting the information in his calendar. I could tell the woman at the desk wasn't a big fan of his.

"Okay Miss Savannah, if there's anything else you need let us know. Otherwise, we will see you at the next visit!" she said to me sweetly.

"Thank you so much."

"No problem. You get home safe," she said with a more serious look. Awkwardly Hector and I walked to the elevator together. I felt like I should say something, but I didn't know what to say. We got on the elevator and went down to the ground floor. When we exited, he went to the left towards his car, and I went to the right. There was no conversation, no goodbye, nothing. It was an incredibly empty, emotional type of torture. I mean, I knew I didn't want to be with him anymore, and I knew I was doing the right thing. But we still had a baby on the way, and I didn't want him to hate me. How could we co-parent well if we hated each other? I got in my car and started crying. I moved my car to a more private area so nobody could see me and just cried. I had loved this man and spent so much time and effort trying with him. My feelings were genuine. I know leaving him hurt, but he had to see *why* I left, right?

I was messaging back and forth with my mom and Giovanni, telling them about the awkward visit. My phone received a text from Hector. My heart sank into my stomach. I opened the text that read "If you aren't doing anything tonight, I would like to take you to dinner. But I don't want to talk about anything going on between us right now. I just want to take you out for Valentine's day." *Wait, what?* I re-read the message several times, confused. He was just acting like he hated me and now he wanted to take me to dinner? Knowing we would have to break this ice eventually, I agreed to go.

"Okay, when and where, and I'll be there," I replied.

"Olive Garden 6:30 p.m."

That was it. That's all we said to each other all day. I screenshotted the conversation and sent it to Giovanni. When he got home from work, we discussed it further. He and his coworkers all had bets going on how the evening was going to go. There were several different scenarios in the air that I found amusing. Understandably, he, along with his coworkers, underestimated me. I was serious about staying gone. I had to do this for my child, and I couldn't go back to lying anymore. I was done.

I arrived at the restaurant 10 minutes early and could barely find a parking spot. I texted Hector when I found one and saw him pulling in and having the same trouble. Seeing there was a line out the door, I went in to get our names on the list. There was already a one-hour-and-20-minute wait for a table. I came out and told him the wait time. He had on a suit and was clean shaven. He seemed happy to see me, but still distant. We sat down in the waiting area and he got on his phone. It was awkward and silent again.

He would ask me different random questions: "Do you separate my work clothes and stuff when you wash them? Or do I just throw everything in together?" or "When do you pay the bills in the house?" Basic life questions. But all things I had always just done for him. "Well, I'm going to give you one of my credit cards so you can keep up on the bills. It's all in your name, anyway; just let me know when you have to pay them," he said.

"Okay." That was a relief. Must be Jose had gotten to him a little bit. "To be clear, it is *not* to pay your car note," he said sternly.

Finally, we sat at a booth and were ready to eat. It was like he changed into a totally different person. He was smiling and making jokes with the waitress and me. He was beaming with pride when he told her we were having a baby. Finally, dinner came to an end and he threw his card down to pay for it. When she returned, he told her to hand it to me.

"You keep that one for the bills and if you need anything," he said.

"Okay, thank you." We still hadn't discussed anything. But it was a relief to know he wasn't going to ruin my credit by not paying the utilities that were in my name. He walked me to my car and gave me a hug.

"Thanks for dinner," I said.

"Yeah, thanks for coming," he responded, giving me a half-hug.

"Are we going to sit down and talk about things soon? We have a lot to work out," I said gently.

"I can't yet, but we'll figure everything out," he said, opening my door for me.

"Okay, well, happy Valentine's Day" He laughed uncomfortably.

"Yeah, you too," he said.

Giovanni was surprised to see me come in before 9 p.m. He was sure I would end up going home with him and making up.

"Wow" he said when I came in. "I wasn't expecting to see you again tonight." He got up from his desk.

"Yeah, I told you it was just dinner," I said.

"Well how did it go?" I filled him in on the awkward evening.

"But he gave me his credit card so I can keep paying the house bills. So at least I know I won't have ruined credit anytime soon!"

"Well that's good. Does that mean you can pay your car note with it?"

"No, he was clear about that," I said shaking my head. "I'm not to even supposed to ask him to help me with it since he hates Gia so much."

Feeling emotionally drained, I took myself to bed. Grateful for the blow-up mattress my father got me, I climbed in fully clothed. Hector messaged me. "I don't know what to do," he said.

"What do you mean?" I asked him, thinking it was something stupid like how to work the dishwasher.

"I want you to come home, but I know I'm no good for you." I took a minute to let that sink in before responding.

"I don't know what to do either. I'm just taking it one day at a time right now and trying to do what is best for our daughter," I said with tears in my eyes.

"I know you will do whatever you think is right for her, that's one of the things I love the most about you." Tears started streaming down my face.

"I don't want to hurt you, but I can't do this anymore."

"I know, I don't want to keep hurting you either," he responded.

I felt myself softening towards him during our texts. I wanted to give him a hug and make him feel better. I was thinking maybe Jose was right and this would finally make him go get help. Maybe there was still hope. I hated the thought of being responsible for his broken heart.

"You just left," he said after a few minutes of silence.

"My biggest fear was coming home one day to find you were gone. And that's exactly what happened," he said.

"I told you if you ever hit me again it would happen. I'm sorry, but I just won't let you do this to me anymore," I said.

"It was an accident."

Immediately my heart ache and broken feelings turned to annoyance.

"That was not an accident. That was you throwing a tantrum," I said.

"It wouldn't have happened if you weren't calling your ex all the time."

Really? I thought to myself. *So, this is still all my fault? How could he possibly see it that way?*

"Don't start. I already tried to tell you that HE called ME and why he called. If you weren't out with HIS friend like some cocaine groupie all the time starting shit, he wouldn't have a reason to call," I said, regretting sending the message as soon as I did. "But it doesn't matter. NOTHING YOU DO is ever YOUR fault, right? YOU'RE the victim. I forgot." No longer feeling soft or heartbroken for him or myself, I continued. "If you want to blame everything on me to make yourself feel better feel free. If it has nothing to do with our daughter, you and I have nothing else to discuss. I'm praying for you to wake up one day, but I have no intention on waiting around for you to do it. Good night," I said, putting my phone on silent.

I got up and changed for bed. My hands were shaking, and my palms were sweating. I wanted to punch something. Clearly, I was wrong for thinking even for a second that this was going to help him see clearly and clean up his life. But he was more focused on making me feel crappy than he was on what we were going to do once our daughter arrived.

CHAPTER TWENTY-SIX

Nobody Told Me!?

The next two weeks went by very quickly. I had been taking a pregnancy and parenting class every Tuesday at a church program a friend of mine was the director of. She was the sweetest woman ever. I met her when I was working out all the time. She was a Zumba instructor and I really liked her. When I had first announced my pregnancy, she and I met for brunch one day, and while we were sitting there, I felt the urge to be honest with her. I didn't even know her that well at the time, but when I started talking there was no stopping it. Having gone through a similar experience earlier in her life, she knew exactly how to be there for me. I found it extremely comforting to have someone not only know what I was going through but also understand how I was feeling and thinking. We became closer quickly. I loved the church 'earn while you learn' program. It was a wonderful tool to use, not only to learn about God and get some real parenting tips, but to earn things like diapers, wipes, clothes, car seats, everything you could think of. I loved the program. Such wonderful amazing people doing God's work in a fantastic way.

Finally, it was time to go follow up with my OBGYN. As instructed by the lady at the specialist office, I did advise the staff of the situation. They were immediately on board with making sure I was 100 percent safe while in their care. I knew Hector was coming to the appointment, so I quickly filled out the paperwork saying that he had no right to access any of my health information. They wanted to make sure that if he called at some point it was in my file not to discuss anything with him and to notify me immediately if he contacted them.

As I sat down to wait, Jose called me.

"Hey," I said.

"You at the doctor yet?" he asked.

"Yeah, I just got here. Why?" I asked.

"We can't get ahold of Hector, so nobody knows if he's going to come in today. Have you heard from him?" he asked.

"No. I don't even know if he's coming today." I hadn't heard from him in a few days.

"Well he'd better be, he told Titi and I yesterday that he was. But he's been fucking everything up left and right and pissing off customers. He's been doing nothing but getting fucked up and partying."

"Well that sucks. I don't really hear from him a whole lot. Mostly people just send me screen shots of all the stupid shit he posts on social media to get my attention," I said, rolling my eyes.

"Yeah, he really is losing it. I thought this would wake him up, but since you left, it's only gotten worse." The nurse called me back to the room.

"I have to go."

"Okay, let me know how your appointment goes." Just as I got in the exam room a nurse came and asked if I wanted to let Hector come back.

"Yeah, that's fine," I said, rolling my eyes. He came in and looked and smelled homeless. I could smell him the second he opened the door and it made me instantly nauseous.

"Wow, what happened to you?" I asked. As he came in and moved my purse so he could sit down.

"What's that supposed to mean?"

"You look awful, and you smell even worse. Are you going to work like that?"

"I'm a chimney technician, people don't care if I'm dirty."

The doctor came in and we went over everything. She wanted me to keep my appointments with the specialist until further notice. I still hadn't had anymore bleeding. When we went to leave Hector was parked right next to me.

"So, when are you going to drop off the baby stuff you stole from my house?" he said. I stopped and looked at him.

"What the hell are you talking about? I literally earned all that stuff, and it's still *our* house."

"Well, I know Frankie gave you a bag of clothes and some other stuff, that's from my family so it needs to be returned to my house immediately," he said, ready to start a fight.

"Okay, well then I'll need you to be out of the house so I can come get all the rest of *my* stuff, and I'll happily drop off the items I was given for *our* daughter," I said not wanting to argue.

"What the fuck ever," he said, "I fucking hate you."

"Well, that's unfortunate, but okay," I said, opening my car door. "You can hate me all you want, but you *do* need to learn how to respect me. I'm the mother of your *only* child and I will *not* tolerate this shit around her *ever*. So, grow up!" I said, putting my purse in the car.

"Yeah fuck you! You're not in control of shit bitch, watch your fucking mouth! I can take that credit card and that phone back right now if I fuck-ing want to," he said, threatening me.

"Then go ahead," I said, putting my phone on the roof of my car. "Be my guest. I'll have all the utilities shut off before you get home," I said, calling his bluff.

"Fuck you!" he screamed at me, getting in his car. He slammed the door and sped off. Needing someone to talk to, I called Frankie to see if she was home with their daughter. She said she was and happily invited me to come over.

She had known Hector a long time and was around to see all the relationships he had been in. She was surprised to see how he was handling this situation, though.

"I really thought this was going to be his big wakeup call. Jose and I were certain if anything would change him, it would be you leaving. I can't believe he's acting like such and ass," she said, almost laughing. "He's showing out on social media like he's some hot shot, when we all know he's a fucking loser asshole. I don't want to start anything, but he's been reaching out to any girl on his friends list for attention," she said.

"Oh really?" I said. "Yeah, like he messaged my best friend from New York, she knows him, she was married to my husband's brother before he died, she thought it was ridiculous that he would even try her like that," she said.

"Yeah, he posted a picture of him and that old ass blond chick he used to fuck when he and Genna were together," I said.

"Oh, the one on Facebook!? Yeah, I saw that. You can tell he's doing all this just so it will get back to you. He's being so fucking stupid," she said. "Wait, he was fucking her when he was with Genna?"

"Yeah he ended up getting her pregnant. I guess she had an abortion before even telling him, so according to him, he hated her for that. Or at least that's what he told me," I said, rolling my eyes.

"Jesus Christ," she said, looking disgusted. "Is there anyone he hasn't fucked?" she asked laughing.

"Not in Georgia."

"Well, how's the baby doing?" she asked.

"So far so good," I said. "They're keeping a close eye on things." I leaned back on her love seat. She was standing hovering over her daughter, but I noticed her behavior had changed. She seemed nervous.

"What's wrong?" I asked.

"Oh, nothing, I just really want to ask you something, but it could start a lot of shit, so I don't know if I should. But I feel like you may be in the dark and literally need to know," she said playing with her fingers. I got chills down my body. *What is it now?* I asked myself.

"Well now you have to tell me," I sat up bracing myself for the bomb she was about to drop on me.

"You know about Genna right?" she asked.

"What about her?" I asked. She started pacing nervously looking like she was about to throw up.

"Did he ever tell you about her health?" she asked, not wanting to look at me.

"Why would he?" I asked anxious to find out where this was going.

"I knew it! He's such a fucking liar!" she said visibly disgusted. "I need you to know something. But you can *not* let him or Jose find out where it came from," she said nervously.

"Jesus Christ, Frankie, just spit it out!" I said, getting overanxious.

"She has AIDS!" I could feel all the blood draining from my face and my nausea setting in. I was getting hot and clammy and shaky all at the same time.

"What?" was all I could manage to spit out.

"He told all of us he was up-front with you about it and to mind our own business, I thought you knew for the longest time. But people were all starting to wonder since you've been having problems with your pregnancy," she said still pacing.

"Wait a minute. Are you saying she had AIDS before he left her?" I asked.

"She had it when he met her!" I felt like I was going to throw up.

"But they were swingers, you can't have a known STD of that nature and still be out fucking everyone! Aren't there laws against that!?" I asked.

"Yeah I think so. But nobody knew for the longest time," she said. "I believe it was his cousin Jimmy that discovered it years ago."

"What?" I said in disbelief. Jimmy and I were still close. No way he knew this and didn't tell me. "How did he discover it?"

"I don't know the exact story, but he was at their house one night and found a bottle of medicine laying on their bed. He didn't know what it was, so he looked it up on his phone and it was for people who were HIV positive or had full-blown AIDS," she said not realizing what she had just unlocked. Everything fell into place! That was the *same story* he gave me when I found out the boys living with us had AIDS. Excepts he changed the details to *him* finding the medicine that allegedly belonged to his uncle! I felt sick.

"Who all knew about this?" I asked.

"Just the family."

"And *nobody* ever thought to tell me!?" I said, furious. "We thought he did, but I see now we were very wrong. I'm so sorry, Savannah, but you need to call your doctor and get tested if you haven't already," she said.

"I had a STD test a little over a year ago when Gia got herpes and I was at risk because Hector had been with her unprotected just before he and I got together. I was clean then," I said trying to breathe and hold back the stomach bile that wanted to come up. *Oh my God! Gia! Did she know this!? His family not telling me is one thing, but if she knew this and kept it from me, it would be an entirely different matter.*

"Hector fucked Gia?" she asked in complete shock.

"Yeah they were fucking back when he and Genna were still married. Listen, I have to go. Thank you for telling me, but I need to go," I said getting up.

"I'm so sorry! Please don't tell him I told you," she begged.

"I won't."

With shaky hands I messaged Gia to call me as soon as she could get a chance. It didn't take long to hear from her.

"What's wrong?" she asked.

"I need to ask you something, and I need you to be honest with me," I said, unsure of whether she knew.

"Okay, what is it?" she asked concerned.

"Did you know Genna has AIDS?"

"*What*!?" she screamed, already revealing that she was unaware. I breathed a sigh of relief for *that*.

"I was just told that she had AIDS and that she had it before she knew Hector. So, people are concerned enough to say something *now* since I'm pregnant and could be affected by this if he has it and didn't tell me," I said with rage in my voice. I pulled into the driveway of Giovanni's house still shaking.

"Fuck no, I didn't know! That motherfucker! After all he had to say about *me* when I came up with what I have, and I handled it like a fucking adult! That piece of shit!" she said, rightfully angry.

"I wouldn't have touched him if I knew this! Oh my God! Does Hector have it?" she asked.

"Nobody knows," I responded.

"Listen, don't say a fucking word yet. I'm going to meet with Jimmy tonight, he's taking me to a movie, and I am going to confront him first. I need to make sure this isn't just a rumor, okay?" I said.

"That motherfucker! I won't say anything, but you need to let me know *immediately* when you talk to him! Because I could have been at risk for this too!" she said.

"I'll call you right after I meet with him, I promise. Just keep your cool until then, *please*," I said, getting off the phone.

I messaged Jimmy to make sure we were still going to the movies later. He replied, "Of course unless you need to do it another day." I responded, "No I'm looking forward to it! See you then!" not letting him know just yet what I needed to find out. My phone rang; it was Bruce. I went out on the back porch to answer it.

"Hello?" I said, still trying to control my anxiety.

"What the hell is wrong with you? You sound scared, are you okay?" he asked. I broke down and told him what I just learned, crying once again.

"Okay, calm down, I'm sure you're fine. If you had something wouldn't you already know?" he asked.

"I don't know, the last STD test I had was two years ago when I first got with him. I was clean then but, we had only been together maybe two months by then," I said. He let out a long sigh.

"Well, I was calling to make sure you were good. Do you need anything?" he asked.

"Not unless you want to pay my car note this month," I said, laughing. "I swear with all the drama and stress, it's hard for me to even *want* to Uber people around."

"You shouldn't be doing that shit anyway. It's not safe," he said.

"Yeah well, I still have to pay my car note, so I don't have much choice."

"How much is it?" he asked.

"$365."

"How much do you have already?"

"$125," I said flatly.

"Okay, if you want to come get it, I'll give you the money." My heart leapt with joy and relief.

"Are you serious?"

"Yeah, I told you I got you. I'll call you tomorrow afternoon and we can meet up then, okay?"

"Yeah, that's perfect. Thank you!"

"No problem, it's the least I can do," he said.

By the time Giovanni came home from work, I was already showered and ready to go meet Jimmy for the movie. I still had a couple of hours before it was time to go, but my anxiety wouldn't let me relax.

"Everything okay?" Giovanni asked, suspecting something was wrong.

"I have to go meet Jimmy in a couple of hours. He's taking me to a movie," I said plainly.

"Who is Jimmy?"

"Hector's cousin."

"You're going to a movie with Hector's cousin?" he asked, confused.

"Yeah but trust me, it's not like *that* at all. I need to talk to him about something I found out today," I said nervously.

"Do you want to talk about it?"

"I don't know," I answered with tears welling up in my eyes.

"Well, something pretty bad must have happened; you look like you're about to cry."

I broke down and told him. I wasn't sure that it was true or that I was even at risk. But I didn't want Giovanni to think even less of me than I had convinced myself he already did. It *had* to be getting ridiculous to him to watch all this drama unfold.

"Well, it sounds like it's probably true," he said calmly. "I mean, it's the exact story he gave you about his alleged uncle when he was advising you on the boys having it. But I understand your need to confirm it." I rocked impatiently in one of the chairs on the back porch. It was March now, and the weather was getting beautiful. We were spending a lot of time out on the deck overlooking the pool.

"Do you trust him?"

"What?" I asked, spaced out on the pool, imagining myself floating around in it with a golden tan not worrying about anything.

"Jimmy. Do you trust him?"

"Oh, yeah, I do actually. He and I have gotten close. He doesn't lie. He may tell you he won't talk about something or that he can't, but he doesn't lie. Not that I've ever seen anyway."

"Okay, well. I hope he answers your questions. But you should probably call your doctor tomorrow regardless," he said.

"Yeah, I know. I asked Gia if she knew about it and she flipped out. She's pretty pissed off too. So, everyone wants to know the truth."

Finally, the time came where I had to leave to meet Jimmy. I said my goodbyes, and Giovanni wished me luck. When I made it to the theater, I was almost late, so we rushed in and got our seats while the advertisements began. The movie wasn't bad. It was nice to get swept away from my anxiety for a couple of hours. When it ended and the credits were rolling, I told him I had to use the bathroom. He did as well, but he waited for me to come out.

"So, how are you?" he asked. "I miss you", he said, hugging me. I smiled; he always had a way of putting me at ease. He was about my height with black hair and a heavy build. He had a few tattoos and a tongue ring, so first glance didn't do him justice. His appearance wasn't nearly as welcoming as his personality. He was usually happy and fun. But was always there for you if you needed him.

"I need to talk to you about something," I said to him when we reached our vehicles. He lit a cigarette.

"What's up?" he asked.

"A little birdy told me today that Genna has AIDS and that she had it the whole time Hector was with her." I could tell by the way he looked up at me from still trying to get his cigarette lit that it was true.

"Who told you?"

"It doesn't matter," I said, pushing on with the conversation. "I need you to tell me the truth now, Jimmy. I could be as risk; my *daughter* could be at risk and *nobody* fucking told me!" I said, starting to cry angrily.

"We thought you knew. Hector told us he had been up-front with you from the beginning, we didn't have a reason to bring it up to you. But we have all wondered if he was telling the truth," he said, shaking his head.

"Well, he didn't. So, I need to hear it from you. Tell me how *you* found out." He let out a sigh.

"I was at their apartment, Hector and Genna had a fight again and she was threatening to kill herself, so Hector asked me to go over there and make sure the kids were okay," he said, taking a drag off his smoke. "They were always doing dramatic shit like this, so it wasn't new." He rolled his eyes. "I went in their bedroom at one point and found a pill bottle laying on the bed. I was supposed to be making sure she wasn't killing herself, so I picked it up to see what she had taken. I didn't know what it was, so I looked it up on my phone," he said, shrugging his shoulders. He told me that Genna came in while he was reading it and he confronted her. She confessed right then.

"So, it *is* true," I said leaning, back on my car for support. "That fucking bastard!" Angry tears of betrayal fell from my swollen eyes. "How have they gotten away with being swingers and fucking everyone in the world with something like this!?" I asked.

"Nobody really knows outside the family. And nobody ever talks about it," he said.

"I wish someone would have told me!" I said, upset at everyone.

"He swore us to secrecy, and it wasn't our business. I'm sorry you had to find out in this condition. But I'm glad you know the truth," he said, hugging me.

"I'm glad I know now as well," I said.

"Have you said anything to him yet?" he asked me.

"No, not yet," I replied, wiping my nose. "I want to do it in person. I want to see his fucking face when I throw this at him and watch him react."

"It's not going to go well. He's going to want to know who told you," he said.

"I don't care what the hell he wants anymore," I said flatly.

"He's already spinning out of control. He's going crazy for real. He went to see a lawyer this morning," he said.

"What? Why?"

"To see what he can do when the baby's here," he said.

"Meaning?" I asked, getting defensive.

"He thought he could just take the baby home from the hospital, so apparently when he found out that he has zero legal right to do anything since you guy's never got married, he flipped out at the office," he said, laughing.

"Jose had been telling him he was wrong, but it took a lawyer to tell him he has no power until he takes certain steps."

"I told him that too, he's stupid. He really doesn't listen." It did make me happy to hear that he finally learned the truth. Maybe he would stop being such an ass now.

I thanked Jimmy for the movie and the honesty and told him I would see him again soon. I gave him a hug, and we went our separate ways. When I got home, the house was quiet and dark, and I figured everyone was in bed. I went to the back porch and called Gia. She was calmer now, but still upset about the situation.

"So now what?" she asked.

"Well, I want to confront him tomorrow face to face," I said.

"I don't know if that's a good idea," she said nervously.

"I don't care. I need to see his face when I ask him about this. I'll tell him to meet me somewhere public, a restaurant or something. But I need to do this," I said.

"Do you want me to go with you?" she asked, eager to confront him as well. "I will!" I laughed.

"No, but I need to do it tomorrow." I wished her a good night and told her I would keep her posted.

The first thing I did the next morning was call my doctor. I told the nurse what I had learned and that I was worried.

"Well, since you don't have any positive tests yet, that's a good sign. But with something like this it can remain dormant for 6 months to a year in some cases. So we will need to have you retested a few more times throughout your pregnancy just to be thorough," she said sweetly.

"But if I get it what will happen to my daughter?" I asked, worried.

"If you test positive at any point then we have medication that will protect the baby from getting it. Your daughter should be fine. Is the father willing to provide proof of a blood test? It would help to know if he has it or not," she said.

"I'll see what I can do."

I sent Hector a message to see if we could meet at Applebee's when he got off to talk.

"Sure, that's fine," he said. The plan was set, I would let everyone know when and where I was meeting him just to be safe and confront him in a public place just in case it got ugly. I went over what I was going to say and do with Giovanni when he got home. Nervously awaiting the moment. Finally, it was time to go. My palms were sweating the whole way there. I saw his car when I arrived and parked right next to it. When I walked in, I spotted his bald head right away. I walked up to the booth and sat down. He had already had a martini and eaten an appetizer and was looking at his phone. I sat down asking the waitress to bring me a small glass of red wine. I needed some liquid courage and my doctor had told me I was safe to have red wine on occasion if it calmed me down since my anxiety had been so bad.

"So what is this about?" he asked, annoyed that I was bothering him.

"We have a lot to discuss," I said flatly.

"Yeah, like are you giving my daughter my last name?" he asked.

I laughed. "No." He was already pissed off.

"Why?"

"Because you and I are not married. My daughter will have *my* last name and there's nothing you can do about it." The waitress sat down my glass and asked if I needed anything else. "No thank you," I said politely.

"Well, I got a lawyer yesterday, and I have rights, so act however you want to, but I'll be getting full custody of my daughter as soon as I can," he said, unaware of the fact that I already knew about his meeting the day before that sent him into a fit.

"I already know you had a *free* consultation yesterday dear. As do I already know that you lost your shit in a whole ass hissy fit when you found out that you in fact have *no* legal rights at this time," I said laughing and taking a sip of my wine. I was here to fight, and the gloves were off.

His whole demeanor changed, he sat up wide eyed and angry that I already knew the truth to his bullshit lie.

"Well, you're wrong. But who the fuck told you that?"

"Irrelevant honey, that's not even why I'm here," I said interlocking my fingers on the table in front of me.

"No, you're going to tell me where the fuck you heard that."

"I'll never do a mother fucking thing that you command me to do, my dear, so get that out of your head," I said stronger than I meant to.

"Why didn't you tell me Genna had AIDS and that not only I could be at risk, but more importantly my daughter could be at risk?" I said, dropping the atomic bomb on the table. Every bit of blood drained from his face and arms. He looked like I just told him he was dying of cancer and had a week to live. The shock and guilt all over his face was exactly what I came to see firsthand. I was now 200 percent sure this was the absolute truth!

"What?" he said, trying to find words.

"What a piece of shit you have to be to keep something like that secret while you're out at swingers' events and fucking anything with a wet hole. You *do* know there are laws against that sort of thing, right?" I asked, taking another sip of my wine.

"Who told you that?" he asked, looking like a cornered animal about to strike.

"Doesn't really matter now, it's already out."

"Well it's a lie," he said laughing uncomfortably. He adjusted himself and looked around the restaurant.

"See, I knew you would say that because you're too much of a fucking *coward* to own up to anything you do, so let me tell you how I know it's true."

"You do that," he said in a condescending tone.

"You remember when the boys were with us and they told me about their AIDS and you told me the story about finding your uncle's pills and looking up what they were to discover his truth?" He twisted his face in confusion.

"Yeah, so?"

"You stole Jimmy's story!" His face drained of even more blood as I assembled the puzzle of lies in front of him. "Jimmy was at *your* house on suicide watch and found *Genna's* pills and looked them up to discover *her* secret. She confessed to him, and *you* had everyone keep their mouth shut about it so it wouldn't get in the way of you being able to be a whore," I said, satisfied to be spilling the truth to him.

"It wasn't nobody's business," he said nervously.

"There it is!" I said, clapping. "*Finally*, the fucking truth!"

"I didn't admit to shit," he said, laughing nervously.

"You're too stupid to realize that's exactly what you just did dude," I said, laughing. "What a piece of shit you are. I bet when everyone finds out, there will be some people who are pretty pissed off at you and your ex-wife!" I said, leaning back in the booth, relieved that it was out in the open now.

"Nobody's gonna know shit because it isn't fucking true. So, you need to keep your mouth shut," he said pointing his dirty finger in my face.

"Oh, I'll be screaming this from the rooftops dear. *Everyone* is going to know the truth about you," I said, sipping my wine again. I had no fear at all. I didn't care how he felt or what he threatened me with; he couldn't hurt me anymore, and he was losing his grip on me very quickly. I was starting to see him more as the monster he was than the wounded boy I needed to save all the time. He was much more deceptive than I gave him credit for, but not smart at all.

"You better not say a fucking word bitch, I'm not kidding," he said in a threatening tone.

"Oh honey, I already told Gia, and she knows *everyone* you know. She's livid with you, and her mouth is far bigger than mine could ever be," I said, laughing.

"She's just waiting for this little meeting to be done and I'm sure you'll be hearing from her shortly. As will most of Georgia. Just like you did to her when she came up positive for herpes remember? What goes around comes around. But a few bumps are a LOT less of a problem than a life-threatening illness. And you and your nasty-ass ex deserve everything you get for hiding this from all the people you were sleeping with." He got up from the table and put his knuckles down on it in front of me leaning into my face.

"I will kill you and that fat whore. *Nobody* is going to take her seriously, she's a cum dumpster for everyone in Georgia!"

"Then why are you so upset right now?" I asked, sipping my wine and blinking excessively. He walked away and then came back to the table throwing down cash for his meal.

"Did Jimmy tell you this?" he asked.

"A little birdie told me."

"It was fucking Jimmy; I'm going to kill him," he said walking off.

"It actually *wasn't* Jimmy, but why kill anyone? It's not true right!?" I laughed.

I called Gia while I sat there finishing my wine, and I filled her in on everything. "You should have seen his face!"

"I would have punched him in his face! I can say something to him now right!?" she said.

"Do whatever you want, I got what I needed."

When I got home, I went on the back porch and filled Giovanni in. My phone started blowing up. Jimmy called me first to see if I had said something to Hector.

"Yeah I just met with him, he was livid," I said.

"You didn't tell him it was me, did you?" he asked. "No, I wouldn't tell him who told me anything, he just kept saying he knew it was you," I said.

"But it wasn't me! I just answered you honestly when you confronted me, I didn't let the cat out of the bag," he said.

"Yeah I know. But I *did* tell him it wasn't you, but he didn't seem to buy it. He'll get over it. Why what did he say to you?" I asked.

"Nothing, I just got a couple of texts from him asking where I was and if I wanted to ride, and then he called me since I didn't respond quick enough. So, I figured you had confronted him already," he said.

"Yeah, I did, but I didn't tell him who told me what so don't let him try you. He's just throwing a tantrum right now because he got caught."

When I hung up the phone, I had several messages from Gia. She sent me screen shots of her conversation with Hector. It wasn't long, but it was unfriendly to say the least. About an hour later she sent me some more screen shots. This time Genna had reached out to her. The fact that Hector had called her and gotten her to contact Gia was even more an admission of guilt as far as we were concerned. What nobody seemed to be able to tell me was if Hector ever tested positive. That's all I really cared about. The rest of it was just the two scum bags trying to save what reputation they thought they had, and I didn't care about that in the least. Gia was more understandably on a war path because of how Hector had behaved towards her when her situation occurred. So, whatever she did with it, was completely up to her. I just wanted to know that my daughter and I were clean and safe.

The next morning Titi called me. "Hey Savannah," she said sweetly. "How are you feeling?" she asked.

"Well, aside from completely stressed out by your nephew all the time, I'm good. How are you?"

"Well, apparently someone told you some things yesterday, and now every-thing is blowing up. Hector is on a rampage and he is ready to kill Jimmy for telling you. So, I just wanted to call and first apologize to you. I asked this motherfucker a million times if he told you the truth and he lied to my face and said you knew. So, I'm sorry, I would have said something if I didn't think you were already aware of it," she said. "But I need to ask you who told you, because he is threatening the life of my nephew right now. And it's not fair for Jimmy to take the brunt of this if it didn't come from him. Jimmy lives in my house, and I'm not having any of this drama at my front door, so I need to know how this came about," she said calmly.

I didn't want Jimmy to get hurt; she was right it wasn't fair to him. But I also knew how ridiculous Hector was with his threats. Most of the time he was all talk. So, I wasn't too worried. I was more worried that Frankie would be in danger if they all knew it came from her.

"Well, I'm not going to tell anyone where it came from right now. I understand how you feel, and I will make it clear to Hector once again that Jimmy was *not* the original source. But until this all dies down, I'm not putting this person in unnecessary danger," I said calmly.

"Okay, I get that. But it wasn't Jimmy, right?"

"No, it was *not* Jimmy. The only person Hector should be mad at is himself. If *he* would have been honest and let me decide for myself whether or not I wanted to be involved with someone who could be putting me as risk, then all of this shit could have been avoided. He has *nobody* else to be mad at but *himself*," I said flatly.

"I told him the same fucking thing this morning. *He* is his own worst enemy. But everyone else has to pay for it. He makes me sick!" I could hear the disgust in her voice.

"I know the feeling," I said.

"So, what are you going to do now?" she asked.

"Well, my doctor wants to see a blood test from him to know for sure whether or not he's contracted it. But I will be tested throughout the rest of my pregnancy just to be sure, whether he provides it or not."

"Well, he needs to go get a test done at the health clinic then."

"It would be *that* easy if he has nothing else to hide, yes."

Later, I got another call from Jose, asking the same questions.

"I'm not telling anyone anything else. It wasn't Jimmy and I'm not reveal-ing my source until things die down."

"Jimmy can't fight Hector, so just tell Hector I said it or something because he doesn't need this kind of heat, and Hector really wants to kill him," he said.

"If you want to tell Hector you did it, then you go ahead and do that. I don't give a shit. I'm not catering to his tantrum. This is all *his* drama. *He* created this by being a fucking liar. He needs to stop blaming everyone else."

"Oh, we agree on that. It wasn't my wife was it?" he asked.

"I'm not telling you. What is the big deal? If he's clean, tell him to go get a blood test *today* at the clinic and show it to me. Case closed, drama over. Why is he dragging this shit out?" I asked.

"That's what we told him to do, but he said he doesn't owe you shit, and he doesn't have to prove anything to anyone," he said with a heavy sigh.

"Then why keep going after who told me what?"

"Because he thinks you're going to keep the baby away from him now." I rolled my eyes.

"Whatever, I have to go; I have shit to do," I told him, getting off the phone. It was too much to deal with having to answer to everyone. I wasn't the one who did anything wrong. So why did I feel like I was the one being reprimanded? He never would go get a blood test. But luckily my daughter and I didn't contract anything from him. To me, that's *all* that mattered.

CHAPTER TWENTY-SEVEN

Head games.

66 "I got a dog," Hector texted me. When I opened the message, it was a little black and brown puppy that resembled Rafiki in every way. I felt a pull in my stomach bringing up unpleasant feelings.

"I named him Ra," I started shaking. Why would he do that? Did he think this was funny?

"Why did you get a dog?"

"He looked like Rafiki," he said, as if I hadn't noticed that. "I don't know what to get for him, and I don't have any dog stuff. Since you still have my card can you go get whatever he needs and meet me at the house? I can't shop with a puppy." I was out Ubering at the time, so I figured what the hell. I went to Walmart and bought everything he would need. I went over to the house and messaged him to make sure I wasn't walking into something I wasn't ready for. I hadn't been back here since I left almost a month ago. He assured me that everything was fine and he would be there shortly.

I went inside and started setting up all the stuff I just bought. He came in a few minutes later and this tiny little Rafiki look alike ran over to me happily. He was adorable. Clearly a different breed than Rafiki was, but same coloring for sure. It brought back every heartbroken feeling I had with the passing of my sweet boy. I tried to hold back the tears but failed.

"Are you okay?" he asked.

"Yeah, I'm fine," I lied. I was *not* fine.

"I named him Ra after Rafiki."

"Why?" I asked with tears in my eyes.

"Because I miss him, and I wanted another dog that was smaller. He's not going to get much bigger, and he won't hurt the baby." I got up off the floor.

"Well here's everything you'll need for him," I said, pointing out what I had purchased. "I'll be going now," I said wiping tears from my face.

"You don't have to leave."

"Yes, I do," I answered with my lip quivering. "I can't be here."

"Are you still coming to the baby shower this weekend with me?" he asked quickly. I completely forgot. One of his best friends and his wife were expecting a new baby soon, they still wanted me to go since I still was on good terms with everyone and their daughter really liked me.

"I guess I can."

"Will you pick me up? I don't want to ride out there alone," he said.

"Where is it?"

"It's like an hour away." Not really wanting to drive that far alone, I agreed to do it. We needed to start trying to get along anyway, if we were going to co-parent together. I told him that was fine and I would see him Saturday. On my way out to the car I decided to go over to the grave for Rafiki.

"I'm sorry baby bear," I whispered crying. "I wish you were still here. I miss you so much. I love you." I felt like I was going to be sick. I went back to my car and got out of there as fast as I could. Being in that house again didn't feel the same. It smelled different. It *was* different. I didn't want to be there with him at all. And I didn't like the way that dog made me feel.

When I got home, Giovanni was already there. I told him what happened and showed him the picture of the dog.

"Wow," he said. "That's fucked up." He reached down and grabbed a cigarette out of his pack and lit it.

"Let me see that again," he said reaching for my phone. "Yeah, that's fucked up. And he named it *Ra*!?" he almost laughed.

"Jesus Christ this man is a fucking terrorist."

"It *is* emotional terrorism, right? I don't know how to feel, but I don't like it," I said.

"Yea, he did that on purpose."

When Saturday came around, I picked Hector up. He wanted me to see his puppy again, so he was outside with him when I pulled in.

"Look, it's mama," he said to the dog. What? I thought to myself.

"I'm almost ready, do you want to come in for a minute?" He didn't have a shirt or shoes on.

"I don't mind waiting out here." The look on his face changed to a less pleasant one.

"Just come inside for a minute please." I did as he asked. It smelled like stale smoke in there. There were cigarette butts piled up in an ash tray. All I could think of was that I needed to get my things out of there.

I waited in the living room for him to come back out while the puppy played friskily in my lap.

"Okay, I'm ready," he said, coming out of the hallway. I stood up and started to head towards the door. He locked the dog in a little cat carrier so he wouldn't run free for hours peeing on everything. The dog immediately started yelping loudly. We could hear him all the way out to the car. On our way out there, he told me that he was going to be leaving town the following weekend with his club to go to Las Vegas.

"Didn't you just go to California last weekend?"

"Yeah, what's it to you?"

"What are you going to do with Ra?"

"I was hoping you would just come stay at the house and watch him," he said softly. *That was a brilliant idea! He would be gone all weekend! I could finally get all my stuff!!*

"I can do that," I said.

"Good," he said, seeming pleased.

The baby shower went well. I got to see Titi and some of the ladies from the club I'd missed seeing. The guys, of course, were outside drinking most of the time. I could tell Hector was getting tipsy each time he came in. On the drive home he told me again that he wanted me to stay at the house next weekend while he was gone.

"I told you I would. It would be nice to sleep in my expensive bed again instead of an air mattress."

"Where are you staying?"

"Somewhere safe."

"You'll have to tell me eventually. I'll need to know where my child is at all times."

"We'll cross that bridge when we come to it," I said, trying to avoid a fight. On the way there he made some calls. He was planning to go out and party all night at the clubhouse.

"You can't keep leaving that brand-new puppy alone like that, Hector. You've already been gone for four hours," I said concerned. "Well, I'm going out, so if you're worried about it, you can stay here with him," he said, grinning.

"No." He sighed and rolled his eyes.

"Then I guess he'll be in his cage. I'll be back eventually," he said, not caring about the dog's well-being at all.

"That's really not cool. He's just a baby," I said, feeling protective of this poor little puppy.

"He'll be fine." When we pulled in, I went inside with him. Before he could even get the door unlocked, the poor dog was yelping. I rushed in and let him out of his tiny crate taking him outside to relieve himself. He was shaking. He hadn't even had him four days and was already going to start neglecting him. I couldn't deal with it.

"Are you going to be gone all night?"

"None of your business." I rolled my eyes.

"I don't give a shit; I just don't want him cooped up in this cat carrier for 12 hours. It's cruel."

"I told you to stay here with him."

"No, but I'm going to take him with me. I will be by first thing in the morning to drop him off before church," I said, gathering his things.

"Why don't you just stay with him?"

"Because I don't feel like it." I picked up the crate and put Ra and his food and toys in it. "I'll be here by 9 a.m.. Service is at 9:30," I said, walking out the door. "Okay, I'll be here. Go with mama," he said to the dog, giving him a kiss. *Why does he keep calling me that?* I asked myself internally.

When I walked in the door Giovanni was out on the back porch. I put Ra's things down and tucked Ra in under my arm holding him with one hand. I walked outside and Giovanni looked up at me. He didn't expect me to walk in with this dog and was *not* happy.

"What the fuck is that?" he asked, irritated.

"It's Hector's dog."

"I see that, why is it here?" he asked.

"Because he had it in this tiny cat carrier and was going out all night and was just going to leave him there," I said nervously. "He tried to get me to stay at the house with him," I said sitting down.

"Of course he did," Giovanni said, getting up to pace.

"I'm sorry, I didn't know what to do," I said, starting to get emotional. "He looks *just* like Rafiki, and I know how irresponsible Hector is, and he's just a baby! I couldn't leave him there! I'm sorry. Please don't be mad!" I said, bursting into unexpected tears. "It's just this one night I promise!"

Still pacing back and forth Giovanni took a few deep breaths and a few drags off his cigarette.

"Please don't be mad at me! I don't know what the fuck I'm doing. I just couldn't leave him there crying and scared and alone all night!" I cried, hugging Ra tighter to me while Halo sniffed the tiny creature in my lap.

"I'm not mad at you. I'm irritated with *him* for sure. And this will *never* happen again. But I know how you are, and I know you couldn't walk away from that. I get it," he said. "I'm not happy about it, but I get it. That fucker really does know how to get to you doesn't he?" he said, shaking his head and pacing.

"What do you mean? You think he did this on purpose?" I asked.

"A hundred percent. He probably thought you were going to stay there with him tonight. He's playing hard ball now," he said, shaking his head.

"Well, he said he was going to Las Vegas next weekend and wanted me to stay at the house with the dog. I told him I would, but I think we should get a plan together to move all my stuff out when he's gone."

Nodding his head, he said, "That's actually not a bad idea. How long will he be gone?"

"I think he leaves Thursday or Friday and won't be back until Monday. So that will give me time to actually pack things and get all hands on deck for the big move."

The next morning, I got ready to meet Bessie at church and stopped by to drop off Ra. Nobody was there. It was 9 a.m. and he still hadn't returned home. I walked through the house to be sure and it was empty. I called Hector. He didn't answer. I called him again.

"Hello?" he answered sleepily like I just woke him up.

"Where the hell are you?" I asked irritated.

"Um, down the street, why?"

"Down the street? You were supposed to be home. You knew I had to drop Ra off before church."

"Oh yeah, well my bro and I had to stop and get a hotel room. He couldn't make the ride home." Everything inside me knew that was a lie.

"Listen, if you want to stay out all night with your groupies that is your business. But you need to find a new home for this dog, because he's going to die. I'm not your fucking dog sitter and I won't be watching him again," I said, hanging up the phone. I locked Ra up, said goodbye and told him I was sorry he was pulled into this life with Hector, and left.

He had obviously taken advantage of me. Giovanni was right. But if he was this irresponsible with taking care of an innocent puppy, then how was I supposed to ever trust him to take care of my daughter? I couldn't. I decided then and there that he would *never* be alone with my daughter unless a judge told me otherwise. It was too much to risk. I went to church, and Bessie followed me home. I told Giovanni what happened.

"I think it's a good idea to stick with the plan for next weekend," he said.

"I agree, I'll ask my dad and brother if they can help," I said, picking up my phone. Everyone agreed the plan was good to go. I was finally going to get all my things out.

The following week, I stopped by to see Frankie on my Uber route. She sent me a message of a picture with her white puppy and Ra, asking why she had to watch his dog. When I got there, Ra was happy to see me.

"Why is he here?"

"Because Hector is never home. All he wants to do is fucking party, and he doesn't have time to take care of his own dog," she said, annoyed.

"So why did *you* get stuck with him?" I asked.

"Just lucky I guess." She looked exhausted. "I heard you got pissed at him last weekend when you dropped Ra off."

"I sure did. How am I supposed to allow him to be alone with my daughter if he can't even be responsible enough to take care of a new puppy?"

"I was thinking the same thing," she said, laughing. "But he said you were pissed because you thought he was with another girl."

"I've already seen proof of him with other girls, what the fuck would that matter at this point? I was pissed because he knew I didn't want the dog to be left alone, and he wasn't fucking home when he said he would be," I said.

"That makes more sense. He really goes out of his way to make you look like the crazy jealous baby mama," she said, laughing.

"That's probably what he wants me to be. These bitches can have his ass. All I care about is my daughter."

"Are you staying there this weekend?" she asked.

"I told him I would yes, since he's going to be in Vegas," I said.

"So, does that mean you guys may get back together?"

"Absolutely not."

"Oh good, I was worried when I heard that. But I should have known better."

"After the AIDS lie, I'm all the way done with him." I got a text from Jose asking me where I was and if I could talk. I told him I was at his house and asked what was up. "Don't tell Frankie it's me, just call me when you leave," he said. That's strange, I thought to myself. I told her that I had to go back to work and that I would stop by again soon.

"Hello," Jose said, answering the phone. "Yo, did you leave?" he asked.

"Yeah, I'm on my way home."

"Alright look, Hector said you were going to stay at his house this weekend while he's out of town, is that right?"

"Yes, why?" I asked.

"If I was you—and you aren't hearing this from me right now so keep it to yourself, or I'll know you through me under the bus!" he said.

"Okay," I said.

"You need to get your brother and dad and get all your shit out the house while he's gone." I grinned, already knowing I was going to do that.

"Why is that?"

"Just trust me please. Don't say anything, not even to Frankie. I will help you move; I will help you pack; I will do whatever you need to get your shit and get out of there," he said.

"Okay, but what aren't you telling me?" I asked.

"He told me that once the baby is here, he was going to do whatever he had to. He wants to take the kid from you whether it's legal or not." I laughed.

"He can't take her from me, you know he can't. He would have to prove me unfit and that won't happen." I said.

"Savannah, you aren't listening to me. You need to get *all* your shit out of there, cut off anything in your name and be done with this nigga. Trust me."

He seemed serious. The conversation was making me nervous for some reason. What was Hector saying that had his cousin so concerned? Was he threatening to kidnap our daughter from the hospital? What didn't I know? Whatever it was, I took it seriously.

"I already have a plan in place. Nobody knows, so if he finds out I will know it was you," I said.

"I won't say shit, I just told you I would help you fucking pack. It's time to go for real."

"Okay, well, I'm not taking that dog."

"I'll keep the dog at my place, he's not your problem, but promise me you will go. *This weekend*," he said.

"It's already set," I said. "As long as he doesn't find out," I snapped.

"He won't from me! And we never had this conversation," he said in a warning tone.

"Agreed." I told Giovanni about the bizarre warning.

"Well, obviously he knows something you don't," he said.

"Clearly, Hector would flip out if he knew he called me, let alone offer to help me move. So, it must be terrible."

"Yeah, well we don't need his help, we'll get everything out of there this weekend for sure," he said. I couldn't wait to get it over with. I was anxious all the time. I couldn't sleep or eat; my stomach was in knots every day and night.

Finally, it was Friday, and my plan was going to begin. I got a message from Hector first thing in the morning.

"You're still going to watch the house, right?"

"Yes," I responded.

"Okay, well I'm leaving. I won't be back until Sunday night." He told me he was heading to the shop and that his cousin would take him to the airport when it was time to go. So, I waited. I gathered a few things I needed. Giovanni had a bunch of Home Depot boxes in the attic he had used to move years ago, so he brought them down and put them in the car for me. He was such a nice man and was quickly becoming my best friend. He made me feel safe, never caused me any drama, just genuinely accepted me and all my baggage into his peaceful home. He had no idea how much I respected and appreciated him.

I called my dad and asked him if he could bring some moving tape and any extra boxes he could find at work. He was nervous about me staying in that house alone for the night, but he understood that we needed to get this done. He agreed to meet me at the house on his way home with what I needed. Finally I got the call from Jose.

"Hey," I said answering quickly.

"I just dropped him off at the airport. Are you already at the house?"

"No, I was waiting to make sure he really left."

"Yeah, he's gone. His flight leaves in about an hour."

"Okay, I'll head over there then."

"I still have another appointment, but I can come by after if you want help."

"Well, my dad is going to come by and help. And I don't want to cause you any trouble," I said.

"Fuck that nigga," he spat out like venom.

"I can't wait for him to come home to an empty ass house! He's a fucking asshole, and he deserves everything that's coming to him!"

"Well, he's definitely in for a rude awakening when he gets home," I said.

"I'll stop by later to check on you."

"Don't feel like you have to go out of the way for me, you've been helpful enough." I said.

"It's no big deal, be careful, I'll see you later."

Pulling up to the house gave me a sick feeling. I opened the garage door and pulled in entering from downstairs. There was a pile of his dirty laundry in front of the washing machine. I picked it all up and put it on top of the washer, clearing the path that we would need the next day. I took a left and turned on the light for the party room. Flicking on the lights I noticed he had definitely had some guests over at some point. There was empty beer bottles and cans sitting everywhere. The pool table looked like it was covered in cigarette ash. I was going to have to wipe down everything as I took it. There was the white powdery residue and clear line markings on the octagon table my father made. I didn't want to touch anything without gloves on. Shaking my head, I went into the office. It had been untouched. Taking a right, I approached the door to the dungeon I created for us. We never used it, so my stomach sank when I opened the door, afraid of what I would find. It too had been untouched. I don't know why that made me feel better, but it did.

I climbed up the steps and saw the living room was messy. Empty beer bottles and half full cups of juice everywhere. Full ashtrays and potty pads everywhere for Ra. Most of which were dirty. *My God, does he ever take that dog outside?* I asked myself. Inspecting the kitchen, it was a mess as well. Half-eaten day-old food on the stove. Dirty dishes in the sink, the garbage was overflowing. The guest bedrooms were both untouched. What used to be my bedroom was a mess. So was our bathroom. When I left, the cleaning lady we had quit going to work for him as soon as she found out why I left him. It was evident that he hadn't cleaned anything in the few weeks I had been gone.

I got a text from my dad that he was on his way, so I took a deep breath and got to work. I had to wash the dishes because they were all mine and, whether I needed it or not, it was *all* coming back into my possession. I went outside to get my things and boxes out of the car when my dad pulled in at the perfect time.

"You want a hand?" he asked, getting out of his car.

"Yeah that would be great!" He grabbed some things and followed me inside.

"I don't even like being back here," he said.

"Yeah, it's not the same is it? I loved this house, I made it a home. It was beautiful," I said sadly.

"Yeah it was, but now it's the place some pussy-ass bitch put his hands on my pregnant daughter," he said emotionally.

"I wasn't pregnant the whole time," I said trying to lighten the mood.

"Yeah, that doesn't make anything better for me."

"I know, I'm sorry," I said, looking down at my fingers. "I'm just a little nervous," I said. We walked through the house together, going over everything I wanted to take.

"I say we take everything," he said.

"Well, the pool table and the dining room table are both his," I said. "Oh, and the two guest beds." We were in the living room discussing what time to get started the next day when there was a knock on the door.

"Are you expecting someone?"

"Not right now. Jose said he would stop by later but it's way too early to be him," I said looking at my phone. I went down to open the door with my dad standing a few feet behind me protectively.

I opened the door to see my neighbor from across the street standing there with a bottle of red wine and a big smile.

"Hey there! I thought I saw you back!" she said, offering me a big hug. She was an older transgender woman who had bought the house across the street a few months before I moved in. She and I got along amazingly. She would cook too much and bring me extra food, and I would go have a glass of wine with her at her place on occasion. Her name was Mary. She wasn't much taller than I was but was about 70 years old with long natural fingernails and glasses. She had natural hair, but it was quite thin on top and longer in the back. She was obviously born a male but identified as female, and I thought she was awesome.

"Yeah, I'm actually just here for the night," I said hugging her.

"Come in," I said introducing her to my dad. She came up and followed me to the dining room table.

"I know you're prego, but red wine won't hurt, and we need to catch up," she said opening my wine cabinet and grabbing two glasses.

"You want one, Dad?" she asked my father.

"Oh no, none for me. I'm actually going to hit the road if you don't need me."

"Okay, that's fine, I'll see you in the morning."

"You call me if anything happens."

"Will do."

"And don't lift anything too heavy, just pack what you can and let the boys deal with the rest tomorrow," he said, giving me a hug.

"Yes sir."

"You have your gun?" he asked.

"Yes, I have both of them, Dad," I said, laughing. Satisfied with my response he went out the front door.

"So, you aren't moving back in then?" Mary asked me, pouring a glass of wine.

"No, Hector is in Vegas for the weekend and he asked me to watch the house. He doesn't know he will be coming home to no furniture," I said pettily.

"Good girl. I noticed you had left but you need to give me your phone number. I want to keep in touch with you!" she said handing me a glass.

"Of course," I said.

"So, what happened?" I filled her in on all the events that had transpired since the last time I had seen her. She didn't like Hector since the day she moved in across the street. She thought he was a rude, inconsiderate douchebag.

"Well, I knew you were gone but there has been another woman here a lot, she looks just like you, so I had to do a double take when I saw her," she said, sipping her wine.

"Oh?" I said.

"Yeah, you're much prettier in the face and she has man arms, but same black hair and general look as yours."

"Well that's interesting." I didn't have any clue who she was talking about.

"Well, I hope she has some furniture," I said picking up my glass and heading to the living room. "Because they won't have anything to fuck on when he gets back!" I said laughing.

"You aren't packing all this yourself, are you?"

"Yeah, I'll be packing all night. I want to get everything out tomorrow. I just need this to be done with."

"Well," she said putting her glass down and picking up an empty box.

"Let's get started, I'm staying to help," she said, rolling up her sleeves.

"You don't have to do that." She raised her hand in the air, stopping me.

"I'm not leaving, so deal with it," she said grabbing a handful of DVDs and putting them neatly in the box.

"Well thank you," I said, appreciative of the help.

We spent the next couple of hours packing and chatting. With her help we got it done rather quickly. I thanked her for everything, and we exchanged phone numbers so we could keep in touch.

"I'll probably come by tomorrow while you guys are moving."

"Okay, that's great, thank you!" I gave her a big hug and she went across the street to her home.

My phone rang. "Hello?" I said to Jose.

"Hey, what are you doing?"

"Just got done packing up what I can."

"You're done already?"

"Yeah a neighbor came over and stayed to help so it wasn't that bad."

"Do you need me to stop by?"

"Not really, everything is done, so I was going to take a bath and try to get some sleep. Big day tomorrow."

"If you want me to come help you move, I'm fine with that." I didn't want him to meet Giovanni or Gabriel, and I didn't want him to know where I was living. I wanted the two worlds completely separate from each other.

"I do appreciate that, but we have it covered. You don't need to be involved in this. He would freak out if he found out," I said, sitting on the couch.

"Yeah, I know, but he deserves this. Will you send me pictures of the empty house?" he laughed.

"I was going to take pictures anyways so I can prove there was no damage caused by me when I leave."

"You're smart," he said.

"I don't know about *that*, but I'm at least smarter than Hector! The neighbor said there's been some girl that looks like me over here frequently," I said.

"I don't doubt it, you know he's a ho."

"Do you know who she's talking about?" It had only been a few weeks and I still had all my stuff there. It was irritating to know he was already fucking someone else.

"He has been trying to fuck anything with legs since you left. But I don't know who and when."

"Well, that makes me a little sad," I said honestly.

"I know, but he's an insecure ass, and that's how he tries to make himself feel better about fucking up his whole life and ruining the best thing that ever happened to him," he said flatly.

"I know, but it still hurts."

"It will pass one day. And you're going to be an awesome mom," he said, trying to cheer me up. "Plus, I have no doubt in my mind you are going to find a man *way* better for you than Hector. He never appreciated you. Someone will, trust me."

"Thanks, but that's the last thing on my mind right now," I said, laughing.

"Good, it should be," he laughed in agreement. "Make sure you shut off all the utilities that are in your name."

"I already called them. Everything is in my name."

"I can't wait to see his fucking face when I bring him home Monday," he growled.

"Why are *you* so mad at him?" I asked curiously.

"Because he's a fucking asshole. He treats everyone like shit. He thinks he's a badass since he's buying this company, but me and Titi are the ones running it. He throws fits all the time, pisses off customers, treats me like shit constantly and then makes me drive him around like a fucking chauffeur." He went on for several minutes about how angry he was with him. Understandably so; they didn't have to live with him, but they still had to deal with his shit every day. "That's okay though, cause one day he's going to lose the company, and Titi and I are going to scoop it up. He's fucking everything up. He's got the temper of a toddler, and he actually believes he's going to take your daughter from you." He laughed.

"Why would he want to do that? He knows I'm going to be a good mom, and I'm not trying to keep him from our daughter," I said.

"Because you hurt him. This is all about you, not your daughter. He will do anything to make you feel like shit. He told us you were threatening to not let him see her. He's pissed you won't allow her to have his last name so now he's even saying the baby isn't his!" Instant rage set in.

"Are you fucking kidding me?" I asked.

"No, that's what he's telling people, that you were cheating with your ex and the baby may not even be his." I was so furious I got up and started pacing around the living room.

"I *never* fucking cheated on him! Although I wish I fucking had!" I said. "How dare he try to make me out like one of these trashy whores he's fucking!"

"I know, he's fucking stupid. You still planning on letting him be there for the birth?"

"Yeah, I'm not going to keep him out of that unless he is being awful at the time. But that's not something I can exclude him from. Like I said I'm *not* trying to keep her away from him. He just won't be alone with her. *Ever*. I will always be there to supervise until a judge tells me otherwise," I said.

"Shit, you don't even have to give him that! My first baby's mom told the judge some fucked up shit about me, and I wasn't even allowed anywhere near my kid. She fucking lied and had no proof, but they believed her," he said.

"I didn't know that," I said, feeling sorry for him.

"Yeah, that's why I kept trying to help him, but he doesn't listen, and I'm sick of it. If you want to let him be there for the birth, that's your choice. But don't let him out of your sight with that baby. I mean it. You should really just keep her away from him. He's a piece of shit just like his dad. And I'm sure you heard about how *he* was toward his kids. Do you want that for your daughter?" he asked.

"No, that's why his visits will be supervised. I'm going to go take a nice bath and pass out," I said.

"Sounds good, you call me if you need anything."

"Will do," I said.

"Good night," he said, hanging up the phone.

I decided to log into Hector's bank account since he had the app on my phone. I checked it every so often, but normally didn't care what he was doing. I just wanted to make sure he was really in Vegas; there it was a $75 purchase in Nevada just a couple of hours ago confirming he was really gone. That put my mind at ease. At least *he* wouldn't be showing up tomorrow. I went to lay in the bed and noticed the faint smell of piss in the air. I assumed the dog had been using the carpet in the entire house as a toilet, so I ignored it and lay down. I fell asleep rather quickly and slept better than I had since before I left this house. I woke up to my alarm going off and realized I felt great. I needed that sleep more than I thought.

I noticed as everyone walked in, they each had a gun on their hip just in case. I was so happy Giovanni was there. I thought I would be nervous having him on this hostile ground, but as soon as he walked in smiling with his blue eyes and smelling better than anything in this nasty house did, I was instantly at ease. My brother went right to work. It didn't take long at all to clear out the living room. Giovanni asked where my bed was and followed me back to the room.

"So just the mattress and box spring are actually mine," I said pulling off the comforter and pillows. "The frame he bought so we will leave that."

"Okay," Giovanni said, laughing. When I pulled off the sheets, I saw the source of piss smell. There was a dirty towel on top of my $2,500 mattress covering a huge piss stain! I moved the towel and the rest of the sheets, and there were pee stains everywhere! Not only was I livid, but I was disgusted.

"What the fuck!" I yelled.

"Looks like your boy lets the puppy pee all over your bed," he said with an unpleasant look on his face. "Are we still taking this?" he asked.

"Yeah, I don't have another bed. I'll just have to shampoo and bleach the shit out of it. I told you he was lazy, but this is a whole another level," I said.

"This looks worse than lazy," Giovanni said, pulling on the dirty mattress. "This looks like he passed out so hard from his drug benders that he didn't even realize he was getting pissed on," he said, shaking his head. "The puppies too small to jump off the bed." he had a point.

"Jesus Christ. Just load it up. I'll clean it later."

"I wish we had a place for the pool table," Giovanni said.

"That's actually his," I said.

"Oh, I wouldn't care, if it would fit anywhere, we would take that bitch," he said. We all got in our vehicles and headed out to Giovanni's place. We got everything unloaded quickly. I was so happy to have all my things.

"So, can we use your stuff?" Giovanni asked me.

"Of course, whatever you want to use. It's all yours."

"Okay, because I want to set up the bar," he said, laughing.

"Go ahead." I drenched my nasty mattress with carpet cleaner for pet stains and wanted to let it soak. Since my dad and brother were calling it a day, I decided to go back to the house and finish up.

"I'll be back soon, but if you want to use or unpack anything, feel free," I said to Giovanni and Gabriel, who were hanging my floating shelves in the new bar area.

"Okay, be careful!"

When I got to the house, I decided to leave a note. I pulled out some old junk mail from the mailbox that hadn't been checked and used the backs of two envelopes to write my letter. I left my key to the house and the garage door opener with the letter on the kitchen counter and took a picture of it. I swept up a little and took the garbage out, but for the most part left it as dirty as it was when I got there the day before. I went through the house taking pictures of each room and saying goodbye to the house I once loved. It was more emotional than I had anticipated. I started crying quietly remembering how happy I was to move in here. The memories of Rafiki running through the halls, Gizmo squawking at me from the countertop demanding food. It was a crushing realization that I was closing this door for good. There was no going back now.

I went around the back of the house to say a final goodbye to Rafiki. Seeing his grave made me cry again. "I wish I could take you with me, I miss you so much. I'm sorry I let this happen to you baby bear. But I must go now. I don't know if or when I'll be back, but I will always love you and keep you with me," I said with tears streaming down my face.

My phone rang on the way home.

"How's it going?" Jose asked.

"I'm out!"

"Like gone?"

"Yeah, I just left for the last time, I left a note and the keys and shit, but we already got my stuff out and unloaded," I said, feeling more relieved the farther I drove from the house.

"Jesus that was fast! Was it just your dad and brother?"

"I had some friends help," I said not answering the question he was really asking.

"Did you take pictures?"

"Oh yeah."

"Send them to Frankie, this phone doesn't get pictures very well. But we're dying to see them!" he said, laughing.

"Oh, you told her?" I asked.

"Yeah I told her this morning."

"Okay good, I'll send them as soon as I'm not driving."

"I can't fucking wait! This nigga is gonna trip!" he said excitedly.

"Did you tell anyone else?" I asked.

"No, I want it to be a surprise on Monday," he said laughing.

"Okay, good," I said.

"Have you heard anything from him?" He asked me.

"No, nothing, he's partying with his club, that's the only thing that matters in life to him. I doubt he'll contact me at all," I said.

"Yeah that's true. Alright, send me them pictures as soon as you can."

It took a lot of effort to clean my mattress. I couldn't eliminate all the stains, but I managed to get rid of the smell and convince myself it was sanitized. I kept fans on it the rest of the day while I unpacked things. Luckily Giovani had a mattress cover that he wasn't in need of that he gave me. I went down and sat on the porch with Giovanni and told him about the phone conversation I had with Jose the night before. I told him about the neighbor saying there was already a Savannah replacement lurking around and how shitty that felt.

"He's telling people the baby isn't his now," I said.

"What?" he asked in disbelief.

"Yeah, he's trying to convince everyone that I'm a whore."

"That's just the actions of a desperate boy not wanting to face the fact that *he* destroyed the best thing he had. It can't be his fault, obviously," he said, shaking his head.

"Well, it still sucks," I said.

"Yeah, it's incredibly shitty," he agreed.

Then I got a text. "You stupid fucking bitch. You steal all my shit while I'm gone? I hope your happy with what you've done. I'm gonna need that ring off your finger!"

"Hector's home," I said to Bessie, showing her the text I just received Monday evening. She rolled her eyes and laughed. "He's so pissed!" she said giggling.

"I didn't take anything that wasn't mine, I left you the keys and everything you purchased," I wrote.

"Whatever, that's my ring I want it back now or I'm calling the cops!" I busted out laughing. Did the big scary biker outlaw wannabe just threated to call the cops on me?

"Well, the number is 911 but I'm sure they have a non-emergency number for situations like this." I said pettily.

"Okay so you're just going to steal from me you fucking loser? That's cool I'll have all new shit tomorrow!" I didn't respond. "I hope you're happy with what you've just done. You destroyed us." I laughed.

"No dear YOU destroyed us. Go call that bitch you've already been having in MY house. Tell her you need some furniture and lights!"

My phone rang. It was Titi.

"Hi Savannah, can we talk for a few minutes?" she asked.

"Sure, what's up?" I said, stepping outside. Bessie and I were at her parents' house.

"Well, I just got an interesting phone call from my nephew."

"I bet you did," I said grinning.

"So, what happened? He said he came home expecting you guys to talk and work things out, and the house was empty." Confused, I asked what she was talking about. "He told me that you were going to stay at the house and wait for him to get back from his trip. He said you guys were getting along better and that you told him you would be there when he got back to discuss how to move forward." I laughed.

"That literally *never* happened! You know me well enough to know that after all this shit the *last* thing I'm going to do is sit around waiting on him to come home while he's out partying all weekend," I said.

"Yeah I was confused because last time we spoke you were pretty upset with him about the AIDS thing, so I didn't think you'd be dumb enough to go back to him," she said.

"No, I saw my chance to get all my shit out peacefully, and I took it."

"Good for you, I hope you took everything!" she said, cheering me on.

"I took everything but the pool table, the dining room table, the guest beds and the frame for my bed. He bought that," I said, looking at my chewed-up nails.

"I would have taken the fucking tacks out of the wall and the ketchup packets out of the junk drawer!" she said.

"Oh, my brother did! I left him one plate, and one fork, one spoon and a butter knife," I said, making her laugh even harder. "I *did* leave my washing machine; we didn't feel like moving it since I don't need it. So at least I was nice enough to do that," I said.

"What about the utilities? Do you still have his card?" she said.

"Yeah, I do for now, and I already cancelled everything. I'll pay the final bills for everything before he cuts the card off, hopefully. But if not, I'll figure it out. I always do," I said.

"Well I gotta hand it to you Savannah, I'm fucking impressed. Jose and I have been hoping you would do something like this for weeks. We were worried that you hadn't gotten anything out of the house yet. Nobody wants to see you back with him. He's trash. And he doesn't need to be around that baby!" she said.

"He won't be without me present," I said.

"He's blowing up my phone, I'll talk to you later," she said.

I asked Bessie if she would stay one more night and go to the doctor with me the next day. I forgot I had an appointment and I didn't want to be there and get ambushed by Hector. She agreed to come and was happy to be there for me. She couldn't stay all day, but it was an early appointment and she could head back to the city afterwards. On our way home, Jose called me.

"That was the best moment of my life!" he yelled excitedly into the phone, laughing. "You should have seen his fucking face!" he said.

"I can only imagine," I said, putting him on speaker phone.

"We pulled up and the house was dark as shit. He couldn't get the garage door open. When we went in the front door, the lights wouldn't work, and I was trying not to laugh! I put my flashlight on my phone and went up the steps behind him shining the light into the empty living room," he said.

"What did he say?" Bessie asked, loving the story.

"'What the fuck? Where's all my shit?'" He laughed. "I told him it looked like it was all gone. I walked all through the house with him trying to act shocked and concerned. I read the note you left to him and pointed out the keys and garage opener," he said.

"Did he cry?" Bessie asked with an evil grin.

"Not yet, he was so shocked and pissed off that he just started flipping out. He called Titi and told her what happened. He said he was going to call the cops on you for stealing the ring and shit. He's such a fucking loser," he said.

"Yeah, I gave him the number to call," I said.

"What number?" he asked.

"I told him the number was 911 but there was most likely a non-emergency number he could look up." He busted out into laughter.

"Oh my God! You kill me girl! He already told me and Titi he wasn't coming to work tomorrow, he's gotta go buy furniture and shit. I'm sure he'll use the company money for it," he said, sounding annoyed.

"Oh, you can count on that! Did he say if he was going to show up to the doctor's appointment tomorrow?" I asked.

"No, he didn't mention it. Does he know about it?"

"Yeah, he was there when I made it."

"Well, he might, just to start a fight," he said.

"I'll be going with her," Bessie said.

"Okay good," he said. "Let me know how that goes."

CHAPTER TWENTY-EIGHT

I didn't know

The next morning, everything went well at the doctor's. Hector never showed up, and the baby was still growing strong. Bessie walked out with me, happy to have gone, and hugged me goodbye. I had parenting class, and she had work, so we went our separate ways. Frankie messaged me asking if I wanted to come by, so I told her I'd be there in 30 minutes. When I got there, she had a few items she wanted to give me for the baby that her daughter had grown out of already.

We sat there discussing all the drama that had been transpiring all day because of my evacuation from the house. Jose had told her that Hector called the two office women that worked there to come to his house so they could help him shop for furniture, leaving Titi at the office alone and Jose the only one to go out to jobs.

"What kind of grown man can't go shop for his own furniture," Frankie said, laughing.

"He needs to get the utilities on as well. He is a child and has always had someone to live off of or take care of him. So, he doesn't know how to do anything for himself," I said, laying back on her love seat.

"He told Jose he was going to cut off your card and phone," she said.

"Not surprising," I responded. My phone was sitting on the coffee table in front of me when it chimed. She looked down at it seeing it was her husband texting me.

"Is that my husband?" she asked. I sat up and opened it.

"Oh yeah, he was just asking how the doctor appointment went this morning," I said thinking nothing of it.

"Are you fucking serious?" she said, bursting into tears. She stood up from the sofa and started pacing. I put the phone down on the coffee table leaving it open so she could see there was nothing going on.

"Look I swear, it's not like that," I said, raising my hands in the air.

"No, I'm sorry, I probably look like a crazy person!" she said, crying harder.

"What did I do?" I asked concerned. She wiped the hair out of her face and pulled it back into a ponytail.

"Nothing, I know you don't know what's going on, I'm *not* upset with you *at all*, I promise!"

"What don't I know?" I asked, confused.

"We haven't told anyone yet; he doesn't want people to know," she said, pacing.

"Take a deep breath, Frankie. Calm down and talk to me. Are you okay?" She sat back down on the sofa and took a few long deep breaths calming down.

"I have cancer." I got chills throughout my body.

"What?" I asked cautiously.

"I got pregnant right about the time you did and when I went in for the visit, they discovered I had a tumor inside my cervix. They recommended I have an abortion and start chemo immediately."

"I remember Hector telling me you had an abortion just before I found out I was pregnant," I said.

"Well that's why." I knew she didn't have a car or even a driver's license, so I asked how she had been getting to chemo.

"I Uber," she said.

"Wait, you uber to your chemo appointments? What do you do with the baby?"

"Take her with me."

"Why doesn't he want anyone to know?"

She started crying again. "Because he wants me to suffer! He never asks me how I'm feeling, never comes to the doctor with me, doesn't help with the kids when I'm too sick to do anything. He told me he wants to watch me die," she said, standing back up to pace again. "That's why when he asked about *your* doctor's appointment, I lost my shit. Why does he care about *you* and *your* baby more than me?" she asked, crying.

"No offense."

"None taken. Hold on, this doesn't sound like the Jose I know. He loves you. Why would he want you to die?" I asked.

"He has everyone fooled! He beats the shit out of me all the time! It pisses me off, because he'll come running to rescue you all the time and get onto Hector for how *he's* been treating you. But he's ten times worse behind closed doors."

My body was numb from the shock I was in. This sounded nothing like the man that I knew. The man that went out of his way to help me and provide me information and advice all the time. I had never seen anything but a sweet loving husband and father from him. But then it hit me. That's exactly how everyone felt about Hector when I started coming out about my situation to my family and people who didn't know him. It was no surprise to his family and friends because they knew he was a piece of shit. But *nobody* suspected Jose of being the same way, if not worse. I had a million questions to ask but was completely speechless.

"I know, you don't believe me, right?" she said, sounding defeated.

"What?" It wasn't that I didn't believe her, it was just a lot to take in.

"I'll show you," she said, walking back to the bedroom. She came back out with two pill bottles.

"Look them up," she said handing them to me.

"You don't have to do that. I believe you." She opened her phone and googled them herself, proving that they were chemo pills.

"Why do you think I don't have a driver license or a job? Or friends for that matter?" she asked.

"He said you didn't want to," I answered.

"He won't let me. He doesn't even like you coming over here during the day. He told me if I said anything to you, he would torture me and make my death slow and painful. You know he's stalking you right?"

I shook my head in disbelief. "What?"

"Yeah Hector's obsessed with finding out where you live, so any little thing you say he has taken note of already. He narrowed it down to some guy on your Facebook." My stomach knotted up.

"What? Who?" I asked, praying he was wrong.

"Hold on, I'll know it when I see it," she said, pulling up my profile on her phone.

"This Giovanni guy," she said, showing me the familiar profile. "That's where he thinks you are, he put it together last night." I felt like I was going to be sick. I was a terrible liar, but I felt like I had to try my best right now since Giovanni could be at risk. I let out a laugh like it was the stupidest thing I had ever heard.

"That's hilarious, what makes him think that's where I am?"

"Because he was the only person in Georgia that has an in-ground pool on your friends list." Me and my big mouth! I *did* tell him that I was spending a lot of time by the pool.

"Well that's not where I am, but I'll let him know that he's on the suspect list in case anyone tries to mess with him," I said as casually as I could. My phone rang, it was Jose. She looked at it and started laughing,

"You see? He's obsessed with you," she said. She showed me her call log and had called him twice, he didn't answer her, she messaged him in the morning and got no response, but twice in the past five minutes he had tried to get ahold of me. "If you don't answer, he'll suspect you're over here. If he knows I told you anything, he will kill me or hurt my kids. Please just text him and tell him you're working or something," she said, shaking her head with disgust.

"Okay." I sent him a quick text, "At parenting class, the baby's fine, I'll hit you back later."

"Okay, just call me when you leave."

"How long has the abuse been going on?" I asked Frankie.

"For at least 10 years," she responded. Like me, once she got the secret out of her mouth, it just poured out of her. She told me that he would take unflattering pictures of her doing degrading sexual acts and create Instagram pages of her. That way if she misbehaved, he would friend all her contacts and they could all see her with a dick in her ass to embarrass her. She said he would hide her chemo pills or take them with him to work so she missed her treatments, if she was laying down, he would hit her feet with a little hammer or something while he walked by casually.

"When I was in the hospital after having our daughter last year, he made me suck his dick three hours after she was born," she said.

"What!? In the hospital room?" I asked.

"Yeah, the day I came home from the hospital he made me bend over and get fucked in the ass. I was bleeding everywhere, since I just had a baby three days before," she said in a zombie like state. "I remember my daughter was on the bed crying in front of me and I was trying to focus on comforting her while he did what he was doing," she said with a tear falling from her eye. "He makes me suck his dick and or fuck him every day, doesn't matter if I'm throwing up from chemo, he wants it, he takes it," she said shamefully.

Tears were streaming down my face listening to her confession. I didn't know what to do. How could I do anything? I had no way of helping this woman and her kids in my position.

"I'm so sorry," I said reaching for her hand. "I had no idea!"

"I gave up on trying to get help. When I first moved here, I started to get close with Angel, Tucker's wife, since he was the president of the club Jose was in," she said.

"I like them. They're fun people," I said.

"Yeah well, Angel caught on and said something to Tucker one night about it. Tucker is against domestic violence, his sister was killed in a domestic violence situation, so he has no tolerance for it," she said.

"Oh wow!"

"Yeah, well anyway all he did was come over and take Jose's gun out of the house, he gave it back a few days later and I got the shit kicked out of me for talking," she said, shrugging her shoulders. "So why bother? Not to mention it's *his* fault I even have cancer!"

"How's that?" I asked.

"When he was living down here with Hector, and I hadn't come down yet, he fucked that trashy ass Azalea chick. The little blond junkie that fucks everyone for drugs."

"I know who she is," I said, nodding.

"Well she gave him HPV, and he gave it to me. The HPV he gave me is the cause of the cancer I have now," she said.

"This is a lot to take in," I said rubbing my head.

"Yeah I know. But you can't say anything please! And no matter what you do don't *ever* let Jose touch your phone!"

"Why would I?" I asked.

"Just don't. you have no idea the kinds of things he can unlock or install to track you with in a matter of seconds. He's dangerous. And he's determined to find out where you are and who's hiding you."

"Well, nobody's hiding me, I'm just staying to myself until things die down a little. Listen, I have to go, but should we develop a safe word or something?" I asked. "Something only, you or I would know that we would only use if we were in danger?"

"That's actually not a bad idea" she said. "If you need anything, call me okay? I don't know what I can do in my situation, but I'll do what I can," I said, giving her a hug.

"Thank you, and please promise you won't tell anyone. If you even act different toward him, he will suspect I told you," she said.

"I won't say a word."

When I drove off, I pulled up to the stop sign feeling exhausted. "Lord please help that woman and her kids," I prayed. I felt betrayed. He made me believe he was a nice guy, that he was always trying to do the right thing. How could he be such a hypocrite? When I got to Giovanni's house, I sat on the back porch to soak up some sun and wait for him to get home. My phone rang. It was Jose. I didn't want to talk to him, but I made a promise, so I cleared my throat and mind and answered the phone.

"Hey, sorry I picked up some customers along the way home, my bad," I said.

"You're good, I just wanted to check on you." I rolled my eyes.

"Well it was just a regular doctor visit today, not the specialist, so nothing fun. Just checking my vitals and the baby's heartbeat," I said, keeping the conversation casual.

"Well that's always good. Have you heard from Hector?"

"No, why?"

"He called the office bitches to his house to take him shopping for all new furniture and to get the utilities back on. He couldn't do any of that on his own. Titi's pissed off. She's sure he's spending all the company's money," he said.

"I would almost guarantee it. He doesn't know how to write a check, so she should be able to see the charges for the day."

"She doesn't have access to the accounts."

"Are you kidding me? She's running that business for him, why wouldn't she?" I asked.

"Because that's how Hector wants it, the other two bitches can access it all they want, but they aren't allowed to let Titi see shit," he said.

I rolled my eyes. "He's such a child. Treats the office sluts like gold whilst treating his own flesh and blood like a flea-ridden dog on the side of the road! I still have access to them," I said.

"You do?" he asked.

"Yeah, unless he changed the password today. I just looked at his account Friday to make sure he was in Vegas."

"Can you look on there now and tell me what you see?"

"I can screen shot it and send it to you if you want. I have access to all of the accounts. He put the app on my phone when I had to quit working and start using his money."

"Yeah go on there." I put him on speaker and pulled it up.

"I'm in! His first purchase was a $1,300 mattress at Mattress Firm. He put down almost a $300 deposit to the power company, looks like $270 for the cable company. There are several smaller purchases: Dollar General, Target, and a sizeable purchase at Ashley Furniture for about $4,200," I said, reading them off.

"Screenshot all that shit," he said.

"You realize if he knows I'm doing this he will cut of my access right?" I said.

"Yeah, I'm not telling him shit, I just want to show Titi. We've had enough of his shit. We're gonna take this fucking company from his ass," he said.

"Okay, I'll send it."

When Giovanni got there, I was eager to tell him everything and get his thoughts on all of it.

"Hey, do me a favor," I said when he came out back. "Make everything you can private on Facebook. Frankie told me today that her husband was up all night trying to figure out where I was and narrowed it down to your house."

"Are you fucking kidding me?" he asked, opening his phone.

"No, I'm not. Has he or Hector said anything to you?"

"Not a word."

"Well I don't know what all he has found out about you, but it can't hurt to make things less easy on him. I would never forgive myself if something ended up at your doorstep because of me," I said, shaking my head.

"It looks like everything is private, so I don't know what he could possibly find out other than my name," he said.

"He's a hacker, a name is *all* he needs, and he already has that. According to Frankie, he's obsessed with me," I said.

"I already told you that," he said lighting a cigarette.

"Oh wait, it gets worse," I said. I told him about how the entire crazy conversation went down. He was as shocked as I was.

"That is one dangerously crazy motherfucker. Don't you *ever* be anywhere alone with him," he said.

"I would have no reason to be."

"At least with Hector it's like dealing with an unruly child who just throws a tantrum at the slightest upset or when he doesn't get his way. This motherfucker is sick and twisted. If what she's saying is the truth, she's never going to get away from him. He would kill her first," he said, sending chills down my spine.

"I hope that doesn't happen," I said sadly.

"Maybe you should stop going over there for a while," he said.

"I can't just abandon her; I know how alone she feels. The woman is battling cancer on top of being abused and tortured," I said, getting upset all over again.

"I know, but you still have to put you and your baby first."

"I will, but she needs a friend right now. She made me promise not to act differently towards Jose or he would suspect I knew. I literally just got off the phone with him. I handled it like a boss," I said proud of myself.

"What did he call you for?" he asked.

"To check on me and vent about Hector."

About a week later, my phone rang. It was my ex-sister-in-law. She didn't really call me, so I thought it may be an emergency with my nephew.

"Hello?" I asked, worried.

"Hey, have you seen Hector's Facebook?" she asked.

"No, why?"

She took a deep breath and proceeded to tell me that there was a post about getting his nursery together for the baby and there was some woman all over it talking like *she* was the one having the baby.

"What do you mean?" I asked.

"She's answering questions like she's the one putting the nursery together and raising the kid with him, I swear to God! I'm sending you pictures." I put her on speaker phone so I could look at what she was showing me. Sure enough, some random bitch I didn't know was on there, explaining the whole underwater themed room *they* were creating for *my* child! "Who the fuck *is* this bitch?" she asked.

"I have no idea, but if he thinks he's ever going to have *my* child alone he's lost his mind, so she doesn't even matter." My other line started ringing and I was getting flooded with messages. Everyone was freaking out over his newest stunt.

I answered the other line, it was my friend who used to work for Hector and got pregnant a week after me. "Have you seen this shit?" she asked.

"Yeah I just found out. Do you know who the bitch is?" I asked her.

"Yeah, that's Janet. The welder chick he uses. I thought she was a lesbian. But it looks like she's playing house with your baby daddy. Where the fuck does *she* get off planning the nursery for *your* baby?" she said, annoyed. Giovanni was sitting there on the back porch with me when I found out and looked the woman up on his Facebook. My friend was right, she was a welder. And judging by the description I was given by the neighbor last week it was most likely the woman who had already made herself at home in my old house. Before I could even get my shit out. So clearly, she had no class or self-respect, but my big issue was with *him*.

I sent Hector the screen shots of his ridiculous post and let him know that he was trash for behaving this way. I was so angry hateful words just poured out of me like lava. I was hurt and I wanted him to hurt as well.

"How DARE you have some groupie fucking whore trying to act like step mommy when I haven't even given birth yet?" I typed angrily. "I haven't even gotten a chance to be a mother yet, and you think I'm going to let some bitch that KNEW you were just ENGAGED TO ME five fucking minutes ago step into a role in MY daughter's life!? You are TRASH, she is TRASH and you can fucking have each other!" I messaged him back and forth for at least an hour fighting.

"Well, who even knows if that baby is mine," he said finally.

"That's rich coming from you! CLEARLY the guilty mind is the accuser once again. You have a bitch living with you right now and I haven't had my stuff out for a week. She was just a 'friend' who you saw sometimes right? But she's got pictures on her Facebook of being at club events in Alabama that I was at, yet never met her once?" I responded, completely aware of how blind I was in this relationship.

"Whatever you wouldn't stop talking to your ex," was all he could say.

"You mean just like you wouldn't stop talking to yours? You wouldn't even delete the naked pictures and fuck videos you made together. I found them on your fucking phone, remember. I hope you warn her that you could be HIV positive but are too coward to go get tested! Have a great fucking life you douchebag!"

I put down my phone and started to cry. I was so hurt by one thing after another on a constant basis, I just couldn't deal with much more.

"It's fucked up," Giovanni said. "But it's going to work out. *You* have all the control of this situation. Unless a judge tells you otherwise, *you* don't have to do a single fucking thing for that piece of shit!" I sniffled and wiped my nose.

"I know. He's clearly too stupid to realize that, but I know. It just breaks my heart because *this* is *not* what I wanted. If he would have done what he said he was going to do and gotten the help he needed, we could have worked things out. But everything is so fucked up now, I can't even trust him to care for her when she's here," I said, rubbing my belly. "I don't want her to be around any of this drama. I want her to be happy and safe and have an amazing life!"

"Maybe you're going to have to give that to her without him in it," Giovanni said.

"I don't know if I can do that. It still seems wrong to not let him try to be a father. And I don't know what kind of father he will be until she's here," I said.

"That's fair. All you can do right now is take it a day at a time," he said.

"I know, I just feel so stupid. I feel like he was more of a monster than I could ever imagine, and everyone knew it but me," I said.

"I can see how you feel that way, but that doesn't mean you were stupid. You just have a kind, forgiving heart, and assholes like that take advantage of people like you. I'm sorry you're having to go through all this. You don't deserve any of it," he said, sickened by the situation.

We were only about a week away from my baby shower. Bessie was planning it. It was to be held in the firehouse at my church. It was a coed guest list, and everyone had been invited. Against Bessie's wishes, I told her that I wouldn't be excluding Hector or his friends or family from the event. I was still trying to get along and try to get on the same team so we could cooperate together. But I didn't know if Hector was going to come or not, so we decided to meet up and talk about it. Earlier that day I had gone to the jewelry store to see what I could get for the ring he had given me when he proposed. Since he was with someone else now, I figured it was safe to just get rid of it. Not knowing anything about diamonds or jewelry, I walked in with the barely worn ring, the packages they came in, and the receipts.

"Hello, how can I help you?" the nice lady asked me.

"I want to sell these back to you. My ex and I are no longer together, and I never really wore this. I have the receipts and the original packaging," I said sweetly.

"Okay, let's see what you have," she said. When she looked at the receipt, she asked if we had any insurance on the rings.

"No, we broke up just five weeks after he gave it to me. So, it never crossed my mind," I said.

"I see," she said opening the ring box.

"Okay, well, I can get a price for you, but I do need to warn you that you won't be happy with it," she said.

"Why is that?" I asked.

"This is a cluster ring, which means that it's just tiny specks of a diamond clumped together to look shiny and pretty. But it's valueless," she said uncomfortably.

"He paid almost $6,000 for this," I said, shocked.

"Yeah, if he would have bought a ring that was a 'rock' instead of a 'cluster,' it would have maintained much more value. But unfortunately, once it leaves the store and passes the 30-day return policy, you'd probably be better off selling it online and seeing if someone would actually buy it," she said.

"Okay, well, I would like to see how much they would buy it back for here," I said.

"No problem, just one moment."

When she came back, she had a business card with the prices written on the back. They offered me $530.00 for the engagement ring and $30.00 for the wedding band.

"That's just based on the weight of the ring," she said, handing me the card. "The diamond cluster is valueless on these pieces." She looked sad for me.

Staring at the numbers in shock, I asked, "So, you're telling me, that this man walked in here and was sold a valueless ring for almost $6,000 cash? And he wouldn't even get $600 for it if he sold it back to you?"

"Yeah, even a pawn shop or anyone that knows diamonds. It's worthless," she said. I burst into laughter. I laughed so hard and so long that my cheeks hurt.

"I'm sorry," I said in between laughs. "This is the funniest shit I've ever heard!" I took a deep breath and gathered my things.

"Can I keep this card?" I asked wanting proof of what I just learned.

"Of course," she said smiling.

I went home and told Giovanni. We laughed for a while back and forth about it.

"So, what are you going to do? Try to sell them online?" he asked.

"No, I'm supposed to meet Hector in a little while to talk about the baby shower. I think I'm just going to give them to him. They won't do me any good," I said.

"You're just going to hand them over to him?" he asked.

"Yeah, why not? I *am* trying to get along with him for my daughter's sake, and it satisfies me to think of how angry he will be when he takes them to the store expecting thousands of dollars back like a pompous ass, and walks out angrily," I said grinning.

"Plus, I look like a champion for returning them to him as asked."

"Yeah that's true," he said.

An hour later, I was at the restaurant that Hector and I used to eat crab legs at all the time. I went in and found him sitting at the bar with an empty shot glass and a half empty beer in front of him.

"Hey," I said nervously.

"Hey."

"Here," I said, putting a small gift bag in front of him.

"What's this?" he asked, putting his beer down and looking in the bag.

"Your rings."

"Are you serious? What made you give them back?" he asked.

"It's a peace offering. The baby shower is a week away; our daughter is due in a month. We have *got* to do better for her. I don't want things to be like this anymore. I can't do it," I said.

"I agree. You want some dinner?" he asked.

"Sure, if you're buying," I laughed. We sat and had small talk. Avoiding any big or hurtful topics.

"My sisters are coming down for the baby shower," he said.

"Well that's nice, I'm glad they could make it," I said.

"So, we're still invited?" he asked nervously sipping his beer.

"Yes, but I don't want any drama there. And your little girlfriend will *not* be invited," I said flatly.

"I don't have a girlfriend. She's nobody, I'm just hanging out with her," he said.

"You mean fucking her." He laughed nervously. "Look, I don't care, it's not my business what you do on your own time. But I'm not having any of your hoes around my child. Ever. I have no problem bringing her by to visit with you, but I will *never* leave her alone with you," I said as nicely as I could.

"Well too bad you don't have a fucking choice," he laughed arrogantly.

"I actually have ALL the choice in the world. This doesn't have to get nasty; I'm not taking her away from you, but you are a junkie, an abuser, and a gang member. I can prove all three in court, and I will. I will do anything to keep her from being affected negatively by you and your illnesses. And I don't care who doesn't like it," I said.

"Who the fuck do you think you're talking to?" he whispered to me in my ear.

"Nobody I'm ever going to be afraid of again," I said powerfully. "Thank you for dinner, please let me know if you will be attending the shower. But I will ask you to leave if there is any trouble," I said.

"Trouble?" he asked.

"Yes, and I mean it. I don't mind you coming, but my whole family and most of my friends will be there. They're all pretty upset with you, as you can imagine, so if you start anything, I will ask you to leave."

"They're mad at me because you just had to open your fucking mouth!" he yelled at me, gaining the attention of those near us. I stood up and grabbed my purse.

"I sure did. I'm not lying to protect you anymore. I have someone more important to worry about," I said rubbing my belly.

"Yeah well you're a fucking liar, so nobody believes you," he said.

"Okay, have a good night," I said, walking away. I was almost to my car when I heard him behind me.

"Fine I'll just do my own fucking shower then," he yelled.

"Okay, that's fine. Saves me the trouble of worrying about how you'll behave," I said.

"I'm serious. I'll do my own fucking shower," he said as if that was supposed to make me upset.

"I'm sure you can get one of your whores to throw it for you," I said, reaching for the handle on my car.

"You're just jealous," he said, laughing.

"No Hector, I'm not jealous," I said turning around to face him. "I'm shattered. You wanted me to be hurt? Congratulations. You won, I have *never* in my *life* been more heartbroken than I am now." I said with angry tears in my eyes. "You have destroyed parts of me that I'm not sure I'll ever see again and ruined what was once beautiful about me. This may be all fun and games to you, a sick contest of who can hurt the other one more, but to me it is utter heartbreak and a whole new twisted form of abuse. I fucking *loved* you...so much...I would have done anything for you. I *did* do anything for you! And you can't even treat me like a fucking person, let alone a person you created life with. I had that ring on my finger *weeks* ago and you have some new bitch living in the house that I have my name on still. You had her in there *days* after I left when you threw that lamp at me. So *please* fucking *stop*. I can't take anymore," I said, now crying.

He had a shocked look on his face. "Well, you didn't act like you cared! You just fucking abandoned me without a word. And then when I came home to my empty house expecting you to be there, I thought we were going to talk and work things out," he said.

"We *never* said that, Hector. This is what I'm talking about. Your mind is *so* fucked up off those drugs you just make shit up out of thin air," I said in defense. I sighed and wiped my face, feeling my daughter move around inside my belly. She must have been sick of be crying and being upset by now. It happened daily at this point. Rubbing my belly and taking some calming breaths I leaned back against my car defeated. "It doesn't have to be like this. This isn't what I want for her," I said tears dropping onto my tank top.

"Is she kicking?" he asked. "She's rolling around, do you want to feel it?"

"I don't know" he said nervously. I rolled my eyes and grabbed his hand placing it on my lower stomach. "I don't feel anything," he said.

"Hold on," I said, jabbing her from the other side with my fingertips. He laughed nervously

"Oh shit. That's crazy."

"That's our daughter," I said. He moved his hand and brushed away a tear.

"Well, I have to go," he said.

"Me too," I said, opening my door.

"When is the next appointment?" he asked.

"I don't have a doctor's appointment until Wednesday after the baby shower, but the hospital tour is this week on Tuesday at 4 p.m. if you want to come," I said.

"What's that?"

"It's a tour of the birthing area so you know where to go and what to expect," I said.

"Okay, I'll be there."

I got in my car and went home, crying the entire way. I was relieved that he didn't want to come to the baby shower because he was always guaranteed to start shit. Plus, my dad and brother wouldn't exactly be trusted to behave if they saw him either. Maybe it was for the best. The next morning, I started getting hateful messages from his sisters. They were upset because Hector had told them I uninvited them to the baby shower.

"What? That's not true," I responded. "You are more than welcome to attend. HE said HE wanted to do two separate ones. That wasn't MY idea," I told them. Once again, it led to an all-day drama fest. I even got a call from Titi asking if that was true.

"No, we literally just discussed this *last night* and *he* decided he wanted to do two separate things! You know I want you to come! This is absolutely ridiculous!" I said.

"That's what I thought, this nigga is coked up so fucking bad that his brain is mush! Savannah, I will be at *your* baby shower. I just wanted to make sure first." By the time Giovanni got home and I told him about everything and showed him all the messages I was so emotionally exhausted I couldn't even cry anymore.

"Well, at least it looks like he won't be at the baby shower," he said, trying to cheer me up.

"Yeah, but why did he go and tell everyone that I uninvited them? He has me looking like the asshole and I've been chasing my fucking tail trying to be the bigger person here!" I said angrily.

"So stop," he said.

"What?" I asked blinking in confusion.

"Stop trying. You are wearing yourself out here. You don't sleep, you don't eat, you are trying so hard to please everyone and everyone still seems to be pissed at you. So why bother?" he said.

"Well, that's an interesting observation." He was right though. What good was it doing me?

The next day I was laying by the pool and got a message from Frankie asking me to come over. I hadn't been back over there since she told me about Jose. When I got there, she was throwing everything she owned in garbage bags frantically.

"What's going on?" I asked.

"I'm leaving. I just wanted to give you a few things and say goodbye."

"Where are you going?" I asked.

"I don't actually know. I found a program and they have a place for me and the kids. They offer counseling for kids who have been exposed to domestic violence in their home, they have everything we need to escape!"

"Well that's great! What can I do?" I asked.

"Oh, nothing, I just wanted you to have these things for the baby. Jose doesn't know this yet, but he's being evicted in three days," she said while running around like a chicken with her head cut off.

"What?" I said.

"Yeah, I haven't been paying the rent, they left the eviction notice on the door weeks ago. I'm sorry, I couldn't say anything to anyone. I can't risk him finding us," she said.

"I understand."

"I tried to leave a couple weeks ago but he showed up when the Uber got here to pick us up and sent them away. He beat the shit out of me and then took my son off the school bus the next day and took him to work with him so I couldn't leave," she said frantically.

"We are leaving as soon as the school bus gets here to drop off my son," she said.

"I'll take you wherever you need to go," I said, picking up two black garbage bags.

"No, I'll have an Uber come. I can't ask you to be involved in this, it's too dangerous," she said reaching for the bags.

"I am an Uber. I'm already here, and if you get out and he doesn't find you, nobody will ever know I helped you." She thought about it for a second, looked at the eviction notice and finally agreed I was right. While she was running around frantically collecting things, she told me that Hector had gone to Medieval Times recently with she and Jose.

"He had some girl with him that was acting like his new girlfriend. She's on his Facebook. I don't know if you've seen all that shit yet but she's planning your daughter's nursery," she said.

Not wanting to discuss my life's drama I brushed it aside with a quick "Yeah, I know," and kept moving.

"Well apparently he's been trying to fuck that ho from the office too," she said moving into her daughter's bedroom with a fresh bag. "He and his father showed up to the club or whatever after she checked in somewhere on her birthday. Apparently, she was uncomfortable with it, she told Jose she was quitting soon because she doesn't want Hector and he doesn't seem to want to take no for an answer," she said.

"Not surprising, he's desperate to make himself feel better. Clearly I shattered his ego when I left," I said.

"Yeah but the other girl that he's been fucking is all up in the office all the time and follows him around like a puppy. She has no idea he's fucking and chasing anyone with a vagina," she said laughing. "When the shit hits the fan, I want you to have all the baby stuff," she said, throwing the last of her daughter's things in a bag. "The crib, everything," she said. "I'm not worried about any of that right now."

Finally, her son arrived. He was 12 years old at the time, so when she told him we were leaving and he needed to grab whatever he needed in 5 minutes, he knew what was happening and understood it was time to go. On the way to the motel, she asked if I could stop at the gas station so she could get some snacks for the night for her kids. While she was in the store, I asked her son if he was okay.

"Yeah, this is the best thing," he said leaning his head against the window. "I don't want mom to be hurt anymore," he said sadly. That broke my heart. I imagined what it would be like to see what he had seen at his age. Watching my mother be brutally beaten and tortured, it made me sick. In *that* moment, talking with him, I knew no matter what I was going through it was all worth it. *My* daughter would *never* be exposed to this disfunction. Not while I was alive.

We found a motel and she went in to get a room. I got all her things unloaded and sat with her in the room for a minute. Her daughter wouldn't stop screaming, and it was making her frantic.

"I'm so fucking scared," she said, patting her daughter on the back while pacing around the room.

"I know. When do you have to meet the lady from the program you're going into?" I asked.

"Tomorrow afternoon at the police station," she said.

"Listen, if you need a ride, just let me know," I said.

"No, you've done enough. I'll probably never see you again." I stood up to give her a hug.

"We don't know what the story will end up being. But just in case, I love you guys, and more than anything you need to be safe and keep your children safe. You're doing the right thing. I'm proud of you," I said.

"Thank you," she said with tears streaming down her face. "I love you too. And I hope you have an amazing life! I'm so glad you got out before your daughter is born. What are you naming her again?" she asked.

"Harmony" I said.

"That's beautiful. You are going to be an amazing mommy," she said hugging me one last time. Pulling away from the hotel, I felt scared and uneasy. It wasn't a calm relief that I expected. I could feel the anxiety and fear radiating from this woman so heavily that leaving her alone with the kids in a motel room felt somehow incomplete. I felt like I'd just abandoned a puppy that had been hit by a car; I moved it off the road not to get hit again, but didn't take it to the hospital or treat its injuries in any way.

Later that night, around 11 p.m., I got the call from Hector. "Do you know where Frankie is?" he asked.

"Home?" I answered acting like it was a stupid question.

"No, Jose is freaking out, he came home and her and the kids were gone. Don't fucking lie, if you know where she is you need to tell me. You were the only friend she had here, and I know how bitches stick together," he snapped.

"I don't know shit," I said calmly.

"Did you know they were getting evicted?" he asked.

"No, why would I know any of this?"

"You better not be lying. You know he'll find her, it's only a matter of time. And if he finds out *you* had something to do with this, he's going to be pissed."

"Good night Hector," I said, hanging up the phone.

The next day, I was sitting on the porch with Giovanni, and Hector messaged me that Frankie and Jose had just left his house, so if I was involved with anything I was going to pay.

"He found her then?" I asked casually.

"Yeah, he found her hiding in a hotel room." My heart sank into my stomach. How did he find her? Now what? I could only imagine the beating that was coming her way if it hadn't happened yet. My heart broke for her all over again. Even more so for her children.

CHAPTER TWENTY-NINE

Cut Off.

The following afternoon, I was lying in bed and got a call from Hector. "Hello," I said sleepily.

"So, you *are* a lying fucking whore!" he yelled.

Not sure if I was hearing him correctly since I was just woken up, I asked "What?" rubbing my eyes and sitting up.

"You're living five minutes from my dad's house! You live with the man you gave Halo too! You probably been fucking his ass since before you left me!" My heart sank into my stomach. How the fuck did he find out? Fucking Jose!

"Yeah, I know everything about him, I know his sibling's names, his address his phone number where he works. *Everything*! How long you been fucking him!?" he growled at me. I could tell I was on speaker phone, so he was putting on a show for someone.

"I'm not fucking him. I never have. He's just a friend. I'm not having this conversation on speakerphone to entertain your little whore, so you can take me off or we can talk later after you calm down," I said.

"Yeah, I don't have anything more to say to you. I want my phone and my card back when I see you at the hospital walkthrough tomorrow. You can let *that* nigga support you." He spat at me and hung up the phone. I ran down to tell Giovanni.

"He knows, fucking Jose stalked me and found out everything for him, he knows your name, where we live, where you work, everything!" I said, panicked. "I'm so sorry! I don't want to bring you or your brother any harm! I'm so fucking sorry!" I said

"Okay, calm down. Take a few deep breaths, this is *not* the end of the world. He was going to find out eventually."

"I know, but now he thinks I was cheating on him with *you* and that we're fucking, and he's pissed. He told me he was taking my phone and his card and cutting me off tomorrow."

"Okay, so we'll go to my service provider today and get you a new phone, no big deal," he said, not seeming upset at all. I heard a Harley Davidson pulling into the neighborhood we lived in and went into a fear-stricken frenzy. I darted over to the fence to see if it was coming down our street. *This is it!* I thought to myself. *He's coming to hurt Giovanni and it's 100 percent my fault!* I started crying frantically, waiting for the bike to appear and whoever else he talked into coming to follow. But it didn't. nothing happened.

"There's a guy on the other street that owns a Harley," Giovanni said, calmly moving toward me with his hands out. "It's not him, he's not here, I'm fine, *you* are fine," he said wrapping his arms around me. I fell into his chest, balling like a baby. I felt completely ridiculous! I just had a whole freak out over nothing!

"It's okay, we're all okay," he said soothingly.

"I'm sorry," I said, embarrassed that I just lost my shit in front of him. In my head, he already had to think this whole situation was ridiculous and I was pathetic for having gotten myself into it. But, once again, he came through like the strong champion I didn't know I needed.

"You have been put through so much. You're handling it very well, better than most. You are a strong woman, but you're still human and it's okay to be afraid sometimes. Who could blame you?" he said as I backed away from him, wanting to sit down. "Look, I'm not afraid of Hector, if he comes for me, he comes for me. But I won't live my life waiting for it to happen. If something does happen it is *not* your fault. But I will be more cautious of my surroundings and carry my gun if that makes you feel better," he said.

"Yeah, that's good. Sorry I lost my shit," I laughed through my tears.

"It was bound to happen eventually," he said. "Now, let's go get you a phone," he said putting his cigarette out.

The next day I arrived at the hospital tour, and Hector wasn't there yet. I texted him to see if I should wait for him outside. I was a little nervous for some reason. This tour was going to be a look into my very near future. He responded that he was running late but, on the way, and to head inside. The hospital tour was already halfway done when he finally arrived, looking homeless and smelling the same once again.

When we walked out of the maternity ward together, I asked where his car was. "I got dropped off," he said.

"Oh, do you need a ride home?" I asked, being nosy.

"No, they'll be here any minute," he said looking anxious.

"They?" I asked, already knowing it was a female.

"She," he said.

"Oh nice, one of your whores is coming. Super," I said sarcastically.

"She's not a whore, you would probably like her if you got to know her. She's half lesbian," he said laughing.

"You are disgusting," I responded, reaching into my purse for his phone and card.

"Here is your phone," I said handing it to him.

"Why do I want this?" he asked stupidly while I retrieved the card from my wallet.

"You told me yesterday you wanted it back," I said, handing him the card. He snatched the card out of my hand and handed me the phone.

"I'll let you keep the phone I guess; I'll need to be able to get ahold of you," he said, putting the card in his wallet.

"I got a new one already," said handing the useless thing back as we got to my car.

"From your little boyfriend," he asked angrily.

"Yes, but he's not my boyfriend. And unlike *you* I haven't fucked *anyone*! But that's not your business anymore," I said. His eyes turned dark and he clenched his teeth.

"You know what I want?" he asked.

"What's that?" I asked, irritated, while opening my car door and putting my purse down.

"I want you to have *nothing*. I can't wait for the day when you show up on my doorstep *begging* to come in. *Begging* to have me back. I can't wait for you to be so poor and so homeless and so hungry that you *have* to come crawling back to me so I can spit in your fucking face!" he said with a pure evil in his voice. It brought chills to my entire body. It hurt me more than I would allow him to know that he hated me so much. Still after all this I didn't hate him, I didn't want him to hate me, and I didn't want my daughter to be punished for me breaking her father's heart.

"Well, I'm sorry you feel that way Hector, but it's never going to happen. For some reason, you seem to have it in your head that I'll never be able to work again," I said crossing my arms at my wrists and setting them on top of my open car door. "But in fact, in about 10 weeks, as soon as I recover from giving birth, I'll be back on my feet again in *no* time. I'm not some helpless victim, I'm just pregnant. This baby has given me more strength than I have ever had in my life. Everything I do now is for *her*, not to hurt *you*. So try not to forget where I was when you came into my life, and where *you* were." I said in a challenging tone. "*You* didn't have shit when you met me, and I helped you grow! You wouldn't have gotten this opportunity with the company if it wasn't for *me*, and you know it. So you should be careful what you wish upon me, doll, karma is a filthy bitch and God don't like ugly," I said like I was preaching a sermon.

"Yeah we'll fucking see," he spat at me. "I hope your little boyfriend knows what he got himself into fucking with you."

"Meaning?" I asked defensively.

"He just wants to fuck you, Savannah, don't fool yourself," he said not answering my question.

"Yes, I'm sure he wants to fuck me Hector. But you know what else he would like to do. He would marry me, take care of me, raise my daughter and provide us an amazing life if I let him. Hell, he would probably adopt Harmony if I would allow it," I said. Hector stepped closer to my car door, getting as close to me as he could.

"What the fuck did you just say to me? Don't get that nigga murdered. Don't you ever say anything like that to me again, you fucking whore!" he yelled.

I saw Hector's car pulling in cautiously, she was going annoyingly slow. Clearly not wanting to get involved in the conversation we were having. "Speaking of whores, there's your girlfriend! Tell her to enjoy my house!" I said getting into my car.

"Fuck you," he responded, slamming my door closed. I blew him a dramatic kiss just to irritate him more, but what he said had gotten to me. I went home and started crying as soon as I walked in discussing the situation with Giovanni.

"I'm sorry I said that to him. I shouldn't have, I never want to put you in harm's way, I was just *so* upset after what he said that I didn't think. I wanted to hurt him like he just hurt me," I admitted.

"That's understandable, and I'm not worried about Hector," he said, reassuring me.

It was Friday, the day before my baby shower, and I had just gotten out of the shower. I had just gotten done drying my hair when my phone rang.

"Hello," I said, annoyed.

"My sisters want to meet you," Hector said.

"They'll meet me tomorrow at the shower, won't they?"

"Yeah, but they want to meet you today."

"I'm working today."

"Well, can you just meet us for a few minutes? We're coming out your way anyways, so we can just meet at the tavern for like 20 minutes." Realizing I wasn't getting out of this without more drama I finally agreed. I called Giovanni and Gia both to let them know where I was going and who was coming just in case anything happened to me.

"Is this a good idea?" Giovanni asked.

"I don't know, but the shower is tomorrow, and I don't want any more drama," I said. Gia was already off work, so she offered to come meet me up there.

"No, but I'll let you know if I need you," I laughed.

"I live two seconds from there! I'll be close!" she said loudly.

"I'm sure I'll be fine," I said, laughing.

When I walked in, they were all sitting in a booth to my left. I walked over and introduced myself politely. I grabbed a chair and sat on the end of the table. Hector and one sister on my right and the younger sister and her toddler on my left. We sat there having small talk and avoiding 'hot topics' that would start drama. I was grateful for that. I thought they were both very nice girls. The younger one seemed much less educated, but sweet enough. The older one was married with three kids of her own. She had just had her third child recently. They had plans to go out and party that night, so they didn't have much time to visit. But neither did I, so that was fine with me. They told me I looked great for as pregnant as I was and that they were excited to see the new baby.

"I'm excited to see her as well. I can't wait but I'm nervous," I said honestly.

"Are you going to do a vaginal birth?" they asked.

"Yeah, and I don't want any medication if I can handle it," I said.

"Good luck with that!" the older one laughed.

"Yeah fuck that shit," the younger one said, laughing.

"I have a pretty high pain tolerance, so I'm hoping I can manage."

"Yeah we saw your little dungeon room! I've seen stuff like that on porn, and it looks painful," the older one said.

"It's not really painful," I said.

"None of it?" she asked curiously.

"Nothing I experienced was. I mean, there is pain involved but it's more like a quick sting to your skin. It can be pretty sexy though," I said.

Leaning into the conversation, more intrigued, she asked, "Was there anything you didn't like?"

Hector laughed uncomfortably. "A ball gag," he said.

I laughed. "Yeah, I hated that."

She shook her head. "I like my hair pulled and a slap on the ass sometimes, but I don't think I could let someone whip me," she said.

"Don't knock it till you try it! The flogging isn't bad at all, there's not much pain involved in that, but it still makes your all cheeks red like he's actually doing something," I said.

"Yeah," he agreed.

"I am *not* going to touch *that* room. You two sound like you fucked all over it" she said laughing. Hector got quiet and looked down at his hands knowing what I was going to say.

"We actually never used it," I said. Shocked, they both looked at me confused.

"What? Why?" she asked.

"Well, I put the room together to surprise him when he was in New York for the funeral. Then he brought his uncle to stay with us. Between that, fighting and not getting along, and the pregnancy, we just never did," I said.

"That's kind of sad," the oldest sister said looking at Hector.

"Yeah," he said sadly.

"Well, at least he still has it. It's all his now," I said uncomfortably.

"Yeah, that's still sad. You did a sweet thing for him and surprised him and then never got to enjoy it," she said.

"It's never been used," he said looking at me when he said it.

There were a few seconds of awkward silence and then his sister said, "Aw, maybe there's still hope! Maybe after the baby comes you two will get back together and live happily ever after!" Hector didn't react at all. I just laughed nervously looking at my watch.

"Well, I really have to get going. But it was very nice meeting you ladies, and I hope I see you tomorrow," I said politely standing up.

"Yeah, we need to get moving as well," Hector said, standing up. We all walked out front and they politely said their goodbyes.

"We'll be there tomorrow, we just wanted to get a chance to meet you so it wasn't awkward for us all," the oldest one said.

"I understand," I said.

"You want to know what you two can do if you want me to keep the house?" Hector said randomly.

"Keep the house?" I asked, confused.

"Beat those fat bitches' asses at the shower tomorrow," he said laughing.

"What bitches?" they asked confused by this new awkward conversation.

"The two fat bitches, the one with multicolored hair and the *really* big *really* loud Italian bitch from Jersey," he said giggling like a mischievous schoolboy. I shook my head in disgust.

"See, that's exactly the dumbass bullshit you always have to pull to ruin shit," I said.

"What? I want them to beat their asses, then I'll keep the house," he said. The two women stood there awkwardly.

"You realize how stupid you sound right now?" I asked.

"It's not stupid, they ruined my fucking relationship and tore apart my family, they deserve it!"

"Oh right, because it couldn't possibly be anything *you* did to make me leave right? There will *not* be any fucking drama at my shower tomorrow, and these poor girls didn't come down here for this shit. It was very nice meeting you, I'm sorry things are so hostile right now. But I do hope you enjoy your stay," I said politely shaking their hands. "Grow up, Hector," I spat at him walking towards my car.

Finally, it was the day of my shower. I wanted Giovanni to come, but I was so nervous about it I that he didn't mind staying home. I felt bad; he was such a huge part of my life now, he should have been there. But the fear of having Hector storm in and start a war kept me from letting the both of us enjoy the day. The shower was beautiful. Bessie had done a fantastic job. There was a photo booth set up with props to take pictures with and everything. The decorations were gorgeous the food was laid out beautifully and everyone was in good spirits. My mom had even come into town to be there. The only thing I was missing was Giovanni. I was happy to see Titi walk in. Jimmy was right behind her.

"I'm so glad you both came!" I said happily, greeting them.

"You know I wouldn't miss this Savannah. Even though that fuckboy baby daddy scheduled *his* stupid shower for right now as well," she spat out angrily.

"What?" I asked.

"Yeah, his shower is happening right now! It's stupidest shit I have ever fucking heard of!" she said.

"I'm not going," Jimmy said, giving me a kiss on the cheek and heading over to Gia for a hug.

"I didn't realize he was doing it on the same date and time as mine," I said, shocked.

"Of course he is. He wants everyone to go to his and not yours. Everything is a stupid competition. It's all for the *same* baby, he's just a fucking child!" she said angrily.

"Well I hope you stay for a while," I said sadly. "I'm not going anywhere. I'll get to his house when I fucking get there, fuck him," she said.

There were a few people missing, but even though he tried to make my party suck, it was still a good turnout. His sisters never showed up, but halfway into the games I was elated to see Big Mama walk in! I hadn't seen her in a long time, and I was *so* happy she came! After the games and gifts were over, I was able to catch up with her for a bit while the other guests were leaving. Titi had never met her before, so I introduced them to each other.

"Thank you so much for coming," I said to them both. "I'm sorry you're being pulled into two different directions with this shit."

"Girl, I ain't being pulled nowhere, I'm not going to two showers, I'm here and that's it. My husband and I wanted to show our support," she said.

Titi chimed in, "It's fucking ridiculous that he's having a shower of his own right now," she said.

"I wasn't gonna say it," Big Mama laughed in agreement.

"I will," Titi said. "Well I guess that's why his sisters didn't come. After all that drama I went through about it I'm almost annoyed they didn't come. I literally just met with them yesterday and they said they would be here," I said.

"You met his sisters?" Titi asked.

"Yeah I met them and Hector around lunch time at the tavern. They insisted on meeting me, so the shower wasn't awkward. But I told him that I didn't want his little girlfriend here and no drama."

"Oh, so you know about her?" Big Mama asked.

"Yeah, she had the nerve to think she was going to be planning my child's nursery and playing stepmom," I answered.

"Oh wow, we've met her a few times. She seems to be nice enough, but I did have to stop her when she started talking about you at the clubhouse," she said.

"What the hell?" I said.

"She was just misinformed. She was told a very different story by your baby daddy than how things went down with you two. I stopped her and corrected her before she made a fool of herself, but you know I wasn't about to have that," she said.

Titi chimed in, "What story? She may not have ever met Savannah, but she knew damn well she was engaged to Hector and pregnant with his fucking child," she said, upset.

"Well, she was told that Savannah left for another man and the baby wasn't his," she said.

"Then why the fuck is she trying to build a nursery?" I snapped.

"Exactly. The whole thing is bullshit, you know Hector *has* to be the victim no matter what. And that's fine, because whether he knows it or not, we support *you*," Big Mama said, pointing to me.

"Well, thank you." I said. "We aren't standing by his stupid ass either," Titi said.

I walked out with the ladies and wished them good travels. When I got home, Giovanni and Gabriel helped me unload everything. I had moved downstairs by this time, so it was like my own little apartment. I had a bedroom, bathroom, and living room down there. It was everything I needed. I looked at my phone and had several messages from different women who were apologetic that they didn't make it to my shower. They were forced to go to Hector's by their husbands but were disgusted by the entire thing. Later that evening I got a message from both of his sisters, apologizing and asking how my shower went. Later that evening, when I got on Facebook, I saw the pictures from his baby shower. They looked sad. He looked sad and empty in the eyes. It didn't look like anyone was having a good time, it just looked uncomfortable. They decorated and got him a cake, served food and had a few gifts, but it all just seemed very awkward. Janet was there, she was talking in one of the videos and sounded like a man. I hated myself for not having Giovanni come to mine, but then dismissed the thought by telling myself he wouldn't have wanted to go anyway.

The following Monday I had a doctor's appointment. I didn't expect Hector to come, but he showed up. When we went out to the parking lot, he asked me how my shower went.

"Fine, even though you tried to ruin it by throwing yours the exact date and time. Don't you realize that the petty things you're doing make everyone uncomfortable? Not just me," I said.

"I don't fucking care," he said smugly. "Yeah, that's clear."

"Did your boyfriend go?"

"No, but I see you had YOUR boyfriend at yours," I said pettily.

"What?" he asked.

"Janet, I saw her on the video your sister posted, she sounds like a dude. She kind of looks like one too," I spat out hatefully.

"She wasn't even there," he lied.

"Stop it, I literally *saw* her there. What's the point in lying about it? Isn't that why you are doing all this anyway? To upset me?" I asked. We reached our cars and I went for my door handle.

"Wait, you're leaving?" he asked. Looking up at him, confused, I asked, "Why wouldn't I be?"

"You want to come to the house? So we can talk?" he asked, crossing his arms. "You can come see all the stuff I got for the baby," he said, smiling.

"Not really, whatever you have to say you can say here," I said, confused.

"It's safe, my youngest sister is still there. We won't be alone."

"What do you want to talk about, I'm not coming over to your house right now. And don't you have to go to work?"

"No, I'm the boss, I have peasants for that," he laughed.

"Get to the point. What do you want?" I asked as I sighed.

"Well, I have been thinking a lot about when you have the baby. I won't be letting you take my child home to some other nigga," he said, as if he had a choice in the matter. "So I want you to come back home."

I scrunched my face up in confusion. "Have you lost your mind?" I asked.

"Hear me out," he said. "You and the baby can have one of the bedrooms, and when the adoption goes through for Janet her new son can have the other room," he said, grinning.

"Are you implying that I move in with you and your new whore?"

"Basically, yeah. She and I both have good careers, so you could just stay at home and take care of the kids and the house all day," he said, smiling.

"Have you lost your fucking mind?" I said, so surprised by his complete stupidity that I wasn't even getting mad yet.

"It was just an idea, I had a dream about it the other night, and she's into chicks, so I thought maybe we could work something out," he laughed nervously.

"You are about the stupidest person I have ever known in my entire life! You think it's cute to ask me such a ridiculous question?"

"Well, yeah, I had thought about this working."

"Mm-hmm, and what are her thoughts on this little fantasy of yours?" I asked, crossing my arms.

"Well, I thought I would try to get you on board first," he admitted. "The fact that you have the audacity to even ask me this dumbass question realistically just shows what trash you are. If you actually thought for a fucking second that I would want to move back into the house that is still *ours* that we moved into together and raise *our* child while I was in the fucking guest room with *our* baby, and your new bitch was in what was *our* bedroom and I was raising *her* kid while you two fucked all the time, you don't know me at all. Nor do you respect me as a fucking person," I said, becoming angry.

"Well, I thought eventually we would all be fucking. You two would really like each other," he said seriously.

"Get the fuck off my car!" I said, opening my door. "Okay, I'm sorry, I guess it was a bad idea. She doesn't have to move in with us!" he said, stepping in my way.

"*We* are never moving in together again. I will allow you to be at the birth, and I will bring the baby to see you, but she *is* going home with me," I said.

"That's not gonna happen," he said in a warning tone.

"There's not a goddamn thing you can do about it! Get out of my fucking way!"

He stepped out of the way while I got in my car. I felt sick.

"This conversation isn't over," he said as I closed the door. "I'm serious," he said through the closed window. "You aren't taking my baby to that fucking house!" I threw up my middle finger while I started the car. "Yeah fuck you too! Real mature!" he yelled at me. Driving away, my palms got sweaty and I felt like I was going to throw up. I pulled over in and empty parking lot and messaged Giovanni. Even he couldn't have seen *that* coming. Thinking I was going to throw up, I rolled the windows down trying to breath. Why was he doing this to me? I wasted all that time and effort on loving him genuinely. But he treated me like I was a leaky bag of trash. What the hell was wrong with him? I was so *sick* of crying, but I felt shattered in a whole new way. Just when I thought things couldn't get worse, he found a new form of torture. I had never been made to feel this worthless by anyone.

The following week, I had my final visit with the specialist. Hector was going out of town to get certified as a chimney technician with Jose, and I didn't want to go alone, so I asked Giovanni if he wanted to tag along.

"Yeah, I could do that," he said.

"Are you sure? It's in the morning on a Tuesday," I said.

"Yeah, I can just take the day off. I'll still get paid, it's fine," he said. It was strange walking into the specialist office with Giovanni. But it was nice to have him there. He had never experienced anything like this before, so it was fun to watch his response. The specialist said most everything looked good but noticed the baby's fluid sac looked a little lower than she liked.

"When is your next doctor's appointment?" she asked.

"One week from today with my OBGYN."

"Okay, we'll let her take another look at you then, I'll send this over to her. If the fluid goes down any more, she may have to induce labor." I was due soon anyway, but I wanted Harmony to stay in there if she could to grow and be healthy. "Nothing to worry yourself about, just take it easy and if anything changes, if you experience any fluid leaks or anything like that, call your doctor immediately" she said. It made me nervous, but thankfully Giovanni was there with me this time. He was great at easing my mind.

Hector was back in town a week later. I told him what the specialist had said, so when he showed up to the OBGYN appointment, he was hoping they would induce me. We went in and discussed the results the specialist sent over and then took me in to get another ultrasound.

"Yeah, okay, we're going to go ahead and get this going," she said. "The nurse is going to get a wheelchair and wheel you over to the maternity ward now," she said. My heart started pounding. I had my hospital bags packed and, in the car, just in case this happened, but I was *so* nervous.

"Is the baby okay?" I asked.

"Yes, she's low on fluid though, and since your due date is in two days, I just don't want to wait. Let's go have a baby!" she said, trying to get me excited.

"Why do I have to go in a wheelchair?" I asked.

"Oh, that's just hospital policy. No reason to panic," she said, asking the nurse to collect a wheelchair.

"Well, I have to go to my car and get my bags," I said, on the verge of a full-blown panic attack.

"No need, dad can do that, I need to get you moved now. You're okay, the baby is okay, but I need to get things moving now so baby and mom *stay* okay," she said.

I took a deep breath. "Okay," I said.

I picked up my phone and messaged Giovanni. "They're keeping me, I have to be induced," I said.

"Well, good thing you're prepared for that. Don't freak out you got this," he said.

"Can you call my mom? She'll need a place to stay," I said.

"Of course. Let me know if you need anything." Already I was sad he wasn't there with me. Looking over at Hector made my stomach turn. I didn't want him there. I wanted Giovanni.

The nurse came in and asked if we were ready.

"I guess," I answered nervously.

"Change into this gown, mom, and I'll be back," the nurse said.

"Can I wear anything under it?" It was freezing in there.

"You can wear a tank top or something and socks, but no pants or under-wear," she said.

"Okay, thank you." I walked over and looked out the window to the parking lot. "We're about to meet our baby," I said.

"Yeah, this is finally happening," he said.

"Can you go down and get my bags please?"

"Yeah, get changed," he said, not moving.

"I wanted my bags first. I have some tank tops in there I wanted to wear underneath, so I don't freeze," I said.

"Well I don't have my car, so I'll be running to the house anyway, I need to get my stuff," he said.

"Can you bring my bags up first?"

He laughed. "No." Already he was being difficult. *Is it too late to make him leave and ask Giovanni to come instead?* I asked myself internally. My phone rang, it was Bessie.

"Hey," I said.

"Hey! We're having a baby!?" she asked excitedly.

"Yeah, I just got in the room. I'll put you on the list to come back," I said.

"Okay, I'm on my way already!" she said.

"Okay see you soon."

"Who the fuck was that?" Hector asked.

"Bessie."

"She's coming?"

"Yes, she's on her way," I said, walking over to my gown.

"She ain't staying," he said.

"She's not staying for the birth no, nobody is," I said.

"I am," he said defensively.

"Yes, I realize that Hector, but I'm not interested in sharing this private moment with everyone. She can wait in the waiting room when it's going down," I said, wishing he would go away.

He got up and went to my purse digging inside it.

"What the hell?" I said.

"I told you I want to go get my shit and come back," he said.

"You could ask," I said, annoyed.

"I don't have to fucking ask. I'll be back," he spat over his arrogant shoulder. I stood there, taking a deep breath and rubbing my temples.

"You're doing this for Harmony, it's the right thing to do," I said out loud to myself. The door opened, and the nurse came back in with some bags of fluid.

"Oh, I'm sorry honey, I thought you'd be ready," she said.

"I'm sorry, I got sidetracked. Can I talk to you please?" I asked her before she tried to leave.

"Yes, of course," she said putting her things down on a metal tray.

"I need to let you and the other staff know that the man I'm here with is my ex-fiancé. I'm allowing him to be here for the birth, but he is a very violent man with an extreme temper. My doctor is aware of it, but if at any time I feel unsafe or uncomfortable, I can make him leave right?" I asked. Her body language changed from relaxed to alert.

"Yes, if at any time you want anyone out of here, they will be asked to leave and, if need be, escorted out by security. But thank you for letting me know. I will alert the rest of the staff to stay aware of the situation," she said as I started to change.

"But anyone *you* don't put on the visitation list *won't* get in," she said.

"Well that's good to know. But I'm trying to do the right thing, so I'm going to try to stick it out with him for the birth," I said.

"Would you like me to step out so you can change?" she asked.

"What's the point? You'll be looking at my ovaries soon," I laughed.

"I like you," she laughed along with me while she started getting ready to proceed.

When Bessie walked in, she had a bottle of our favorite Champagne and a little vase of flowers and a balloon. I was already in the bed with the IVs stuck in my arm.

"Hey mommy," she said happily.

"Hi!" I said so relieved someone was going to be here with me besides Hector.

"Where's the idiot?" she asked, rolling her eyes.

"He took my car to his house to get his bags," I said, annoyed.

"Your car? Why?" she asked.

"He said Jose dropped him off. He wouldn't even bring up *my* bags from the car first, so I'm dying of thirst," I said.

"He's such a fucking asshole," she said, shaking her head. "Are you *sure* you want him here for all this?" she asked, hoping I would ban him from being involved.

"No, but I'm trying to do the right thing for my daughter. Plus I already let the nurses know, so if I want him to leave I just have to say the word, and he's gone. They won't even let him back in," I said.

"Does it have to be *you* that requests that?" she asked, laughing.

"Yes," I laughed with her. "Well, mom is on her way. Pops isn't coming until the baby is here, he doesn't want to see Hector."

"You feel anything yet?" she asked

"No, not really. Nothing more than some cramps here and there like when you're really constipated and can't poop."

"Well it's working then."

Hector strolled in about that time with his bags.

"Hey, where are my bags?" I asked.

"I couldn't get it all at once and my friends are on the way, so I have to go back down anyway. I told them I'd meet them outside. Put their name on the list," he said, walking back out.

"What friends?" Bessie asked me with her hands on her hips. I told her it was the ones whose baby shower we had recently gone to. She already had the baby and he wanted some support, so I agreed to let them come visit. I actually liked them a lot. Their oldest daughter was awesome, and the whole family was very sweet.

Once the Pitocin started to kick in and my contractions got bigger, my patience for Hector was getting shorter. Every time he put his feet up on my bed or ate the food in front of me, someone got onto him about it. I was doing okay without pain meds so far, but *man* were those contractions getting strong. I was so grateful that Hector had invited his friends; the wife was doing a wonderful job helping me breath through the contractions and calm me down. Eventually, the doctor wanted to break my water since it didn't seem to want to do it naturally. All my guests tucked themselves behind a curtain for the event. They put my legs in stirrups and told me to lay back and relax as much as I could.

"This may be painful so you may have to hold her down," the nurse said to Hector. Taking the opportunity to touch me, he got in my face and leaned his body on my chest, pinning me down. I severely underestimated how much this would hurt. Her first attempt failed, and all we accomplished was I ended up screaming my face off.

"I'm sorry, but we're going to have to try again; it didn't work," the nurse said gently. We waited for the next contraction to come and go, and she told me to take a deep breath. The pain was sharp and excruciating but having Hector pin me down and breathe in my face was torture. I didn't want him touching me. It brought back horrible memories I didn't want to relive. I started to panic. Flash backs of how he used to force himself on me mixed with the pain of the nurse breaking my water were too much for me to handle. I screamed and yelled at Hector to get the fuck off me. Finally the stabbing pain stopped, and she told him to let me go. After she broke my water the contractions became almost unbearable very quickly. I couldn't get comfortable for longer than a minute at a time. I didn't want to lie down, but walking wasn't much of an option either. I hadn't anticipated it going on this long.

"You are one tough cookie," the nurse said to me. My guests had already gone home. I tossed and turned and moaned and groaned all night. Hector kept getting mad at me for making so much noise while he was trying to sleep. "You can fuck *all* the way off! Go fucking home! You aren't helping me at *all*!" I snapped.

"Yeah, no chance in hell," he said.

"Then shut the fuck up!"

Finally, at about 6 a.m. the next morning, the doctor came in to check on me. I wasn't dilated enough to push, which to me was unfortunate news.

"Okay, I know you don't want any medicine. But you've been at this for 12 hours, and I'm guessing haven't gotten any sleep?" she said.

"How would I get sleep? The contractions barely stop, and then another one comes," I said, trying to catch my breath.

"Well, unfortunately, I'm going to need you to either get some rest so you can push, or we will end up having to do a C-section," she said.

"I'm not getting a C-section. I can do this," I said.

"Then I need you to consider a low epidural. You'll be able to get a little rest and then hopefully be able to push. But I need you to get it now because if we wait much longer you will be too far along to receive one," she said.

"Just do it," Hector said. "I'm tired, and you won't stop moaning," he laughed nervously seeing the look the doctor and the nurse were giving him.

"Well, I don't want a C-section," I said, considering my options quickly. "Fine, let's do it."

"My shift is almost over, but my associate will be taking over and he is wonderful," she said.

"*He*?" I said, not fond of the idea.

"Yes, but he has done this a million times. He is fantastic, don't worry. I was hoping to do it for you, but I've worked too many hours and the hospital is kicking me out," she said, smiling.

After they administered the epidural, I was finally able to get a little rest. I requested the lowest dose possible, so it didn't get rid of the pain, but it made it more bearable, which was a blessing. Three hours later, the nurse finally told me it was time to get ready to push. She picked up the phone and paged the doctor and then sprang into action. While she was breaking down the end of my bed and getting me positioned, she noticed my rubber bracelet.

"Oh my! We go to the same church!" she said excitedly.

"Really? Which service?" I asked.

"Second service when I'm not here."

"Me too! This will be awkward!" I said, laughing.

"Oh no, it happens all the time," she said. "Okay, on your next contraction, I want you to take a deep breath and push like you have to go to the bathroom," she said.

"Shouldn't we wait for the doctor?" I asked.

"He will be here long before this baby comes out, trust me. Dad, you can hold a leg and talk her through this while she's pushing. Your job is to encourage her. This isn't going to be easy, but the more helpful *you* are, the better it will go," she said nicely. "Okay, mom, here comes a contraction. Deep breath! Now push!" I held my breath and pushed through the wave of pain. It was painful but pushing through it felt like the natural thing my body wanted to do. So I couldn't wait to do it again.

"Good morning!" I heard a man's voice say happily from the door. "How we doing, mom?" he asked. When he came in, I recognized him immediately.

"Oh wow, you delivered my nephew!" I said laughing.

"Did I? How old?" he asked. "He'll be 10 this year, but I was in the delivery room when his mother gave birth, and it was you who delivered him!" I said, feeling relieved.

"All I do is catch, you ladies do the delivery," he said lightly. "Here comes another one, mom, deep breath," the nurse said while the doctor got prepared.

"Looks like you're doing great!" the doctor said sitting down in front of me.

After an hour of this, I was getting frustrated. They showed me how close I was with a mirror and gave me a glove so I could feel her head, but I just couldn't seem to get her out.

"Okay, if we don't get the head out soon, I'm going to have to help her along," the doctor said. He ordered some suction device to put on her head and pull her out. As it arrived and he was opening the package, I got another contraction. I held my breath grabbed, Hector's arm, and dug in with everything I had inside me. I could feel her head tearing through me, but I didn't care.

"Head's out! Guess we don't need that anymore," he said handing the device back to the nurse.

"Good job mom. Okay now here comes the hard part, the shoulders are tough to get out but, you're halfway there and you are going to meet your little girl in the next few minutes. Here comes a contraction!" Hector grabbed my phone and started taking pictures, distracting me.

"*No pictures!*" I yelled with a demonic voice I had never heard come out of me.

"Okay, sorry," he said, putting my phone back down. He wasted my contraction, and I was pissed.

"You fucking douche," I said under my breath. Another one came and I used the anger I had towards him and pushed this giant creature out of my body. I had never in my life experienced a relief so great. I went from the worst pain of my life to feeling instantly amazing. I did it!

They plopped the slimy new baby on my chest, and she started opening her eyes while the nurses clamped off the umbilical cord. I didn't even care that she was covered in slime. She was the *most* beautiful thing I had ever seen. *This* was the tiny person I had gone through hell for, and she was worth every bit of it.

"Hello Harmony," I said emotionally. The doctor cut the umbilical cord, and the nurse grabbed my baby.

"I'll give her right back, mom, we just need to clean her up and check her," she said sweetly.

"We still have one more push, mom," the doctor said. "We need to get everything out of there so I can see what we need to do to get you all fixed up," he said. I didn't care, I didn't feel any pain anymore. All I could focus on was my daughter on the other side of the room crying.

"Go let her hold your finger and talk to her, comfort her," I snapped at Hector who stood there watching what the doctor was doing to me.

"Is she okay?" I asked the nurse.

"She's perfect" she responded. I started to cry.

"Almost done, mom," she said.

"I've never been this far away from her," I said. They all laughed.

"That's true," the doctor said, nodding his head and finishing up my stitches.

"She's 6 pound 8 ounces, born at 10:30 a.m." the nurse said.

"Can I have her back now?" I asked eager to hold my little angel. The doctor got up and the other nurse came over to adjust my bed and get me comfortable.

"You did great, mom, congratulations," he said smiling.

"Thank you," I said. The nurse finally brought over my daughter. "We like to recommend two hours of skin to skin right now so you two can bond, and she may even feed—if you're breast feeding, that is," she said.

"I'm going to try," I said.

"I'm going to undo your gown and lay her on your chest," she said, explaining everything as she was doing it. "Keep her hat on, and feel free to keep yourselves covered, but the goal is to have her lay naked on your bare skin," she said. We adjusted everything as she suggested and immediately Harmony latched on to my left nipple and started to feed. I cried. This was the most beautiful moment of my entire life. I had never felt this kind of love before ever. This little girl had no idea how much I had already gone through for her, and I was wrapped around her skinny long finger already. I was completely in love.

Hector and I had already agreed not to post any pictures of her in the delivery room. We wanted to wait until they moved us to the visiting room and get her dressed in a cute little outfit. He started texting everyone, letting them know the baby was finally here. I let Bessie and Giovanni know first. Bessie had already been instructed to tell everyone for me once it was done. She was in the hospital waiting room already. I sent Giovanni a picture of her sweet little face while Hector was distracted.

"She's beautiful. Congratulations Savannah, no matter what happens, you're going to be an amazing mom," Giovanni said, bringing tears to my eyes. I looked over at Hector, who was now having his bonding time with her, and my heart ached. I wanted Giovanni there, not Hector. Just the sight of him disgusted me. Something inside me had changed since meeting my daughter. I felt strong. Any feelings I still had for this monster had vanished. I no longer saw him as a broken little boy, no longer felt the desire to help fix or please him in any way. My only job now was keeping him from hurting my daughter.

CHAPTER THIRTY

New Me.

The hospital stay was horrible. As soon as we started getting visitors, he started behaving like a delinquent. Some visitors he charmed; when my pastors came by, for instance, he put on a show. They were already aware of the reality of our situation, but Hector didn't know that. When my parents and Bessie came in you, could feel the tension in the room. My dad had it written all over his face that he wanted to kill Hector, and Hector had a similar look. My mother asked to hold the baby first. About the time she sat down, a heavy-set dark-skinned woman with glasses walked in.

"Hello mom, congratulations! I'm here to do the birth certificate with you, if you have a few minutes," she said. The atmosphere in the room became extremely uncomfortable.

"Is this dad?" she asked.

"Yes," Hector said, sitting up tall.

"Okay, are you married?" she asked.

"No ma'am," I answered.

"Okay, so mom, is she getting your last name or dad's?" she asked.

"Mine," I said, feeling the daggers stab me from Hector's eyes.

"Really?" he asked, alerting the lady that this was going to be uncomfortable.

"Yes, she's getting *my* name," I said, turning to look him dead in the eye while I said it. I wasn't afraid of him anymore. He shook his head angrily, wanting to say terrible things to me. He stood up, turning red.

"Okay, well, I can just leave this paperwork with you mom," she said, placing the paper on the table next to me.

"I can see this isn't the best time, so I'll just come back a little later," she said, backing out of the room.

"Thank you," I said politely.

"I'm leaving. I'll be back when everyone leaves," Hector said hatefully, grabbing his things.

"*Bye!*" my dad said, happy to see him leave.

I was so happy they were there while that transpired. I knew it would have gone a lot worse if they weren't. That evening, his friends had returned, happy to see that I was doing much better than when they left the hospital the night before. Hector decided he wanted to go get himself some beer, so he left, leaving his friends there with the baby and me.

"So, have you thought about what you're going to do now?" his friend asked me.

"What do you mean?" I asked watching his wife sway back and forth with my newborn lovingly.

"Like, are you going home when you leave here?" he asked. It hit me that he left his friends here to try to talk me into going back with him since he failed at it.

"Yes, I *am* going home. To the house I currently live in, with my daughter," I said politely.

"Well, you know he wants you to go home with *him* right?" he said smiling.

"I know he wants me to live with him and his new whore, yes. It's not happening. I have my whole life set up for her, and I'm not changing the plan," I said crossing my arms leaning back on my bed.

"They aren't together anymore. He wants *you*; he knows he's fucked everything up, and he doesn't know how to get everything right again," he said.

"Well he can't. I don't want him; I will never want to be with him again. I have no problem bringing Harmony over to see him, but as I've already told him, he will never be alone with her unless a judge tells me otherwise. He is a junkie and an abuser, and I won't have it. I'm sorry he put you in this position, but there is nothing anyone can say or do to make me want to be with him ever again," I said.

"Okay, I just had to ask, I respect that."

The next day, Hector told me he had to go to the bar for a few hours because he was hosting a club event there. Gia had just shown up, and she and I both rolled our eyes.

"It's the second day your daughter is alive, and you already have to leave her to go party? Why are you even here? Just take your shit and go the fuck home, we don't need you," I said.

"I'm not going home. I won't be gone long. I have no choice," he lied.

"You *always* have a choice. Everyone knows you just had a fucking baby, if you didn't go to work today how do you justify going to fucking party? Just fucking leave," I yelled. Gia and I were both relieved to see him go.

"I *will* be back" he said. A little while later a nurse came to get a few tests done on Harmony. She discovered she had a slight case of jaundice and told me she would need to lay in under a UV light all night to try to clear it up.

I messaged Hector, but it didn't seem to matter. He "couldn't" come back yet; the party was just starting. They brought in the incubator with the UV light and took her out of my arms, undressing her. She immediately started screaming. I sat up uncomfortably.

"She can stay in here with you, mom, but she needs to remain under the light, so you won't be able to hold her unless she needs to feed, then put her right back," the nurse said. She was screaming the whole time. They put some soft goggles over her eyes and laid her down under the light. She was screaming and thrashing her little hands and kicking her feet. It was heartbreaking. This went on for hours. I was so exhausted and sad; I was crying with her. I couldn't do anything to quiet or comfort her. I was freaking out just as much as she was, and I was completely alone. I tried to comfort her however I could, but nothing worked.

I messaged Giovanni and told him what was happening. With everything inside me I wanted to beg him to come to the hospital and be with me. I didn't want to do this alone I didn't want Hector to come back; I wanted Giovanni. But I couldn't ask him to put himself in that position. I knew Hector would come strolling in eventually and I didn't want to cause any drama at the hospital. All I could do was cry. I sent Hector pictures of his daughter screaming under the UV lights and let him know what a piece of shit I thought he was.

"You have already proven the priority in your life will always be the club and the partying. MY priority is MY DAUGHTER! She's terrified, she's been screaming for HOURS and your fucking partying!! FUCK YOU I fucking HATE you! I hope you fucking overdose!" I said hatefully. I screenshotted the entire conversation and sent it to Titi.

"I love how he missed work today because he 'wanted to spend every minute he could' with his new daughter, but the second the sun started to go down, he darted out the door to go host a club party at the fucking bar! Your nephew is a piece of shit!" I told her.

Finally, two hours later, he walked cautiously through the door.

"Get the fuck out," I told him. "I don't want you here."

"I'm sorry," he said like a scared kid whose mom just found out he skipped school.

"You definitely *are* sorry," I shot back at him.

"Do you hear her? She's been screaming like this since 9 p.m. What time is it now?" I asked, knowing the answer.

"I don't know," he said, standing with his back against the door.

"It's 2:15am," I said. I picked my child up, hoping she would latch on finally; she was so upset she hadn't eaten in hours and I knew she was starving. The nurse came in.

"Still crying?" she said.

"Yes, and I still can't get her to eat," I said crying.

"Well, I brought in these little bottles of formula, I know you don't want to feed her this, but she has to eat something," she said delicately.

"It's been hours, so if we can get some of this in her, she may finally go to sleep," she said.

"Okay, let's try it," I said, defeated.

Finally, she drank. It was so nice to have a moment of quiet.

"Thank you, Jesus," I said just above a whisper.

"Good, this is good," the nurse said.

"She will probably cry when you put her back in, but with a full belly, hopefully she will fall asleep. You need to get some sleep too, mom," she said.

"I would like nothing more trust me," I laughed, more exhausted than I had ever been. She left the room, and Hector went in the bathroom. I could hear him sniffing in there. I knew exactly what he was doing, and it was disgusting.

"Are you fucking serious? You're snorting coke in the hospital room?" I hissed at him while he came out of the bathroom.

"No, I'm not," he said guiltily.

"I fucking *hate* you," I spat at him.

"Yes, you've made that clear," he said, going over to the bed he was sleeping on. I put Harmony back in the incubator, and she started screaming again. I don't know how long she went on this time. But eventually she and I both passed out from exhaustion. I woke up to Hector's alarm going off for work.

"Do you want me to skip work and stay with you today?" he asked me.

"No," I said, still angry with him.

"Well, I'll call you when I leave and see if you want me to pick up something to eat for dinner or something. Keep me posted on any progress," he said with his tail between his legs.

We had to stay four days total due to the jaundice. But, finally, it was the day of release. Everyone offered to be there with me, but I decided to do it myself. I didn't want any more drama, and there was nobody I trusted to behave themselves. I knew this was going to be a hard day for Hector, and I didn't see the point of pouring salt in the wound. While the nurse wheeled me down, I had Harmony already strapped into her car seat in my lap. I was *so* excited to take her home and let Giovanni and Gabriel meet her! I hadn't heard form Giovanni much, and I was anxious to see him. When we came out the hospital doors, the nurse asked if we wanted her to take a picture of the three of us leaving.

"Sure," I said. I was so happy to be leaving that I was beaming in the picture. Hector less happy, did force a sort of smile. He took the car seat and put it in the car for me. Hearing it snap into the base safely, I was satisfied. He said goodbye to his daughter and turned around to face me.

"You really aren't going to come home with me?" he asked with tears in his eyes.

"I can't. We are no good for each other. She deserves better than us fighting all the time, and you know it," I said. He seemed to be genuinely heart broken. This was the most vulnerable I had seen him. "I'm sorry; I know this hurts, but I can't go back. I will bring her to see you soon," I said, giving him an awkward hug and climbing into my driver seat. As I drove away, he stood there crying. I hated making people cry, even if they were jerks. But I soon had a smile of excitement on my face knowing I was taking my daughter *home.*

When I pulled in Giovanni and Bessie came out to help me carry everything in. We got everything inside, and I asked who wanted to hold her first. It felt a little awkward for a moment. I didn't know why, but I figured it was just that I had been gone for four days. I took my sweet angel out of her car seat and handed her to Giovanni. She seemed even smaller in his giant hand. He could hold her in one hand without a problem if he wanted to. It was love at first sight. I went about unpacking and getting things in order while he sat with her on the couch. Finally, Gabriel got a turn, and it was the same reaction from him. Instantly she had them both wrapped around her tiny finger. I was so happy to be home. They stayed down there and talked a bit for a long time. Finally, the boys felt comfortable enough to go up to their normal lives and leave us girls to fend for ourselves. I was completely exhausted and was hoping I could get some sleep soon. The baby had fallen asleep and was laying peacefully in her bassinet and I had to pump before I could try to sleep. Bessie was staying with me as late as she could, but she did have to go home since she had to work in the morning.

"So, I should fill you in on what's been going on around here while you were gone," she said. She had stayed here the entire time I was in the hospital, along with my mother, who had now gone home.

"The second night was rough," she said.

"Tell me about it, that was the worst night of my life," I said.

"Yeah, well Giovanni had been drinking pretty heavily so he didn't drive himself crazy while you were at the hospital. And I guess you had texted him telling him about Hector being out at the bar while the baby screamed, and you were all upset."

"Yeah, it was awful. All I wanted was Giovanni to come, but I didn't want to deal with the drama or put him in Hector's path of destruction," I said, remembering how shitty I felt about the situation.

"Well, he didn't know you were even thinking about him, and he got pretty upset," she said gently.

"Why?"

"Because he's in love with you," she said flatly.

"Nobody understands why you allowed Hector to be there, but it was your decision and he respected it, as we all did," she said.

"Okay, so why was he so upset?"

"Girl, he was shit faced. He went over to Leah's house and cried out his feelings and then came back and jumped in the pool butt naked," she laughed.

"So he's mad at me?" I asked, not wanting any more drama.

"No, he's not mad, and we've talked about it since, he was just really drunk and wanted you to want *him* there. He was hoping you would snap out of it and tell Hector to fuck off and have Giovanni there instead," she said.

"I *did* want him there! From the second I got there, I was so mad at myself for putting myself through the torture of Hector. But I *had* to be able to know that I tried. I really tried to be fair to him," I said.

"You were *more* than fair to him," she said.

"Well, I don't want Giovanni to be upset with me," I said sadly.

"I don't think he is, but it wouldn't hurt to talk to him when things get settled," she said.

"Yeah, I'll definitely do that, he's my best friend," I said.

"Um, excuse me bitch?" she said.

I laughed "Okay, he's my best *guy* friend."

"That's better," she laughed. "Now, I know he was stupid drunk, but I do want to be honest and tell you that he hit on me."

I laughed, "Oh did he? Well, he's not my boyfriend," I said laughing.

"I know, but I just wanted to be honest about it. He was stupid drunk, so I don't think he meant it. I just think he was hurting and worried about what you would decide to do. We all were," she said honestly.

"Well I'm here now, and unless he kicks me out, I have no plans of going anywhere," I said.

"I don't think he's going to kick you out. I think he wants to marry you."

"Oh my god, you're so dramatic," I laughed, pulling the breast pump off me.

"I'm serious," she said.

"Well, we'll see what happens then I guess, won't we?"

Surprisingly I didn't get a request from Hector to see the baby for the first few days. The first time he saw her was at her first checkup with her new pediatrician. It was four days after we left the hospital. When he showed up, he was dragging his feet lazily, his clothes were dirty, and he smelled awful. When we went into the exam room, he lay on the exam table with our newborn, and they both fell asleep. It was kind of adorable, but I knew why he was exhausted. I could smell the drugs and stale smoke on him. He was so disgusting, I didn't even want him touching Harmony. But I just wanted to get through this encounter with as little drama as possible. The doctor came in and checked everything. We scheduled the next appointment on the way out. On the way to the car Hector asked when he could see us again.

"Whenever you want, just let me know in advance, and I'll need some gas money," I said, since I still wasn't working.

"Why would I give you money to see my kid?" he asked.

"Because Giovanni isn't going to be paying for the gas to run back and forth for *you*. You're going to have to help me," I responded, annoyed.

"I'm not paying for gas," he said.

"Well then I guess you won't be seeing her. That's up to you. I already supplied everything she needs, and Giovanni pays for everything else. If I took you to child support, you wouldn't have a choice," I said.

"You're not doing that."

"I will if I have to. But I'd rather you do the right thing on your own," I said, locking the car seat into the base and closing the back door.

"This is fucking bullshit. Already you're trying to keep me from my kid?"

"Are you high? I literally just said you could see her whenever you wanted, I just need the gas to get over here and back. I didn't ask for your soul," I said sarcastically.

"Well I'll just come to your house and visit."

"Not an option."

"Why?" he asked.

"Because all you want to do is start shit. I'm not having it."

"I won't start anything unless *he* does."

"*He* is a fucking grown up. If I felt like you could be as well, maybe one day that might happen. But no time soon."

"Whatever, I want to see my daughter!"

"Okay, let me know when you have time and gas money," I said, getting in my car to leave.

That week he requested visits twice. I went out there and took my daughter to him as requested. He wouldn't change diapers if they were dirty, just wet ones. And since I was breastfeeding, I had to feed her or pump so he could feed her. Both times he gave me $10 for gas. That was fine with me. He never offered to buy anything for Harmony but would always have wine or beer to offer me. He would order food for us or cook dinner. But we didn't really talk much. I just sort of sat there reading or playing on my phone until she needed to be fed or changed. Both times when it was time to go home, he tried to get us to stay the night.

"It's not going to happen," I would say. He would get upset and tell me what a whore I was, and then we would leave on bad terms. Two weeks went by and he saw her once. He tried to get me to bring her over a few times, but they were always at night.

"She's a new baby. I'm not bringing her over at 7 o'clock at night, I'm trying to get her on a schedule. You're going to have to see her earlier than this. I'm putting her to bed at 8 o'clock," I told him several times.

"So come put her to bed here."

"I'm not here to be at your beck and call, we need to sit down and figure out a schedule. You can't expect me to drop everything when you decide to carve out a free hour to see her." She was only three weeks old, and it was already annoying. He even had the audacity to ask me to bring her to the clubhouse for a family day event they were doing so all the bros could meet her.

"Come on, everyone misses you anyway," he said.

"She is *three weeks* old. You have lost your mind if you think that I'm taking her anywhere besides your house any time soon. And she will *never* be going to the clubhouse," I told him. He told me I was being unreasonable and "keeping him from his daughter" every time I turned down one of his ridiculous requests.

Titi finally came to visit when Harmony was almost four weeks old. "She is *beautiful*, Savannah, but she looks exactly like her father," she said, disappointed.

"Yeah I know, they're twins, but I don't hold it against her," I laughed. She gave me a few parenting tips and then asked how it was going with Hector.

"He hasn't seen her much. Every time he asks me to bring her over, it's at night, and I'm not doing that. I'm trying to get her on a schedule, and he's not going to just request to see her when it's convenient for him," I said.

"I agree, I told him you two need to make a set schedule, but he just wants to keep telling people you're keeping her from him," she said, shaking her head.

"Is that what he's saying?" I said.

"Oh yeah, you won't let him see her unless he gives you money, and then when he asks you never bring her over," she said.

"What a fucking asshole!" I said.

"You got that right! In my opinion, she shouldn't even know who the fuck he is. He's trash! When I went to his stupid baby shower, he made a complete ass of himself," she said.

"Not surprising," I said, rolling my eyes.

"He literally tried to throw his own mother down the stairs," she said, wide-eyed.

"Wait, what?" I asked. I knew his mother had appeared out of nowhere looking for a place to stay. I'd never met her, thank God. I heard horrible things about the woman. Hector told me she was a junkie and a whore. She would post half-naked pictures on her Facebook page all the time. Frankie told me when Hector was 3 and 4 years old, she would be out sucking dicks and fucking guys for money and drugs, and Hector would be sitting there in the stroller waiting for her to get done. So she wasn't exactly someone I wanted to meet. Nor did I want my daughter anywhere near her.

Hector had mentioned her staying with him. And I knew she was gone now, but I didn't know the whole story.

"Yeah, he and his mom got into an argument because as people were leaving the shower, she was offering them plates of food to go since there was so much left over," Titi said. "Hector didn't think it was her place since he bought all the food, so they got into it. He told her to get the fuck out after it got heated so she started packing up her shit. Apparently, Jackie saw her putting some beers in her bag, so when she walked away, she told Hector. That's when he blew the fuck up. He went ballistic in front of everyone, calling her a whore and a loser. They went back and forth verbally until he finally grabbed her and started pulling her toward the top of the step! He tried to throw her down the goddamn stairs in front of everyone! His own mother! Jose and another guy stopped him just before she went down, and then it was a big 'fuck you I'll kill everyone' situation," she said, shaking her head. "Now don't get me wrong, his mother *is* a piece of shit, but he's telling everyone *you* lied about the abuse, and then does that in front of a house full of people? He's lost his fucking mind. Don't you ever leave this baby alone with him," she said.

"I won't be. He didn't tell me any of that, obviously. Hell, he tried to lie and say Jackie wasn't even there! I saw the bitch in the video his sister posted on her Facebook, and he still says she wasn't there," I said.

"Oh, she was there all right. She was playing hostess all day. When I got there, she started trying to introduce people to each other. I stopped her and said 'Jackie, we all know each other. And why are you playing hostess? This is Savannah's house; you are way out of line here.'"

"Oh wow, what did she say to that?" I asked curiously.

"She didn't know what to say. I was trying to be as nice as possible, but at the end of the day, this whole situation is so fucked up, I had to correct some untruths! After what happened with his mother, I pulled her aside and said, "That's the *real* Hector, the one you didn't believe hit Savannah, don't think he won't do it to you one day.""

I remembered when I was in the hospital and his friend casually let me know that Hector and Jackie weren't seeing each other anymore, I wondered if that party had something to do with it.

"I told her she was out of line. She knew he had a fiancée and a baby on the way, and the second he tried to get at her she should have turned him down, but she opened her legs instead. Who's to say they weren't fucking long before you even left? He had a working relationship with her, did you ever even meet her?" she asked.

"No, I knew about her. He talked about her sometimes, but he said she was a lesbian."

"Well clearly she swings both ways." She went on to tell me about how bad he was making the business look. "We just had to move into a new building because the owner sold the one we were in. It's disgusting. I'm not going to work there until he gets it together. I can work from home; I'm not going into that place! Have you seen it?" she asked.

"No. Are you guys already moved?" I asked.

"No, we're in the moving process. I'm the only one in the office now. Nobody else could put up with his abusive temper tantrums," she said.

"Well, that's not surprising, I guess. He's like an angry child all the time," I said.

"Well it's only getting worse. Ever since you left him it's been a downward spiral. All he does is party. He's spending money left and right at bars and hookah lounges. He'll take all his little friends out and blow $600 in one night just trying to look cool, but he's draining the company. There was $40,000 in it when he took over. I checked it this morning, and there is $3,000 in it," she said.

My jaw hit the floor. "Are you kidding?" I asked.

"No, I have access to it since everyone quit so I'm keeping records of all his spending. You should do the same, you may need it for court one day. If you still have access to it. Start printing shit out," she said.

"I'll have to do that. I have screen shots of all his traveling. He bitches about me needing gas money to bring his daughter over, but he's still traveling and partying and showing out for his followers on social media. Trust me, if I have to take him to court, I'll be showing them all of it," I said.

"You're going to have to get child support; he'll never give it to you otherwise. Has he even bought anything for the baby?" she asked.

"No, not one thing," I said. "See, he's a piece of shit, take his ass to court."

"It's starting to sound like I may have to," I said.

When Titi left, I put the baby down for a nap and went to the computer. She was right, the spending he was doing was outrageous. I printed out his statements and created a file for each bank account. The card he was letting me use months ago was now maxed out and overdue on payments. His personal account had $600 in it and the business had just over $3,000. I was shocked. He was buying plane tickets, furniture, and massive bills at bars and lounges every weekend.

The next week he messaged me, asking me to bring the baby to the new location for his business so we could map out a visitation schedule we could both agree on. I gathered everything up and met him at the address he sent me. Titi was right; the place was disgusting. It wasn't mapped out like a business at all; it looked more like an old biker club house. It was full of trash and smelled like rotting wood and mold.

"What the hell is this place? A clubhouse?" I asked. He laughed nervously.

"Yeah, actually, it was a clubhouse. There was a stripper pole right there," he said pointing to the old location.

"Wow. Where is everyone?" I asked.

"Titi is at the other office, and I have a guy bringing a load over shortly. Jose is at a customer's house." We sat down in the disgusting "office" and started talking about when to do our visitation. We agreed on four days a week. He wanted Saturday, Sunday, Monday, and Tuesday. we agreed that if he had to work too late, then he wouldn't be a dick if it was too late to bring her over. It seemed like we were making progress and actually getting along for once.

"She's almost out of diapers," I said.

"How is that my problem?" he asked.

"She's your fucking daughter" I said.

"You have tons of diapers. I saw the picture," he said.

"Yes, but she's not wearing that size yet, I just need one more pack of New-born diapers."

"Then ask your boyfriend."

"That's fine, but don't bitch about another man helping me raise *our* child when you aren't doing it."

"He better not be going anywhere near her!"

"I can see it's time to go," I said, not wanting to fight. He walked us out to the car, putting the car seat back. When we came out, the power company was there shutting the power off to his new building. He told the gentlemen there must be a mistake, but there wasn't. Nobody had switched the utilities over to the new building. As he called Titi and started screaming and cussing at her, I got in the car to leave.

"I don't have a vehicle here, and now the power is shut off, and you're just going to leave me here?" he asked.

"You said someone was on the way. I have to get her home for a nap," I said, shrugging my shoulders. I wasn't about to cater to his needs; he just told me getting diapers for *his* daughter wasn't his problem, so *nothing* in this situation was *my* problem. I rolled up the window and drove away.

Even though we had a set visitation schedule, he *never* stuck to it. He would call or text me on the days he was supposed to see her and explain that he had to be at a club meeting or help a friend fix their motorcycle, which was bullshit because he didn't know how to fix a bike to save his life. Or work issues. In the first seven weeks of her life, he only saw his daughter a handful of times. He bought *one* small pack of diapers and gave me a total of $40 for gas to get back and forth. He traveled every other weekend and partied so hard he wouldn't even answer his phone on weekends until the late-night hours when he was finally awake and ready to go party again. I had enough of it. I had enough evidence to prove that I'd tried to get him to help and that he was doing nothing. Because I was on state assistance for my daughter, I had no choice but to report who the father was. The state goes after the father of the child to make them step up financially in cases like this. One day, I had just come out of my parenting class and got a phone call from a mutual friend of ours who used to work for Hector and was still close with Titi.

"We need to talk right now," she said. Knowing it was serious I pulled off into a parking lot.

"I'm listening."

"I was told not to tell you, but Hector handed over the company this morning. He's gone, honey," she said. My heart sank into my stomach.

"What the hell are you talking about?"

"He handed the keys and the contract back to John and told him he didn't want it anymore. He said he was moving to Florida with his new girlfriend, and they were leaving today!"

"Shut the fuck up," I said in disbelief. "Are you kidding? He left his daughter? And what girlfriend?"

"Nobody knows, some Spanish chick who doesn't even speak English."

"Hector doesn't speak Spanish."

"He speaks drugs and money, and apparently she likes both and has them."

"Why wouldn't he tell me?" I asked.

"Because he's abandoning his daughter," she said. I started to cry. This is exactly the heartbreak I wanted to save her from! So, because he couldn't have me, he didn't want his daughter?

"I'm so sorry girl, but you needed to know. I'm sorry!" I took a deep breath and wiped my face.

"It's fine. I'll handle it. She'll be better off without him anyway."

I put my Bluetooth headphones in my ears and called Mary, who lived across the street from Hector.

"Hey stranger!" she said.

"Hey, I just got a phone call that Hector handed over his company and fled the state this morning," I said.

"Oh my god. Well, there's three chicks over there. They all look strung out. He's not there much, but I did notice he got rid of that broken-down vehicle, and the work van is gone," she said.

"So he left the house full of junkies? My name is still on that house! I've been in contact with the leasing office, and they said they would have it removed, but I still get the email every month that the rent hasn't been paid," I said.

"You need to go down there and talk to them face to face, and you need to go to the courthouse right now and press abandonment charges against him!"

"I can do that?"

"Absolutely."

"Okay, I think I will." I called Bessie and told her I needed her to be at my house as soon as possible so she could run some errands with me. She said she would be there as soon as she could.

I called Giovanni and told him what had happened.

"Are you sure you don't just want to let him go?" he asked.

"No! Fuck him! Why does he get to get away with *everything*?"

"Okay, do what you think is right." We went and filed the charges immediately. I went by the child support office to see if they could tell me if he had been served yet.

"We haven't been able to locate him. We've been trying, but he's never home," she said. "Have you considered abandonment charges?"

"Yes, I actually just filed them before we came here."

"Good, that's really all you can do until someone finds him."

How dare he do this to the child he claimed to want so badly? My heart broke for her. I loved her *so* much, I changed my whole life for her, what the hell was wrong with this man? Why would he do this to her? She's *so* amazing, he didn't know what he was missing. I messaged him to tell him what a coward he was and how fucked up he was for doing this. He tried to play stupid at first until I told him I already knew what he did, where he was going, and that he was with some Spanish chick nobody knew but that she drove a white Dodge Challenger.

"What the fuck? So you're spying on me?" he asked.

"No, but you're such an asshole, people can't wait to tell me about all the dumb shit you're always doing. You go live your life; I don't give a shit. I already filled charges against you so what goes around comes around, enjoy your life. But keep in mind it's *your* decision to walk away from your daughter." I said.

"Yeah okay, whatever."

When I finally got clearance from my doctor to return to work, I started the next day. Gabriel volunteered to look after Harmony for me, since he didn't have a job and was at home all day anyway. I took it slow at first, only working a few days a week, but at soon as people started hearing that I was back at it, my phone was ringing more often, and sooner than I anticipated I was back to work full time. I hated leaving my daughter behind, but I knew she was safe at home, and Gabriel was amazing with her. I was so happy to be back to earning my own money again. I was falling in love with my new life. One evening Giovanni and I were downstairs. I was folding laundry and pumping, and he asked me nervously what my plans were now that I was back to work.

I got nervous and asked, "Why do you want us to go?" He laughed, patting Harmony on the back.

"No not at all."

"Well I don't want to leave, and she adores you. So I'd like to stay if you don't mind."

"I would love that."

He was the best man I had ever know, besides my dad, stepfather, and grandfather of course. Watching the way that he loved my daughter and me, it was only a matter of time until I realized I was falling in love with him. I didn't know what to do with that for a while; I was a mess and, in my head, nowhere near good enough for him. I knew he liked me before, but I didn't know if he still did. But as the days ticked by, we started getting closer and closer. One Friday night we were up sharing a few drinks together and talking. I had just gotten done pumping and was putting everything away. I had talked our neighbor Leah into getting a Brazilian wax with me when I was pregnant since I didn't want to grow a jungle down there, and since then we had been keeping up on it. We had just gone earlier that day. When I came out of the bathroom and sat back down, it was dark. The only light was from the TV and a night light we had on over by the bassinet.

Out of nowhere Giovanni asked how my wax went.

"It was fine, it gets less painful each time, so that's good. The first time was awful," I laughed.

"Does it hurt now" he asked.

"It's a little sore, it will be fine tomorrow though. Why?" I asked, starting to get aroused by his interest.

"I don't think I've ever seen a waxed vagina in person," he said.

"I don't know if I believe *that*. You told me you used to be a ho!" I joked.

"Yeah such a ho," he said, rolling his eyes.

"Can I see it?" he asked.

"My vagina?"

"Yeah, I won't touch you if you don't want me to. But I'm curious to see it." In my head I thought, *why wouldn't I want you to touch it?* but I kept that to myself. I hadn't been with another man in years, and I surely hadn't had sex since I left Hector.

"Sure," I said quietly. I pulled my pajama pants open and he leaned in to inspect the situation.

"Yeah that's nice," he said as I put my pants back where they were. He sat up, looking casual. It was a little awkward; I didn't think I was ready to have sex yet, but my body was definitely turned on.

"Can I go down on you?" he asked. I laughed nervously.

"What?"

"If you don't want to do anything else, that's perfectly fine, but I need to eat that," he said, causing my body to shudder. I didn't know what to say, I *really* wanted him too, but I was still so shut off from physical touch that I didn't know how comfortable I would actually be once he touched me.

"I won't pull my dick out, I won't ask for anything in return, I just want to taste you and make you feel good," he said. The thought of a selfless lover seemed so far-fetched that I remained skeptical at first, but he was such a gentleman, and I was already starting to fall for him. If there were anyone I trusted to touch me, it should be him, right? I thought about it for a few seconds with my body screaming *Please!! Yes!!* and finally agreed.

"I just got waxed though," I said nervously, "So there's probably still wax on me or something," I said while he got on the floor in front of me.

"I don't care," he said hungrily. I pulled my pants off and opened myself up to him. He didn't dive right in like I expected him to. He took his time getting there. He kissed all the sensitive areas in between my legs, avoiding the spot that ached for him, teasing me so much I could barely take it. I wanted him *so* bad, my body was already shaking. Finally he put his mouth where I wanted it. I cried out in pleasure. Whatever he was doing it felt fucking amazing. I dug my hands into his hair and told him to look up at me. He did as I asked, and it was the hot! I came so fast and so hard I was almost embarrassed. My whole body felt euphoric; I couldn't control the trembling. He tried to keep going, but I was *so* sensitive that I couldn't bare it. Giggling, I begged him to stop and pulled his head back.

"That was fun!" he said. Trying to catch my breath, I laughed. "Feel better?" he asked.

Not able to form words just yet, I nodded my head panting and smiling.

"Good," he said, moving away from me. My body yearned for more, but my heart wasn't quite ready. As promised, he sat back on the couch, not asking for anything more. I put my pants back on, impressed.

"I don't know where you learned how to do that, but you need to teach a fucking class or something," I laughed. He smiled.

"So it was okay then?" I laughed, sitting back down.

"It was more than okay. I'm considering marrying you now," I joked.

"Nice," he responded, smiling. I felt kind of bad for not doing anything for him, but I wasn't ready yet, and I didn't want to force myself. I was waiting for him to try something, but instead he just said I should try to get some sleep and wished me a good night heading up the stairs.

"Okay, good night."

CHAPTER THIRTY-ONE

One man's loss is another man's gain.

The first court date, I showed up prepared. I had all the proof I needed to show he abandoned his child, including a text from Hector himself telling me that he moved to Florida and abandoned the house. I brought both Gia and Bessie with me. They sat on either side of me to show their support. Hector walked in giggling and making a joke of the whole thing with his newest whore. They both looked like they were strung out and un-showered. The sound of his stupid-ass laugh made me sick to my stomach. Since everyone else in the courtroom was there for the same charges, they explained the process to the entire courtroom at the same time. Basically, if you could prove abandonment, the father would be arrested and thrown in jail right there. I couldn't wait for my turn. When our names were called, we both stood up. Hector was offered legal counsel to defend himself, which he chose to have, so they went outside to discuss the charges.

While we were waiting, most of the couples that were called opted to try mediation before going in front of the judge. When our names were called again, Hector's lawyer responded to the judge by saying, "Your honor, my client has reason to believe the child is not his." Our jaws hit the floor.

"Is he fucking kidding?" Gia whispered while Bessie rolled her eyes and shifted uncomfortably. Tapping my now-clenched fist, Gia said, "It's okay, we got this, he's only going to make himself look like the idiot we all know he is," trying to calm me down. I was filled with instant rage. How fucking dare he?

"Does your client understand that by claiming this, he has to pay for a $500 DNA test and that he will have four weeks to be back here with the results of said test?" the judge asked.

"Yes, your honor." Seeing the look of disgust and heartbreak on my face, the judge asked the lawyer to pull me outside and discuss what was happening so that I understood what was next. They lawyer held the door for me, and I looked Hector and his whore in the eyes while I walked out. I knew the truth, and I knew this was all just a game to him.

"Okay look," said the lawyer. "I'm gonna level with you, he told me it was probably his, but that he's made everyone believe you cheated on him. So he feels like he has to take the test, or he'll look stupid," he said shaking his head.

"He already looks stupid," I responded.

"Well, I'm going to give both of you the same paperwork when you leave, he has to set up and pay for the test himself. You'll have to take yourself and your daughter to get oral swabs. *But* your next court date will likely be in four weeks. It takes two weeks to get the DNA results back, so there isn't time to waste," he said.

"I think you should make that as clear as possible to *him*, sir," I said.

"I will, I just want you to be clear as well," he answered. "Do you have any questions?" he asked.

"No."

"Okay, I'm going to go grab Hector and explain everything again to you both together, then you can be on your way," he said. Hector came back out, grinning like an idiot, not wanting to look me in the eye. The lawyer repeated what he had just told me and gave us both the paperwork we needed.

"Do you understand?" he asked us both.

"Yes sir," I said.

"Yeah," Hector said anxious to leave.

"Okay, you're free to go. Is anyone in the courtroom with you?" he asked us.

"Yeah," we both said.

"Hang tight, I'll go get them," he said, leaving us alone in the hallway.

"I remember a time you said you wouldn't do this," Hector said, finally looking at me.

"Do what? Fight for my daughter's rights?" I said, irritated.

"Take me to court," he said.

"Yeah, well I remember a time where I didn't think I would have to. It's funny to me that *all* you wanted was a baby, and now you have the audacity to say she isn't even yours in a courtroom full of people. What the hell did I do to you for you to do this to your daughter?" I asked. The door opened and Gia and Bessie stepped out behind Hector's new whore. He finally looked away from me and walked off with her.

"Let's find a bathroom. I need to pee," I said.

"Good plan. Let stupid and stupider leave first so we don't beat their asses," Gia said.

I messaged Giovanni and told him what happened. "That's all this kid does is play games. That's okay, he's going to look *really* stupid when he goes back next time." I knew that, but I was still not only embarrassed but furious. I cried for my daughter. There was nothing in the world I wouldn't do for her, no battle I wouldn't fight. No mountain I wouldn't climb. How could he *not* feel the same way about her? She was beautiful. Everyone who met her fell in love with her, so why didn't *he*?

"Because at the end of the day," Giovanni answered me, "It's not about her, it's about *you*. *You* left, *you* broke his heart, *you* took away the control he had the whole time. *You* are too good for him and *far* too strong for him," he said.

The following week, I called the DNA place as instructed to see if he had made his appointment yet. He had, so she asked if we wanted to come in at the same time to test.

"I'd like to wait at least an hour if I can. We aren't on good terms," I said.

"No problem. Why don't you come in at 12:30 p.m.?" she said.

"Perfect, thank you," I answered, hanging up. I was anxious to get this over with. When I arrived at the facility, I walked in and gave her our names.

"What's the father's name?" she asked. "Oh, he hasn't come in yet," she said.

"His appointment was 10:30 this morning, wasn't it?"

"Yeah, but he hasn't shown up yet. The father has to pay for the test, so we don't swab the mother and child until after that's done usually." I was so sick of this man's shit at this point it was written all over my face.

"Let's just go ahead and get you two taken care of, if he shows up, we can handle it when he gets here," she said.

"What if he doesn't? Am I going to have to pay something?" I asked.

"Oh, no." She had me fill out the information packet and went forward with the test. We were in and out in no time. As I put my daughter in the car, Hector messaged me that he was on his way to take his test and to meet him there. I called him back.

"You were supposed to be here at 10:30 a.m. Our half is done," I said, starting the car.

"So I don't get to see my daughter?" he said.

"I thought you said she wasn't yours. Goodbye, asshole," I said, putting my phone down and leaving.

It was late September and Gabriel's 29th birthday. None of us had been out since I moved in, and I was excited to be getting out to go drink and have a good time with everyone. Leah volunteered to be the babysitter since she lived just next door, adored Harmony, and was fine with keeping her at our house. We decided to go to a strip club. We got dressed up and hit the town. We were having a blast. This was the most adult fun I had in years. It felt good to get out and just let loose! Everyone was having a good time. Giovanni was driving, so he didn't really drink that much, but the rest of us enjoyed ourselves fully. When we got home, I was happy to see my child sleeping soundly in her bassinet. I thanked Leah for watching her and asked what I owed her.

"I don't think so, missy, I love that baby like she's my own granddaughter. You aren't paying me to watch that sweet angel," she said tiredly. Gabriel and Gia seemed to be hitting it off rather well, so Giovanni and I went up to the other living room. Bessie went up to bed in the old room I used to be in upstairs. We had turned it into a guest room.

Giovanni and I were on the couch talking. He had a way of almost making me believe things about myself that Hector had killed in me. Like being beautiful, strong, or funny—those things Hector hated about me, so he degraded me for everything. I had once been confident, and I slowly felt like I was getting that back with Giovanni. I don't remember what we were talking about, but I remember wishing he would just shut up and kiss me. He still hadn't even kissed me. Even the nights he would go down on me, it was just for me, just to make me feel good. But it built not only my desire for him, but a beautiful new trust that I was starting to love. Finally, he kissed me. He was sitting next to me on the couch, but our bodies were facing each other, so when he *finally* went for it, I happily obliged.

He and I hadn't kissed in years, since we dated long before Hector was in the picture. I had forgotten how good he was at it. Everything this man did with his mouth is magic. He made the first move, and we had waited long enough. I wanted him, right here, right now; I needed him inside me. I pulled him on top of me while I laid back on the couch and wrapped my legs around him hungrily.

"Take my panties off," I said. I was wearing a dress, so it didn't take much effort. Even the way he looked at me turned me on. "Come here," I said leaning up on my elbows, wanting his mouth on mine once again. I didn't have to ask twice, he kissed me slower this time, even more passionately than the first, my whole body was aching for him to be all over me. I noticed he was shaking.

"Are you nervous?" I asked, pulling my head back to look at him.

"A little," he laughed shyly.

"You don't know how long I've wanted this," he said.

"Well it's yours now," I said against his lips. "If you want it, that is," I said playfully pulling back a little.

"Oh, I want it," he growled, undoing his pants.

I couldn't wait another second for him, I yanked his pants down and pulled his dick out, he was taking too long. I pulled him on top of me, rubbing him on me so he could feel how aroused I was. He let out a shaky sigh, I don't know why, but the fact that he was nervous made it hotter to me. I slid him inside me, and we both moaned with pleasure. He felt good, and I felt safe and happy. I felt like I wanted this feeling forever. I felt like we weren't fucking at all; this was making love. I wanted to be his in every way, and I could feel that he wanted the same. It was beautiful. I was expecting it to be over quickly, but it wasn't. I was used to Hector being done in just a couple of minutes leaving me unsatisfied, but I had already climaxed twice, and Giovanni was still going strong. I asked if he would mind bending me over the couch since I was getting kind of hot with him on top of me while sinking into the couch.

"Hell yeah," he said slapping my ass while I turned over. I giggled, he was always gentle and sweet, not aggressive in any way, so him slapping my ass was adorable. I was about to come again, and he finally said he was going to as well. We finished together, both panting and shaking. Our bodies trembled together as one.

"Holy shit," I said.

"That was fucking awesome," he said, and we both laughed. We had finally come together, and there was no going back. The next day with a more sober mind, we both discussed it and agreed we wanted to be together as a couple. I was elated. Not only did this man genuinely love me, but he genuinely loved my daughter. He was my best friend, and now he was my man.

I hadn't heard a word from Hector since the day I went to do the DNA test. I was at work, taping off some cabinets I was about to spray when my phone started blowing up with messages.

"I got the results of the DNA test," he said.

"That's good, what do I care?" I said.

"She's mine," he said as if he were giving me new information.

"I know that, stupid ass," I replied, annoyed.

"Well you were always talking to you ex, so I didn't know, plus Weasel was sure you were still fucking him so…I don't know."

"Is that supposed to be an apology?"

"Kind of."

"You told everyone I was a whore and that I fucked Bruce and the baby was probably his. News flash, if she was his, she would be a lot tanner," I said, annoyed.

"Well anyway, thank you for not doing what I thought you were doing."

"Did you just thank me for not being a ho?"

"Yeah I guess lol."

"Right, well see you next month in court," I said.

"I'm engaged, you know," he said randomly as if I gave a shit. "She asked me but that's okay, I'm happy and I want to keep being happy and away from all the drama up there, so we're getting married in December." I had already heard through the grape vine that he flipped out when he saw that Giovanni and I announced our official relationship on Facebook. I just laughed and shook my head.

"Your relationship status in none of my business. If it's not about our daughter, we really don't have anything to discuss."

"Well, I can come up and see her. I want to see her now."

"You mean now that you see I wasn't lying about her being yours, even though she's your fucking twin and looks exactly like you. NOW you want to see her?" I asked.

"I said I was sorry," he said.

"No actually, you never did say that. Not that it matters. I'll see you at court next month."

"Well I want to see her, bring her to the house tomorrow."

"What house?"

"Our house."

"You don't even live there, it's full of junkies!"

"Whatever I'm coming back, and I want to see my kid," he said.

"I'm sorry, but you aren't going to jerk me around anymore, I will see you in court, and the judge can decide what's next. You don't just get to boss me around and come in and out of her life whenever you fucking feel like it."

Before Giovanni and I became a couple, I felt like I was standing in the middle of two separate worlds, trying to keep them apart. Not wanting him to get involved in any of the drama. It was exhausting. We were riding somewhere in the car and I told him we had a court date coming up December 11th.

"Would you like to go with us?" Gia and Bessie were already planning to come support me again, but I felt like if I was going to commit to Giovanni, then I should at least allow him the option of being involved in whatever he felt comfortable with.

"Yeah, I'll come. I'll just take off work," he said.

Court day was here, I was ready. I had even more things printed out, proof of him spending tons of money left and right while he should be helping me out financially with his daughter. We arrived well before Hector did and sat in the front row, eager to get things moving. Finally, Hector walked in. Surprisingly he was alone, and his total attitude had changed since the last court date. He wore a suit and had cleaned up a little. He still looked overtired and had grown a hideous beard that looked silly with his bald head.

"Stupid's here," Gia said louder than she should have. When the judge came out, they went through the whole process again for everyone in the room. They made it clear that mediation was the best option for most cases and tried to push people toward that direction. When the judge called our names, Hector and I both stood up.

"Would you like legal counsel again?" he asked Hector.

"Yes your honor," he replied shyly. Nothing like the pompous ass that had been in here putting on a show the last time.

"Would you like to try mediation first?" the judge asked.

"Your honor, due to the extremely violent past we have, I do not feel safe or comfortable being in a room with him at all," I answered quickly.

That got the judge's immediate attention, and he looked up from the pages in front of him to address me.

"I see, there's a history of domestic violence between you?" he asked.

"Yes sir, he has an explosive temper and can't keep his hands to himself," I responded.

"Noted, have a seat," he said to me.

He looked at Hector, "Your lawyer will find you," he said. I sat down and Giovanni whispered in my ear that he was proud of me. That made me feel even stronger. A while later, a small blonde woman in a suit approached us.

"Hello, I'm going to be the legal representation for Hector. I know you said you don't feel comfortable with being in a room with him, but would you be open to a shuttle mediation?" she asked.

"What's that?" I asked.

"The two of you will be in separate rooms while the mediator and I shuttle back and forth. You will never be left alone with him, not even for a minute," she said. I looked over at my support group and they all had the same "it couldn't hurt" look on their faces.

"What do you think?" I asked Giovanni.

"It seems safe enough, but it's up to you," he said. "If we can't work out a deal, then we will come back out and go before the judge anyway. But this way, he won't go to jail, and you can both agree on some sort of child support and visitation," she said.

"Okay, I'll do it," I said.

"Great, I'll come get you in just a few minutes."

"Your honor," she said, turning around to address the judge. "Miss Savannah has agreed to a shuttle mediation," she said.

"Okay, that will be fine," he said, handing a pack of paper to the officer that stood next to him. He handed it to the lawyer, who signaled for Hector to follow her.

"This could take a while," I whispered. Hector and I agreeing on anything would be a miracle at this point. She came back to get me, and I followed her to the hallway, surprised to see Hector standing there.

"This way please," she pointed me in the direction, staying between him and me at all times. I went to one room and he went to the room next to me.

"We'll start with Hector," she said making sure I was comfortable. I put my massive folder of evidence in front of me and told her thank you. A few minutes later, she came in with an older white gentleman. He wore glasses and had an almost all-gray beard and short hair. He was well maintained and had a pleasantry about him that was very comfortable.

"Okay, so my client said he will agree to paying $200 a month for child support until the actual child support order comes through and requests that you drop off your daughter every weekend to the house you shared together," she said, getting things started. I laughed.

"No," I said.

"Okay, so what do you want?" she asked.

"First of all, he doesn't live in that house anymore. He gave away his company and moved to Florida. I have the proof right here," I said pulling out the printed messages from Hector himself admitting to doing so. I then pulled out a whole other file of messages from several other people, including Hector's siblings, confirming this.

"Here are the screenshots from his social media. As you can see, he checked in several times in Florida while bragging about his new life there."

She took a deep breath. Clearly, he hadn't been up-front with her.

"May I borrow these?" she asked.

"Absolutely, I have copies of everything. Take what you need," I said while she picked everything up.

"What about child support?"

"Well, considering how much he spends on traveling and partying, I think I'll start the bidding at $1,000 a month."

"Okay, we'll be back," she said. They both left the room, and I actually heard her from the other room slam the table and tell him loudly "Do you realize social media can be used as evidence?" That's all I could make out, but it was clear she didn't have time for his shit.

When they came back in, she told me that he would pay $250 a month and that he was moving back into the house this week.

"Well, the house is being evicted, so I doubt that," I said smugly.

"Can you prove that?" she asked, surprised by my statement.

"Yes ma'am," I said pulling the eviction notice out. "My name hasn't been removed from the emails. He hasn't paid the rent in months, and they have to be out by January 1," I said. "I'll accept $800 a month, or we can take all this in front of the judge," I said, knowing the ball was in my court. She sighed heavily.

"May I see that eviction notice?" she asked, holding out her hand. "You sure can," I said handing her the paper. The mediator stayed put this time, taking his glasses off and rubbing the top of his nose.

"I don't know how you do this all day. I would go crazy," I said. He laughed.

"You have no idea," he said.

The lawyer came back in and said, "Okay, although he really doesn't want to, he agreed to $400 a week and weekend visitation," she said, looking tired.

"I think we just need to wrap this up. I'll never agree to unsupervised visitation, and he's just being an ass," I said, fed up with it. I started collecting my paperwork and putting it back in the file.

"Let's just go in front of the judge," I said standing up.

"Wait!" She said eagerly. She didn't want us in front of the judge. She knew he was going to jail, and her job was to avoid that if at all possible.

"Let me try just one more time," she said and asked me for my folder.

"What *would* you agree to for visitation?" she asked looking through my evidence.

"I will agree to public meetings with myself present. I don't trust anyone around him. I don't trust him," I said.

"And support?" she asked.

"No less than $500, I will agree to every other Saturday meetings at a public place and he can pay $250 at each meeting," I said.

"Okay." She was gone a lot longer this time, but when she finally came back, he agreed to my terms. "The one condition he has is that it just be you and him and your daughter on visitation days, no spouses or friends present. Can you agree to that?" she asked.

"Absolutely," I said. We set the first visitation for the upcoming Saturday at noon at O' Charlies. He agreed to have the money for the first payment then, and the judge signed off on the agreement.

We followed her back into the courtroom, where the judge explained that until child support services interrupted, the amount of this order was to be maintained by both parties. If he didn't pay or didn't show up for his scheduled visitation, he was in violation of the order and not only did I not have to comply with the agreement, but I could file the abandonment charges against him again. Satisfied, I walked out of the court room with my head held high. This was the first time Giovanni and Hector had ever seen each other in person. They stared each other down on the way out. Gia and Bessie giggled in celebration as we left. I wrapped my arm around Giovanni's and handed him all the paperwork. Quietly we walked out of the courthouse with Hector following us alone.

I went over the terms we agreed on with my support club in the car. They all agreed it was about the best I could have done.

"I still wish we would have watched him go to jail!" Gia said.

"Agreed," said Bessie. At least they could agree on something. Gia had a Christmas gathering planned at her house that Saturday afternoon, and she lived only a few minutes from our meeting point for visitation. Everyone went there so I could meet them right afterward. That morning, I received a screenshot of his Facebook wedding invitation. He and the girl were getting married on December 19 at a local bar. The same bar that he was at all night the 2nd night of his daughter's life while he left me at the hospital alone, in fact.

"Well, isn't that special," I replied to the screen shot.

"Girl, this is the stupidest shit I have ever seen! Who gets married at a bar! She must really want her green card!" said the individual who sent it to me.

"Why isn't he in jail?" she asked. I filled her in on the mediation and that I was actually taking her to see him later and collecting my first payment.

"I bet anything he doesn't have the money," she said.

"Well, that would be unfortunate for him if he doesn't. The judge made it clear he would be in violation of the agreement if that were to happen," I responded.

"Good, I hope you get his ass locked up!"

I started the shower to get ready for the meeting, and my phone chimed.

"I have late meeting I forgot about; can we meet at 1 instead of noon?" he asked. I rolled my eyes. Already he was trying to change what we just set in stone.

"Fine, but don't make this a habit please." When I showed up at 1 p.m. he was late. I messaged him to see where he was, and he said he was on the way. I waited almost 15 minutes, and he finally arrived. I got out of the car and said hello while grabbing my daughter's diaper bag.

"You want to carry her for me?" I asked.

"Of course," he said getting in to take her out.

"What happened to your car?" he asked, noticing I was in a different vehicle.

"Nothing, I just use it for work all the time, this one is better for the baby," I said.

"Hmm," he replied, walking in to the restaurant. We sat at a table, and the waitress came over.

"Can I get you something to drink?" she asked.

"Water for me," Hector said.

"I'll have the same, and can we get a small mac and cheese for her?"

"Absolutely, anything else?"

"No thank you."

"She eats food?"

"Yeah, she eats soft food, nothing hard yet, she's just starting out. But she loves mac and cheese."

"Does she have teeth?" he asked, picking her up out of the car seat.

"She's teething," I answered. It was clear he never asked about her, these are all things a parent would know.

"Well, hello," he said, sitting her in front of him on the table.

"I'm Daddy, do you remember me?" he asked. I sat there quietly messaging Giovanni, letting Hector have his moment.

"Why are you guys dressed so nice?" Harmony was wearing a red Christmas-looking dress, a headband with a bow, and little black dress shoes, I was just wearing a black dress with a scarf.

"We are going to a Christmas party when we leave here," I responded.

"Oh, that's nice." The waitress brought the waters and the mac and cheese for my daughter.

"Would you like to try and feed her?"

"Yeah!" I dug in her bag for a baby spoon and handed it to him. I picked up the silverware the waitress had on the table and started cutting the noodles up.

"Why are you doing that?" he asked.

"I thought you said she was eating," he said.

"She is, but she's just learning, so the smaller and softer the food, the less likely she is to choke on it."

He tried to feed her, but she wasn't in the mood. She was distracted by everything: his glasses, the hat he had on; anything she could get her hands on, she wanted.

"So what do you do with her all day?" he asked.

"Keep her alive," I said, laughing at the question.

"I feed and change her constantly. She's very curious, so I show her everything I can, she'll sit in her swing and watch me cook or do the dishes, or just chill in front of the TV. She likes Moana," I said.

"What's that?"

"A Disney movie."

"Oh okay," he said, seeming bored with the conversation.

"She's a baby. All she does is roll around the floor and try to crawl," I said.

"So she doesn't crawl yet?" he asked.

"Not yet, she rolls." She started to get fussy, and he didn't know what to do.

"Get up and walk around with her," I said, looking at the time. "We only have about 10 minutes left anyway."

He got up and walked her around, quieting her down a bit. I paid for the mac and cheese and started gathering her things. He saw what I was doing and came back over to place her in the car seat. I pulled out Giovanni's keys and hit the push to start button to warm up the car for her.

"Are you serious?" he asked, rolling his eyes.

"It's cold out," I said defensively.

"I heard your boyfriend had money," he said.

"Not at all your business. But speaking of money, do you have your child support?" I asked.

"Can we talk about that outside," he responded. I knew already he was going to say he wasn't paying. When we reached the car, I waited for him to put the car seat in and say goodbye to my daughter. After he closed the door, he told me he didn't have any money.

"You agreed to these terms, and all you do is travel and fucking party. You have to have money to travel, and drugs and alcohol aren't cheap, so give me what you agreed to pay," I said putting my hand out.

"I don't have any money, Savannah. I don't have the company anymore and I'm not working," he said, looking down at the ground.

"I went to the child support office and they told me I didn't have to pay that, they said they would set an amount when I go back."

"It states clearly in the paperwork that you agreed to pay the agreed upon amount *until* child support gives you the permanent amount. Did you not listen when we went to court?" I asked, irritated.

"Well child support said it's up to them," he said cockily.

"It is eventually their call, yes, but unless you already got an amount and the order has been approved you are still obligated to pay the $250 today that you agreed on. Otherwise you are in violation of the agreement, and I can not only take you back to court, but I no longer have to follow our visitation schedule if I don't want to."

"Oh, so you won't let me see her?" he asked.

"I didn't say that, I said I don't legally have to since you just broke the agreement we *just made* last week. This is absolutely ridiculous. You're priorities are so fucked up!" I said, getting more upset.

"Do you realize your daughter is 5 months old, and you haven't done a single fucking thing for her? Do you have any idea how much diapers cost? How about formula? Wipes? Not to mention how quickly she grows out of clothes. What size diaper does she wear, Hector? What size clothes is she in?" I asked.

"I don't know," he answered with his head hanging down.

"No, you fucking don't, because *you* are *not* a parent! *You* are a fuckboy, you will always be a fuckboy, and your daughter deserves someone who's interested in being a father to her for *every* part of her life! Just fuck off, go enjoy your bar wedding and your life in Florida, we don't need you," I said opening my driver side door. "It's your fucking fault I'm not a parent! You keep her away from me and have all these stupid fucking rules!" he snapped.

"My rules are very simple, you had it made in case you forgot. I agreed to let you see her four days a week in the beginning. I let *you* set the schedule and *not fucking once* did you abide by it. *You* are the reason you're not a parent. So stop trying to blame *me* and everyone else for your fucked-up life," I said, getting in my car and closing the door.

"I'm sorry you had to hear any of that baby," I said to my daughter, who was passed out cold in her car seat.

The next two weeks went by, and I barely heard from Hector at all. I showed up to the second scheduled visitation, documented that Harmony and I were there on the correct date and time, and then left. He never showed up. I saw a post from one of his sisters in New York later that night that he was in New York with her. They posted a picture together. It infuriated me. It was Christmas weekend, and he hadn't bothered to tell me he wasn't going to be in town or show up for the visitation he asked for. I didn't see his new "wife" in any of the posts people started to send, which I found slightly interesting since they had only gotten married a week prior. It was his daughter's first Christmas, and he didn't send her a present or a card or even ask about her. I'd had enough. I was done chasing him to be a father, and I decided to let him know that.

"Since I see you are once again traveling and partying even though you 'couldn't afford' to pay any child support, I have decided I will no longer be chasing you to be a father. You didn't even call and ask how your daughter's first Christmas was, you didn't send a card or a gift for her. You obviously don't care about her, and that's fine. She doesn't need you; she is very happy and well taken care of. I hope you enjoy your little vacation." Immediately he responded to my message.

"I didn't tell you because I thought that you wouldn't let me see her. I can't fight with you anymore. You say horrible things to me and make me feel like a piece of shit. It's too much for me to handle. I DO love the baby, and I DO want to be her father. I just can't take any more of your abuse." I burst into laughter.

"You mean you can't handle hearing the truth about yourself? How ironic that of all people YOU would accuse me of abuse!" I said.

"Well I don't like the way you make me feel about myself," he said.

"Then change. Or don't. I don't fucking care anymore. Have fun and good luck. I'm done trying," I said.

"Please don't say that. Please don't give up on me; everything aside, you are doing an amazing job with her. You're a great mom. I'm just going through a rough time." I shook my head and bit my lip, responding.

"Your self-inflicted rough time. You have nobody to blame but YOU for where you are right now. And until you can own that, you won't get better," I said.

"Of course you would say that, you're a fucking rock! Nothing fucking bothers you; you just keep moving and getting better. You fucking abandoned me and left me behind to die. Sorry if I'm not dealing with that well," he said.

"I'm sorry for hurting you Hector, but I left almost a year ago. Aren't you married now? And furthermore, have you ever considered for a second how hard it was for me to leave in my situation? How difficult it was to be the ONLY person dealing with Harmony by myself at night? I get NO sleep, I still have a fucking career and have NO choice because I have to be the best mother I can be for her because her father fell the fuck off." At this point in our relationship, I still lived downstairs. Giovanni and I were taking things as slow as we could since we were already living in the same house. I wasn't ready to move up to his room and change my daughter's nights just yet. So I did everything at night just like a single mom. I was too stubborn to let he or Gabriel help me, but Hector didn't know any of that.

"Please give me one more chance Savannah, I'm sorry, I've already missed so much. My heart is broken!" I didn't respond. My heart was broken too, for my daughter. I didn't understand why the one person who was supposed to love her like I did, didn't seem to care about her at all.

"Please, just one more chance. You don't know the truth; you don't know what's really going on. I'm sorry, I wish I would have done so many things differently, but just give me a chance. Please, let me see you guys when I get back."

Pettily I responded, "Your next visitation is scheduled in two weeks. That will be the LAST one I show up to if you aren't there. And you better have either money, or something for your daughter," I said. "Thank you, I will, I promise!"

After Hector got back in town, I agreed to meet him at Applebee's for our scheduled visitation. We sat there quietly while he tried to feed Harmony. She just wanted me, so I ended up taking her for a few minutes to calm her down. I handed her back to Hector when my phone chimed. It was Angel. I hadn't heard from her in a while and I was trying to let Hector visit with his daughter, so I sat back down and opened the message.

"Hey, have you heard from Hector?" she asked me.

"I'm sitting across from him at Applebee's right now, why?" I asked.

"Oh girl, don't tell him I'm messaging you! Call me as soon as you leave, I need to tell you something!" she said.

"Okay, we'll be leaving soon."

"Who was that?" Hector asked.

"Nobody."

"Can we meet somewhere more interactive next time? Like a park or something?" he asked, putting Harmony back in her car seat.

"Well, she's a little young for that," I said. "But when she gets a little bit bigger and starts walking, then, yeah, that will be fine," I said.

"So how are things with your little boyfriend?" he asked me, carrying the car seat out to the car for me.

"Better than I could have imagined," I said honestly. "Not that it's any of your business."

"So he doesn't care that you have a baby by someone else?"

"Obviously not, since I was pregnant when I moved into his house. Why are you asking me all these questions?" I asked, opening the back door of Giovanni's car.

"Just curious," he said, shrugging. "Are you happy?" he asked.

"Yes, I'm very happy with him," I answered honestly. He shook his head like that wasn't the answer he was hoping for.

"So, do you have any child support money this time?"

"You know I don't."

"How would I know that? You just had money to go to New York for Christmas and New Year's, so why wouldn't I assume you would make providing for your daughter a priority? Oh, that's right, because you never actually *have* provided a single fucking thing for her," I said, closing the back door. "Have a nice day," I said, opening the driver door. He put his hand in front of me to stop me from getting in.

"I'm sorry okay, look, I have some things for her at the house. I was going to see if you would come by for a little bit so we could talk and I could give them to her," he said nervously.

"Absolutely not, I know what's going on at that house, and aren't you guys supposed to be out of there by now?" I asked.

"We were able to come up with enough to avoid eviction on the first," he giggled.

"No, I'm not coming to that house, and what is it you got for her exactly?" I asked, knowing it was bullshit.

"Um, I don't know," he said.

"You don't know what you got for her?" I asked sarcastically.

"Like, diapers and shit I guess," he said. I laughed. This was ridiculous.

"Lies. Move out of my way please," I asked, not wanting to touch him.

"Well, I didn't get the stuff, but my wife did, so I don't know what it is," he said.

"No thank you. Visitation is over, and we will see you in two weeks, if you show up that is," I spat at him, getting in the car. He stopped me from closing the door.

"Please," he said desperately.

"Please what?" I asked.

"Please, I want to talk to you," he said.

"Then say what you have to say. I'm not going to that house," I said sternly.

"Fuck it," he said, backing away. I closed the door and started the car. *What the hell was that about?* I asked myself.

While he was walking away, I put my phone on Bluetooth and called Angel. "Hey girl," I said when she picked up the phone.

"Are you away from Hector?" she asked.

"Yeah I'm in the car heading home," I said.

"What's up?" I asked.

"I just ran into a homegirl of mine. Apparently, she ran into Hector at an event last night, and he spilled his guts to her," she said.

"Oh? About what?" I asked.

"*Everything!* He told her that he married the wife for money, she agreed to pay him $25,000 in payments if he married her so she could get her green card. He said losing you was the worst thing that ever happened to him, and, no matter what, he was going to come back and win you and his daughter back so you could all be a family," she said.

"*What?*" I asked, laughing.

"Yeah, so when you told me he was with you I started to panic. You aren't going to get back with him, right?"

"No, of course not. He was probably just high when he said all that. Not to mention I would never be willing to go back to him, so it really doesn't matter. My daughter and I are happy, he has no chance."

"Yeah, that's what I thought."

That week I got a letter from the department of child support. They had officially set a child support payment plan in place. Since he was "jobless," they issued the order for a whopping $267 a month. That's it. He was obligated to enroll in a parenting plan that aided jobless fathers in finding and keeping employment that was to begin immediately. He was also obligated by law to provide Harmony with health insurance until she reached the age of 18. It was clear in the paperwork that there was nothing I could do to appeal the order. It was set in stone for the next three years. The state minimum was $260. I was so angry, I could have punched a hole in the wall. I showed Giovanni the papers when he got home, and he shook his head while reading them.

"Wow, that motherfucker really got away with this shit?" he asked.

"Yeah, what the hell is that supposed to even cover? He doesn't even have to start paying until May 1!" I said.

"Yeah, this is bullshit. What's even the point? I mean by then she's going to be almost a year old! Is this how long it normally takes?" he asked.

"I have no idea, but it's fucking outrageous," I said, furious. "But it also says that the state wants their money back first, so what little assistance I got will be taken off the top," I said.

"Yeah, putting you at July to actually receive a payment."

"Correct," I answered, disgusted with the situation.

The next week I got a call from Mary, the neighbor across the street from the house Hector and I shared.

"Well, I don't know if they were avoiding eviction or just in a rush, but there was trucks and bikes in and out of here all night last night, and now the house is empty," she said.

"What?" I asked.

"Hector said he was moving back in to be here for his daughter."

"Well, he lied to you once again honey. The house is vacant, they even tore up my lawn trying to get the moving truck backed in."

"So, he ran again?" I said in shock.

"For good this time from the looks of it," she said.

"He texted me some threatening text a few weeks back to stop telling you things or he would hurt me, so I took my phone down to the police station and showed them. I filed a written report just to be safe, but I never responded," she said.

"What?"

"Yeah, if you get a chance come by when you get off work, I'll show it to you."

"I think I'll do that," I told her. I messaged Giovanni to tell him.

"Yeah sounds like he ran," he said.

"Have you heard from him?"

"No, not a word." I got a text from Mary while I was talking to Giovanni.

"Looks like it was an eviction thing, there's a crew here now going into the house, they just dropped a dumpster in the driveway," she said.

"I'll be by after work," I told her.

When I pulled up and saw the dumpster piled high and all the doors to my old house open, I was anxious to go inside. I parked at Mary's and knocked on her door.

"Hey girl!" she said, excited to see me. "They're tearing that place apart it looks like."

"Do you think we can go look at it?" I asked.

"Sure, let's go! I'm curious to see what it looks like since you left," she said. There was one red truck there with two Spanish-speaking gentlemen working to throw out all the trash. I told them we just wanted to walk through and see the house, and they didn't care. The whole place was trashed. It smelled awful, even with all the doors open. There was trash everywhere. Fist holes in the walls everywhere. In the hallway leading to the bedrooms, there was a giant hole cut out in the sheet rock that they had freshly patched up. The sheet rock mud was still wet.

"What the hell was this for?" Mary wondered out loud. "Who knows," she said.

The master bedroom was disgusting. In the middle of the room there was a massive dark blue stain, it looked almost like someone spilled ink there, but it was as about big as king sized pillow. So we couldn't figure out what it was, we just knew there was no cleaning it. The carpet would have to be replaced. The bathrooms were both disgusting. There were shit splatters all over the toilets and urine stains on the floor. It smelled disgusting.

Every inch of the floor throughout the entire house was nasty. The cabinets were damaged in both bathrooms and the kitchen. The outside deck was full of trash and old bottles and cans full of cigarette butts everywhere. Mary noticed a hole in the wall above the front door that didn't make sense. It was about 6 feet above the door, in a spot that you would need a 10-foot ladder to reach. Clearly something had been thrown there, but we couldn't tell what. She stopped one of the gentlemen working and asked what it was.

"There was a knife stuck in it," he said moving along.

"Wow," I said. You could tell there were plenty of temper tantrums here.

"It was a junkie house," he said matter-of-factly, climbing the stairs.

Curious, Mary asked him, "What makes you say that?" even though we already knew he was right.

"There were needles; we found a melted spoon in the bathroom; there was evidence everywhere. It's all in the dumpster," he said.

"Jesus," Mary said.

"And he just tried to get me to bring my child here last Saturday!" I said.

"Thank God you didn't."

"I want to go say hello to Rafiki," I said.

"Okay," she said, digging through the items left behind. I went over and saw my dog's completely neglected grave. It was so covered up with mud and grass you could barely see the headstone. I wiped it clean and sat down next to him.

"I think this might be the last time you see me at this house, baby bear. I sure do miss you; Harmony would love you. I'm sorry I can't take you with me. I love you, and I hate myself for letting this happen to you. You were the *best* dog," I said as a tear dropped from my eye. "Goodbye baby bear," I said, getting up. For some reason, seeing the house, seeing that Hector was gone, was a huge relief. The journey in this house had been so emotional that I felt free knowing I would never have to step foot in it again.

I went across the street with Mary and chatted for a few minutes. She showed me the threatening text she had received from Hector.

"I'm sorry about that," I said.

"Oh fuck him, I was never afraid of him, and he knew it," she said.

"Well I appreciate you looking out for me," I told her. I updated her on my life, and we agreed to keep in touch. I gave her a hug and went home to show Giovanni the pictures I had taken of the disgusting house. The last picture was a selfie of Mary and I at the dumpster before we left.

"Look how happy you look in this picture," he said.

"I know, I feel free," I said.

"Good, I'm glad," he said.

"We don't need a single fucking thing from him," he said.

"I know," I agreed.

Epilogue

I never heard from Hector directly again. Five days *after* her first birthday, he randomly sent me some BDSM porn. Pictures of women tied up with their skin red from being whipped and flogged. He didn't say anything, and I never responded to him. I showed Giovanni the messages and he shook his head in disgust.

"There is really something wrong with that motherfucker," he said.

"He didn't even ask me about his daughter's first birthday or say anything!"

"Don't even respond, he's just looking for your attention," Giovanni said, pushing my phone and the images out of his sight. Hector never paid a dime towards child support; he never went to the parenting classes or got a legal job. He still went on trying to make everyone believe I was a terrible person and he was just a victim of my wrath. But I didn't mind anymore. I had a new life; I was happy with Giovanni and so was Harmony. As time went on, I became less worried about what was being said about me. I didn't feel the desire to defend myself anymore. My actions spoke louder than Hector's words. Eventually he was arrested in Florida for beating his wife. They were divorced shortly after that.

He came to Georgia frequently to cause trouble, but never approached Giovanni or me. He found the hotel Jose and Frankie were staying at and slashed the tires to the work van in the middle of the night in a drug induced rage. It was caught on surveillance, but since the vehicle was still registered in Hector's name, they couldn't bring charges against him. So instead, Jose posted the surveillance video on social media along with a lengthy message to Hector. He admitted that Hector was a junkie, he told the world that he had seen Hector be physically violent with me, both before and during my pregnancy. He mentioned that he watched him throw the lamp at my head the night I left him and even admitted to researching where Hector could go that child support wouldn't expedite him. He told the truth about a lot of things. Things that I had battled alone for so long. I was relieved someone finally spoke the truth besides myself, but that was the last I ever wanted to know about either of them.

I finally moved upstairs in July of 2018. Giovanni had been so amazing and so patient with me, my love for him grew stronger as the weeks passed. I finally had someone I knew I could trust and rely on for the rest of my life. Harmony had her own room across the hall from ours, and she loves him unconditionally. Their relationship is beautiful and impenetrable. In December 2018, Giovanni asked me to marry him! We decided to go to the courthouse the following month and avoid spending money on a wedding. We had a beautiful reception at the tavern he and I had met at the first night we began talking again. We rented the upstairs banquet room, and Gia set everything up. It was perfect for us. We spoke to a lawyer about doing a stepparent adoption and what that would entail. Giovanni wanted to be Harmony's legal father, and I was thrilled about it. We wanted to make sure Hector couldn't cause any trouble for us later on down the road. We had to wait until we were married for a certain amount of time before we could apply for it. But we were both in agreement that it was the best thing to do.

During the waiting, period we had an amazing opportunity to purchase a company. One of my paint vendors told me this finishing company he worked with for years was selling. The owner's son who had been running it unexpectedly died in the middle of the night. The owner was an older gentleman, in his early 80s with dementia. So he met with me and liked me immediately. He and his other son who came in from out of town to handle things asked me what we could afford, and we agreed on a shockingly low price. So not only was I married to my best friend, I have an amazing little girl, and now I am a small business owner. Business grew busier than I could have imagined!

Harmony is learning and growing so fast, it seems like every day is a new adventure. She is intelligent and curious; she wants to know how to do everything. She has gone from a bald little baby to a beautiful little girl in what feels like a blink of an eye. She has adorable dimples and smiles all the time. She has beautiful curly hair with naturally perfect light brown ringlets that gently fall down her back. Her spirit shines bright and she makes everyone fall in love with her. She is charming and wonderful and more than I ever thought I deserved in life. She wants for nothing; she has everything she needs and more, most importantly, unconditional love and a safe and happy home. I can't believe my life has turned out so beautifully, but I give *all* the credit and glory to God! He pointed me in every direction and stood by me even when I thought I was alone. He gave me an amazing daughter, husband, company, and life.

The purpose of this book is to bring awareness to the different types of abuse one can be experiencing. I didn't realize I was being abused while it was happening to me. Nobody would have suspected someone like me to be in a violent relationship. I was considered too strong. But it can happen to anyone. Recognizing the signs and speaking up can not only change your life; it may save your life. If you or a loved one needs help, contact your local domestic violence agency for assistance.

Helpful resources

Women's Health and Wellness Clinic of Walton offers the following services at no charge:

- Pregnancy testing
- Limited obstetric ultrasounds
- Evidence-based sexual health education
- Consultations on all of your options
- Earn-You-Learn Program (earn baby supplies by participating in educational parenting classes)
- Compassionate and nonjudgmental mental care
- Fatherhood mentorship program
- Abortion recovery support
- Referral for community support services

In addition, we offer Sexually Transmitted Infection Testing and Treatment for Chlamydia and Gonorrhea. A $10.00 lab fee is requested.

To schedule your appointment, go to whwclinic.com or call us at 770-466-3900.

To find a location near you, phone 1-800-712-4357 or text "Helpline" to 313131

If you or a loved one are in danger or in need of help, please call the National Domestic Violence Hotline at 1-800-799-7233. If you are unable to speak safely, log onto thehotline.org or text LOVEIS to 1-866-331-9474.

About the Author

Shannon Ezzo is an incredibly strong-willed wife and mother. She started her cabinet finishing career at the age of 18 and now owns her own cabinet finishing company in Georgia. She never imagined writing a book, but she felt called to do it in hopes that her personal story of survival and overcoming hardships would be helpful to another person who may be in a similar situation. She hopes that her testimony will bring awareness to not only red flags that may be noticed early on in a toxic relationship, but also to shed light on all forms of abuse people in a toxic relationship may be experiencing. She is one of the most genuine, caring people you would ever meet, but she is also a force to be reckoned with. When she wants something, she works hard for it, prays hard about it, and goes after it.

Made in the USA
Columbia, SC
20 December 2020

27513149R00294